P.O. Box 1375
Barrhead
Glasgow
G78 1JJ

Tel: 0141 880 6839
Fax: 0870 124 9189
e-mail: teejaypublishers@btinternet.com
web page: www.teejaypublishers.co.ok

First Edition published by TeeJay Publishers - March 2012

Level 1(b) Textbook

Produced by members of the TeeJay Writing Group

T Strang, J Geddes and J Cairns.

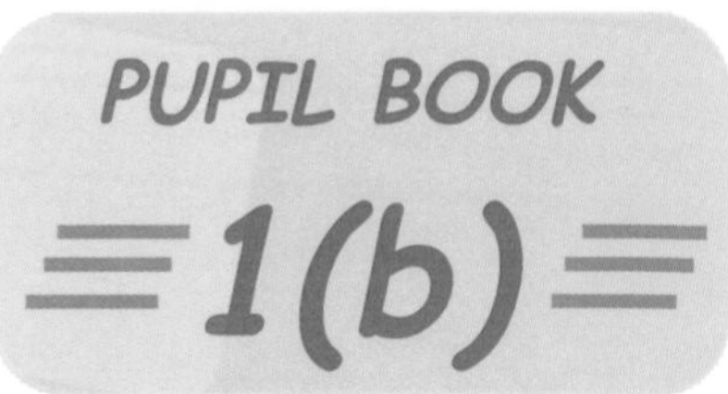

CfE Level 1(b) Textbook

The book, along with CfE Level 1(a) can be used in both Primary and Secondary with pupils who have successfully completed CfE Early Level.

- Most pupils will complete the contents of books 1(a) and 1(b) throughout Primary 2 to 4, some earlier.
  As a guide, Book 1(b) might be started, after completing Book 1(a), with the majority of pupils around half way through P3.

- There are no A and B exercises. The 2 books cover the **entire Level 1 CfE course** without the teacher having to pick and choose which questions to leave out and which exercises are important. They all are !

- Pupils who cope well with the contents of Level 1 should commence work on Level 2 during P5 or even late P4. Books 2(a) and 2(b) can then be used to work through CfE Level 2 during the latter part of Primary.

- Book 1(b), unlike Book 1(a) does not contain a "**Chapter Zero**". Instead, every chapter is preceded by a "**Consolidation Exercise**" which revises the corresponding work from Book 1(a), prior to tackling the new work in the following chapter.

- Non-calculator skills are emphasised and encouraged throughout the book.

- Each chapter will have a "**Revisit - Review - Revise**" exercise as a summary.

- Teachers are encouraged, at the end of various chapters, to consider assessing the pupils using the corresponding **TeeJay Outcome Assessment**.

- Homework is available as a photocopiable pack.

- **TeeJay's Assessment Pack** for each Level, Early to 3, is available and can be used topic by topic or combined to form a series of Level 1 Cumulative Tests.

We make no apologies for the multiplicity of colours used throughout the book, both for text and in diagrams - we feel it helps brighten up the pages !!

T Strang, J Geddes, J Cairns

(March 2012)

* Available for purchase separately.

Contents

Revision of Whole Numbers

1. Write these numbers using **digits** :-

   a seventy five b four hundred and eighty nine.

2. Write these numbers in **words** :-

   a 96 b 207 c 846 d 333.

3. Put these numbers in order, starting with the largest :-

   328, 287, 381, 413, 278, 319.

4. What numbers are the arrows pointing to ?

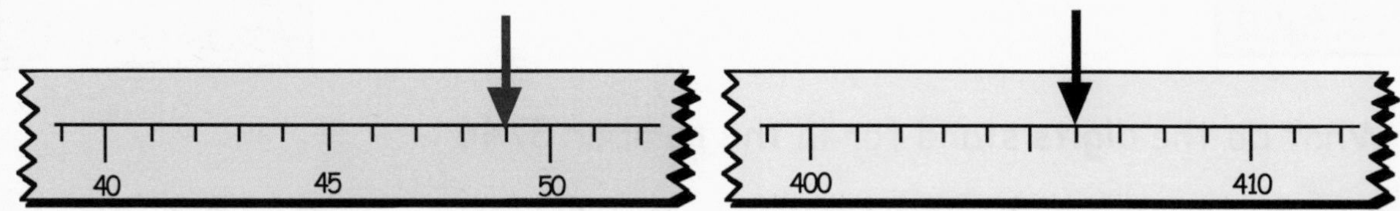

5. Write the number that comes :-

   a **just after** 239 b **two before** 400 c **ten after** 583.

6. Write the number 839 in hundreds, tens and units :-

   839 = ... hundreds, ... tens and ... units.

7. How many 1p coins will you get for :-

   Seven £1 coins, five 10p coins and three 2p coins ?

8. How many £1 coins and 10p coins will you get for :-

   a 410p b 3650p c £7·20 d £20·80 ?

9. Archie went to the football match with seven £1 coins to get in, nine 10p coins and eight 1p coins for juice and crisps at half time.

   How much money did Archie take with him ?

Calculators should NOT be used in this chapter.

Whole Numbers 1

Understand place value for numbers up to 10000.

In the number :- 6295

the 6 stands for 6 thousand	=	6000
the 2 stands for 2 hundred	=	200
the 9 stands for 9 tens	=	90
the 5 stands for 5 units	=	5
	=	6295

Six thousand two hundred and ninety five
6295

Exercise 1

Worksheet 1·1

1. What do the **digits** stand for in the number 3746 :-

   a 3 b 7 c 4 d 6 ?

2. What does the **8** stand for in each of these numbers :-

   a 8163 b 2580 c 6758 d 3817 ?

3. Write out the following numbers **in words** :-

   a 1720 b 3586 c 2908 d 8009
   e 937 f 6340 g 9087 h 9876.

4. Write the following numbers **using digits** :-

   a four hundred and forty four b nine hundred and six
   c three thousand one hundred and seventy two
   d five thousand two hundred and seven
   e eight thousand four hundred and sixty six
   f seven thousand seven hundred
   g eight thousand three hundred and ninety nine.
   h nine thousand and fifty.

I'm only four hundred and forty four years old today.

5. Write down the number that is :-

a 10 after 680
b 400 after 800
c 40 before 950
d 200 before 1300
e 500 after 3800
f 2000 before 7300
g 2000 after 6500
h 6000 before 7300
i 3200 before 9200
j 2100 before 7100.

6. Put the following numbers in order, **smallest first** :-

a 380, 402, 399, 400, 413, 335, 381, 410, 397.

b 3054, 3095, 2985, 2895, 3009, 3100, 2899, 3002.

c 8243, 8432, 8234, 8300, 8200, 8400, 8355, 8249.

7. What numbers do **A**, **B**, **C**, ... stand for in these scales :-

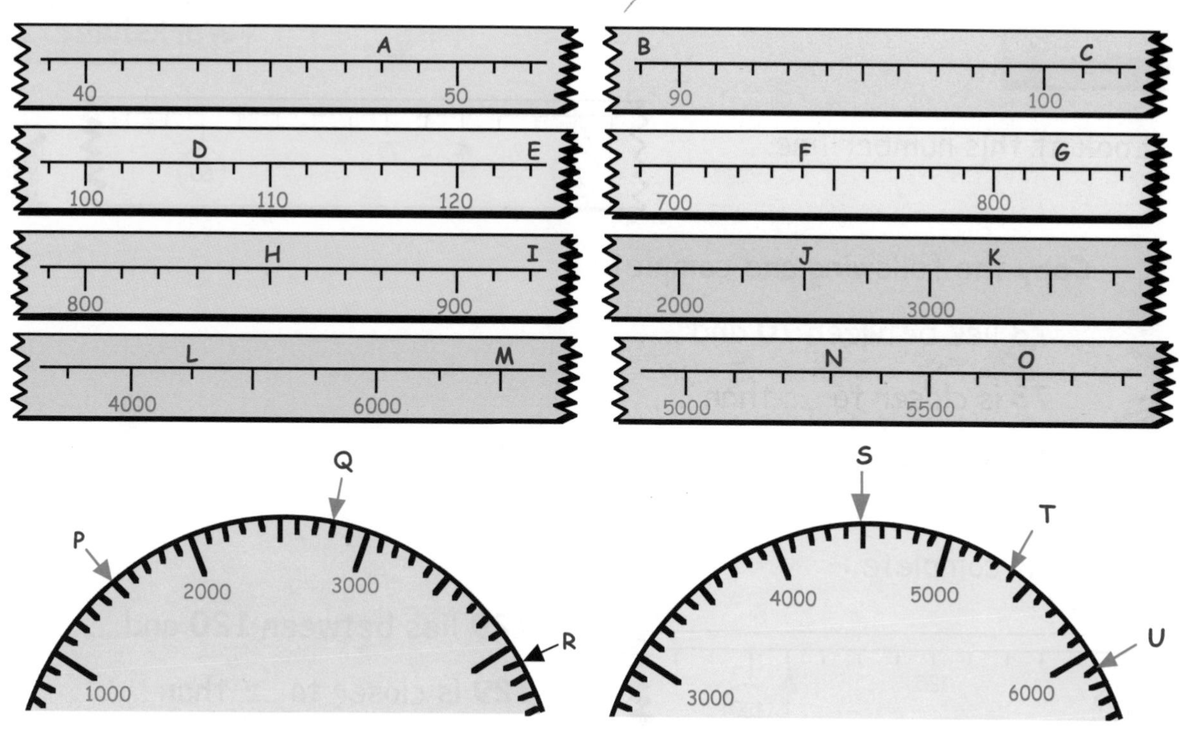

8. What number lies **halfway** between :-

a 200 and 260
b 800 and 1200
c 2000 and 2600
d 3000 and 7000
e 5500 and 6500
f 2000 and 8000 ?

Rounding to the nearest 10

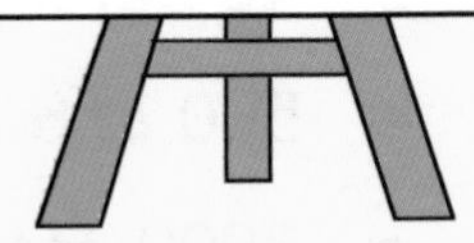

Here is a number line :-

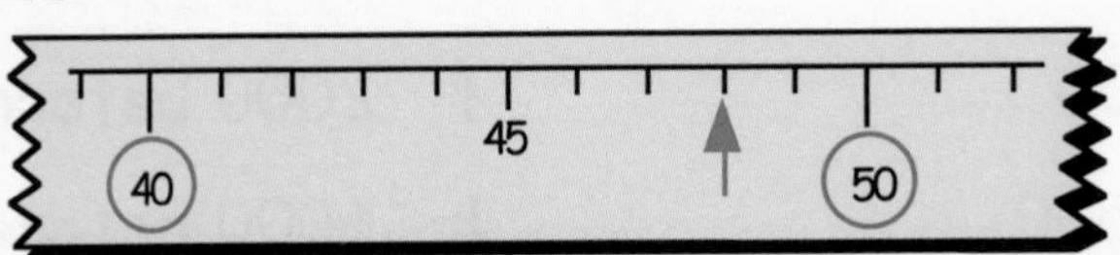

The arrow points to the number **48**.

- Notice that **48** lies between **40** and **50**.
- Can you see that **48** is closer to **50** than **40** ?

We say that, " **48, rounded to the nearest 10, is 50.**"

> ***Rule*** If the last digit is a 1, 2, 3, 4 - **ROUND DOWN**
> If the last digit is a 5, 6, 7, 8, 9 - **ROUND UP**

Exercise 2

1. Look at this number line.

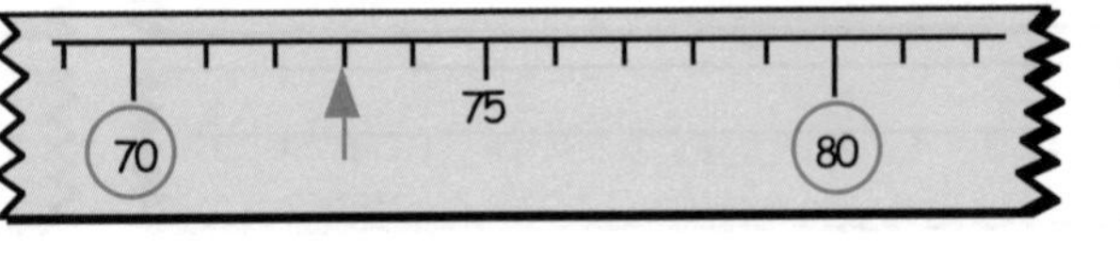

Copy the following and complete :-

- **73** lies between **70** and .....
- **73** is closer to ..... than .....
- **73** rounds to ..... (to the nearest 10)

2. **Copy** and complete :-

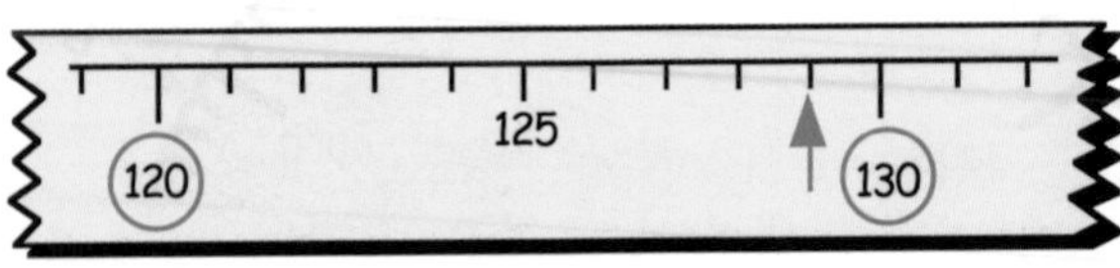

- **129** lies between **120** and ...
- **129** is closer to ..... than ...
- **129** rounds to ... (to the nearest 10).

3. **Copy** and complete :-

- **24** lies between **20** and .....
- **24** is closer to ... than .....
- **24** rounds to ... (to the nearest 10).

4. Imagine the following numbers and decide what each one rounds to, (to the nearest 10). **Copy** and **complete** :-

a **87** lies between 80 and ..... It is closer to .....

b **133** lies between ..... and 140 It is closer to .....

c **458** lies between 450 and ..... It is closer to .....

d **902** lies between 900 and ..... It is closer to .....

> A short way of writing **"68 rounds to 70 to the nearest 10"** is to simply write **68 —> 70**
>
> If a number ends in a **5**, we round up - **75 —> 80** (**not 70**)

5. **Copy** each of the following and round to the nearest 10 :-

a 37 —>	b 71 —>	c 18 —>	d 63 —> ......
e 159 —>	f 141 —>	g 316 —>	h 534 —> ......
i 45 —>	j 405 —>	k 703 —>	l 777 —> ......

6. a The height of this pot is **33** centimetres.

Round this to the nearest **10** cm.

b 

My jet to Tenerife reached **506** miles per hour.

Round this to the nearest **10** miles per hour.

c A tennis professional can earn **£185** per day.

Round this to the nearest **£10**.

d 

Sam reckons he repairs at least **628** pairs of shoes every 3 months.

Round the pairs of shoes to the nearest **10**.

Estimate by Rounding

Estimate answers by rounding numbers to the nearest 10

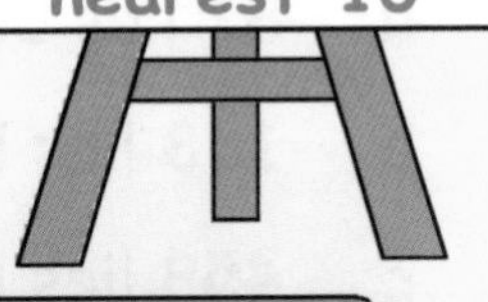

Numbers can be **rounded to the nearest 10** when doing calculations to **estimate** the answers.

Example 1

Example 2

951 – 428
950 – 430
= 520 (approx)

Exercise 3

Worksheet 1·4

1. **Copy** and complete each calculation :-

a	56 + 38	b	92 + 77	c	18 + 49	d	149 + 214
is about	60 + 40	is about	90 + ...	is about	.... + 50	is about	.... + ...
	=		=		=		= ....
e	152 – 27	f	189 – 142	g	454 – 199	h	581 – 216
is about	150 –	is about	190 –	is about	.... –	is about	.... – ....
	=		=		=		= ....
i	727 + 146	j	426 – 128	k	632 + 344	l	998 – 299
is about	.... + ...	is about	.... –	is about	.... + ...	is about	.... – ....
	=		=		=		= ....

2. **Estimate (mentally)** :-

a	29 + 63	b	47 + 99	c	53 + 79	d	171 + 103
e	73 – 29	f	142 – 67	g	252 – 97	h	861 – 459.

3. In a prize draw, **4** girls won tickets to a concert.

   Each ticket was worth **£119**.

   Estimate the total worth of the tickets.

The 3 Я's

Revisit - Review - Revise

1. Look at this part of a number line.

   Estimate what the number 67 rounds to, to **the nearest 10**.

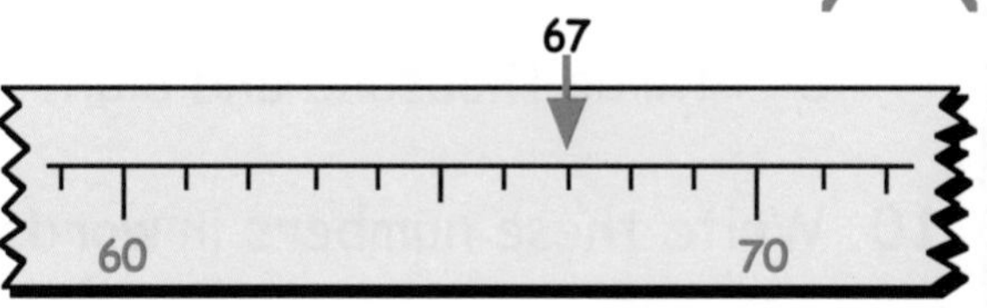

2. Round each of these numbers **to the nearest 10** :-

   a 43 b 69 c 457 d 285.

3. **Copy** and **complete** the sentence below.

   Estimate the answer to **248 + 149**.

   ***248 + 149** is about the same as **250** + ..., which is about ....*

4. In the same way as question **3**, **estimate** the answers to :-

   a 49 + 21 b 239 + 424 c 74 - 18 d 982 - 615.

5. Jason collected 263 computer games over the years, but recently decided to donate 187 of them to charity.

   Estimate to the nearest 10, how many games he kept.

6. 

   Betty bought a microwave oven for £94 and a vacuum cleaner for £325.

   Estimate to the nearest 10, how much she paid.

7. Jessie won £216 on Monday, £82 on Tuesday and £195 on Wednesday at the bingo hall.

   Estimate to the nearest £10, how much she won in total.

8. 

   A baker has a total of 431 apples.

   He uses 288 of them to make apple pies.

   The rest he uses to make apple crumbles.

   Estimate how many apples are for crumbles.

9. Write these numbers using **digits** :-

a forty three

b one hundred and sixty four

c three thousand and eight

d seven thousand and ninety.

10. Write these numbers in **words** :-

a 62

b 738

c 5039

d 8070.

11. Write the number that comes :-

a just **after** 179

b just **before** 599

c ten **after** 360

d ten **before** 700

e 100 **after** 8600

f 1000 **before** 6900.

12. What does the **6** stand for in these numbers :-

a 462

b 3678

c 6941 ?

13. Write the numbers below in order, starting with the **smallest** :-

381, 287, 406, 562, 183, 460.

14. Write the following numbers in order, starting with the **largest** :-

3674, 4102, 5138, 3746, 5381, 4201.

15. What numbers are the letters sitting on ?

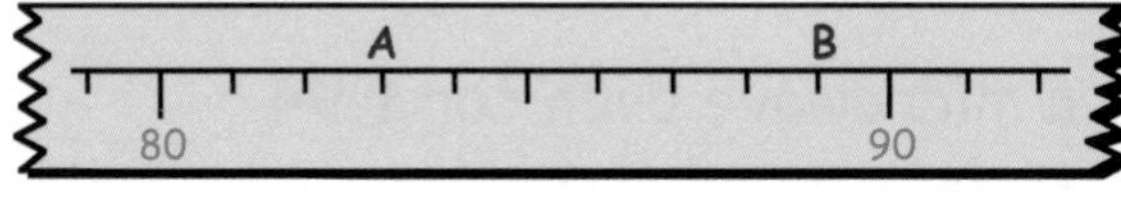

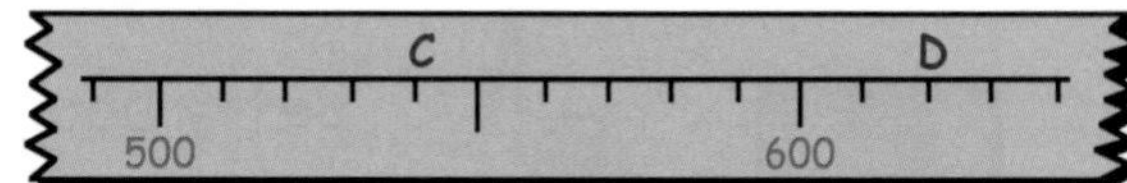

16. Write down the five numbers which come **before** the number **1912**.

17. Three boys, Jack, Simon and Kyle decided to race on their bikes.

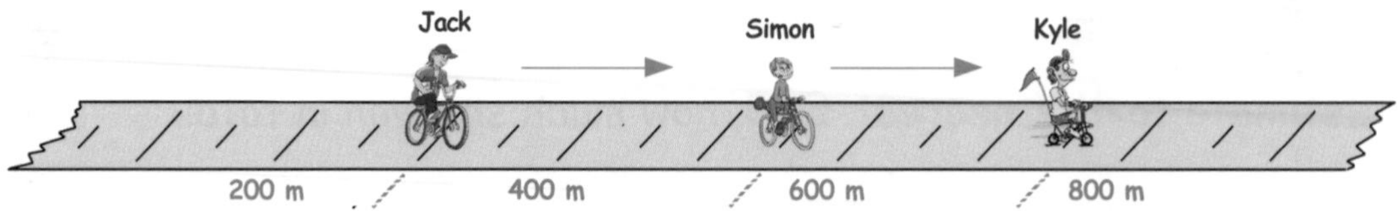

a How far had Jack cycled ?

b How far had Kyle cycled ?

c How far ahead of Simon was Kyle ?

Revision of Symmetry

1. Do these shapes or pictures have **symmetry** ? (Write **Yes** or **No**).

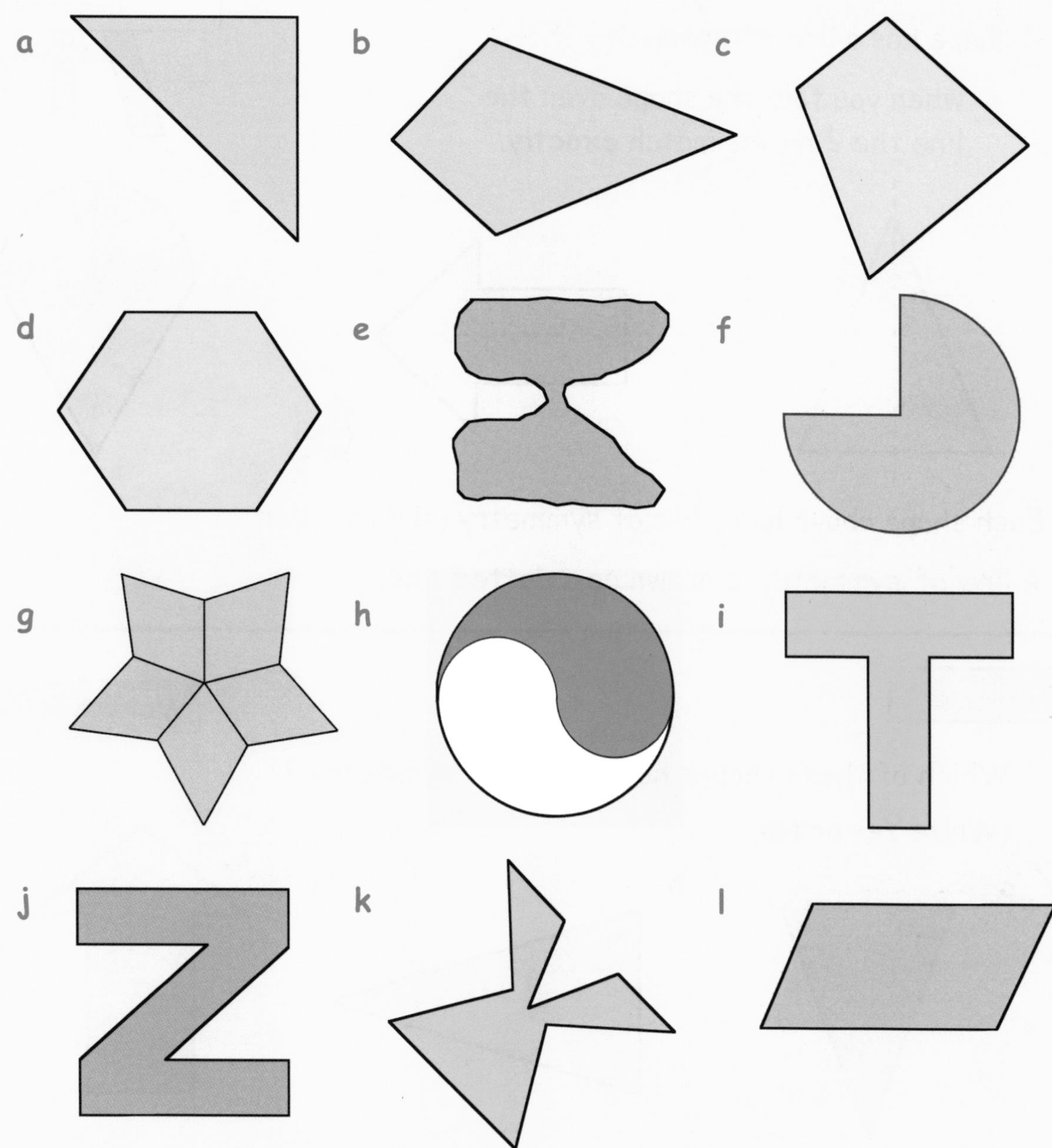

2. Write down **3** things in the classroom that have **symmetry**.

3. Draw a picture of a funny face that is symmetrical.

Symmetry

Be able to identify a line of symmetry in a shape

Line of Symmetry

A shape has a **line of symmetry** if :-

when you fold the shape over the line the 2 halves match **exactly**.

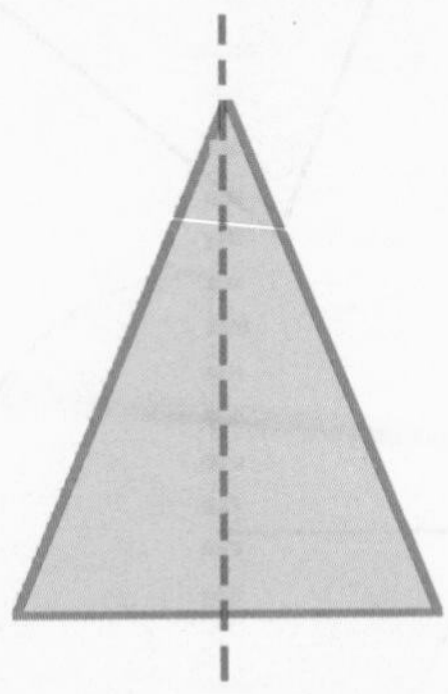

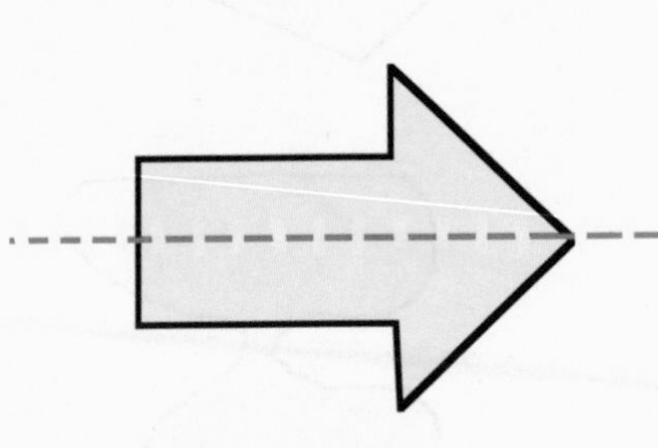

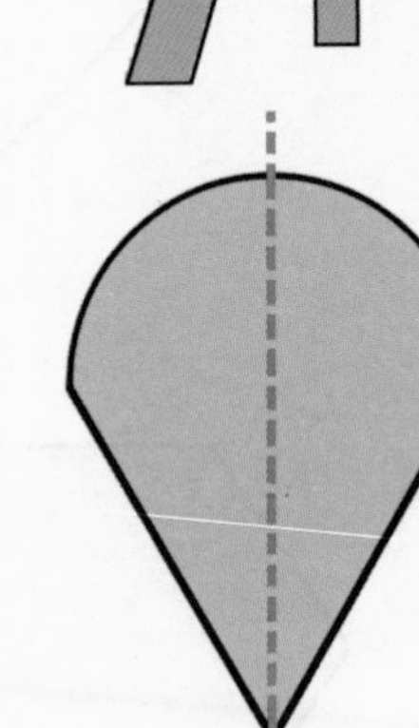

Each shape above has a line of symmetry (shown in **red**).

A **line of symmetry** is drawn as a **dotted line**.

Exercise 1

Worksheet 2·1

1. Which of these shapes have a **line of symmetry** ?
(Write **Yes** or **No**)

a

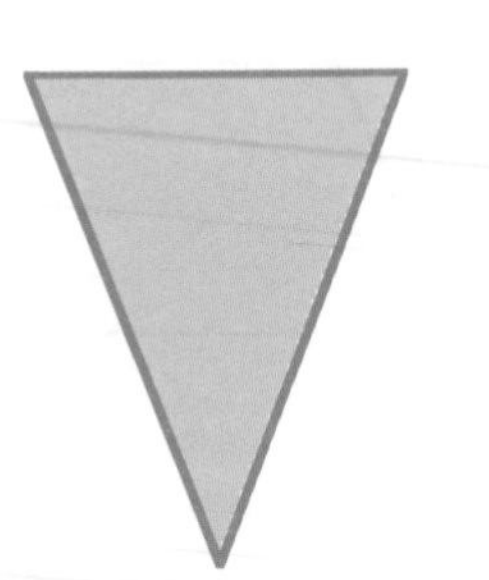

b

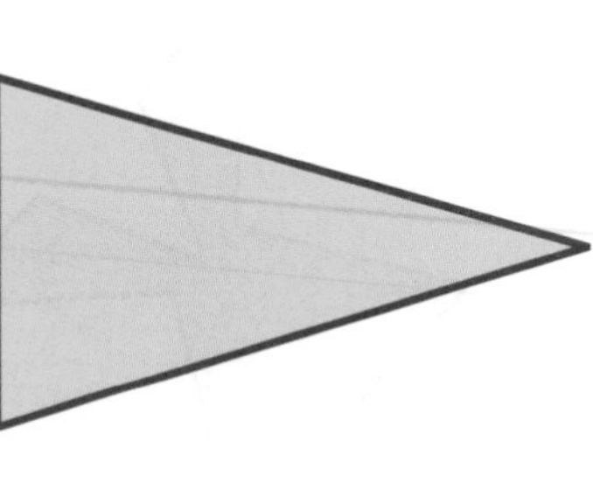

c

d

e

f

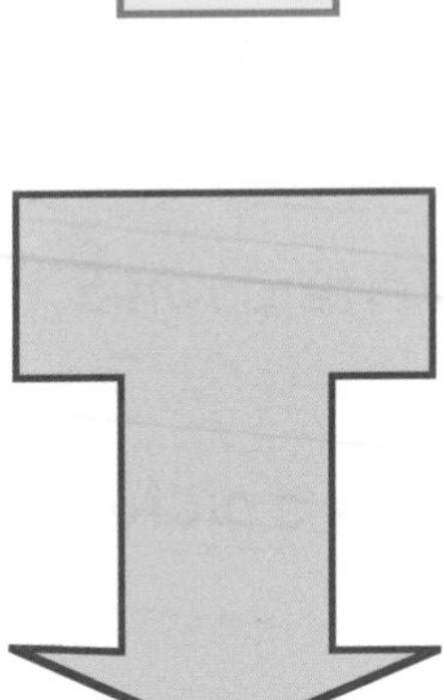

2. Draw (or trace) each shape **carefully** into your jotter and mark any lines of symmetry.

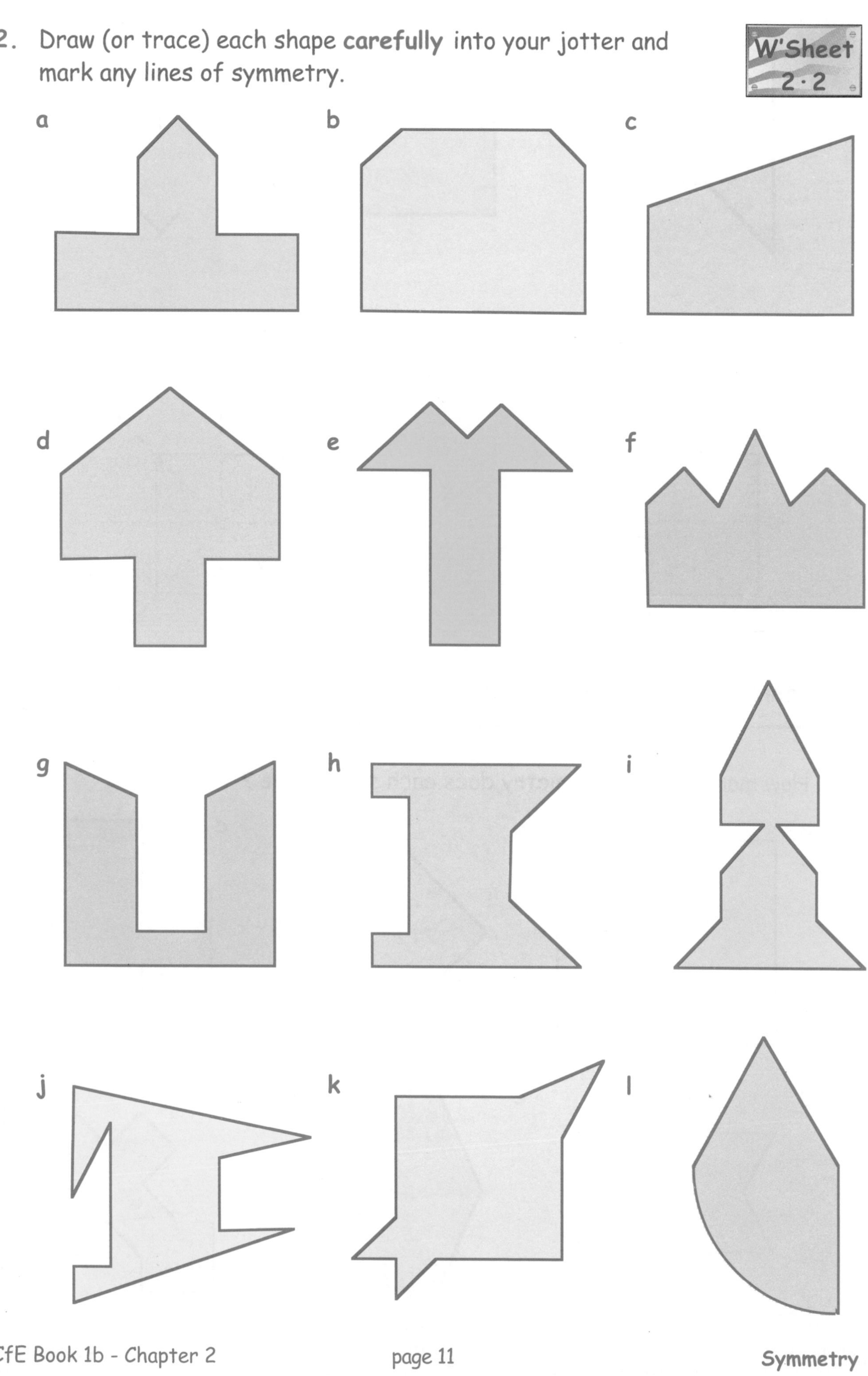

2.

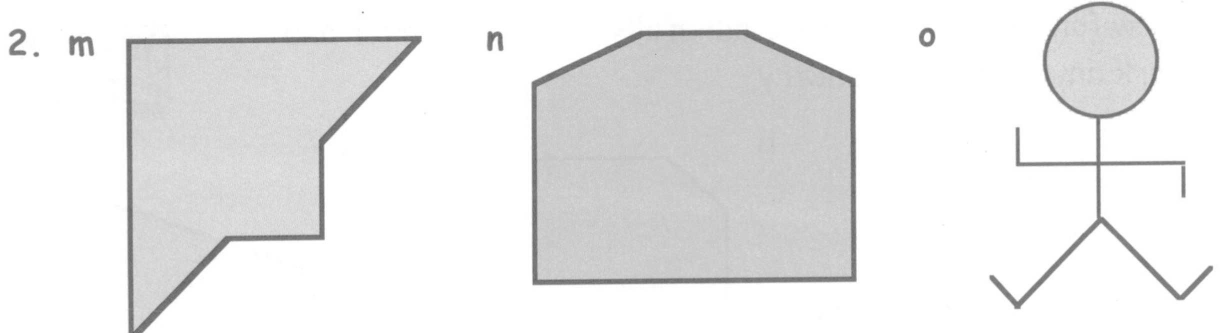

Some shapes have **more than** 1 line of symmetry.

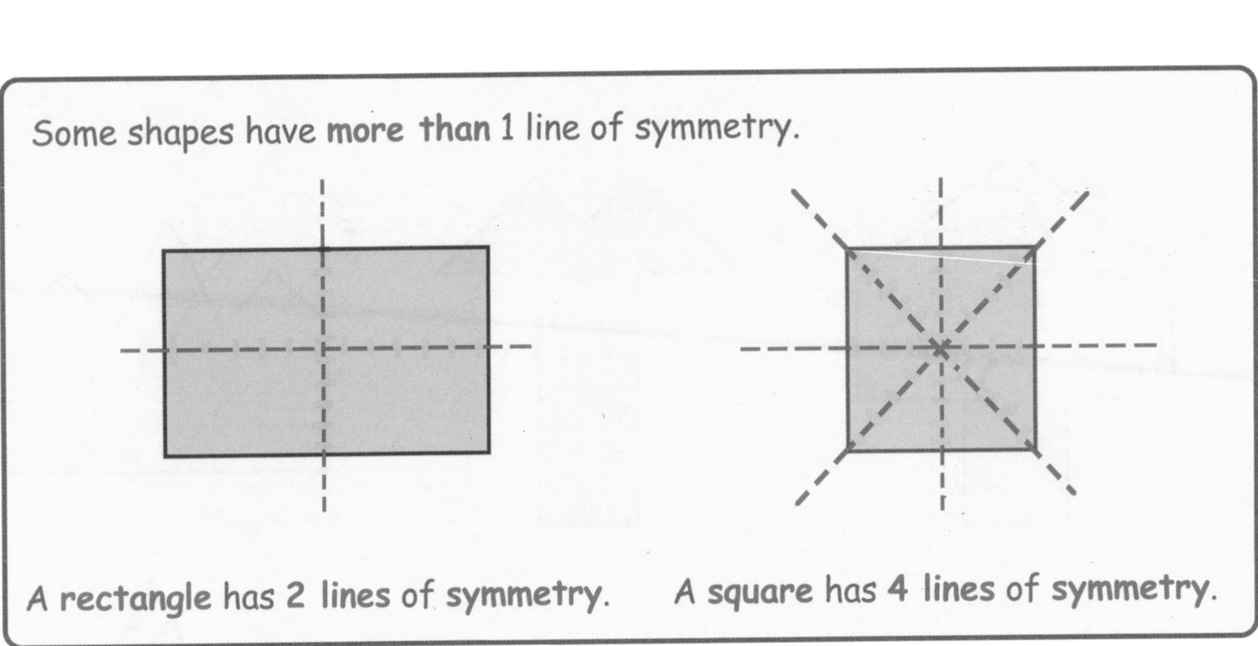

A **rectangle** has **2 lines** of **symmetry**. A **square** has **4 lines** of **symmetry**.

3. How many **lines** of **symmetry** does each shape have ?

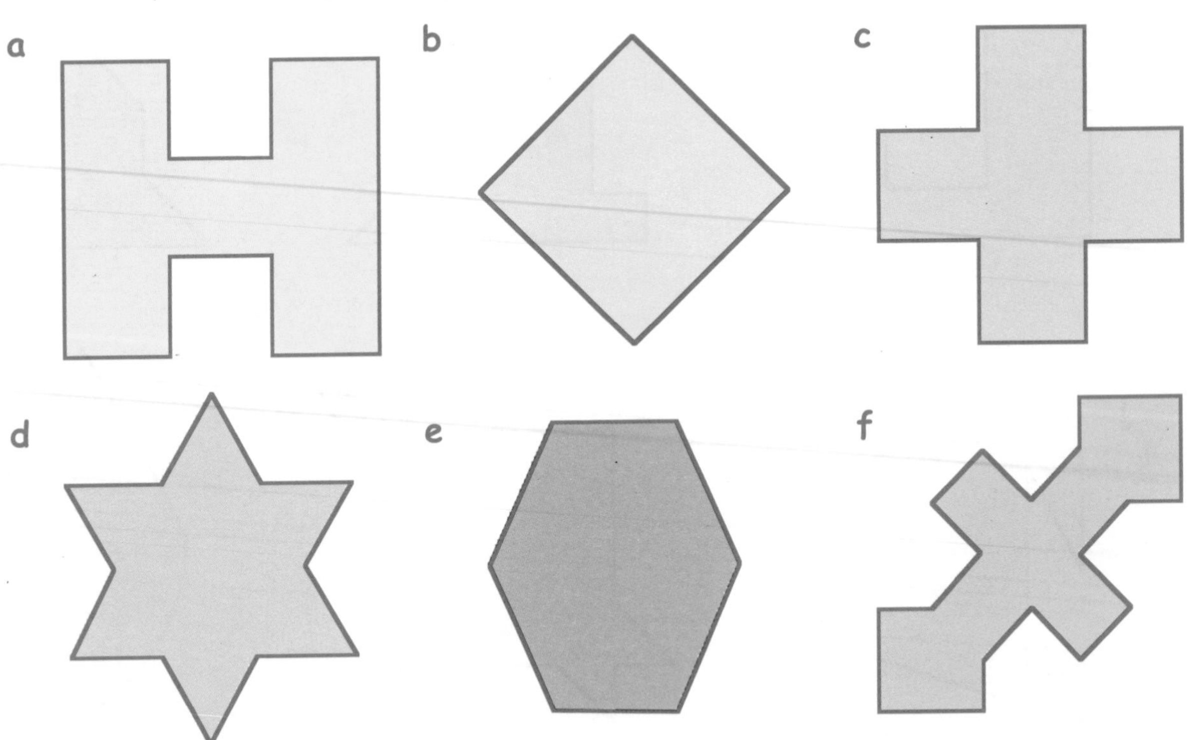

4. **Copy or trace** each shape as carefully as you can. **Worksheet 2·3**

Draw in all lines of symmetry using a coloured pencil.

a

b
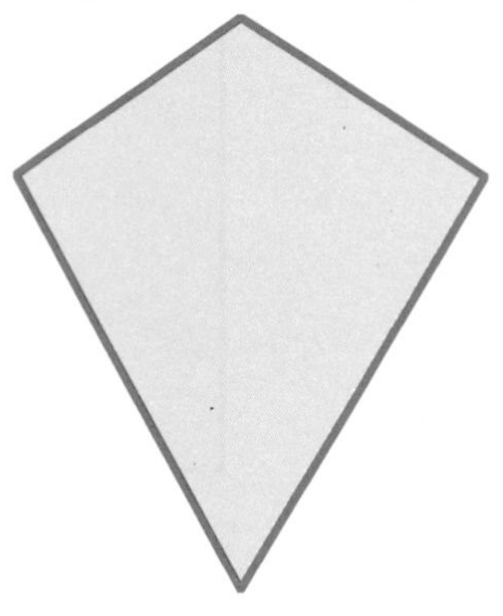

c
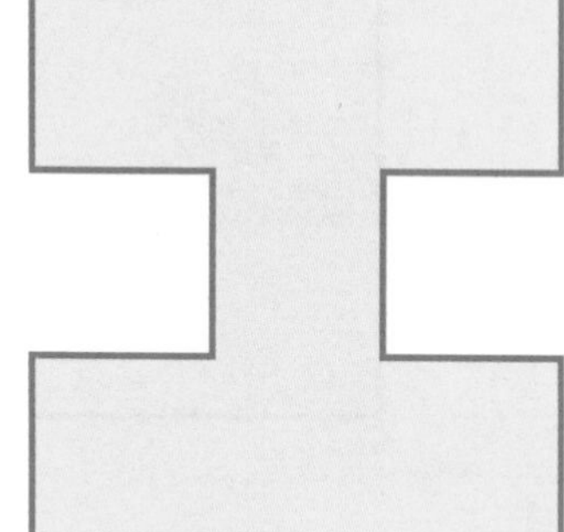

d

e
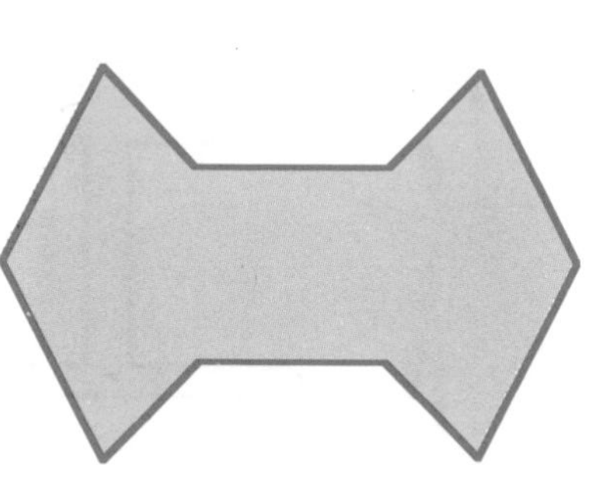

f

g
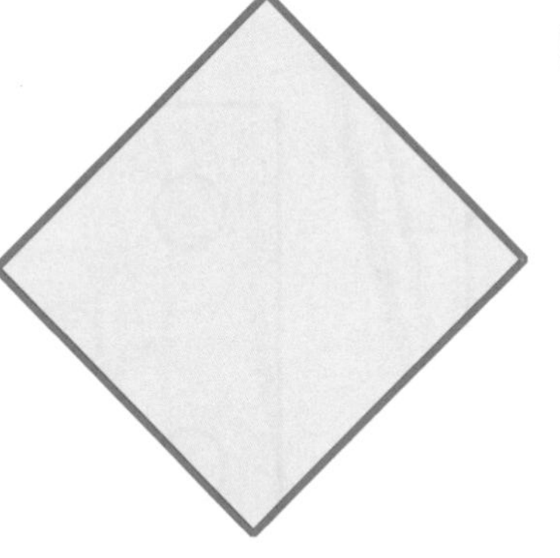

h
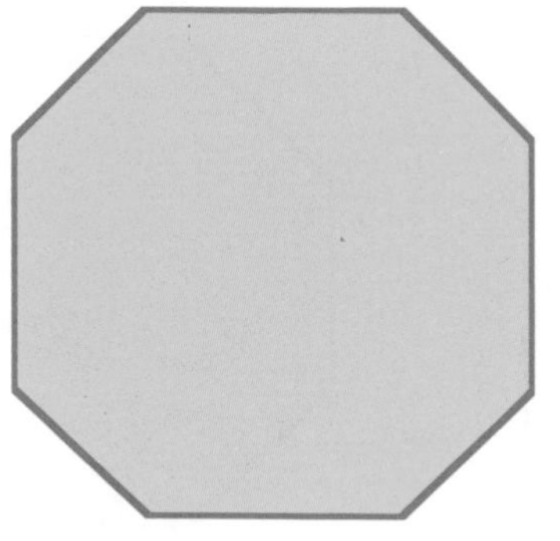

i
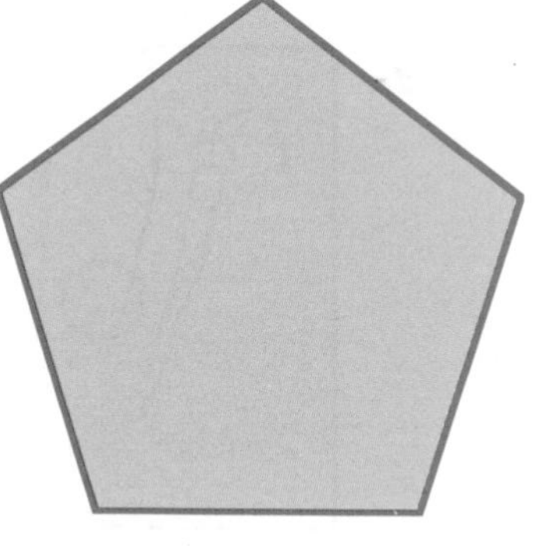

j

k
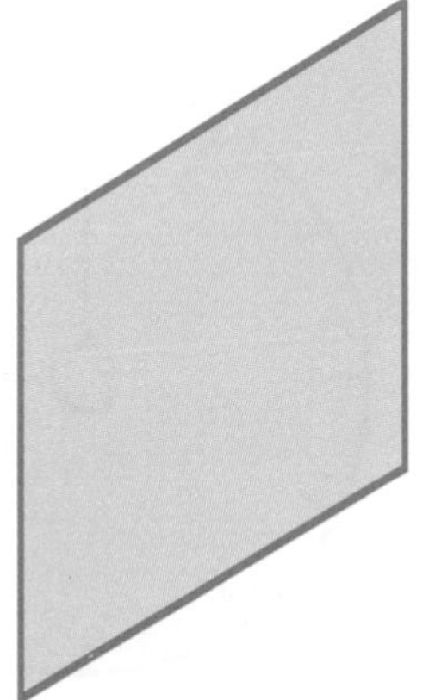

l

5. How many lines of symmetry does each of these shapes have ?

a

b

c

d

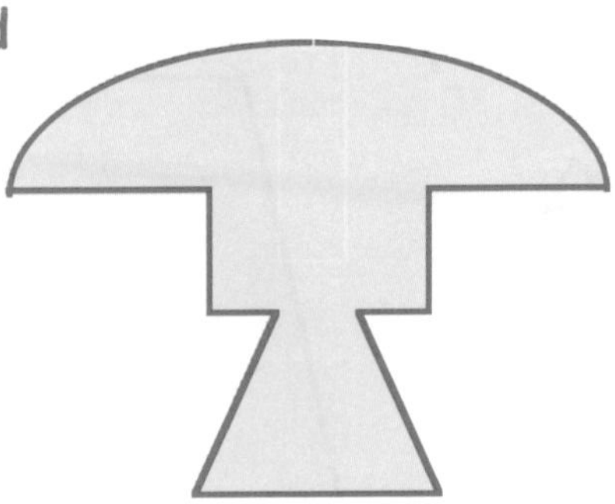

e

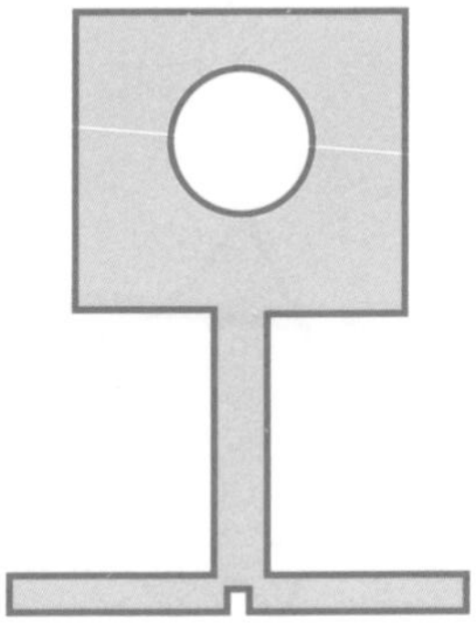

f

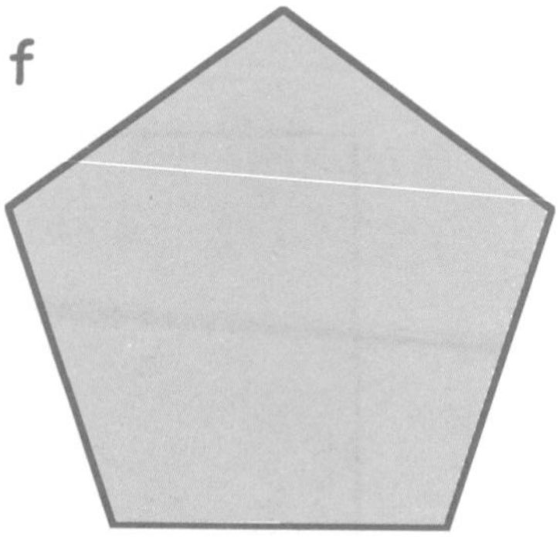

g

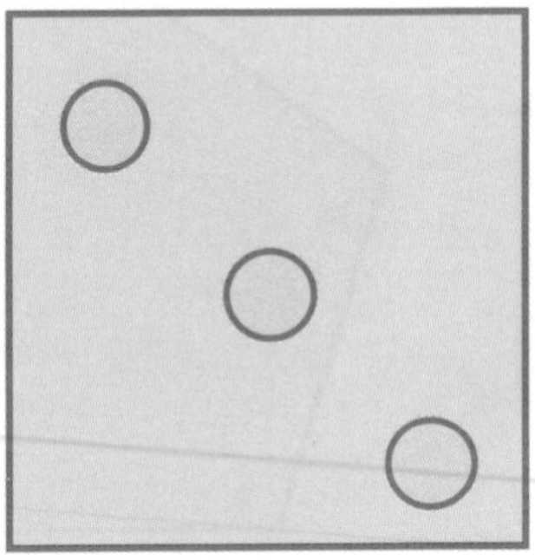

h

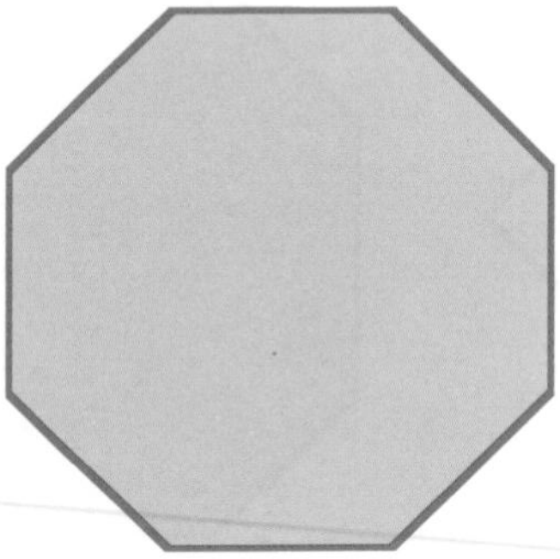

i

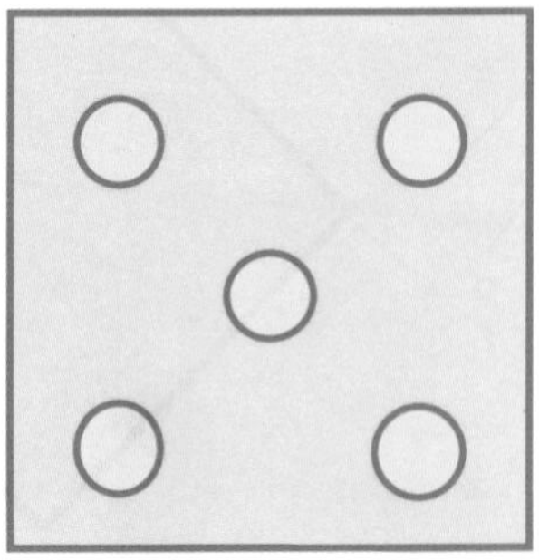

j

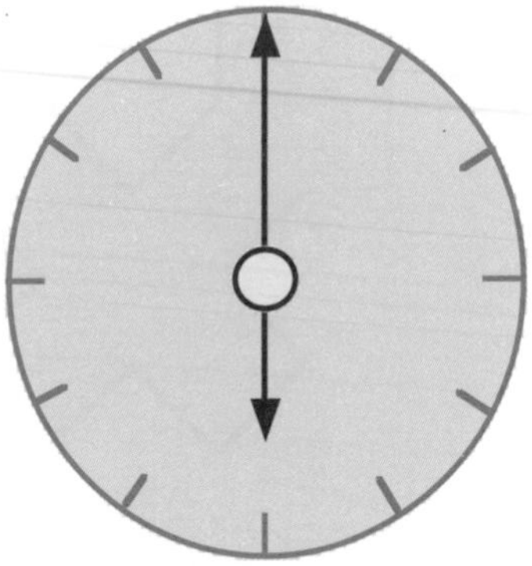

k

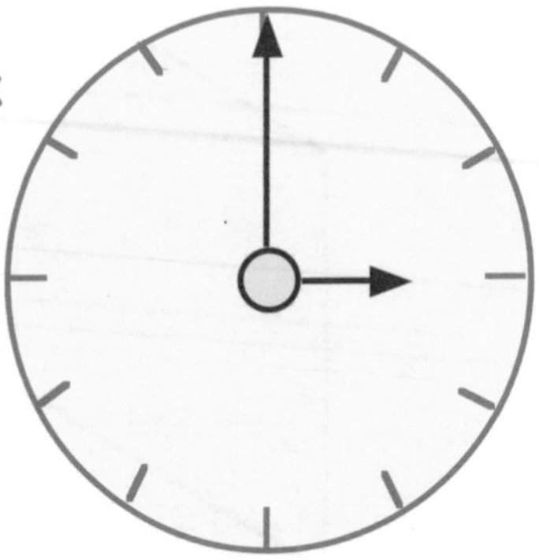

l

Making Symmetrical Shapes

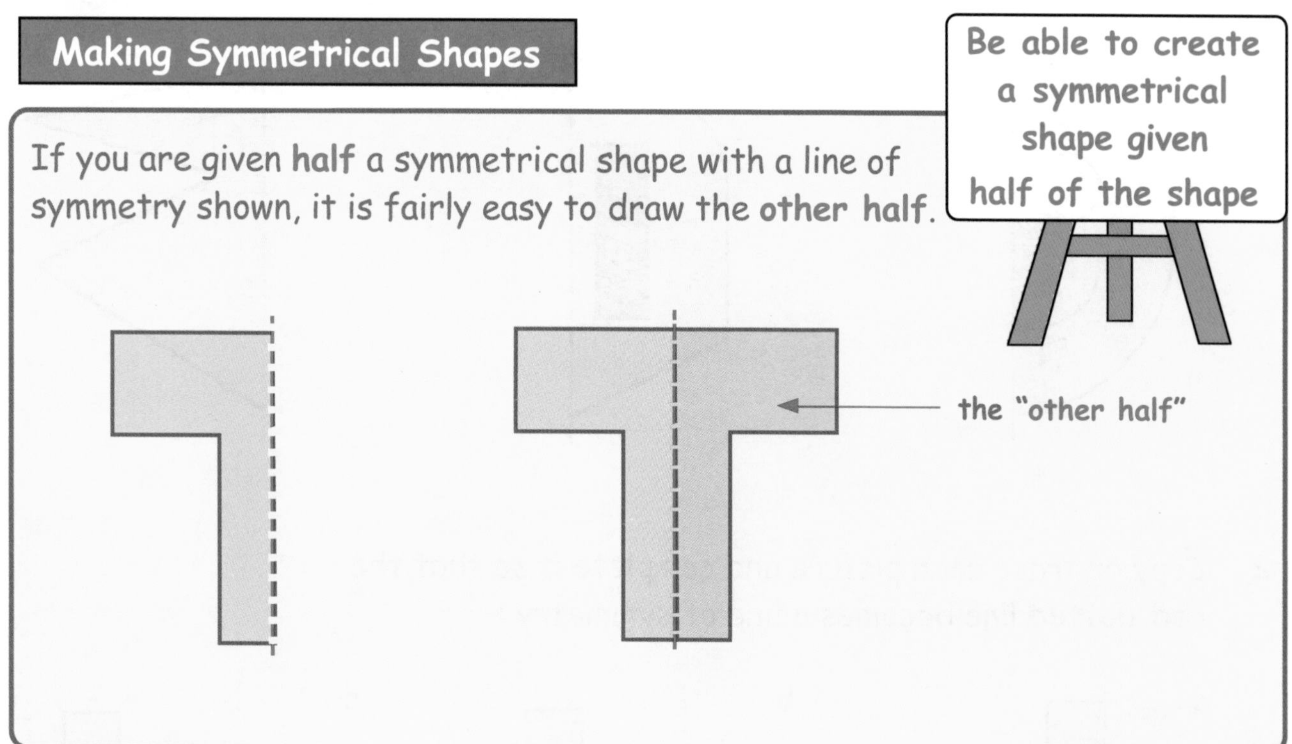

Be able to create a symmetrical shape given half of the shape
If you are given half a symmetrical shape with a line of symmetry shown, it is fairly easy to draw the other half.
the "other half"

Exercise 2

Worksheet 2·4

1. Copy each shape or picture and complete it so that the **red dotted** line becomes a line of symmetry :-

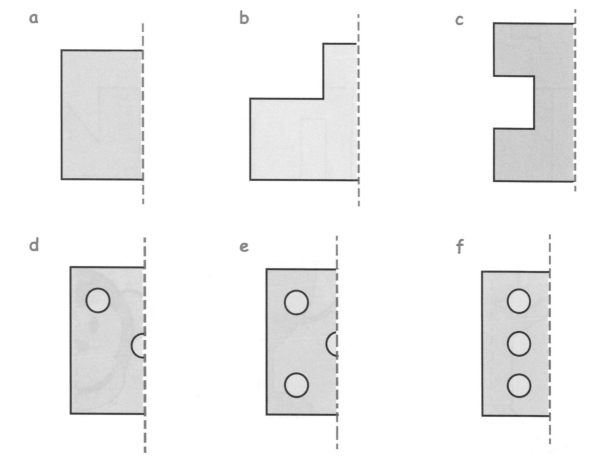

a

b

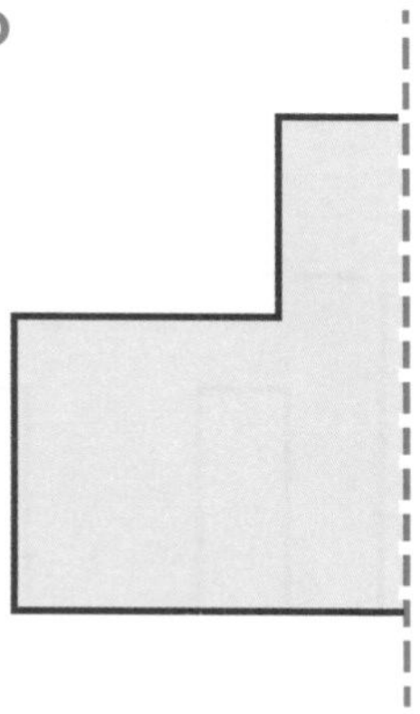

c

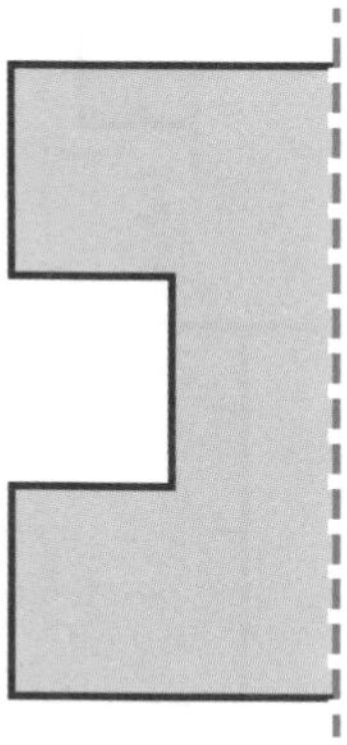

d

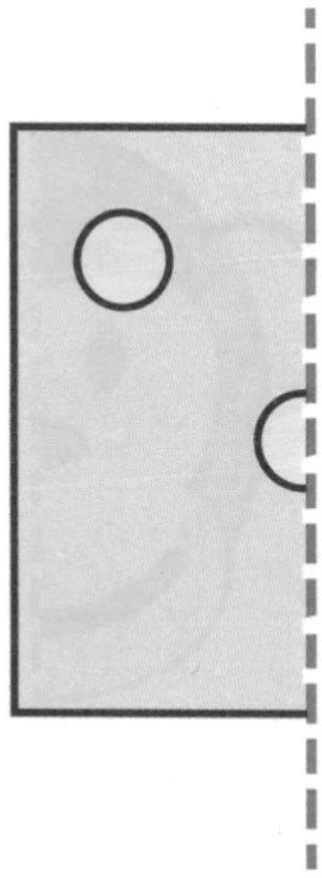

e

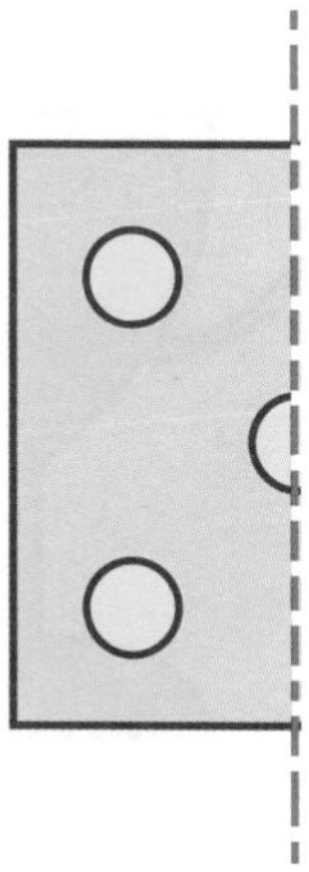

f

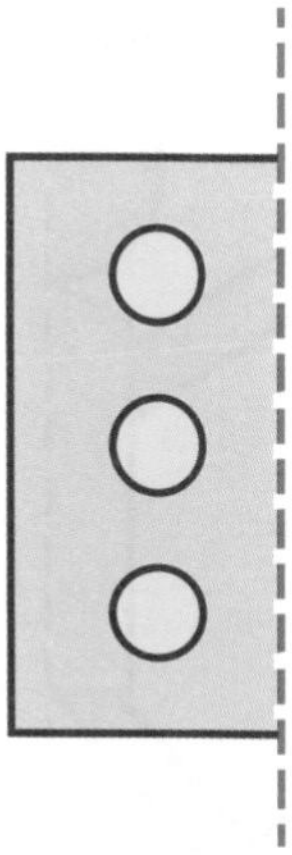

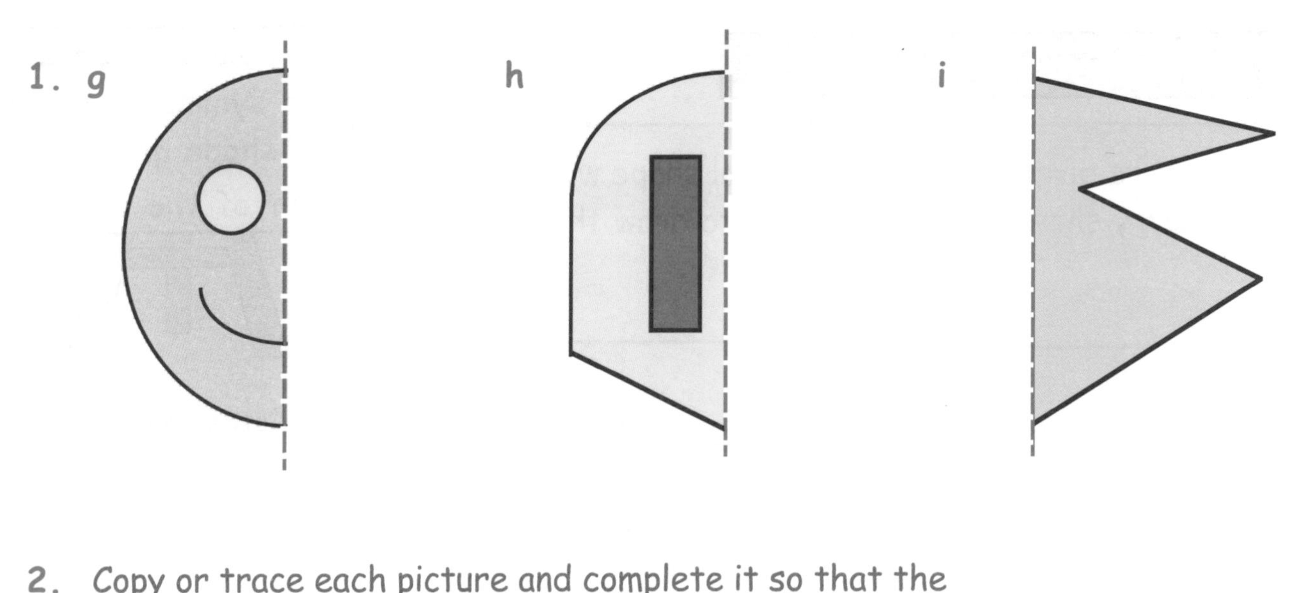

2. Copy or trace each picture and complete it so that the **red dotted** line becomes a line of symmetry :-

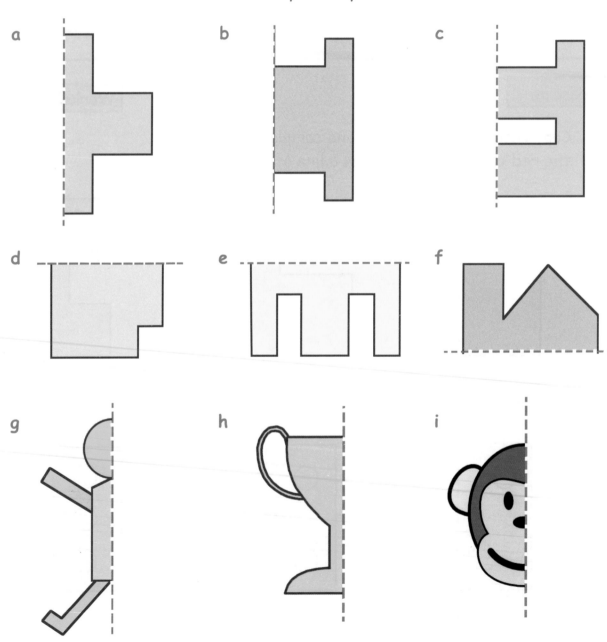

a

b

c

d

e

f

g

h

i

3. *These are much harder.*

Worksheet 2·5

Copy each figure and complete it so that the red dotted line or lines become lines of symmetry :-

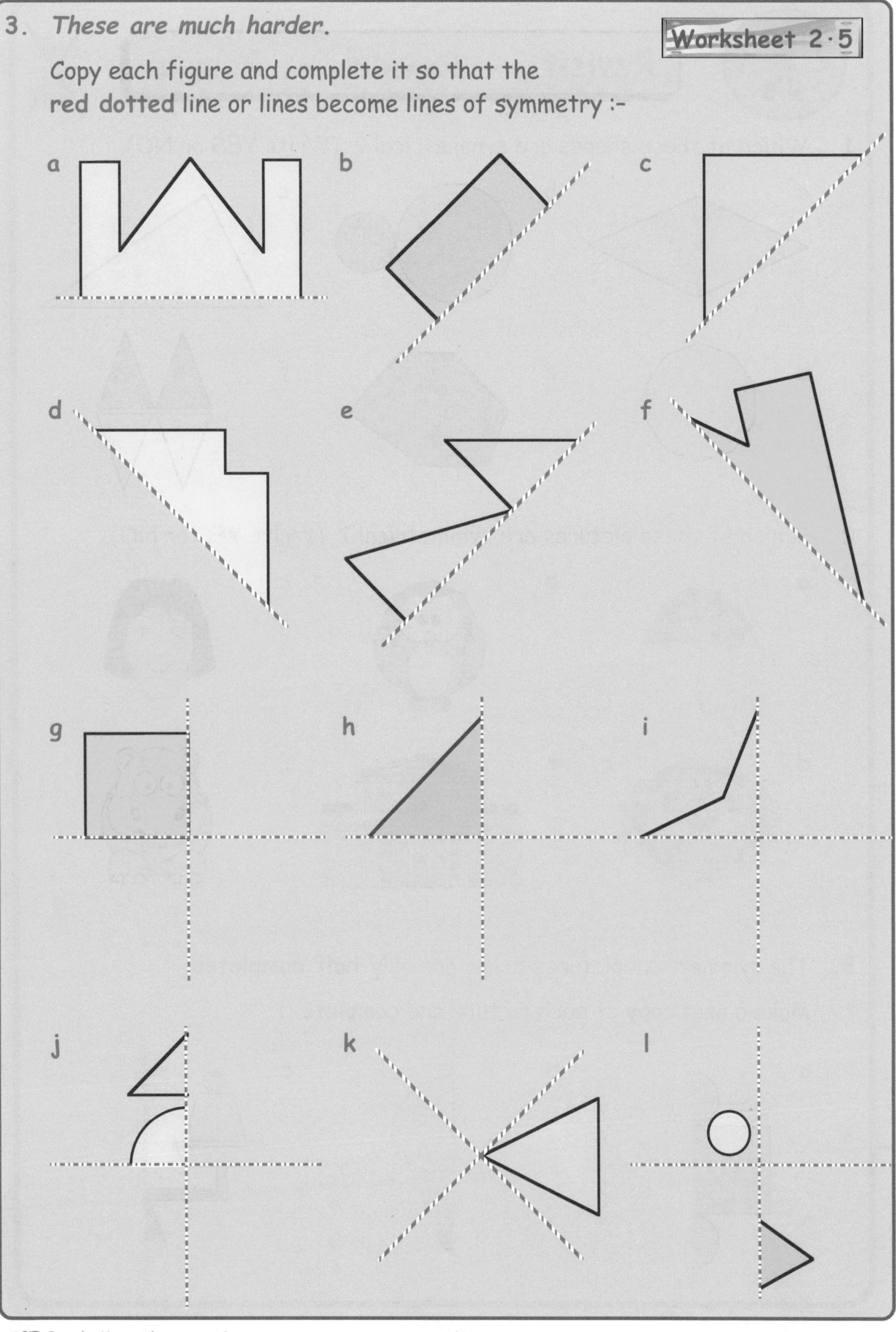

Revisit - Review - Revise

1. Which of these shapes are symmetrical ? (Write **YES** or **NO**).

a 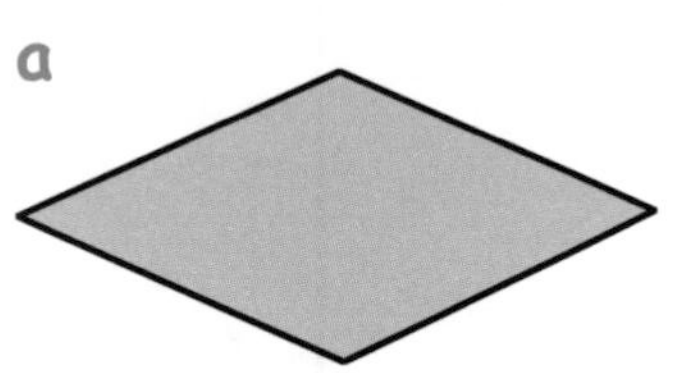

b 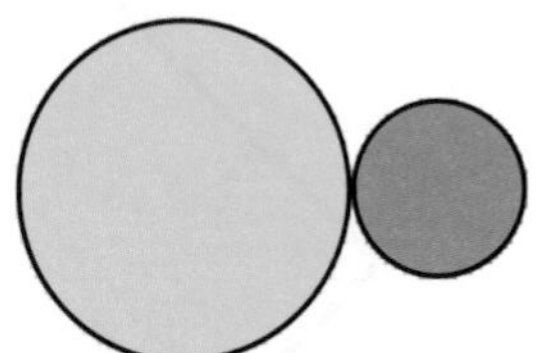

c 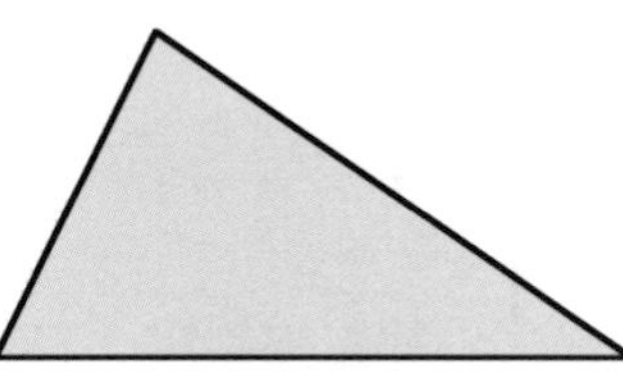

d 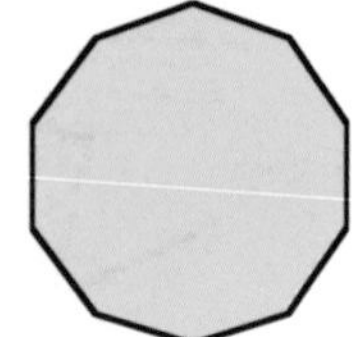

e 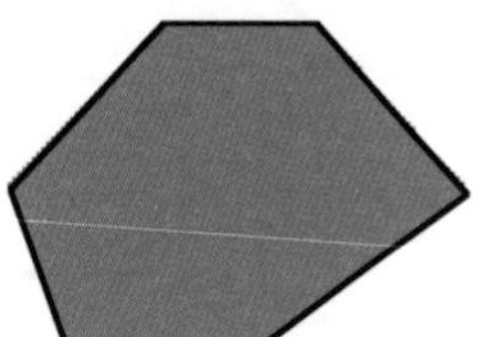

f 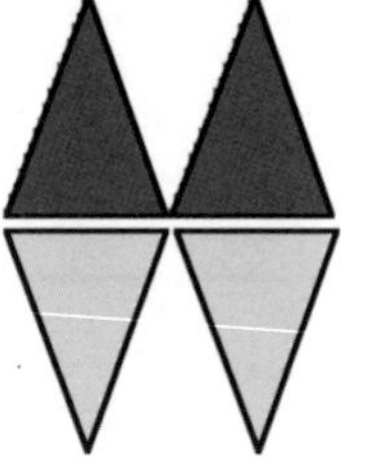

2. Which of these pictures are symmetrical ? (Write **YES** or **NO**).

a 

b 

c 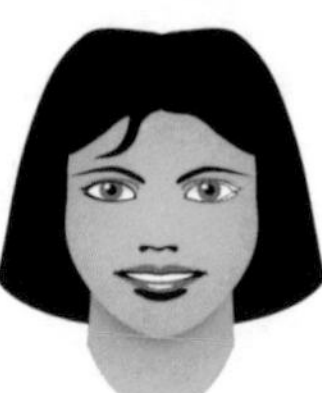

d 

e 

f 

3. The symmetrical pictures below are only **half completed**.

   Make a neat **copy** of each picture and **complete** it.

a 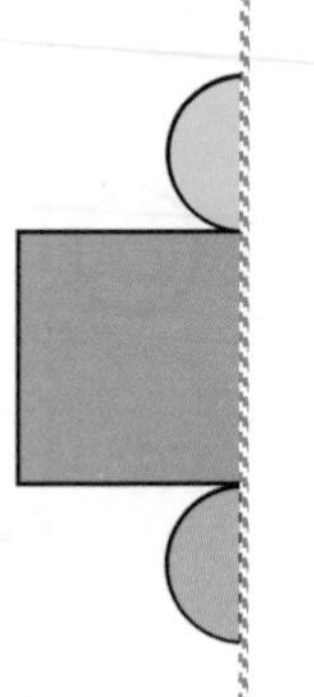

b 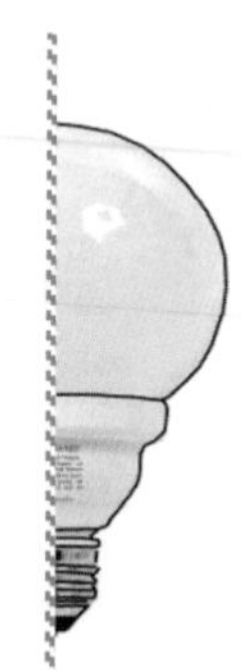

c 

Revision of x, + and -

1. Copy and work out :-

a $\begin{array}{r} 27 \\ +\ 9 \\ \hline \end{array}$ b $\begin{array}{r} 54 \\ +\ 35 \\ \hline \end{array}$ c $\begin{array}{r} 68 \\ +\ 756 \\ \hline \end{array}$ d $\begin{array}{r} 294 \\ +\ 689 \\ \hline \end{array}$

e $\begin{array}{r} 77 \\ -\ 5 \\ \hline \end{array}$ f $\begin{array}{r} 468 \\ -\ 35 \\ \hline \end{array}$ g $\begin{array}{r} 617 \\ -\ 39 \\ \hline \end{array}$ h $\begin{array}{r} 815 \\ -\ 297 \\ \hline \end{array}$

2. Find :-

a 83 + 49 b 325 + 478 c 92 - 57 d 782 - 136

3. Copy and work out :-

a $\begin{array}{r} 54 \\ \times\ 2 \\ \hline \end{array}$ b $\begin{array}{r} 73 \\ \times\ 3 \\ \hline \end{array}$ c $\begin{array}{r} 89 \\ \times\ 2 \\ \hline \end{array}$ d $\begin{array}{r} 68 \\ \times\ 3 \\ \hline \end{array}$

4. Find :-

a 2 x 55 b 3 x 91 c 78 x 2 d 49 x 3

5. Though 73, Sadie still plays tennis every week.

Husband Albert, 8 years older, doesn't play any more.

What age is Albert ?

6. 

At the end of their sale, Boddies Garden Centre still had 83 watering cans left to sell.

After lowering their price again, they sold 69 in an hour.

How many had they left then ?

7. Sandy the slater was quoting £183 to replace two roof tiles.

Roofie Roofers were asking £276 for the same job.

How much dearer were Roofie Roofers ?

8.

In a sand pie making competition on Prestwick beach, the under 10's made 97 pies.

The under 15's made 36 pies more than that.

How many did they make ?

9. McGall's Buses were selling their old buses.

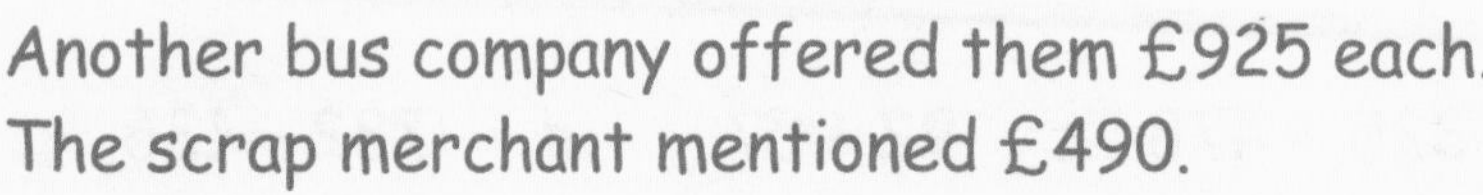

Another bus company offered them £925 each.
The scrap merchant mentioned £490.

How much less would McGall's get if they scrapped the buses ?

10.

These two construction workers are discussing the building of 625 houses in a new estate.

208 are to be detached houses;
360 semi-detached houses, the rest bungalows.

a How many bungalows are to be built ?

b How many more semi-detached than detached ?

11. The cost of a driving lesson is £28.

Jessie books 3 lessons.

How much will this cost her ?

12.

A packet of rich flavoured coffee costs £3 and small cartons of milk are priced at 35p.

What would it cost for a box with 15 packets of coffee and 2 cartons of milk ?

Whole Numbers 2

4 times table

Be able to multiply by 4 and learn.

Can you remember your **3 times** table ?

3 x 1 = 3

3 x 2 = 6

3 x ... = ...

etc

The **4 times** table can be done in a similar way.

Use **Worksheet 3·1** to complete the **4 times** table.

4 sets of 0 = 0	4 x 0 = 0
4 sets of 1 = 4	4 x 1 = 4
4 sets of 2 = 8	4 x 2 = 8
4 sets of 3 = 12	4 x 3 = 12
4 sets of 4 = 16	4 x 4 = 16
4 sets of .. = ...	4 x 5 = 20
4 sets of .. = ...	4 x 6 = ...
4 sets of .. = ...	4 x 7 = ...
4 sets of .. = ...	4 x .. = ...
4 sets of .. = ...	4 x .. = ...
4 sets of .. = ...	4 .. .. = ...

Exercise 1

1. **Copy** and **complete** :-

a 4 x 4 =	b 4 x 2 =	c 4 x 3 =
d 4 x 6 =	e 4 x 5 =	f 4 x 10 =
g 4 x 7 =	h 4 x 8 =	i 4 x 9 =

2. What numbers are **missing** ?

a 4 x .... = 20	b 4 x .... = 8	c 4 x .... = 16
d 4 x .... = 28	e 4 x .... = 12	f 4 x .... = 36
g 4 x .... = 24	h 4 x .... = 4	i 4 x .... = 32.

Example What is **28 x 4** ?

Set down like this.

$$\begin{array}{r} 28 \\ \times\ {}_{3}4 \\ \hline 112 \end{array}$$ ✓

3. **Copy** and **complete** :-

a
$$\begin{array}{r} 14 \\ \times 4 \\ \hline \end{array}$$

b
$$\begin{array}{r} 27 \\ \times 4 \\ \hline \end{array}$$

c
$$\begin{array}{r} 43 \\ \times 4 \\ \hline \end{array}$$

d
$$\begin{array}{r} 52 \\ \times 4 \\ \hline \end{array}$$

e
$$\begin{array}{r} 85 \\ \times 4 \\ \hline \end{array}$$

f
$$\begin{array}{r} 38 \\ \times 4 \\ \hline \end{array}$$

g
$$\begin{array}{r} 70 \\ \times 4 \\ \hline \end{array}$$

h
$$\begin{array}{r} 97 \\ \times 4 \\ \hline \end{array}$$

i
$$\begin{array}{r} 89 \\ \times 4 \\ \hline \end{array}$$

4. Find :-

a 27 x 4   b 53 x 4   c 46 x 4

d 74 x 4   e 81 x 4   f 93 x 4

g 35 x 4   h 13 x 4   i 68 x 4.

5. a There are **4** wheels on a car.

How many wheels are there on **45** cars ?

b 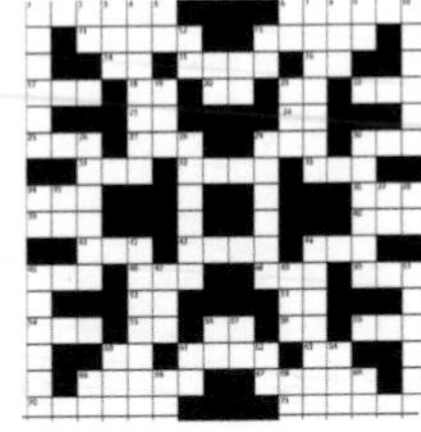

There are **19** words with **4** letters in a crossword.

How many letters in **total** ?

c Most taxis can carry **4** people.

How many people can be carried by **37** taxis ?

5 times table

Be able to multiply by 4 and learn.

You should now know the :-

2 times table, the
3 times table and the
4 times table.

The 5 times table can be found in a similar way.

Use **Worksheet 3·2** to complete the 5 times table.

5 sets of 0 = 0	5 x 0 = 0
5 sets of 1 = 5	5 x 1 = 5
5 sets of 2 = 10	5 x 2 = 10
5 sets of 3 = 15	5 x 3 = 15
5 sets of 4 = 20	5 x 4 = 20
5 sets of .. = ...	5 x 5 = 25
5 sets of .. = ...	5 x 6 = ...
5 sets of .. = ...	5 x 7 = ...
5 sets of .. = ...	5 x .. = ...
5 sets of .. = ...	5 x .. = ...
5 sets of .. = ...	.. . .. = ...

Exercise 2

1. **Copy** and **complete** :-

a 5 x 3 =　　b 5 x 2 =　　c 5 x 4 =

d 5 x 10 =　　e 5 x 6 =　　f 5 x 5 =

g 5 x 8 =　　h 5 x 7 =　　i 5 x 9 =

2. **Missing** numbers again. Find them.

a 5 x .... = 25　　b 5 x .... = 10　　c 5 x .... = 5

d 5 x .... = 15　　e 5 x .... = 35　　f 5 x .... = 45

g 5 x .... = 20　　h 5 x .... = 30　　i 5 x .... = 40.

Example What is **47 x 5** ?

$$\begin{array}{r} 47 \\ \times \ {}_{3}5 \\ \hline 235 \end{array}$$ ✓

Set down like this.

3. **Copy** and **complete** :-

a $\begin{array}{r} 16 \\ \times 5 \\ \hline \end{array}$ b $\begin{array}{r} 42 \\ \times 5 \\ \hline \end{array}$ c $\begin{array}{r} 53 \\ \times 5 \\ \hline \end{array}$

d $\begin{array}{r} 74 \\ \times 5 \\ \hline \end{array}$ e $\begin{array}{r} 35 \\ \times 5 \\ \hline \end{array}$ f $\begin{array}{r} 87 \\ \times 5 \\ \hline \end{array}$

g $\begin{array}{r} 91 \\ \times 5 \\ \hline \end{array}$ h $\begin{array}{r} 78 \\ \times 5 \\ \hline \end{array}$ i $\begin{array}{r} 150 \\ \times 5 \\ \hline \end{array}$

4. **Find** :-

a 27 x 5 b 32 x 5 c 66 x 5

d 44 x 5 e 81 x 5 f 73 x 5

g 5 x 58 h 5 x 93 i 125 x 5

5. a Perfume is sold in **50 ml** bottles.
How many ml in **5** bottles ?

b May hangs **5** T-shirts on to every rail.
How many T-shirts will she put on **24** rails ?

c **5p** for a blackcurrant chew.
How much for **75** of them ?

10 times table

Be able to multiply by 10 and learn.

You should now know the :-

2 times table, the
3 times table, the
4 times table and the
5 times table.

The 10 times table is easy and can be found in a similar way.

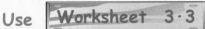

Use 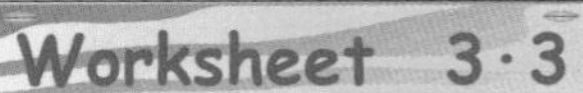 to complete the 10 times table.

10 sets of 0 = 0	10 x 0 = 0
10 sets of 1 = 10	10 x 1 = 10
10 sets of 2 = 20	10 x 2 = 20
10 sets of 3 = 30	10 x 3 = 30
10 sets of 4 = 40	10 x 4 = 40
10 sets of .. = ...	10 x 5 = 50
10 sets of .. = ...	10 x 6 = ...
10 sets of .. = ...	10 x 7 = ...
10 sets of .. = ...	10 x .. = ...
10 sets of .. = ...	10 x .. = ...
10 sets of .. = ...	10 x .. = ...

Exercise 3

1. Copy and complete :-

a	10 x 0 =	b	10 x 2 =	c	10 x 5 =
d	10 x 8 =	e	10 x 7 =	f	10 x 6 =
g	10 x 10 =	h	10 x 9 =	i	10 x 3 =

2. More numbers missing ! What are they ?

a	10 x .... = 50	b	10 x .... = 20	c	10 x .... = 80
d	10 x .... = 30	e	10 x .... = 60	f	10 x .... = 70
g	10 x .... = 90	h	10 x .... = 40	i	10 x .... = 100.

Multiplying by 10

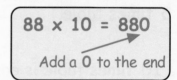

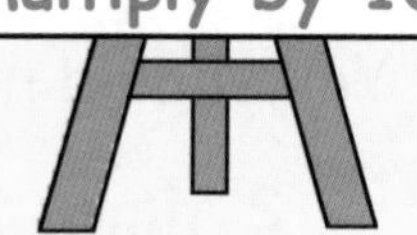
Learn a quick way to multiply by 10

It is easy to multiply a whole number by 10.

Simply, add a 0 to the end of the number

Example 1 49 x 10

$$\begin{array}{r} 49 \\ \times\ 10 \\ \hline 490 \end{array}$$

Example 2 70 x 10

$$\begin{array}{r} 70 \\ \times\ 10 \\ \hline 700 \end{array}$$

Example 3 88 x 10

88 x 10 = 880

Add a 0 to the end

Exercise 4

1. **Copy** and **complete** :-

a $\begin{array}{r} 19 \\ \times 10 \\ \hline \end{array}$ b $\begin{array}{r} 47 \\ \times 10 \\ \hline \end{array}$ c $\begin{array}{r} 68 \\ \times 10 \\ \hline \end{array}$ d $\begin{array}{r} 95 \\ \times 10 \\ \hline \end{array}$

2. Try these **mentally** :-

a 24 x 10 b 37 x 10 c 56 x 10 d 82 x 10.

3. Find the **missing** numbers :-

a 10 x .... = 120 b 10 x .... = 500 c 10 x .... = 1000.

4. a In a safari park, there is **one** keeper for every **10** elephants.
If there are **13** keepers, how many elephants ?

b 

Candles are packed in boxes of **10**.
How many candles in **72** boxes ?

c There are **10** DVD's in a pack.
How many DVD's are there in **47** packs ?

Multiplying 3 digits

Be able to multiply a 3 digit number.

Example 1 154 x 3

Example 2 187 x 4

Example 3 325 x 5

Exercise 5

1. Copy and complete :-

a	104 x 2	b	203 x 3	c	211 x 4
d	112 x 5	e	764 x 2	f	496 x 3
g	525 x 4	h	667 x 5	i	887 x 2
j	758 x 3	k	599 x 4	l	900 x 5

2. Set down as in Question 1 and find the answers :-

a	279 x 2	b	216 x 3	c	163 x 4
d	177 x 5	e	595 x 2	f	614 x 3
g	4 x 448	h	609 x 5	i	10 x 815.

3. Mr Spencer owns **2** factories.

There are **460** workers in each.

How many people work for him ?

4. 

Eva and her two sisters each took **£325** with them on holiday.

What did **3** of them take **altogether** ?

5. Chic earns **£338** per week as a painter.

What will he get paid for a month (**4** weeks) ?

6. 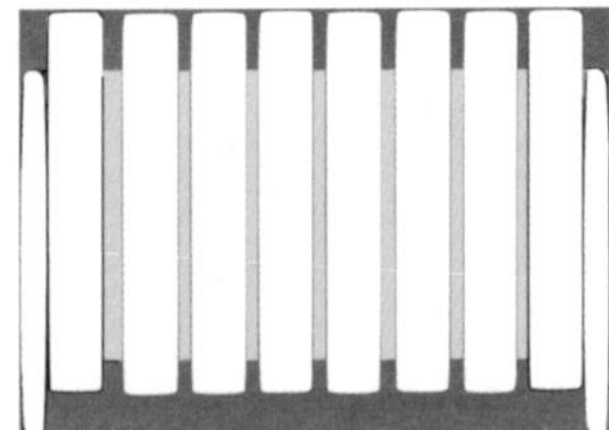

Radiators cost **£183** each.

What's the cost of **10** ?

7. A shopkeeper bought in **275** pens at **£2** each.

How much did she pay for them ?

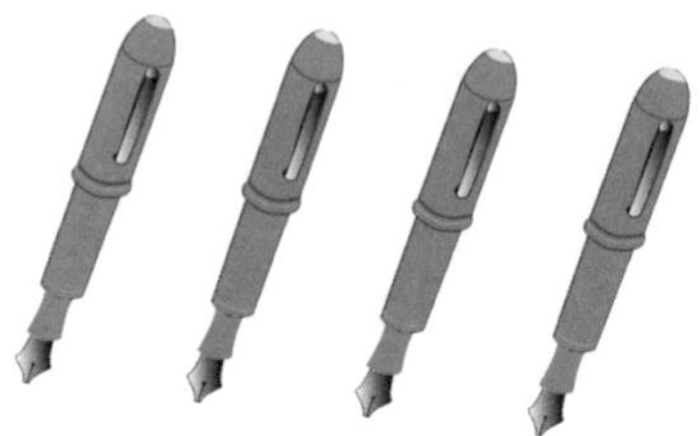

8. 

Each of the **3** levels of a cinema can seat **194** people.

How many people can the cinema hold ?

9. The bucket can hold **4** litres of water.

The tank holds **180** times that.

How many litres can the tank hold ?

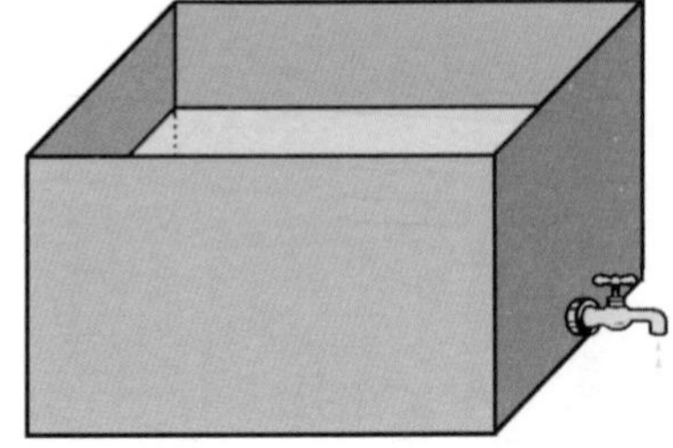

Mixed Exercise

Be able to multiply up to 3 digits by 2, 3, 4, 5 or 10.

Exercise 6

1. Copy and complete :-

a 2 x 6 = b 3 x 7 = c 4 x 8 =

d 5 x 9 = e 10 x 5 = f 40 x 10 =

2. What numbers are missing ?

a 2 x .... = 16 b 3 x .... = 27 c 4 x .... = 12

d 5 x .... = 35 e 10 x .... = 80 f .... x 10 = 210.

3. Copy and complete :-

a 18 x 2 b 46 x 3 c 29 x 4

d 60 x 5 e 86 x 2 f 97 x 3

g 75 x 4 h 48 x 5 i 625 x 2

j 419 x 3 k 263 x 4 l 720 x 5

4. Find :-

a 45 x 2 b 84 x 3 c 68 x 4

d 144 x 5 e 24 x 10 f 385 x 5

g 4 x 716 h 3 x 807 i 637 x 10.

5. Curry pies are on special offer in the bakers at 86p each.

Jim bought 2 of them.

How much did he pay ?

6. 

To carry out an experiment, a scientist used 150 jars, with 3 bugs in each jar.

How many bugs did she use altogether ?

7. Each week, Molly puts £38 worth of petrol into her mini.

How much does she spend on petrol over a month (4 weeks) ?

8. 

Flo's Flowers sold 430 bunches of roses on Valentine's Day.

If they cost £10 per bunch, how much did the shop take in that day ?

9. Last Christmas, Bob the binman got a £5 tip from every one of the 260 people in the village.

How much did this bonus come to in total ?

10. 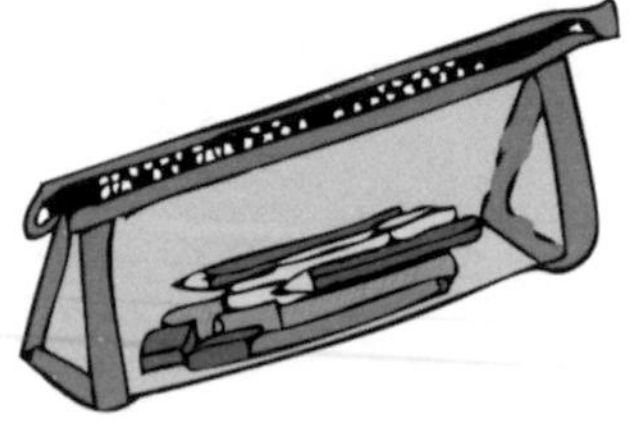

These pencil cases can hold 99 pencils.

How many pencils can 3 of them hold ?

11. A basket can hold 120 apples.

There are 4 vans outside a supermarket and each van contains 5 baskets of apples.

How many apples are there in total ?

Doubles and Trebles

Be able to
double (x 2) or
treble (x 3) any
number

To **DOUBLE** a number, you simply x by 2.

To **TREBLE** a number, you simply x by 3.

double 9 —> **2** x 9 = 18	**double** 46 —> **2** x 46 = 92
treble 8 —> **3** x 8 = 24	**treble** 29 —> **3** x 29 = 87

Exercise 7

1. What is :-

   a double 8   b double 15   c double 34   d double 67 ?

2. What is :-

   a treble 9   b treble 20   c treble 42   d treble 75 ?

In this "funfair" game, you throw hoops at a board to win prizes.

A **green** hoop counts **SINGLE**

A **red** hoop counts **DOUBLE**

A **blue** hoop counts **TREBLE**

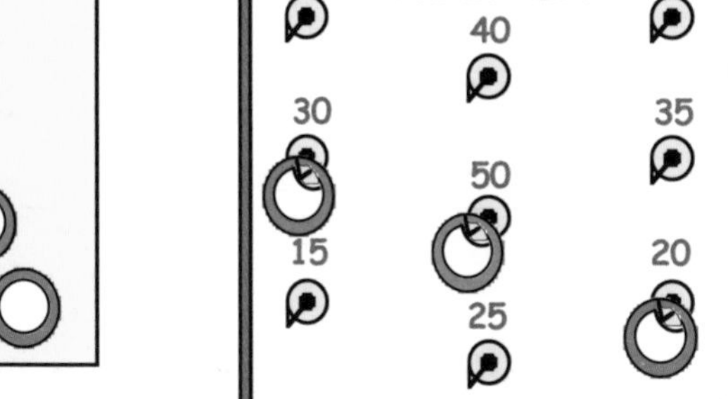

3. a What was the score from the **green** hoop ?

   b What was the score from the **red** hoop ? (**not** 30 !)

   c What was the score from the **blue** hoop ?

   d What was the **TOTAL** score ?

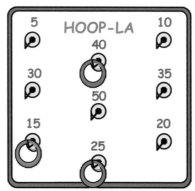

4. For each game, write down the score for each coloured hoop and then write down the **TOTAL** score.

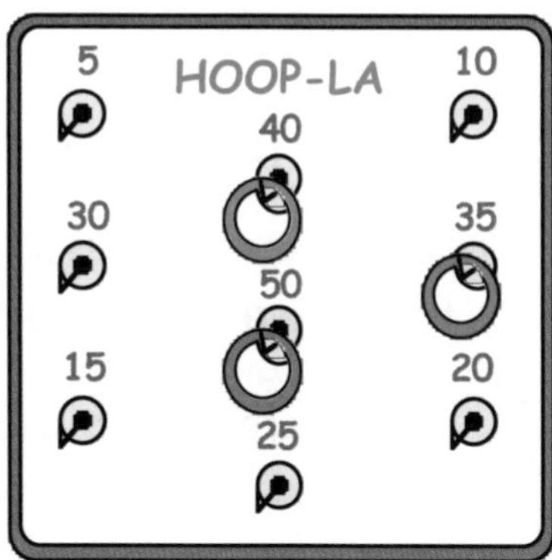

The 3 Я's

Revisit - Review - Revise

1. **Copy** and **complete** :-

a $2 \times 8 =$ b $4 \times 7 =$ c $3 \times 6 =$

d $5 \times 9 =$ e $7 \times 10 =$ f treble 9 = .

2. What numbers are missing ?

a 10 x .... = 40 b 3 x .... = 24 c 5 x .... = 30

d double .... = 18 e 2 x .... = 14 f 4 x .... = 32.

3. **Copy** and **complete** :-

a $\begin{array}{r} 362 \\ \times 2 \\ \hline \end{array}$ b $\begin{array}{r} 197 \\ \times 3 \\ \hline \end{array}$ c $\begin{array}{r} 86 \\ \times 4 \\ \hline \end{array}$

d $\begin{array}{r} 79 \\ \times 5 \\ \hline \end{array}$ e $\begin{array}{r} 372 \\ \times 4 \\ \hline \end{array}$ f $\begin{array}{r} 698 \\ \times 5 \\ \hline \end{array}$

4. Fish and chips costs £4 at Toni's.

Last Friday night, Toni sold 238 of them.

How much money did he take in ?

5. These designer handbags are on sale at £197 each.

What would it cost for the 5 of them ?

6. Water tanks hold 4 litres of water.

There are 3 trays of them stacked outside a factory and each tray has 10 tanks sitting on it.

How many litres of water are there altogether ?

Revision of Time

1. a What day is 2 days **after** Monday ?

   b What day is 3 days **before** Sunday ?

   c What is the month just **after** September ?

   d What month is 2 months **before** June ?

   e Name the **5th** month of the year.

   f What time is it 4 hours **after** quarter to eleven in the morning ?

2. Write the time shown on each clock :-

a

b

c

3. Write the time on each clock **in 2 ways** :-
(***Example*** – *quarter to 7* or *6·45 pm*)

a

morning

b

afternoon

c

evening

4. I arrived in Glasgow Central at four o'clock in the afternoon after a 5 hour train journey from Mallaig.

   When must the train have left Mallaig ?

Time 1

Digital Clocks

Be able to tell the time on a digital clock.

Remember - There are **60 minutes** in an **hour**.

Half Past is 30 minutes after the hour.

Quarter past is 15 minutes after the hour.

Quarter to is 15 minutes before the hour.

Digital clocks show the time using only numbers.

7:15 — hour, separator, minutes

8:00	means 8 o'clock.
2:30	means half past 2.
6:15	means quarter past 6.
3:45	means quarter to 4.

45 minutes past 3 is the same as 15 minutes to 4.

Exercise 1

Worksheet 4·1

1. Write the time shown on each clock **using words** :-

a 4:30 (half past ...)

b 5:15 (quarter past ...)

c 1:45 (quarter to ...)

d 8:30

e 9:00

f 6:45

g 2:30 h 9:45 i 11:15

j 9:30 k 1:15 l 5:45

2. For each clock below, **draw a digital clock** to show the **same** time :-

a
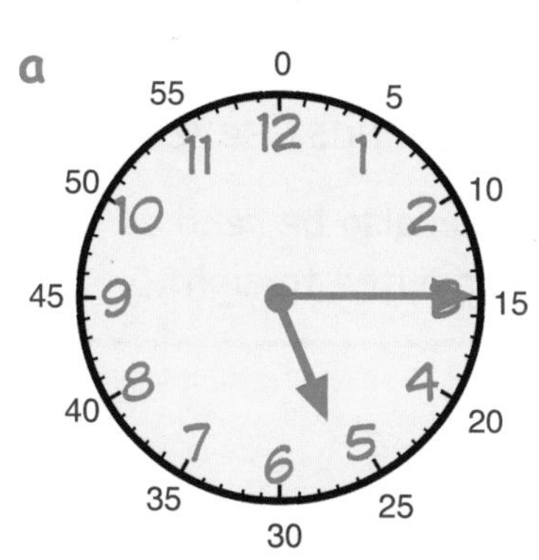

b
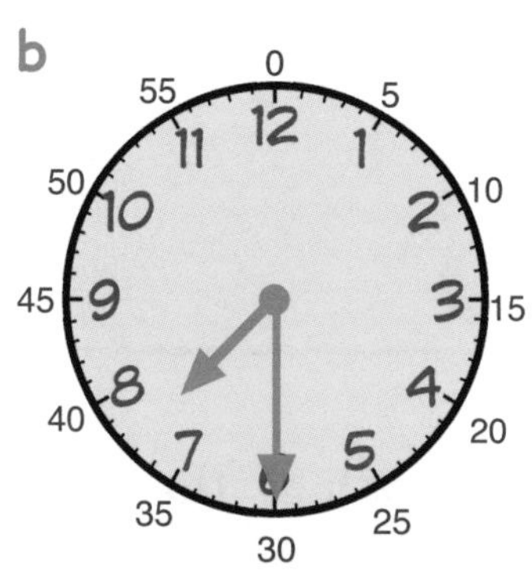

c

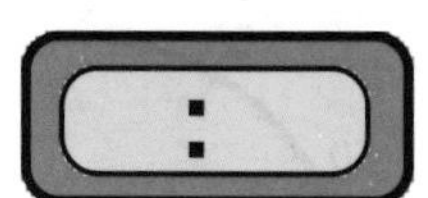

d
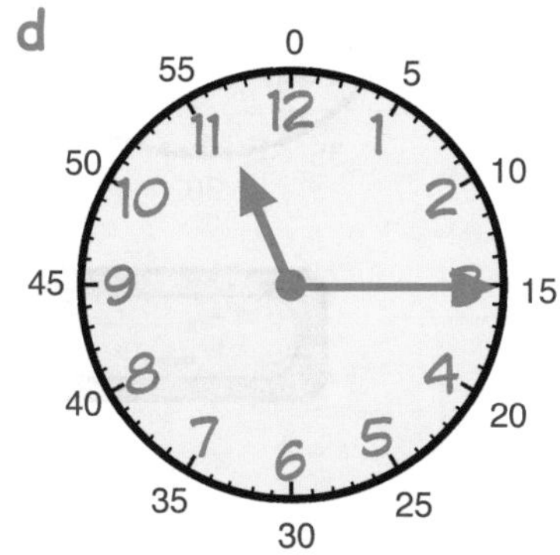

e

f
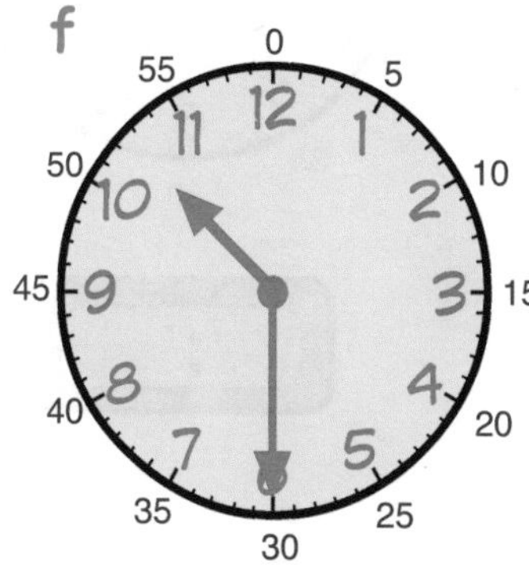

Worksheet 4·2

3. Write each time on a **digital clock** :-

a half past 9
b quarter past 1
c quarter to 9
d quarter past 3
e quarter to 12
f half past 2
g quarter past 7
h quarter to 11
i half past 6.

Examples :-

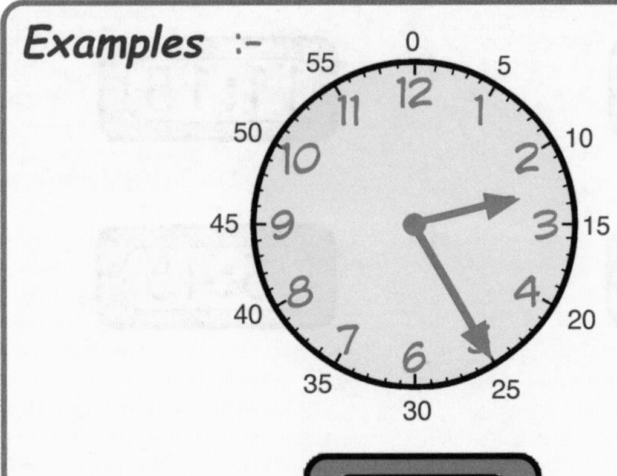

2:25

These clocks read twenty five minutes past two.

7:50

These clocks read fifty minutes past seven.

This can also be read as ten minutes to eight.

4. Write the digital time for each of the following :-

a

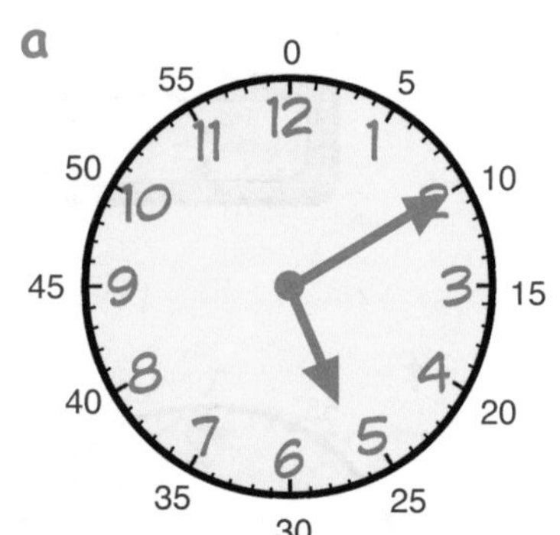

:

b

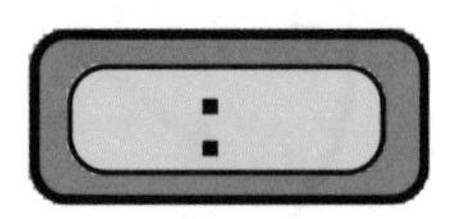

c

:

d	five past **3**	e	ten past **12**	f	twenty past **2**
g	quarter to **7**	h	half past **11**	i	six forty
j	nine fifty five	k	eleven twenty	l	three thirty
m	five to **6**	n	ten to **1**	o	twenty to **4**
p	twenty five to **1**	q	one minute to **2**	r	one minute to **8**

s thirty three minutes past **3**.

am and pm

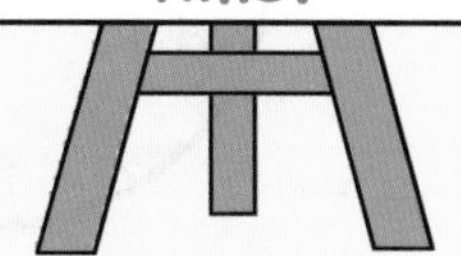

Be able to interpret and tell am or pm time.

Each day is divided into 2 "**halves**".

before - noon (ante-meridian (**am**))

after - noon (post-meridian (**pm**))

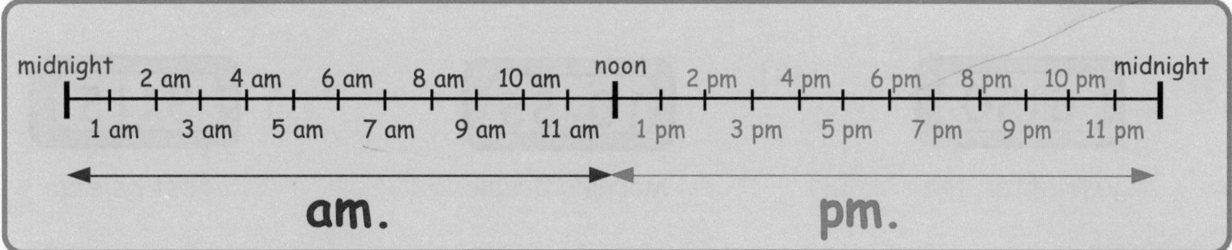

Most children start school at about 9·00 **am**.

Most people have their tea at about 5·00 **pm**.

The clock time shown can be written in 2 ways

"$\frac{1}{4}$ past 8 at night or 8·15 pm"

supper time

Exercise 2

1. Write down the time on each clock in 2 ways :-

a 

in the morning

b 

just before lunch

c 

bedtime

d 

school stops

e 

wake up early

f 

evening

1. g

Sunday morning

h

get up for school

i

asleep in your bed

j

just after tea

k

morning break

l

fast asleep

2. Write each of the following times using **am** or **pm**.

(For example, "**8·20 am**" or "**7·55 pm**") :-

a Ben went to the cubs at **$\frac{1}{4}$ past six** last night.

b Zara watched a film after tea which started at **$\frac{1}{4}$ to eight** and ended at **half past ten**.

c The evening News started at **five past seven** and finished at **five to eight**.

d My doctor's appointment is at **ten past one**.

My optician's appointment is at **quarter past three**.

e My plane left Edinburgh airport at **ten to seven** and arrived in London at **five to 8**. I then had breakfast.

f Jake left school at **twenty past three**.

He arrived home at **twenty five to four**.

7:45 am — 7:45 am can be written as "quarter to 8 in the morning".

3. Write each of the following times out fully :-
(use "**in the morning**", "**in the afternoon**" or "**at night**")

a 2:30 pm

b 9:45 am

c 10:50 pm

d 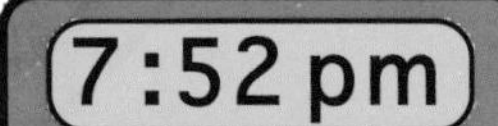

e 6:10 am

f 11:55 am

g 

h 

i 

j 

k 

l 

m 

n 

o 

p 1:11 pm

q 7:27 am

r 8:58 am

Exercise 3 **Simple Time Intervals** Extension

Be able to find simple time intervals.

1. a How many **hours** is it from **2** o'clock to **5** o'clock ?

   b How many **hours** is it from **3** o'clock to **8** o'clock ?

   c How many **hours** is it from **12** o'clock to **3** o'clock ?

   d How many **hours** is it from **5** o'clock to **11** o'clock ?

2. a How many **hours** is it from **half past 3** to **half past 5** ?

   b How many **hours** is it from **half past 6** to **half past 11** ?

   c How many **hours** is it from **quarter past 2** to **quarter past 7** ?

   d How many **hours** is it from **6:15 am** to **11:15 am** ?

   e How many **hours** is it from **5:20 pm** to **10:20 pm** ?

   f How many **hours** is it from **10:55 am** to **3:55 pm** ?

3. The bus station clock is shown.

1:30

   a What time does the clock read ?

   b My bus leaves at **quarter to two**.
   How many **minutes** until my bus leaves ?

   c Jack's bus leaves in **45 minutes** time.
   At what time does his bus leave ?

   d The bus to town leaves in **1 hours and 30 minutes** time.
   At what time does the bus to town leave ?

T33 JAY

Reading Simple Timetables

Be able to interpret simple timetables.

Shown is the 23 bus timetable.

Airdrie	10:45 am
Falkirk	11:25 am
Stirling	11:59 am
Perth	12:20 pm
Dundee	1:05 pm

The bus is at Airdrie at "**quarter to 11 in the morning**".

The bus is at Falkirk at "**twenty five minutes past 11 in the morning**".

Exercise 4

1. Look at the timetable above.

   Write the other 3 bus times out fully **in words**.

2. Look at the train timetable below.

Aberdeen →	Glasgow →	Leeds →	Luton →	London
9·55 am	12·05 am	....	5·40 pm	....

a At what time did the train leave **Aberdeen** ?

b At what time was the train at **Glasgow** ?

c The train arrived at Leeds at **10 past 3** in the afternoon.
Write this time (*using am/pm*).

d Write out in words when the train was at **Luton**.

e The train journey ended in London
at **ten to seven** at night.

Write this time (using am/pm).

3. Eric and his dad arrived at the show at **6·50 pm**.

Were they **late or early** ?

Tonight's
show is at
$\frac{1}{4}$ to 7

4.

EASY-AIR Flight Departures	
Malaga	10:55 am
Palma	11:40 am
Barcelona	12:35 pm
Ibiza	1:05 pm
Tenerife	2:50 pm
Nice	3:20 pm

Amy's mum is checking her flight times.

Her plane to Malaga leaves at **5 to 11 in the morning**.

Write the other departure times in a similar way.

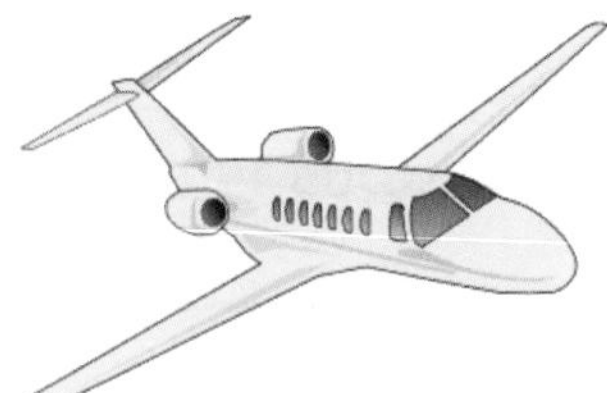

5. Stacey was looking at Channel 6's T.V. programmes for Tuesday.

CHANNEL 6

3:05	Olivio (R)
3:25	Royal Ascot
3:50	Count-Up (game show)
4:15	Ace Adventura (film)
5:25	Away And Home
5:50	Tea-Time News
6:25	Scottish Report
7:05	Seven-Alive
7:35	Sports Roundup
8:00	BIG SISTER (live)
8:50	News In Brief
9:00	Pyjama-Banana (film)

a **Royal Ascot** is on at **25 past 3** in the afternoon.

Write out the times of the following programmes fully in a similar way :-

(i) Count-Up

(ii) Away And Home

(iii) Sports Roundup

(iv) News In Brief

b Stacey was watching Channel 6 at **5 past 4**.

Which programme must she have been watching ?

c Which programmes are showing on Channel 6 at :-

(i) 5:35 pm (ii) 7:50 pm (iii) $\frac{1}{4}$ past 8 at night ?

24 hour Clock Time

Be able to change between 12 and 24 clock time (hours only).

Clock times can also be written using 24 clock time.

am times in 24 hour clock

7 am can be written as 0700 hours

pm times in 24 hour clock

8 pm is written as 2000 hours

mid night	1 am	2 am	3 am	4 am	5 am	6 am	7 am	8 am	9 am	10 am	11 am	noon	1 pm	2 pm	3 pm	4 pm	5 pm	6 pm	7 pm	8 pm	9 pm	10 pm	11 pm	mid night
0000	0100	0200	0300	0400	0500	0600	0700	0800	0900	1000	1100	1200	1300	1400	1500	1600	1700	1800	1900	2000	2100	2200	2300	0000

Morning times like 7.00 am stay basically as they are ——> 0700

Afternoon/evening times - **add on 12 hours** - 8.00 pm ——> 8 + 12 = 2000

Exercise 5

1. Write down each of these times using **24 hour** clock times :-

a	9 am	b	1 am	c	1 pm
d	5 am	e	5 pm	f	7 pm
g	11 pm	h	10 am	i	4 pm
j	10 pm	k	2 pm	l	3 am.

2. Write down each of these times in **12 hour** notation (using **am** or **pm**) :-

a	1400	b	1500	c	0600
d	1100	e	1800	f	0200
g	2100	h	2300	i	1330.

Revisit - Review - Revise

1. The time on this clock can be written as

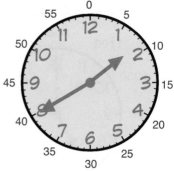

1.40 or twenty to two

Write each of these times in 2 ways.

a 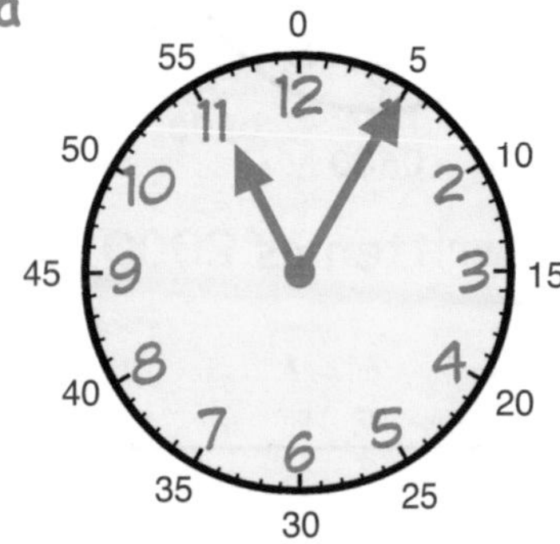

b 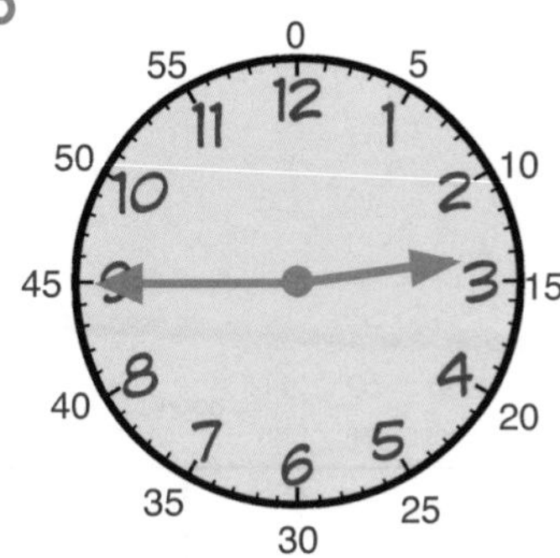

c 

2. Write these digital clock times using words :-

a 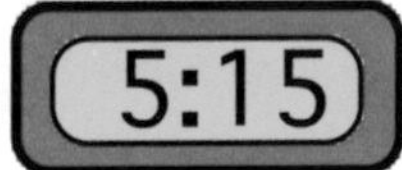

b 

c 

3. Write each time below in 12 hour form using **am** or **pm** :-

a 

Sunday breakfast

b 

supper- time

c 

get up for school

4. Shown below is part of a bus timetable.

Aberdeen —>	Dundee —>	Edinburgh —>	Glasgow —>	Ayr
9·55 am	11·05 am	....	2·10 pm	....

a At what time did the bus leave Aberdeen? (Answer in words).

b The bus arrived in Edinburgh at five minutes to noon.

Write this time using am/pm.

c The bus took 50 minutes to get from Glasgow to Ayr.

At what time did the bus arrive in Ayr?

5. Stan looks at part of a TV Times Guide.

CHANNEL 2

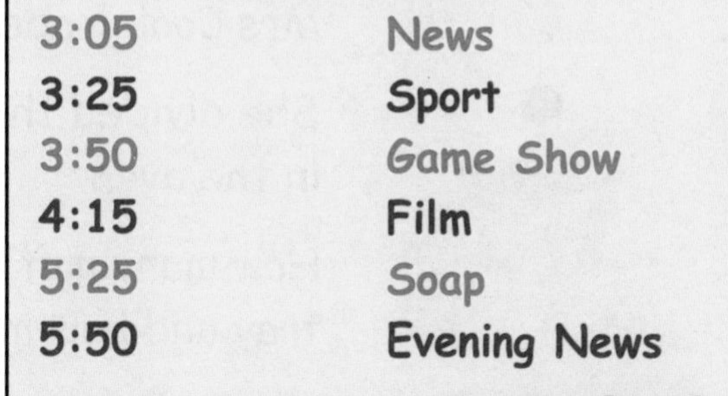

3:05	News
3:25	**Sport**
3:50	Game Show
4:15	**Film**
5:25	Soap
5:50	**Evening News**

Sport is on at **twenty five past three in the afternoon.**

a Write out these times in the same way :-

(i) Game Show

(ii) Soap

b Which programme starts at ten to six?

6. Change each of these times to **24 hour** form :-

a 5 am b 1 pm c 8 pm.

d 10 am e 11 pm f 3.30 pm.

7. Change each of these times to **12 hour** form :-

a 0200 b 1600 c 2100.

d 1100 e 2100 f 1630.

Revision of Division by 2 and 3

1. Copy and **work out** :-

a $2\overline{)28}$ b $3\overline{)39}$ c $2\overline{)35}$ d $3\overline{)48}$

e $3\overline{)64}$ f $2\overline{)71}$ g $2\overline{)98}$ h $3\overline{)77}$.

2. Find :-

a $39 \div 2$ b $53 \div 3$ c $31 \div 2$ d $76 \div 3$

e $51 \div 3$ f $68 \div 2$ g $89 \div 2$ h $87 \div 3$.

3. **3** litres of paint are needed to paint a fence **42** metres long.

1 litre of paint will cover how many metres of fencing ?

4. 

Mrs Cook made enough mix for **59** cherry muffins.

She divided the muffins equally onto **3** trays to put in the oven.

How many muffins did she manage to get on each tray and how many didn't make it onto a tray ?

5. **83** sunflower seeds were planted in **2** rows, one row having one more seed than the other.

How many seeds were in each row ?

6. Teddy bears are on sale in The Toy Store.

The bears must be bought **in pairs**.

a If there are only **35** bears to be sold, how many customers could buy two each and how many bears would be left unsold ?

b The bears sell for **£3** each.

How much will the store take in for the teddy bears it sells ?

Whole Numbers 3

Dividing by 4

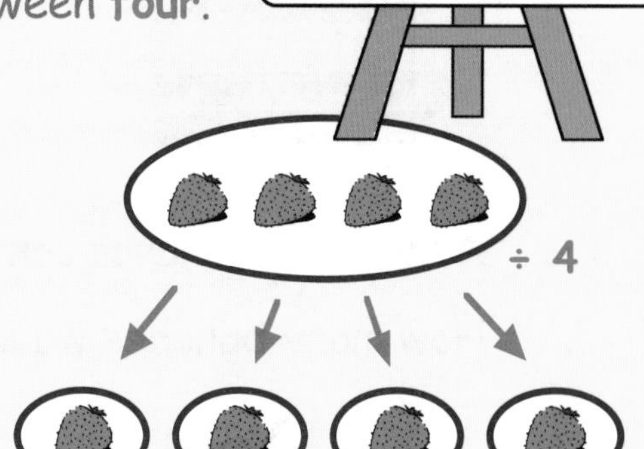

Dividing by **4** is the same as **sharing** equally between **four**.

Sam has **4** strawberries.

He shares them with Aaron, Joan and Pete.
All four each get **1** strawberry.

We say that **4 divided by 4 = 1**.

or **4 ÷ 4 = 1**

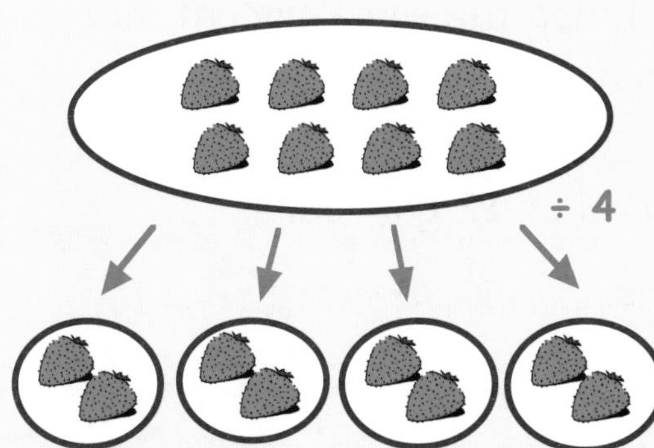

Julie has **8** strawberries.
She shares them with Pat, Nan and Ian.
They each get **2** strawberries.

We say that **8 divided by 4 = 2.**

or **8 ÷ 4 = 2**

Exercise 1

1. **Write** out your **4 times** table and use it to help in this exercise.

2. **Copy** and **complete** :-

a	12 ÷ 4 = ...	b	8 ÷ 4 = ...	c	16 ÷ 4 = ...
d	24 ÷ 4 = ...	e	20 ÷ 4 = ...	f	28 ÷ 4 = ...
g	36 ÷ 4 = ...	h	32 ÷ 4 = ...	i	40 ÷ 4 = ...

3. Find the missing numbers here :-

a	☐ ÷ 4 = 5	b	☐ ÷ 4 = 10	c	☐ ÷ 4 = 7
d	☐ ÷ 4 = 6	e	☐ ÷ 4 = 9	f	☐ ÷ 4 = 8.

4. Try these questions **mentally**.

a 4 children share out 32 flowers equally.

How many does each get ?

b  The total number of pencils in 4 boxes is 40.

How many pencils are in each box ?

c A bunch of bananas contains 4 bananas.

How many bunches would 28 bananas make ?

d  Frank bought 16 biscuits for his **four** dogs.

If he gave each dog the same amount, how many would each get ?

e When 4 girls went golfing they lost a total of 12 golf balls.

They each lost the same number of balls.

How many was that ?

f  It cost £36 for **four** child tickets to the finals of the tennis competition.

What was the price of a ticket ?

*** Remember**

48 ÷ 4 = ... can be written as :-	$4\overline{)48}$ giving 1 2	How many 4's are in the **4** ? answer **1** How many 4's are in the **8** ? answer **2**

5. **Copy** and **complete** these :-

a  $4\overline{)40}$ b $4\overline{)48}$ c $4\overline{)44}$

d $4\overline{)80}$ e $4\overline{)84}$ f $4\overline{)88}$

Set down each question as a division sum and work it out.

6. a It took Tam **84** seconds to eat **4** burgers.

   How long would it have taken him to eat 1 ?

   b 

   Kim bought **4** identical joysticks for a total of **£48**.

   How much did they each cost ?

   c A box of **88** chips was shared between **4** children.

   How many did each of them get ?

   d 

   A pineapple is quartered by cutting it into **4** slices.

   If I have **40** slices, how many whole pineapples must I have had to cut up ?

Dividing by 4 - Remainders

Be able to divide 2 digits by 4 (a remainder)

Example 1

45 ÷ 4 = ...
can be written as :- $4\overline{)4\,5}$ = **1 1 r 1**

How many 4's are in **4** ? ans **1**

How many 4's are in **5** ? ans **1 r 1**

Example 2

52 ÷ 4 = ...
can be written as :- $4\overline{)5\,{}^{1}2}$ = **1 3**

(remainder **1** is carried)

How many 4's are in **5** ? ans **1 r 1**

How many 4's are in **12** ? ans **3**

Example 3

67 ÷ 4 = ...
can be written as :- $4\overline{)6\,{}^{2}7}$ = **1 6 r 3**

(remainder **2** is carried and still another remainder appears)

How many 4's are in **6** ? ans **1 r 2**

How many 4's are in **27** ? ans **6 r 3**

Exercise 2 **Worksheet 5·1**

1. **Copy** and **complete** :-

a $13 \div 4 = ...$ b $11 \div 4 = ...$ c $14 \div 4 = ...$

d $23 \div 4 = ...$ e $9 \div 4 = ...$ f $7 \div 4 = ...$

g $18 \div 4 = ...$ h $15 \div 4 = ...$ i $19 \div 4 = ...$

2. **Set down** and **work out** :-

a $4\overline{)42}$ b $4\overline{)43}$ c $4\overline{)46}$ d $4\overline{)49}$

e $4\overline{)81}$ f $4\overline{)82}$ g $4\overline{)85}$ h $4\overline{)87}$.

** Remember - set down the following as division sums and work them out.*

3. a **17** slices of lasagne were divided between **4** diners.

How many slices did each get and how many were left over ?

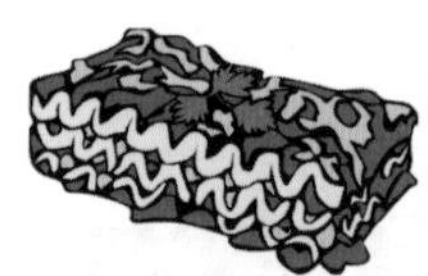

b 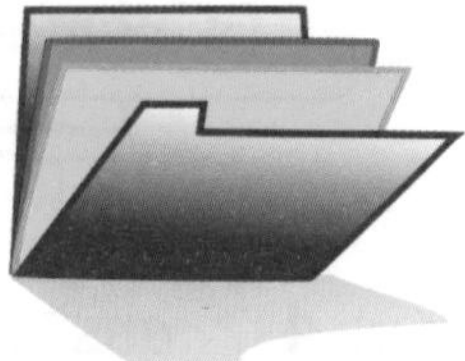

41 receipts were placed equally into **4** folders.

How many receipts went in each folder and how many were left out ?

c **4** envelopes were used to keep **89** stamps in.

Each envelope had the same number of stamps.

How many were in each envelope and how many were left out ?

d 

Playing in the garden, **Joe and his 3 pals** divided **83** water balloons between them and gave the rest to Joe's sister Mandy.

How many water balloons did Mandy get ?

e I'm thinking of a big number. When I divide it by 4, I get the answer 15, remainder 3.

What number was I thinking about ?

4. Copy and complete :-

a $4\overline{)28}$ b $4\overline{)32}$ c $4\overline{)40}$ d $4\overline{)52}$

e $4\overline{)56}$ f $4\overline{)68}$ g $4\overline{)64}$ h $4\overline{)60}$

i $4\overline{)72}$ j $4\overline{)76}$ k $4\overline{)92}$ l $4\overline{)96}$.

5. a My plants have to be fed every **4** days.

If I were to go on holiday for **36** days, how many times would my neighbour have to feed the plants ?

b  **48** tyres have to be put on to **4** identical trucks.

How many tyres will be on each truck ?

c **Four** girls collected a total of **£84** during a poppy appeal.

If they each collected the same amount, how much was that ?

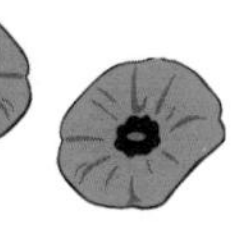

d 

Pizza slices are to be put into boxes, **4** to a box.

How many boxes will be needed for **76** slices ?

e The total cost for **4** pre-theatre dinners came to **£68**.

What was the cost for one dinner ?

6. Copy and complete :-

a $4\overline{)62}$ b $4\overline{)55}$ c $4\overline{)73}$ d $4\overline{)58}$

e $4\overline{)71}$ f $4\overline{)93}$ g $4\overline{)74}$ h $4\overline{)95}$

i $4\overline{)99}$ j $4\overline{)26}$ k $4\overline{)39}$ l $4\overline{)102}$.

7. a Gleamo Cleaning Company bought **63** scrubbing brushes and divided them among its **4** employees.

How many brushes did they each get and how many were left ?

b 

The council made **70** roundabout signs to be put up in **4** of its new towns, each town getting the same number.

How many signs did each town get and how many signs were not used ?

c **65** formula one racing cars lined up in **4**'s on the starting grid.

How many rows of four were there and how many cars were on the back row ?

d 

97 metres of guttering were used between **4** houses on a new estate.

How many metres were used on each house and how many metres were left over ?

e **39** golfers turned up to play in a **foursome** competition.

How many groups of **4** were formed and how many players were needed to make up another group ?

f 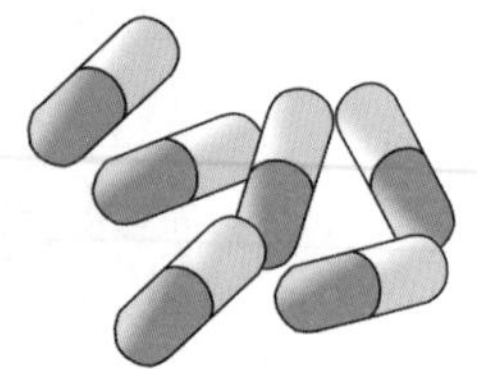

There are **54** headache tablets in a packet.

If Gemma takes **2 tablets twice** per day, how many days will the packet last - but what will Gemma have to do on the last day ?

8. **Copy** these divisions and work them out :-

a $4\overline{)27}$ b $4\overline{)29}$ c $4\overline{)34}$ d $4\overline{)37}$

e $4\overline{)44}$ f $4\overline{)51}$ g $4\overline{)57}$ h $4\overline{)61}$

i $4\overline{)66}$ j $4\overline{)72}$ k $4\overline{)79}$ l $4\overline{)86}$.

Dividing by 5

Be able to divide 2 digits by 5 (no remainder)

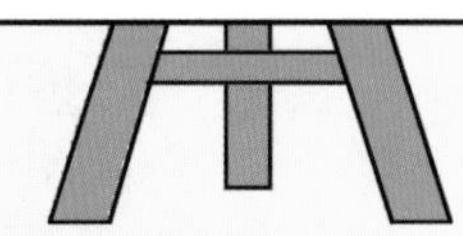

Dividing by 5 is the same as **sharing** equally between **five**.

Lennie has **5** Rollos.
He shares them with Jean, Jim, Irene and Helen.
All five each get 1 Rollo.

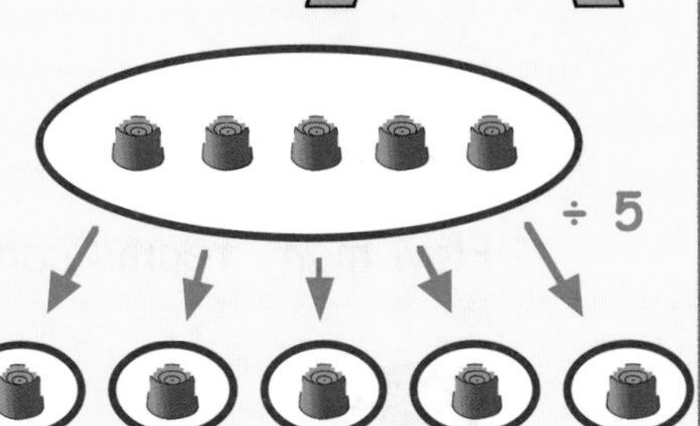

We say that **5 divided by 5 = 1.**

or 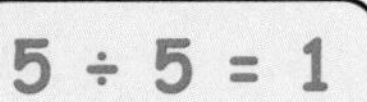

5 ÷ 5 = 1

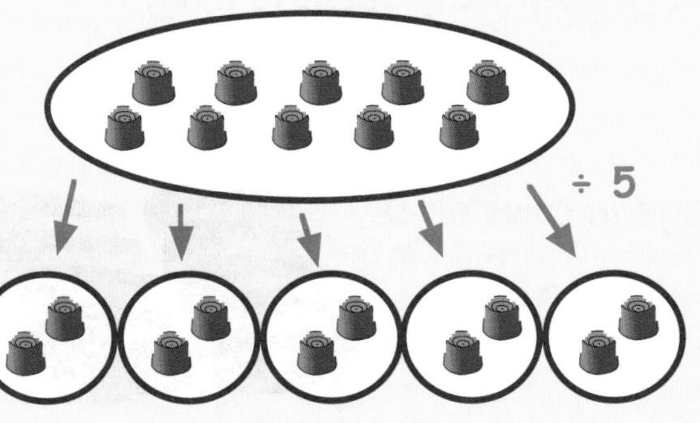

Marion has **10** Rollos.
She shares them with Ella, Annie, Chrissie and Alex.
All five of them get 2 Rollos.

We say that **10 divided by 5 = 2.**

or **10 ÷ 5 = 2**

* Note, also :- **15 ÷ 5 = 3 and 20 ÷ 5 = 4**

Exercise 3

1. **Write** out your **5 times** table and use it to help in this exercise

2. a 15 ÷ 5 = ... b 30 ÷ 5 = ... c 50 ÷ 5 = ...
   d 35 ÷ 5 = ... e 20 ÷ 5 = ... f 40 ÷ 5 = ...
   g 25 ÷ 5 = ... h 45 ÷ 5 = ... i 55 ÷ 5 = ...

3. Find the missing numbers :-
   a ▭ ÷ 5 = 3 b ▭ ÷ 5 = 7 c ▭ ÷ 5 = 10
   d ▭ ÷ 5 = 6 e ▭ ÷ 5 = 8 f ▭ ÷ 5 = 5.

4. Try these questions **mentally**.

a How many **£5** notes would I need for **£45** ?

b 

How many **5p** coins would I get for **20p** ?

c **40** children turn up for **five-a-side** football.

How many teams can be made up ?

d Each mini-packet of Rollos contains **5** sweets.

If I ate **50** Rollos, how many packets must I have eaten ?

e Buses have to be parked at the garage in rows of **5**.

If the bus company has a fleet of **35** buses, how many rows will there be ?

f 

25 counters were laid out in groups of **5**.

How many groups of five were there ?

g A chef at a hotel has **5** frying pans and **30** eggs.

If he divides the eggs equally over the pans, how many eggs will he be able to fry in each pan ?

h 

55 boxes of cereal were split equally between **5** shelves in a shop

How many boxes did each shelf hold ?

i Mr Price bought **5** chews for **25p** and **5** sugar mice for **45p**.

Mr Allan bought 1 chew and 1 sugar mouse from the same shop.

What was the total cost for him ?

Dividing by 5 - Remainders

Be able to divide 2 digits by 5 (a remainder)

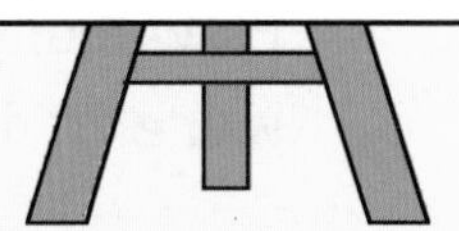

Example 1

57 ÷ 5 = ...
can be written as :-

$$5\overline{)57}\quad = 11 \text{ r } 2$$

How many 5's are in 5 ? answer **1**

How many 5's are in 7 ? answer **1 r 2**

Example 2

75 ÷ 5 = ...
can be written as :-

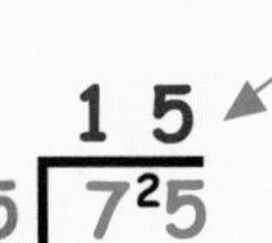

remainder **2** is carried

How many 5's are in 7 ? answer **1 r 2**

How many 5's are in 25 ? answer **5**

Example 3

93 ÷ 5 = ...
can be written as :-

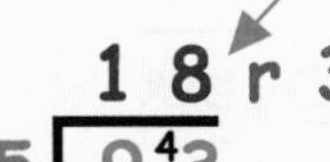

remainder **4** is carried and still another remainder appears

How many 5's are in 9 ? answer **1 r 4**

How many 5's are in 43 ? answer **8 r 3**

Exercise 4

Worksheet 5·2

1. **Copy** and **complete** :-

a	12 ÷ 5 = ...	b	7 ÷ 5 = ...	c	18 ÷ 5 = ...
d	9 ÷ 5 = ...	e	3 ÷ 5 = ...	f	16 ÷ 5 = ...
g	19 ÷ 5 = ...	h	13 ÷ 5 = ...	i	17 ÷ 5 = ...

2. **Set down** and **work out** :-

a	$5\overline{)51}$	b	$5\overline{)53}$	c	$5\overline{)57}$	d	$5\overline{)52}$
e	$5\overline{)58}$	f	$5\overline{)54}$	g	$5\overline{)59}$	h	$5\overline{)56}$.

Set down the following questions as division sums and work them out.

3. a 52 guests at a wedding were sitting at tables for 5 people.

How many full tables were there and how many people were at the small extra table ?

b 

58 folders were packed equally into 5 boxes.

How many folders did each box hold and how many were left over ?

c At a top level meeting, 5 policewomen were to guard each Head of State.

If there were 56 Heads of State present, explain why having 11 policewomen on duty was not acceptable.

4. **Copy** and **complete** :-

a	$5\overline{)50}$	b	$5\overline{)80}$	c	$5\overline{)60}$	d	$5\overline{)70}$
e	$5\overline{)85}$	f	$5\overline{)75}$	g	$5\overline{)55}$	h	$5\overline{)65}$
i	$5\overline{)90}$	j	$5\overline{)95}$	k	$5\overline{)100}$	l	$5\overline{)105}$.

5. a 75 Dvd's were placed into cases containing 5 Dvd's.

How many cases were used ?

b 

80 tins of Scottish Broth were placed on 5 shelves.

How many tins went on each shelf ?

c When chocolate eggs were on sale shortly after Easter, I bought 90 of them and crammed them equally into my 5 shopping bags.

How many eggs was I able to get in each bag ?

6. Copy and complete :-

a $5\overline{)39}$ b $5\overline{)42}$ c $5\overline{)93}$ d $5\overline{)51}$

e $5\overline{)87}$ f $5\overline{)64}$ g $5\overline{)68}$ h $5\overline{)71}$

i $5\overline{)94}$ j $5\overline{)88}$ k $5\overline{)97}$ l $5\overline{)104}$.

7. a **78** sheep were to be rounded and led equally into **5** pens.

How many sheep were left without a pen ?

b 

Baby Jo wants to put her **69** blue counters into bundles of **5**.

How many can she make and how many counters will be left over ?

8. a How many free theatre tickets will you get when you ask for **61** tickets ?

b How many tickets will you have to pay for ?

Special Offer
Pay for 5 tickets
Get another
one
FREE !

9. Buses leave Glasgow for Clydebank every **5** minutes. I arrived just as a bus was leaving.

a How many buses would I then expect to leave in the following **34** minutes ?

b At the end of that **34** minutes period, how long would I have to wait for the next bus ?

10. Copy these "**division by 5**" sums and do them :-

a $5\overline{)62}$ b $5\overline{)74}$ c $5\overline{)83}$ d $5\overline{)96}$

e $5\overline{)85}$ f $5\overline{)79}$ g $5\overline{)98}$ h $5\overline{)107}$.

Dividing by 10

Be able to divide 2 digits by 10 (no remainder)

Dividing by 10 is the same as **sharing** equally between **ten**.

10 strawberry chunks are shared equally between 10 girls.

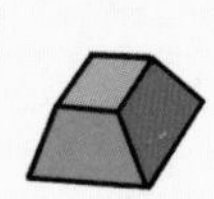

All 10 get 1 strawberry chunk each.

We say that **10 divided by 10 = 1.**

or **10 ÷ 10 = 1**

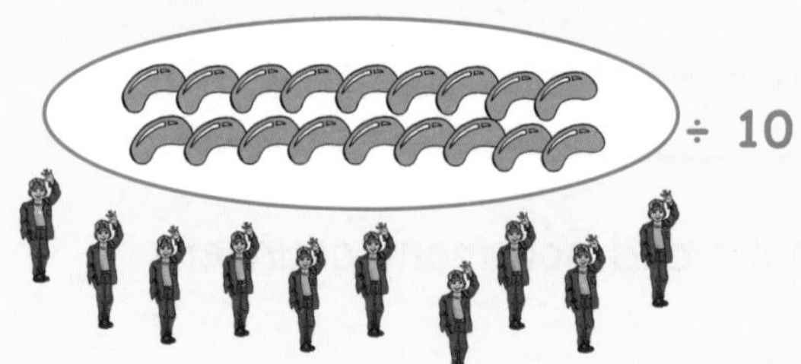

20 jelly beans are shared equally between 10 boys.

They all get 2 jelly beans each.

We say that **20 divided by 10 = 2.**

or **20 ÷ 10 = 2**

* Note :- **30 ÷ 10 = 3~~0~~ ÷ 1~~0~~ = 3.**

*When you **divide by 10**, simply **remove the 0 from the end** !*

Exercise 5

1. **Write** out your **10 times** table and use it to help in this exercise

2. Use the quick, easy method of **removing the 0** to find :-

   a 60 ÷ 10 = ... b 40 ÷ 10 = ... c 20 ÷ 10 = ...

   d 70 ÷ 10 = ... e 10 ÷ 10 = ... f 90 ÷ 10 = ...

3. Find the missing numbers :-

   a ☐ ÷ 10 = 3 b ☐ ÷ 10 = 5 c ☐ ÷ 10 = 9

   d ☐ ÷ 10 = 8 e ☐ ÷ 10 = 6 f ☐ ÷ 10 = 10.

4. Try these questions **mentally**.

a (i) How many **£10** notes would I get for **£70** ?

(ii) How many **10p** coins would I get for **50 pence** ?

b 

Fireworks come in boxes of **10**.

If Harry wants **80** fireworks, how many boxes will he need to buy ?

c Rebecca paid **60p** for cupcakes which the bakers were selling off at **10p** each.

How many did she buy ?

d 

30 balloons were shared equally between **10** kids.

How many did each get ?

e The Cash and Carry warehouse were selling cans of diet cola in trays of **10** cans.

If a shopper wanted to buy **140** cans, how many trays should she pick up ?

5. **Copy** and **complete** *by* ***removing*** *the last zero* :-

a 80 ÷ 10 = ...	b 40 ÷ 10 = ...	c 100 ÷ 10 = ...
d 130 ÷ 10 = ...	e 190 ÷ 10 = ...	f 210 ÷ 10 = ...
g 250 ÷ 10 = ...	h 320 ÷ 10 = ...	i 360 ÷ 10 = ...
j 400 ÷ 10 = ...	k 410 ÷ 10 = ...	l 480 ÷ 10 = ...

6. Kevin bought a computer for **£1200**.

He paid **£200** on the day he bought it and paid the rest of what he owed over **10** months.

How much did he have to pay every month ?

Be able to divide any 3 digit number by 2, 3, 4, 5 or 10

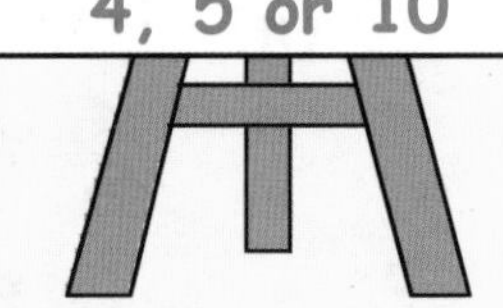

Example 1 143 ÷ 2

Example 2 614 ÷ 3

Example 3 511 ÷ 4

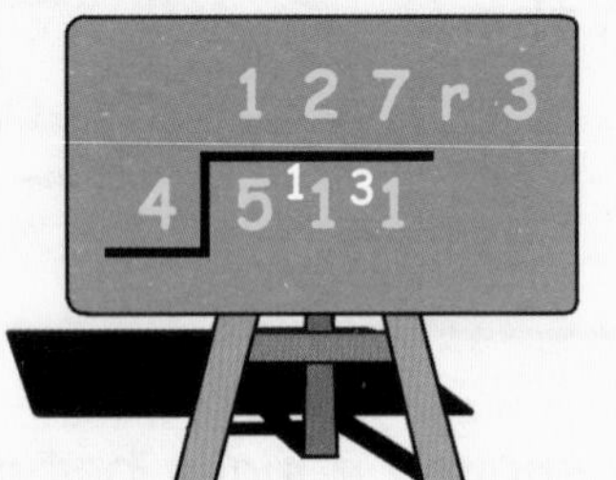

Example 4 731 ÷ 5

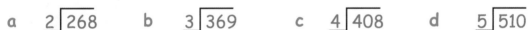

1. **Copy** and **complete** :-

a	$2\overline{)268}$	b	$3\overline{)369}$	c	$4\overline{)408}$	d	$5\overline{)510}$
e	$3\overline{)478}$	f	$4\overline{)746}$	g	$5\overline{)283}$	h	$2\overline{)939}$
i	$4\overline{)357}$	j	$5\overline{)744}$	k	$2\overline{)777}$	l	$3\overline{)827}$.

2. **Set these down** like Question 1 and **work them out** :-

a	305 ÷ 2 = ...	b	206 ÷ 3 = ...	c	362 ÷ 4 = ...
d	600 ÷ 5 = ...	e	300 ÷ 10 = ...	f	721 ÷ 4 = ...
g	512 ÷ 5 = ...	h	613 ÷ 2 = ...	i	200 ÷ 3 = ...
j	881 ÷ 4 = ...	k	839 ÷ 5 = ...	l	900 ÷ 4 = ...
m	870 ÷ 10 = ...	n	618 ÷ 3 = ...	o	999 ÷ 5 = ...

Set down these questions as division sums and work them out.

3. Mr Davis bought a **£258** sofa and paid it up over **3** months.

   How much was each monthly payment ?

4. The total number of runs scored in **2** cricket matches was **578**.

   If the same number of runs were scored in each match, how many was that ?

5. Terry and June took **5** hours to travel **345** miles.

   At the same speed, how far would they have gone in 1 hour ?

6. Geraldine is paid **£936** for **4** weeks work.

   What does she get paid for 1 week's work ?

7. **465** bags of gritting salt was loaded equally onto **2** lorries.

   How many were in each lorry and how many were left out ?

8. It took a worm **3** hours to go **534 cm** across ground.

   How far did it go in 1 hour ?

9. A **500 ml** carton of orange juice was poured into **4** identical glasses.

   How many **ml** did each glass hold ?

10. A supermarket took in **£990** from the sale of **£10** boxes of dark chocolates.

    How many boxes did they sell ?

11. A shopkeeper has put **5** apples into each of **24** bags.

    Charlie buys all the apples.

    He gives **4** apples to each of his mates.

    How many classmates does Charlie have ?

Mixed Exercise

Exercise 7

Be able to add, subtract, multiply or divide by 2, 3, 4, 5 and 10

1. Copy and work out :-

a $\begin{array}{r} 23 \\ +\ 9 \\ \hline \end{array}$ b $\begin{array}{r} 56 \\ -\ 8 \\ \hline \end{array}$ c $\begin{array}{r} 57 \\ \times\ 2 \\ \hline \end{array}$

d $\begin{array}{r} 286 \\ -\ 51 \\ \hline \end{array}$ e $\begin{array}{r} 86 \\ +\ 79 \\ \hline \end{array}$ f $2\overline{)18}$

g $\begin{array}{r} 513 \\ -\ 84 \\ \hline \end{array}$ h $\begin{array}{r} 78 \\ \times\ 3 \\ \hline \end{array}$ i $\begin{array}{r} 45 \\ +\ 397 \\ \hline \end{array}$

j $\begin{array}{r} 158 \\ \times\ 4 \\ \hline \end{array}$ k $3\overline{)102}$ l $\begin{array}{r} 812 \\ -\ 594 \\ \hline \end{array}$

m $\begin{array}{r} 632 \\ +\ 189 \\ \hline \end{array}$ n $\begin{array}{r} 432 \\ \times\ 5 \\ \hline \end{array}$ o $4\overline{)276}$.

2. Set down and find :-

a 7 + 45 b 63 - 18 c 75 x 2

d 600 ÷ 5 e 47 + 73 f 316 - 25

g 194 x 3 h 56 ÷ 4 i 87 x 5

j 926 - 345 k 628 + 295 l 84 x 10

m 537 ÷ 3 n 2100 ÷ 10 o 4 x 725

p 3 x 4 x 5 x 10 q 4 x 250 ÷ 10 r 280 ÷ 5 - 36.

3. Most new cars nowadays don't come with a spare wheel, so you have to pay extra if you want one ....
£68 for a metal wheel and £73 for a tyre.

How much does that come to ?

4. 

A tree has 235 leaves on it.

On each leaf there are 3 ladybirds.

How many ladybirds in total are there on the tree ?

5. To fly with Thomas Crook to Gran Canaria costs £412 return.

Flying with Jet3 costs £289 return.

By how much is Jet3 cheaper ?

6. 

A hotel bought 10 new single beds for the rooms on the top floor, costing £2470 in total.

What was the cost of each bed ?

7. A mechanic puts 4 litres of oil into all the cars he services.

If he serviced 38 cars last month, how much oil did he use ?

8. 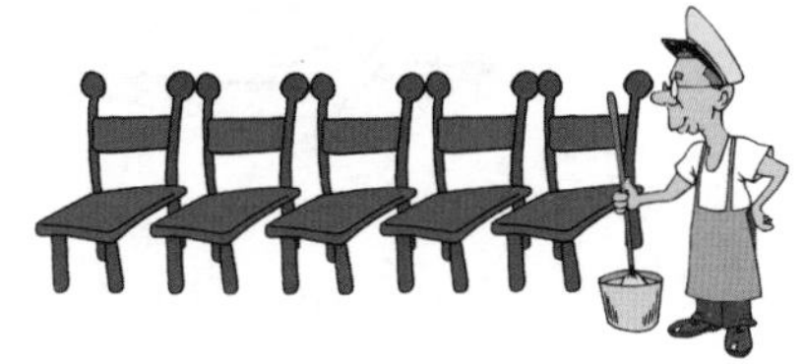

A janitor lays out chairs in rows of five.

If he puts out 80 chairs, how many rows will there be ?

9. There are 60 lollies in this jar.

There are 4 jars of them on display in each of 2 supermarkets.

How many lollies in total are up for sale ?

10. 

Moira pays fees of £285 for gym membership.

She is also in a bowling club, costing £198.

How much does she pay in total ?

The 3 Я's

Revisit - Review - Revise

1. **Copy** and **work out** :-

a $2\overline{)74}$ b $3\overline{)96}$ c $4\overline{)92}$ d $5\overline{)85}$

e $3\overline{)201}$ f $5\overline{)795}$ g $2\overline{)308}$ h $4\overline{)348}$.

2. **Find** :-

a $106 \div 2$ b $117 \div 3$ c $96 \div 4$ d $410 \div 5$

e $389 \div 4$ f $519 \div 2$ g $834 \div 5$ h $294 \div 3$.

3. **5p** for a chocolate bit.

How many will I get for **85p** ?

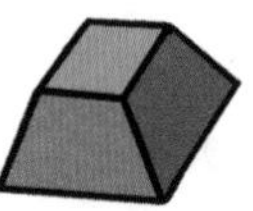

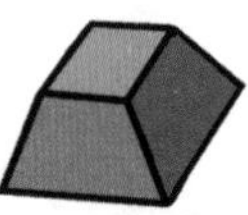

4. 

There are **10** DVD plastic cases in a pack.

A factory produces **450** cases per minute.

How many packs is that ?

5. It cost John and his 2 brothers **£981** altogether to go on holiday to Spain.

How much did they each have to pay ?

6. 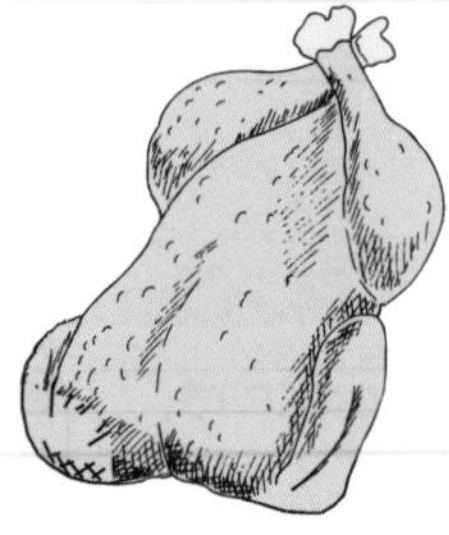

A supermarket removed **74** chickens from their shelves because they were out of date.

They were put in small boxes. Each held **4** chickens.

How many **full** boxes were there and how many chickens were left over ?

7. A cider manufacturer ordered **3000** apples.

They were delivered in **5** vans, each van carrying **4** baskets of apples.

How many apples were in each basket ?

Revision of Angles

1. How many angles do you see in each picture ?

a

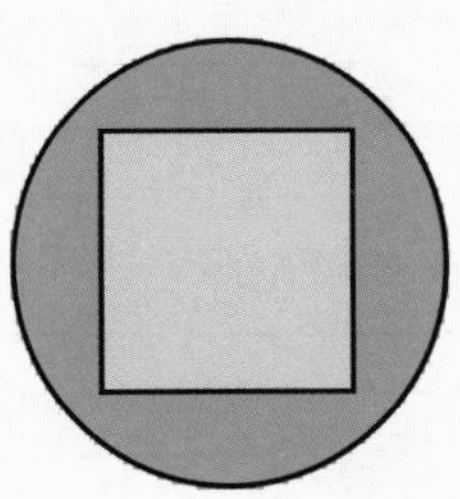

b

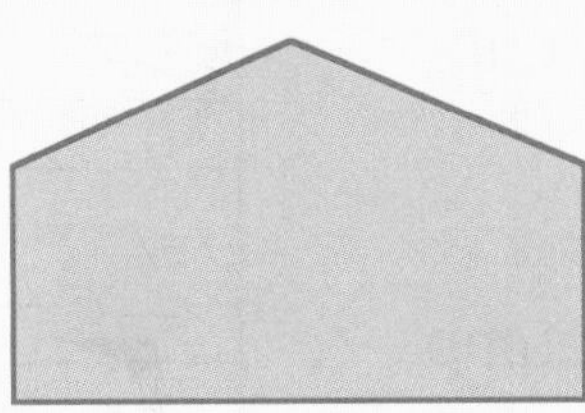

c

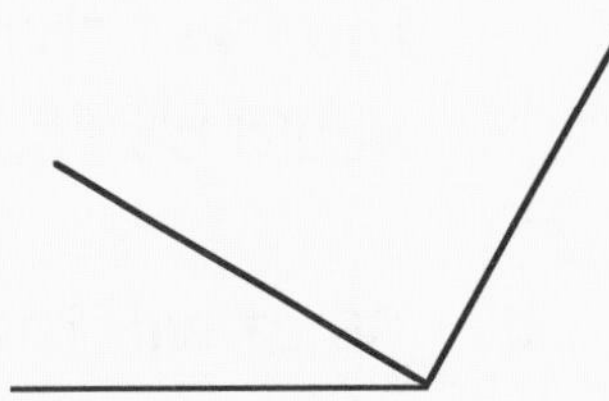

2. Two of these three angles are right angles. Which two ?

a

b

c

3. How many right angles does this shape have ?

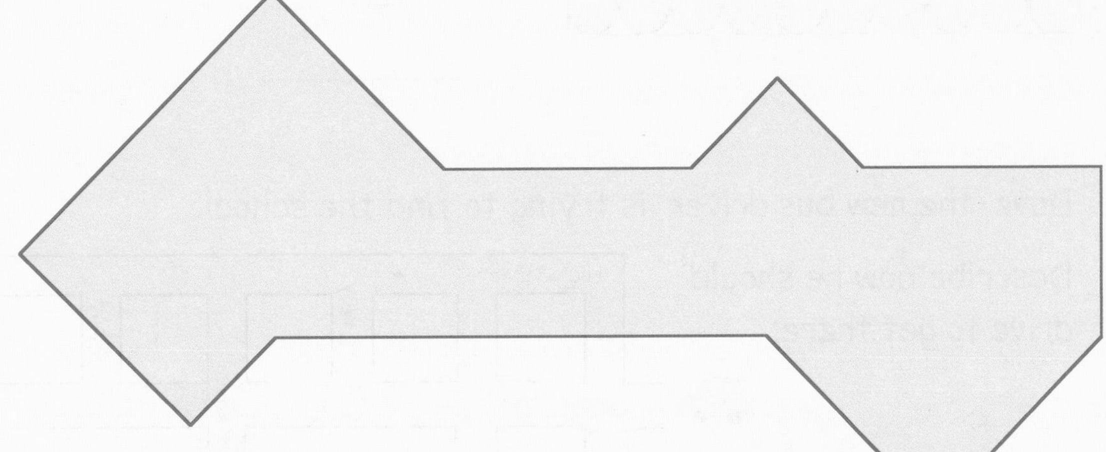

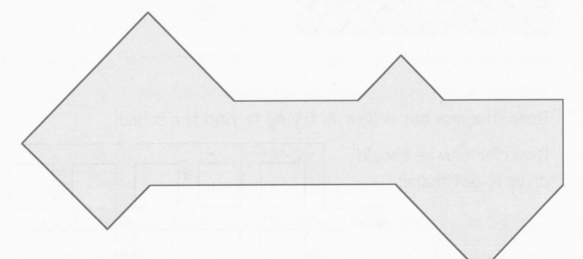

4. a Trace the shape shown in question 3.

   b Mark in all the right angles which you found.

5. Nick's remote control car is heading towards his mum

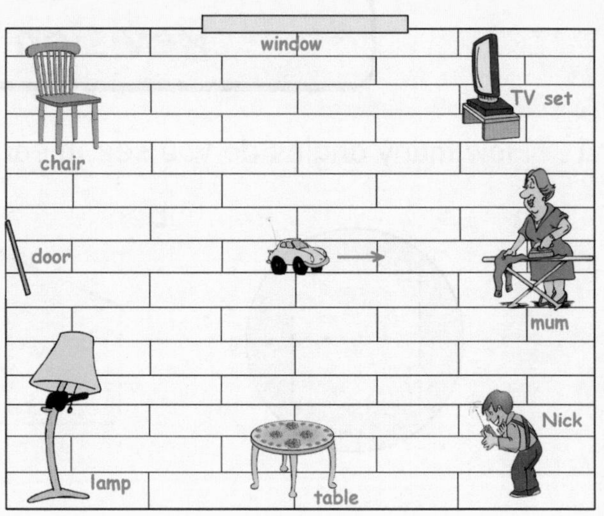

a   If Nick turns the car **anticlockwise**, what is the **first** thing the car would be facing ?

b   What will the car bump into if he turns it instead a **quarter turn clockwise** ?

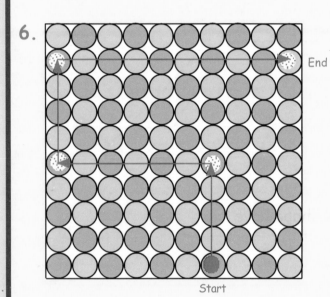

6. This board game has green and yellow circles.

End

Start

Describe how the red counter is moved around the board.

Move ...... **circles forward.**

Turn ....

Move ...... **circles** ....

Turn ....

....

7. Dave, the new bus driver, is trying to find the school.

Describe how he should drive to get there.

Drive along .... street.

Turn .... into ....

....

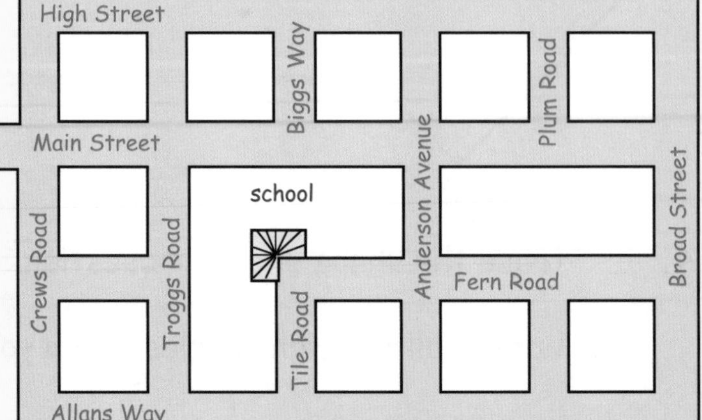

Chapter 6

Angles

Right Angles

Be able to identify a 90° angle

Remember how to make a **right angle** template.

If your template fits exactly into an angle then the angle is a **right angle**.

Angles can be measured in **degrees**.

A **right angle** is said to be **90 degrees**.

It is written as 90°.

An angle may be **smaller** than 90°.

An angle may be **bigger** than 90°.

template

Exercise 1

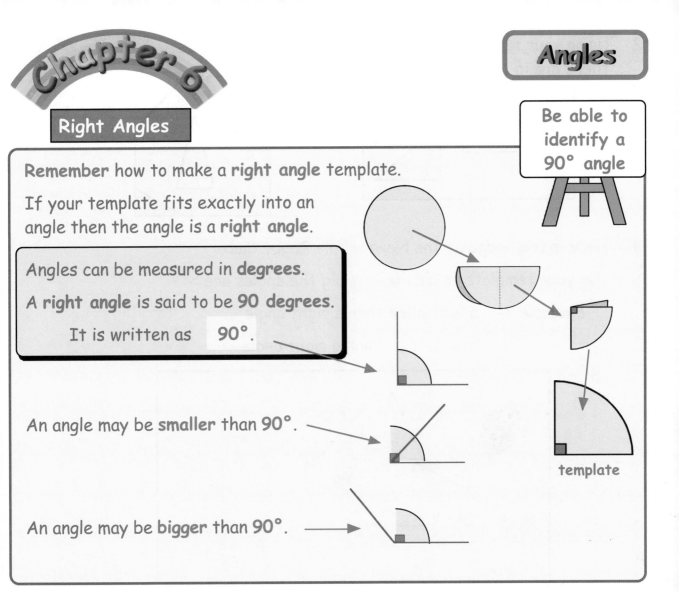

1. Use your template to find out which angles are **90°**, **smaller than** or **bigger than** 90°.

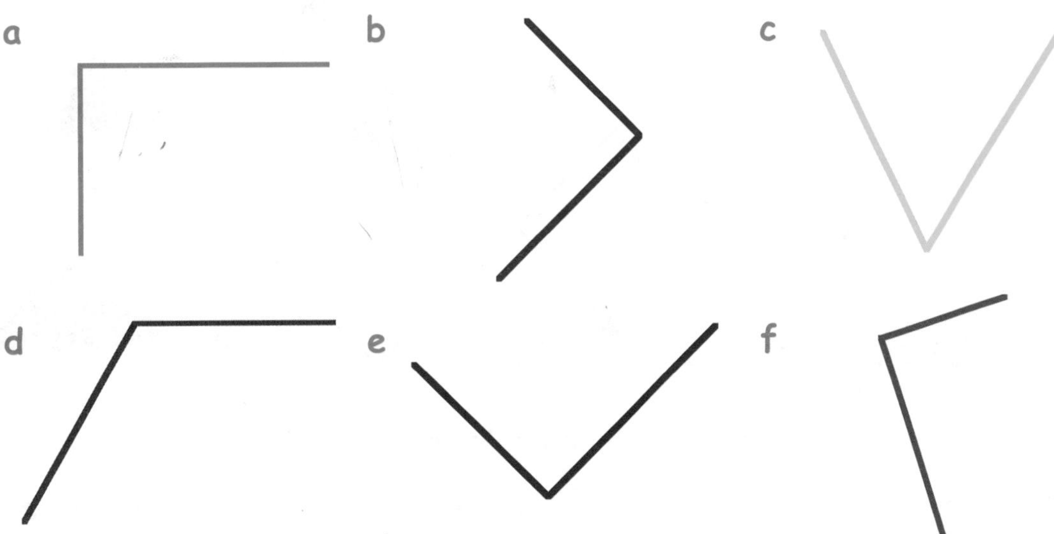

2. Using your template, write down how many right angles there are in the figures shown below :-

a

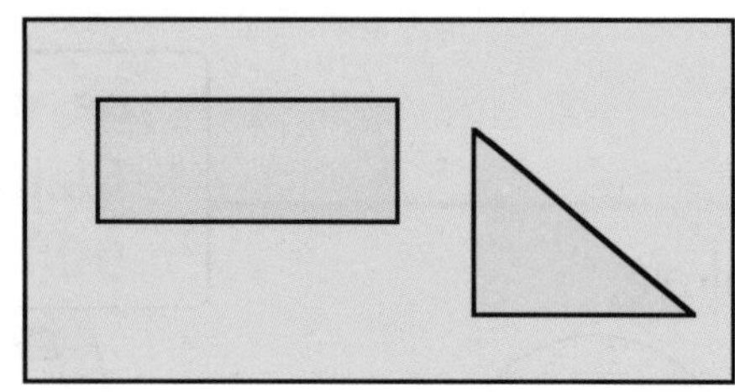

b

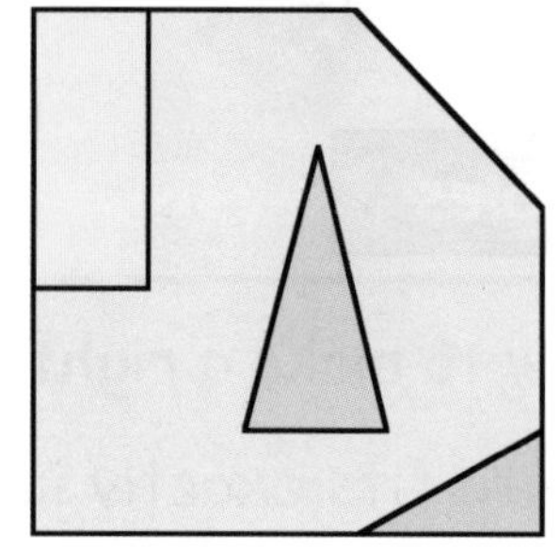

3. Here is the badge of the NewtonVale Rugby Club.

Use your template to decide how big the angles are :-

Example :- a is **smaller** than a right angle,

b is .... than a right angle,

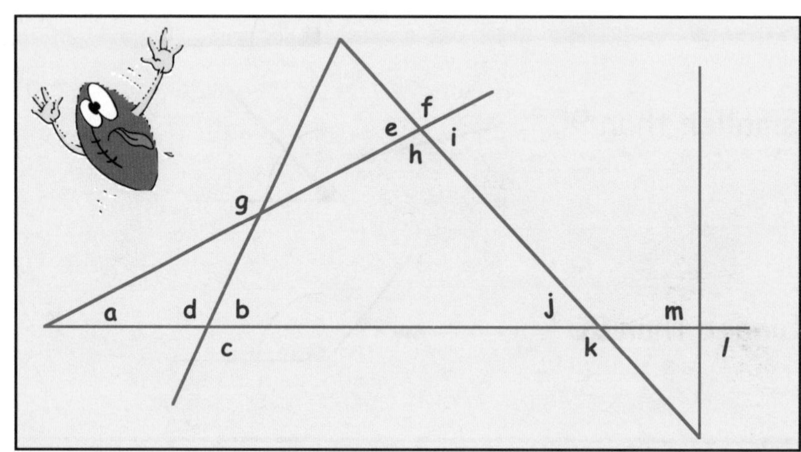

4. Steve potted the black ball into a centre pocket to win a game of snooker.

The path the ball took showed how lucky Steve was to win.

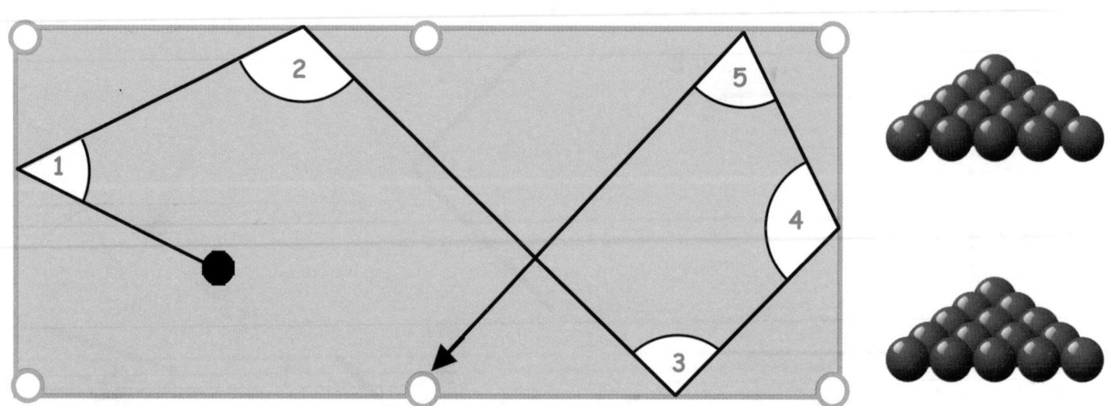

Use your template to find out which angles are :-

a right angled b bigger than a right ..... c smaller than a .....

Quarter-turn, Half-turn and Complete turn

Be able to identify quarter, half and full turns

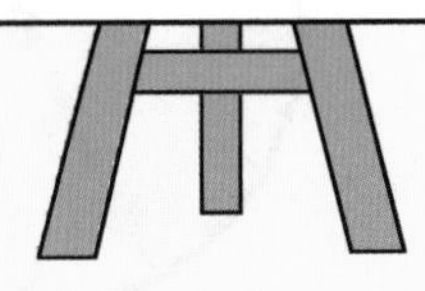

As the hand of a clock moves from the **12** round to the **3** it sweeps through a right angle - **90°**.

This is known as a **quarter-turn**.

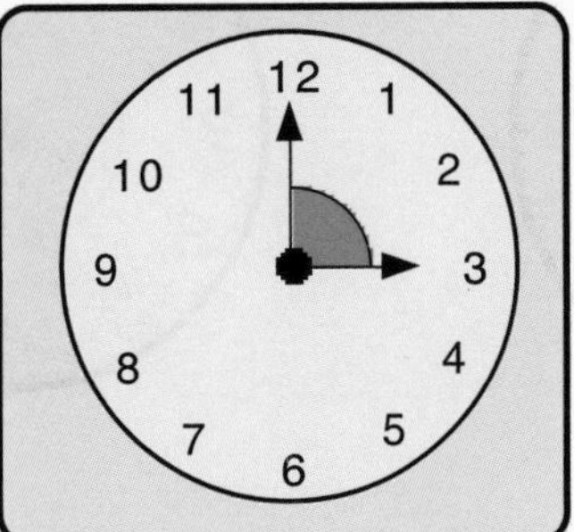

As the hand of a clock moves from the **12** round to the **6** it sweeps through 2 right angles - 2 x 90° = **180°**.

This is known as a **half-turn**.

As the hand of a clock moves from the **12** right round to the **12** again it sweeps through 4 right angles - 4 x 90° = **360°**.

This is known as a **complete-turn**.
or **one whole revolution**.

Exercise 2

1. How many degrees are there in a :-

   a quarter-turn b half-turn c complete turn ?

2. How many degrees does the minute hand move through on these clock faces ?

   a  b c

2. d

e

f

3. On a clock face, how many degrees does the minute hand sweep through when it moves **clockwise** from the :-

a 6 round to the 9 | b 7 round to the 1 | c 2 round to the 5

d 3 round to the 12 | e 5 round to the 8 | f 12 round to the 12 ?

The hands of a clock move **clockwise**.

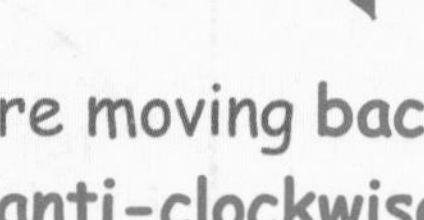

If the clock hands were moving **backwards** they would be moving **anti-clockwise**.

4. Imagine the hands of a special clock move **anti-clockwise**.

How many degrees does the hand sweep through when it moves **anti-clockwise** from the :-

a 9 round to the 6 | b 7 round to the 1 | c 2 round to the 5

d 3 round to the 12 | e 5 round to the 8 | f 8 round to the 5 ?

5. Describe in **two** ways (use **clockwise** and **anti-clockwise**) the movement of a hand moving from :-

a 1 round to the 4 | b 8 round to the 2 | c 7 round to the 7

d 5 round to the 2 | e 11 round to the 8 | f 4 round to the 7.

Compass Points

The four main points of the compass are

North, South, East and West.

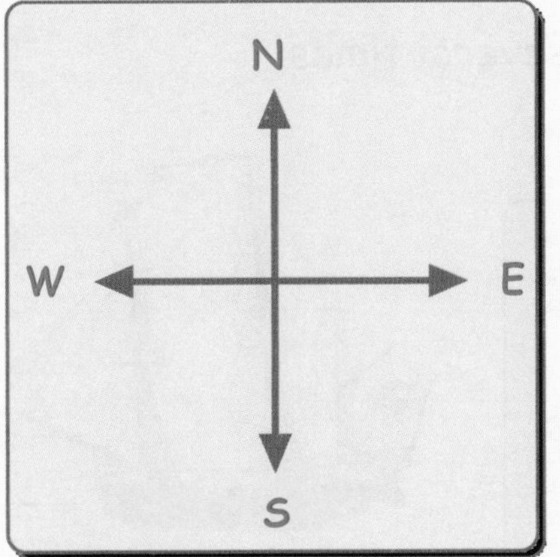

North will always point to the North Pole.

Never - Eat - Smelly - Wellies.

Exercise 3

1. Copy the 4 points of the compass diagram above.

2. How many degrees are there from :-

   a North to East (clockwise)

   b East to South (clockwise)

   c North to West (anti-clockwise)

   d North to West (clockwise)

   e North to South (clockwise)

   f East to South (anti-clockwise).

3. a Ed was walking East. He then made a $\frac{1}{4}$ turn clockwise.

   In which direction is Ed now walking ?

   b Jill was driving West when she came to a roundabout. She then turned her car through 180° clockwise.

   In which direction was Jill then driving ?

   c A jet fighter was flying South. The jet then turned through 90° clockwise.

   In which direction did the jet end up travelling ?

d 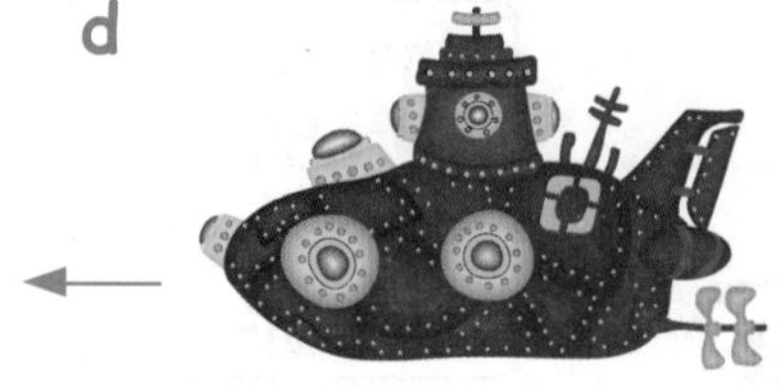

A submarine is sailing West.

The submarine turns **anti-clockwise** and now faces North.

By how many degrees has the submarine turned ?

e A tall ship, sailing **East**, changes direction several times.

The captain issues the following orders :-

- *Turn anticlockwise 180° for 100 metres.*
- *Turn clockwise 90° for 50 metres.*
- *Turn clockwise 270° for 75 metres.*
- *Turn 180° anticlockwise.*

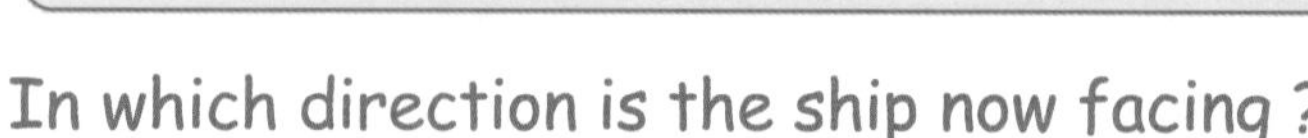

In which direction is the ship now facing ?

4. A helicopter is shown in this picture.

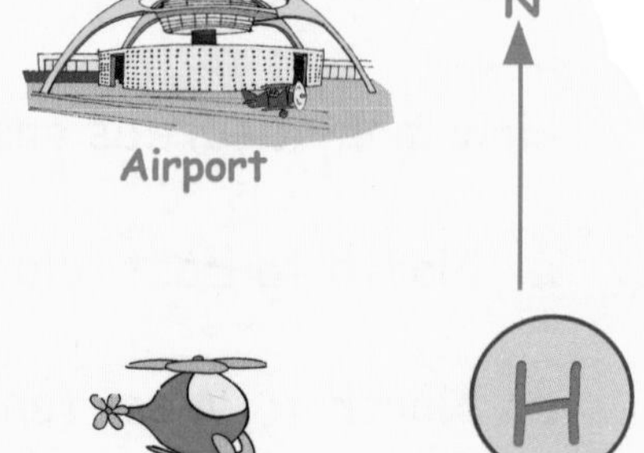

a In which direction does the pilot need to fly to get to :-

(i) the city

(ii) the beach

(iii) the airport ?

b You are standing at the **heli-pad**.

In which direction is the helicopter ?

c Archie cycles from the city to the airport.

(i) Which direction is his journey ?

(ii) In what direction will his return journey be ?

d The helicopter is travelling East.
It then spins 450° (clockwise) out of control.

In which direction is this helicopter now facing ?

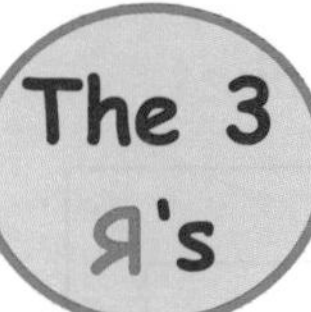

Revisit - Review - Revise

1. This spinner has 12 different coloured parts. The arrow points to **red**.

   a The arrow is spun **quarter turn clockwise**.

   On what colour does it land ?

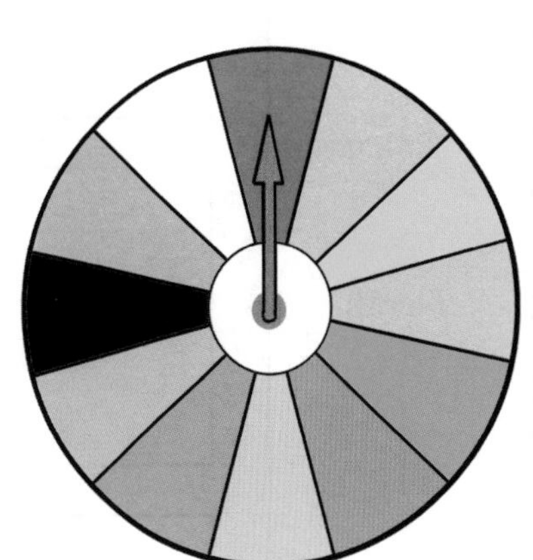

   b From **red**, the arrow is spun **anti-clockwise**.

   What is the first colour it passes over ?

   c This time the arrow starts on **black**.
   It spins a **half turn clockwise**.

   What colour does it end up at ?

   d Now the arrow starts on **brown**.

   It is spun **90° anti-clockwise**.

   What colour does it land on ?

2. 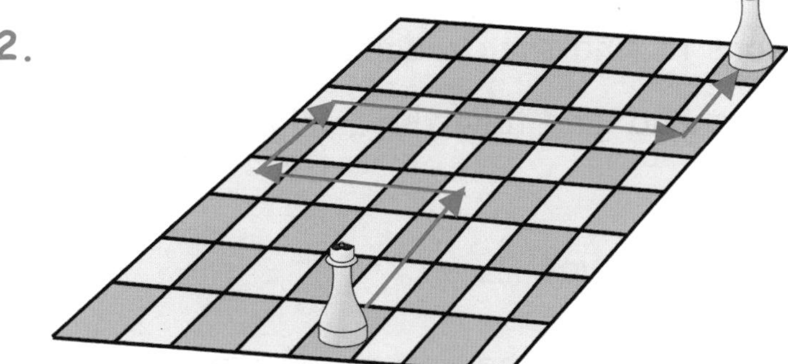

During a game of chess, the Queen moved around the board as shown.

Use **left**, **right** and **forward** to describe the moves.

3. a Sketch this cross to show a compass.

   b Fill in the directions, **South**, **West** and **North** on your diagram.

   c I am facing South. I make a **90° turn anti-clockwise**.

   Which way am I now facing ?

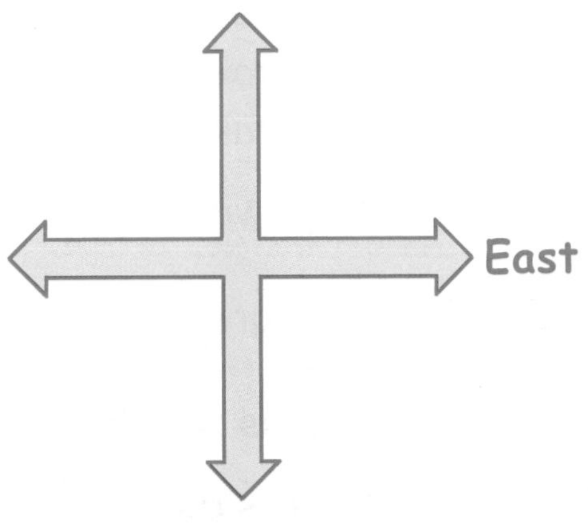

4. This map shows where all the goods are in Adsco's Supermarket.

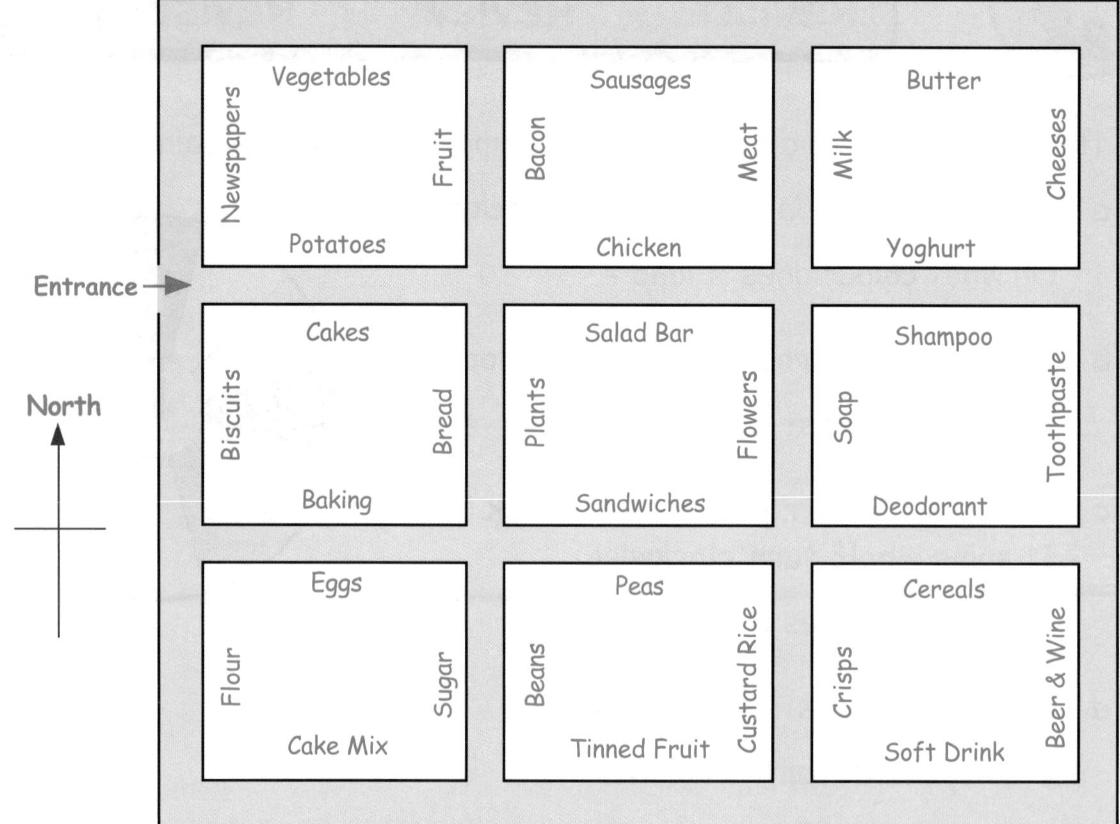

a Mrs Jones is at the **Entrance** and wants to buy some **Cereals**.

Give Mrs Jones directions to find the Cereals.

- Walk straight ahead and take the .... **right**.
- Turn **1st** ....
- The **Cereals** are on your ....

b Give similar directions to get from the **Entrance** to the **Butter**.

c
- I turn **right** at the entrance and walk forward.
- I take the **2nd left** and walk forward.
- I take the **2nd left** and stop.

What will I see on my **right side** ?

5. In the diagram above, the **Fruit** is **North** of the **Bread**.

a What is **North** of the Plants

b What is **South** of the Soap

c What is **East** of the Milk

d What is **West** of the Sugar ?

Revision of Money

1. How many :-

   a 1p coins in 50p   b 2p coins in 30p   c 5p coins in 45p ?

2. List the fewest number of coins you would use to buy this slice of cake.

98p

3. Write these amounts of money using a decimal point :- (68p = £0·68)

   a 37p   b 8p   c 241p   d ninety pence.

4. Set down these additions and subtractions and work them out :-

   a £0·64 + £0·26   b £4·15 − £1·48   c £5·29 + £4·85

   d £6·01 − £3·52   e £5·29 + £1·79   f £1·67 − 78p.

5. How much money does each person have ?

   a Madge   b Trevor   c Daisy

6. a Sharon bought a pack of chicken fillets for £4·20 and 2 lettuces at 40p each.

   How much did it cost her in total ?

   b Alex went to the snooker club with £8.

   He paid £3·25 for his games of snooker and £2·88 for something to eat and drink.

   How much money was he left with ?

Money

Be able to change money up to £20

Money up to £20

Remember

£1 and £2 coins are used in everyday purchases.

These are also used :-

a £5 note **is worth the same as** FIVE pound coins

a £10 note **is worth the same as** TWO £5 notes

a £20 note **is worth the same as** TWO £10 notes

Exercise 1

1. How many **£1 coins** will I get for :-
   - a two £5 notes
   - b three £5 notes
   - c one £5 note and a £10 note
   - d four £2 coins
   - e one £5 and three £2 coins
   - f one £5, one £10 and two £2 coins ?

2. How many **£5 notes** will I get for :-
   - a two £10 notes
   - b one £10 and five £1 coins
   - c ten £2 coins
   - d one £10 and five £2 coins ?

3. Write down how much each person has :-
   - a Tony

   - b Sean

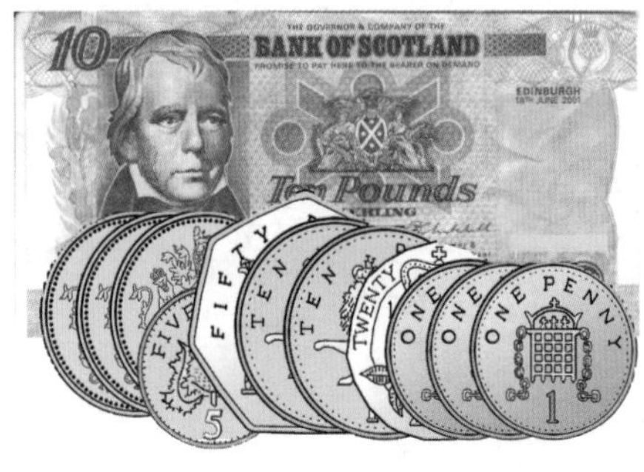

3. c Jenna

d Lenny

Kara buys a magazine costing £18·29.

She gives the shopkeeper the exact money as shown.

There are many different ways of giving the exact money when buying something.

4. Look at how much **Kara** gave the shopkeeper.

   Write down other ways she could have paid exactly.

5. Write down the coins that you could pay **exactly** for :-

   a £7·77 b £10·53 c £11·94 d £18·91

   e £19·05 f £14·87 g £15·55 h £19·99.

6. Harry gave the shopkeeper a £5 note to pay for his £4·12 cake.

   a How much change should he get ?

   b Give an example of what notes and coins might make up his change.

7. 

May's mum handed over a £10 note for her £6·79 scarf.

   a How much change should she get ?

   b Give an example of what notes and coins might make up her change.

8. James paid for a £4·75 box of chocolates with a twenty pound note.

List the coins or notes he could get for his change.

9.

Sammy buys a box of sweets for £2·69. She hands over a £10 note.

a How much change should she get ?

b Give an example of what notes and coins might make up her change.

10. Jason goes to Hamburger Palace and buys food costing £13·27. He pays with a £20 note.

a How much change should Jason get ?

b Give an example of what notes and coins he might have in his change.

11. David has these notes and coins.

He buys an ink cartridge costing £15·85 for his printer.

Which of these notes and coins make up the £15·85 ?

12.

Frank gave a £20 note to pay for his £11·55 weekly newspaper bill.

His change is shown

Has Frank been given the correct change ?

If not, what is missing ?

13. Anika has only a £20 note to pay for her £1·47 sandwich.

Give an example of what notes and coins she might have in her change.

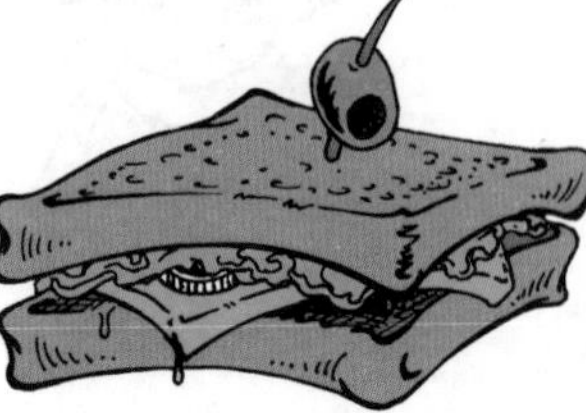

Add, Subtract, Multiply and Divide with Money

Be able to add, subtract, divide and multiply money up to £20.

Addition and Subtraction

When you ADD or SUBTRACT money, you MUST line up the decimal points.

Examples Addition

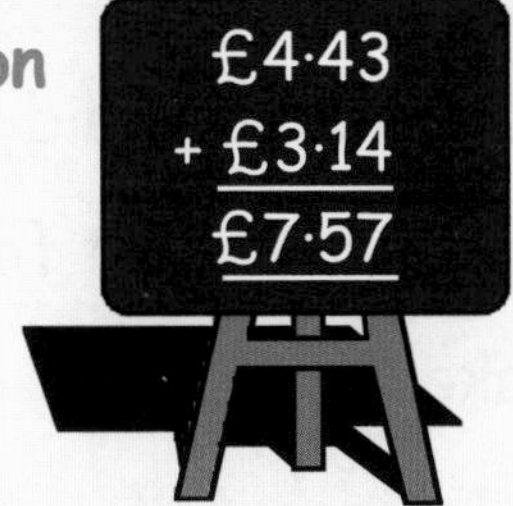

Subtraction

Exercise 2

1. Copy the following and find :-

a	£3·25 + £2·54	b	£6·53 + £3·24	c	£9·35 +£3·46	d	£6·72 + £4·84
e	£7·74 - £3·42	f	£9·45 - £2·65	g	£11·28 - £3·33	h	£18·43 - £7·15
i	£15·98 - £ 4·77	j	£19·43 - £ 8·28	k	£12·25 - £ 9·79	l	£19·67 - £ 9·83
m	£14·49 + £3·91	n	£18·12 - £1·61	o	£2·14 + £ 11·79	p	£17·36 - £13·37

2. Set down these additions and subtractions in the same way as question 1 and work out the answers :-

a	£5·25 + £4·54	b	£9·57 - £7·26	c	£15·84 + £3·19
d	£16·42 - £7·54	e	£14 + £5·42	f	£20 - £7·17
g	£8 + £4·98	h	£15 - £11·98	i	£17·56 + £2·34
j	£13 - £11·99	k	£9·94 + £9·99	l	£18·04 - £12·35.

Mixed Money Problems without a Calculator

Exercise 3

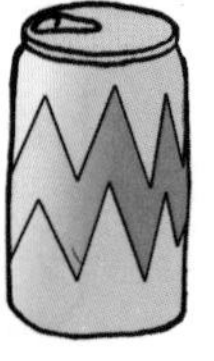

1. Ravi bought a can of cola for 85p and a packet of crisps for 32p.

   How much did this cost him **in total** ?

2. a **Five** chocolate lollies costs £3·35. How much did it cost for **one** lolly ?

   b Joe paid 87p for a pen. How much would it cost for **4** pens ?

   c How much would it cost for **six** cakes if **one** cost 45p ?

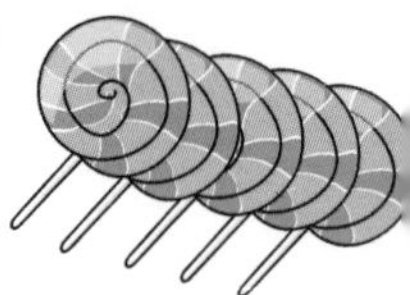

3. Zoheb paid £4·40 for a hamburger and 150p for french fries.

   What change did Zoheb get from three £2 coins ?

4. Ben buys a cooked breakfast.

   Bacon £1·25, Mushrooms 40p, Toast 25p and Fresh Orange Juice 80p.

   a What is the total cost of Ben's breakfast ?

   b He only has two £1 coins and one 50p coin with him.

   Will this be enough ? **Explain !**

5. A fish supper costs £5·10. Mr Chips buys **three** fish suppers.

   a How much change did he get from a £20 note ?

   b Give an example of what coins he might have had in his change.

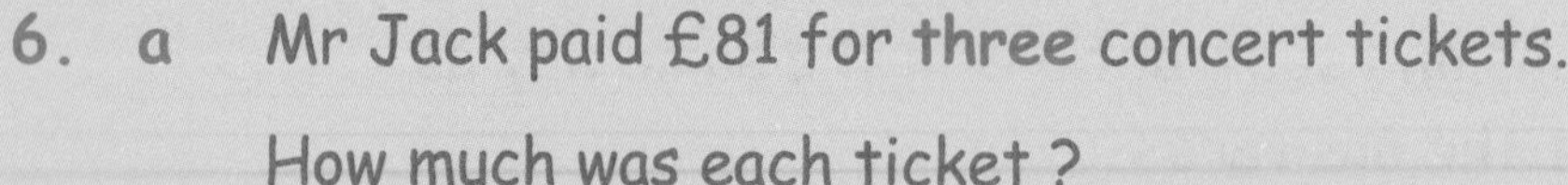

6. a Mr Jack paid £81 for three concert tickets.

   How much was each ticket ?

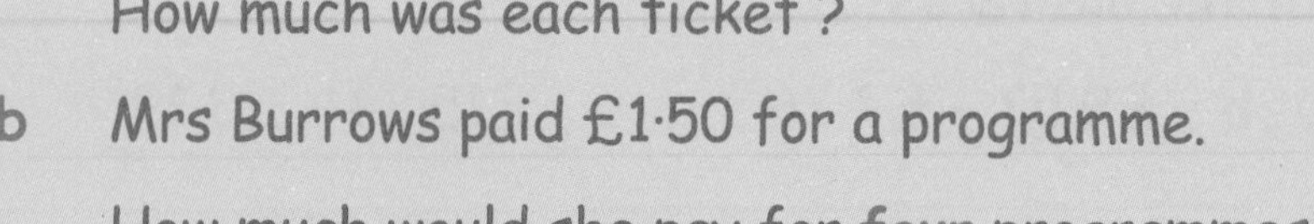

   b Mrs Burrows paid £1·50 for a programme.

   How much would she pay for four programmes ?

7. a A packet of crisps costs 75p. How much would it cost for **5** packets ?

   b How much would one plant cost if eight plants costs £48 ?

Money with a Calculator

Be able to use a calculator when working with money problems

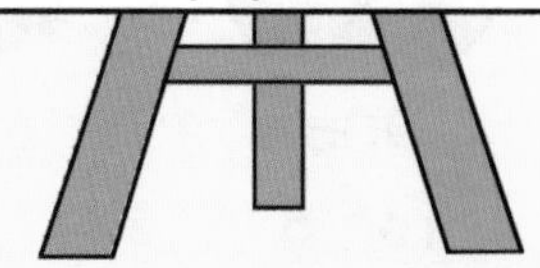

When using money there **MUST** be **two** numbers after the decimal point.

The sum of money shown on this calculator is **£4·02**

(£4 and 2 pence)

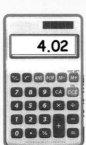

4.02

The sum of money shown on this calculator is **£4·20**

(£4 and 20 pence)

NOT £4·02

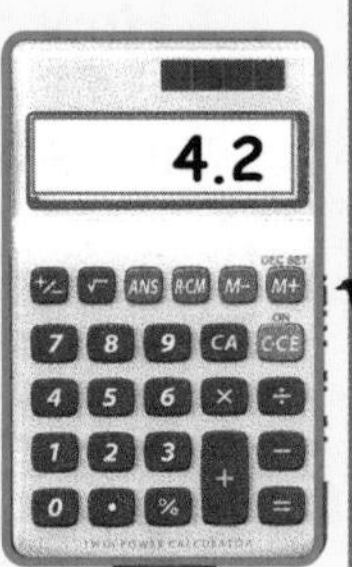

Exercise 4

1. Write down the amount of money shown on each calculator :-

a

b

c

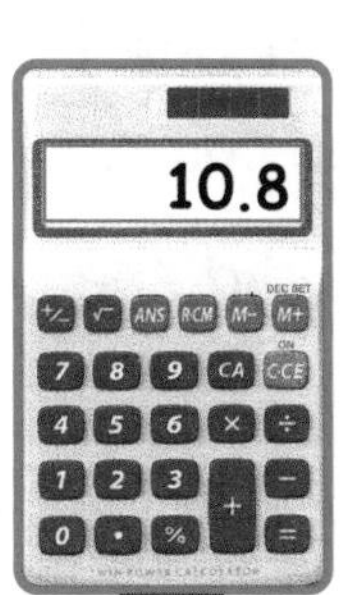

d

e

f

g

h

2. Ollie buys a juice at £1·75 and a sandwich at £2·35.

   How much did he pay **in total** ?

3. Bee bought a scarf at £14·50 and a headband at £8·40.

   How much **more** did she pay for the scarf than the headband ?

4. The local fruit shop sells the following :-

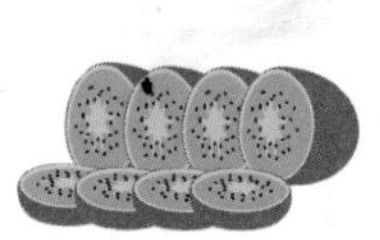

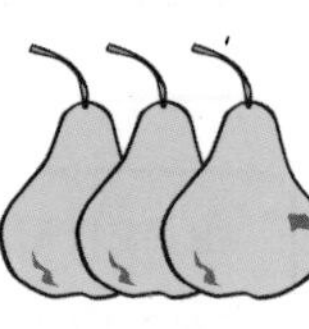

Apples	Watermelon	Kiwi	Grapes	Pineapple	Pears
90p for 6	£2·95	£1·20 for 4	£3·40	£3·90	95p for 3

How much would it cost for :-

a six apples and a watermelon

b three pears and a pineapple

c grapes and four kiwi

d pineapple and two watermelons

e three apples and three pears

f twelve apples and a pineapple

g eight kiwi and three apples

h 6 apples, 4 kiwi and 3 pears ?

5. Sandra looked at her weekly bill from Andy's shop.

a Copy the bill and complete it.

b Sandra handed over one £10 note and four one pound coins.

How much change did she receive ?

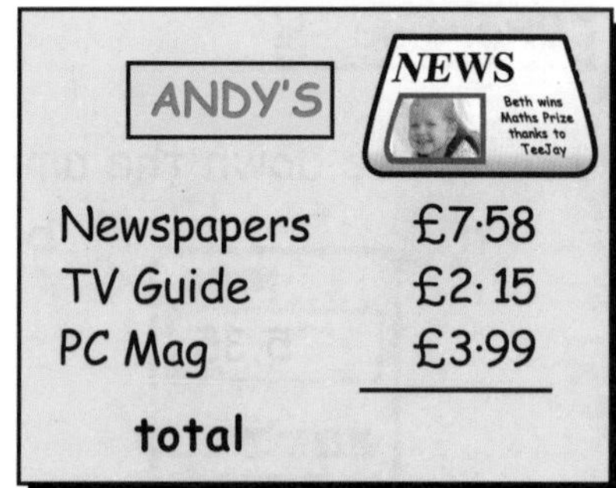

Newspapers	£7·58
TV Guide	£2·15
PC Mag	£3·99
total	

6. Mr Baxter took his 2 children to Gordon's Go-Karts.

Gordon's Go-Karts
(for 10 minutes)

Adult	£7·50
Child	£4·00
Parent/Child (1 adult + 2 kids)	£14·25

a How much did it cost to buy one adult and 2 children's tickets for a ten minute ride ?

b How much would Mr Baxter have saved by buying the Parent/Child ticket ?

7. Mrs Brown took her children to Gordon's Go-Karts.

She paid a total of £23·50 for herself and her children.

(*She did not buy the Parent/Child special ticket*).

How many children did Mrs Brown take Go-Karting ?

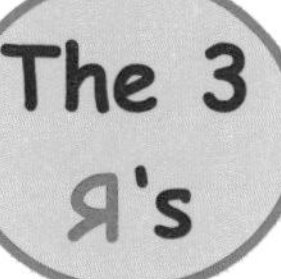

Revisit - Review - Revise

1. Find :-

a
$$\begin{array}{r} £13{\cdot}34 \\ +\ £\ \ 2{\cdot}42 \\ \hline \end{array}$$

b
$$\begin{array}{r} £17{\cdot}47 \\ -\ £\ 4{\cdot}25 \\ \hline \end{array}$$

c
$$\begin{array}{r} £12{\cdot}47 \\ -\ £\ 9{\cdot}76 \\ \hline \end{array}$$

d £12·73 + £5·77 e £16·87 – £6·92 f £20 - £7·85.

2. How many :-

a  are there in  ?

b  are there in  ?

c  are there in  ?

d  are there in  ?

3. a How many £1 coins will you get for 700p ?

b How many pence are there in £6·75 ?

4. List the coins or notes you might use to pay for each item exactly :-

a 

72p

b 

£4·65

c 

£17·84

5. Jack has two 50p coins.

He spent 64p on sweets.

What coins would he expect in his change ?

6. Una paid £3·75 for a magazine and 95p for juice.

a How much did she spend altogether ?

b What change should she get from a £5 note ?

c List the coins she might get in her change.

7. 

Jo went into the shop with a £10 note.

After buying a hat, she had £2·28.

How much was the hat ?

8. Sally has £17 in her purse.

She buys perfume for £8·75, face cream for £3·60 and soap for 95p.

How much does she have left ?

9. 

Ben has a £5 note, four £2 coins a 50p coin and a 20p coin.

His train fare costs £3·74 and he buys lunch for £4·88.

He also buys a book (£3·50) for the train.

How much does he have left ?

10. Copy and complete the bill, working out the total cost.

2 chips at 75p each	=	£
1 burger at £1·65	=	£
3 colas at 68p each	=	£
Total	=	**£**

The Calendar

Time 2

Be able to use a calendar to answer questions.

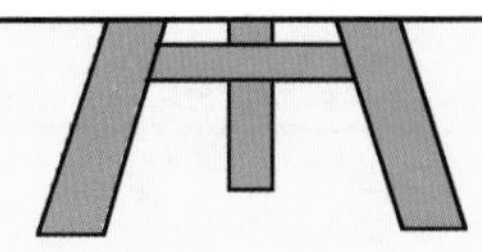

Remember

There are **7 days** in a **week**.

There are **12 months** in a **year**.

30 days has September, April,
June and November.
All the rest have 31, except
February which has 28 days clear
and 29 in each leap year.

January

				1	2	3
4	5	6	7	8	9	10
11	12	13	14	15	16	17
18	19	20	21	22	23	24
25	26	27	28	29	30	31

Worksheet 8·1

Exercise 1

1. a What is the 1st month of the year ?

   b What is the **last** month of the year ?

   c Which day comes 2 days **after** Thursday ?

   d Which day comes 3 days before **before** Monday ?

   e Which month comes 3 months **after** July ?

   f Which month comes 4 months **before** May ?

2. How many days are there in the month of :-

   a January b February c April d June

   e August f October g November h December ?

3. What is the :-

   a 6th month b 3rd month c 10th month d 8th month ?

The date, 3rd of January 2012 can be written using 6 digits.

3rd Jan 2012

2012			JANUARY			2012
SUN	MON	TUES	WED	THU	FRI	SAT
1	2	3	4	5	6	7
8	9	10	11	12	13	14
15	16	17	18	19	20	21
22	23	24	25	26	27	28
29	30	31	*	*	*	*

3rd January, 2012 = 03 : 01 : 12 or 03/01/12

day month year

4. Write each of these dates using **6 digits** as above :-

a 23rd February 2014 b 19th April 2013 c 22nd July 2014

d 18th August 2017 e 7th June 2009 f 3rd March 2021

g 10th December 2007 h 1st January 2016. i 4th February 2016.

5. Write each of these dates in words :-

a 14/01/13 b 01/03/14 c 11/11/11

d 23/04/05 e 12:12:12 f 07:08:15

g 09:03:20 h 31:06:16 i 30/02/10.

6. What is wrong with questions **5 h** and **5 i** ?

7. Look at the month of April 2014.

April 2014						
Su	Mo	Tu	We	Th	Fr	Sa
		1	2	3	4	5
6	7	8	9	10	11	12
13	14	15	16	17	18	19
20	21	22	23	24	25	26
27	28	29	30			

a How many Wednesdays are in April 2014 ?

b Ellie has her birthday on 03/04/14.

What day is her birthday on ?

c Teri has her birthday exactly 3 weeks **after** Ellie.

Teri has her birthday on what date ?

d Chad's birthday is 3 days **before** Ellie's.

What date is Chad's birthday ?

8. Look at the two calendar months shown.

May 2015

Mo	Tu	We	Th	Fr	Sa	Su
				1	2	3
4	5	6	7	8	9	10
11	12	13	14	15	16	17
18	19	20	21	22	23	24
25	26	27	28	29	30	31

June 2015

Mo	Tu	We	Th	Fr	Sa	Su
1	2	3	4	5	6	7
8	9	10	11	12	13	14
15	16	17	18	19	20	21
22	23	24	25	26	27	28
29	30					

a How many Saturdays are there **altogether** in May **and** June 2015 ?

b My birthday is on May 14th.

My sister has her birthday exactly 3 weeks later.

What date is my sister's birthday ?

c What is the day and date :-

(i) one day before 1st of May 2015

(ii) two days after 30th of June 2015

(iii) a **week** after 24th June 2015

(iv) a **week** before 12th June 2015 ?

(v) 2 **weeks** after 8th May 2015

(vi) 1 **week** after 25th May 2015 ?

9. How many days are there between (*do not include the dates*) :-

a March the 4th to 15th

b April 11th to 29th

c 02/02/14 to 23/02/14

d 30/05/13 to 02/06/13

e the 20th of June to 3rd of August ?

10. You need a calendar showing the present year. Look at your calendar. How many weeks are there from the :-

a first Monday in June to the last Monday in June

b last Friday in May to the first Friday in June

c first Monday in January to the first Monday in March

d last Saturday of November to the last Saturday in December ?

Units of Time

Be able to decide what unit of time to use to measure an activity.

There are **60 seconds** in **one minute**.

There are **60 minutes** in **one hour**.

There are **24 hours** in **one day**.

Exercise 2

1. Would you measure each of these in **seconds**, **minutes**, **hours**, or **days** ?

   a walking to school

   b walking across the classroom

   c walking all round Scotland

   d doing a 500 piece jigsaw

   e writing your name

   f a marathon run (26 miles)

   g boiling an egg

   h watching two DVD films

   i swimming one length

   j growing a plant ?

2. Time yourself for some of the activities in question 1.

3. List two or three activities that would take :-

   a seconds   b minutes   c hours   d days.

4. How many seconds are there in :-

   a 2 minutes   b 3 minutes   c 5 minutes   d 8 minutes

   e half a minute   f 9 minutes   g 10 minutes   h $2\frac{1}{2}$ minutes ?

5. How many minutes are there in :-

   a 2 hours   b 4 hours   c 5 hours   d 9 hours

   e 3 hours   f half an hour   g a quarter hour   h $1\frac{1}{2}$ hours ?

6. Copy the diagram and match what time would go with which activity.

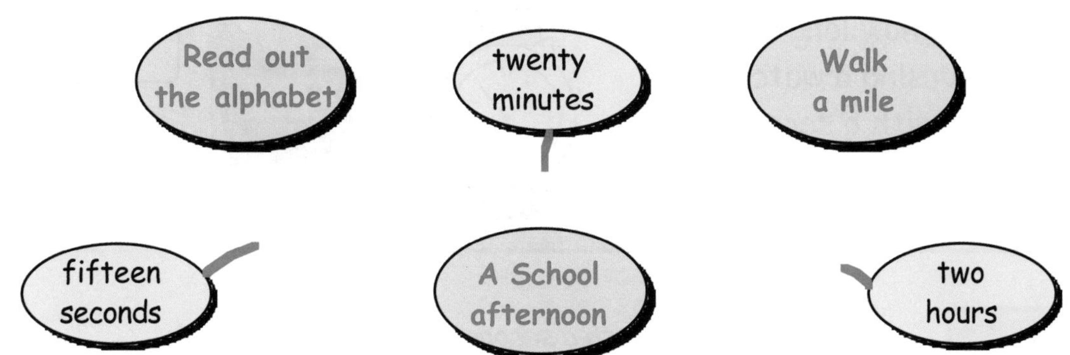

7. Copy the diagram and match what time would go with which activity.

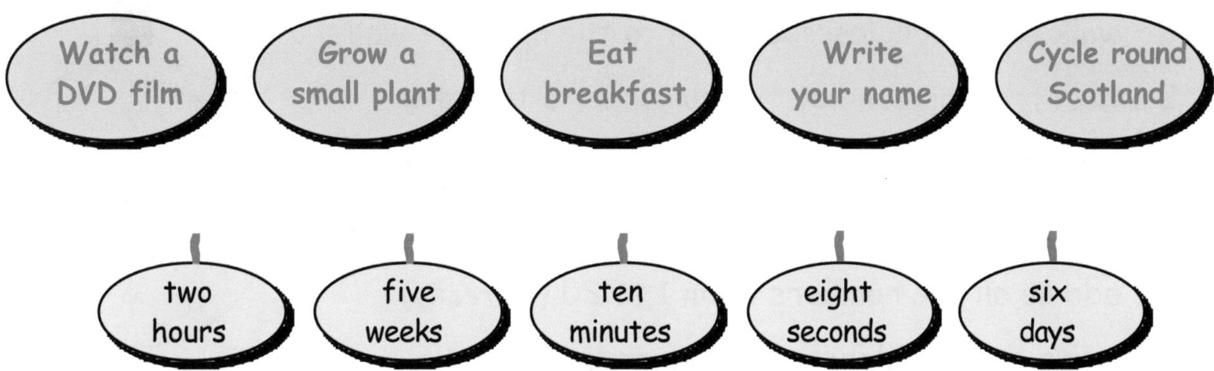

8. Use an encyclopaedia or the internet to find information about the fastest man or woman to run :-

a 100 metres b one mile c a marathon.

9. Make a poster for one of the following or pick a topic yourself. (*Use an encyclopaedia or the internet to find information*) :-

a How fast different types of penguins can swim compared to how fast a human can swim.

b Different speeds of aircraft (small plane, jumbo jet, fighter jet, ...)

c Different speeds of boats (rowing boat, speed boat, cruise liner, ...)

d The slowest moving animals.

Timing Events

Be able to time events using a watch or stopwatch

You can time how long something takes to do using a watch, (preferably with a second hand) or a stop watch.

Exercise 3

(You need a watch with a second hand or a stopwatch)

1. **Estimate** how long it would take you to complete each of the following :-
   (Some might be in seconds and some in minutes and seconds)

   a walk from one classroom wall to the opposite wall
   b walk from one end of the corridor to the other
   c walk all the way round the outside of the school
   d jog all the way round the outside of the school
   e add up all the numbers from 1 to 20 (*correctly*)
   f write out the alphabet ***backwards*** (*correctly*)
   g solve a puzzle or tangram given to you by your teacher
   h get up from bed and get ready for school yourself
   i make and eat your own breakfast
   j walk (or be driven) home from school
   k jog home from school (*remember to stop and check at roads*).

2. Now time using a watch or stopwatch some or all of the activities in question 1.

3. Stopwatches can have "read outs" that look like this.
   a Find out the meaning of this read out (*especially the 7*).
   b Investigate what sports or activities use this kind of read out.
   c Why do you think they have to use these kinds of read outs ?

MODE
3:29:7
stop watch
PS-50

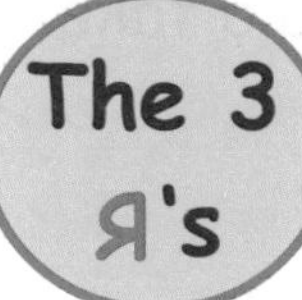

Revisit - Review - Revise

1. a What is the day just **before** Wednesday ?

   b Which day comes 3 days **after** Friday ?

   c Which day comes 2 days **before** Thursday ?

   d Which month comes 3 months **after** June ?

   e Which month comes 4 months **before** January ?

2. How many **days** are there in :-

   a January   b June   c one year ?

3. What is the :-

   a 6th month   b 3rd month   c 10th month ?

4. Write the **seasons** in order starting with winter.

5. Write each of these dates **using only words** :-

   a 12 / 05 /15   b 01 / 01 / 20   c 07 / 06 / 05.

6. Write each of the following **using only numbers** :-

   a fifth of May two thousand and sixteen

   b twentieth of October two thousand and nine.

7. Shown is the calendar tab for July 2015.

   a How many Fridays are in July 2015 ?

   b What day is the 1st of August 2015 ?

   c What day is the 29th of June 2015 ?

July 2015

Mo	Tu	We	Th	Fr	Sa	Su
		1	2	3	4	5
6	7	8	9	10	11	12
13	14	15	16	17	18	19
20	21	22	23	24	25	26
27	28	29	30	31		

8. What **unit of time** would you use to measure how long it would take :-
(Answer as ***seconds***, ***minutes***, ***hours***, or ***days***).

a an aeroplane to fly to Africa

b to walk home from school

c to add all the numbers from 1 up to 5

d to walk from Glasgow to London ?

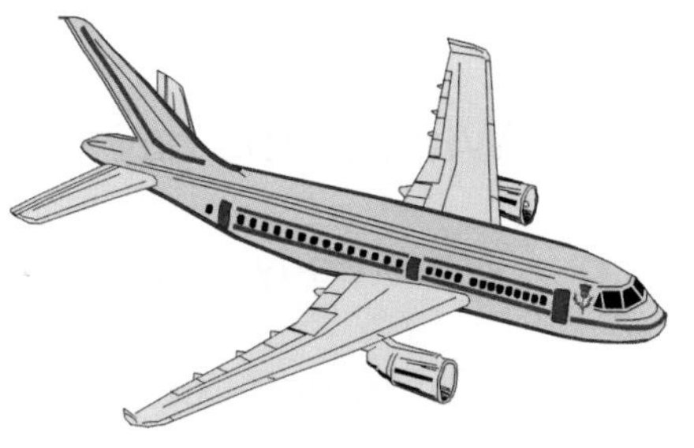

9. Write down an activity you might do which would take about :-

a 10 seconds b 10 minutes c 10 hours.

10. Match each of these times with each event :-

A 3 seconds	**1** drink a pint of milk
B 30 seconds	**2** do your homework
C 3 hours	**3** watch two DVD films
D 4 days	**4** sneeze
E 15 minutes	**5** paint the whole school.

11. a How many **seconds** are there in **two minutes** ?

b How many **minutes** are there in **ten hours** ?

12. Joe is planning a sponsored walk to raise lots of money for charity.

Which of the following times would you expect Joe to walk to raise lots of money :-

10 seconds, **10 minutes,** **half an hour,**

3 hours, **5 days,** **3 weeks.**

Revision of 2 Dimensions

1. Name these 2 dimensional shapes :-

a 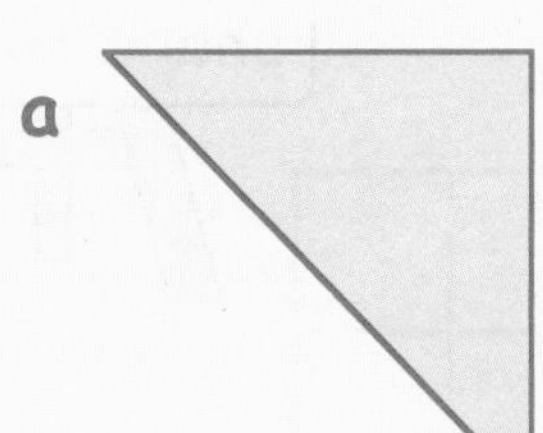 b  c  d 

2. Name the 2 dimensional shapes in the picture and say how many of them there are.

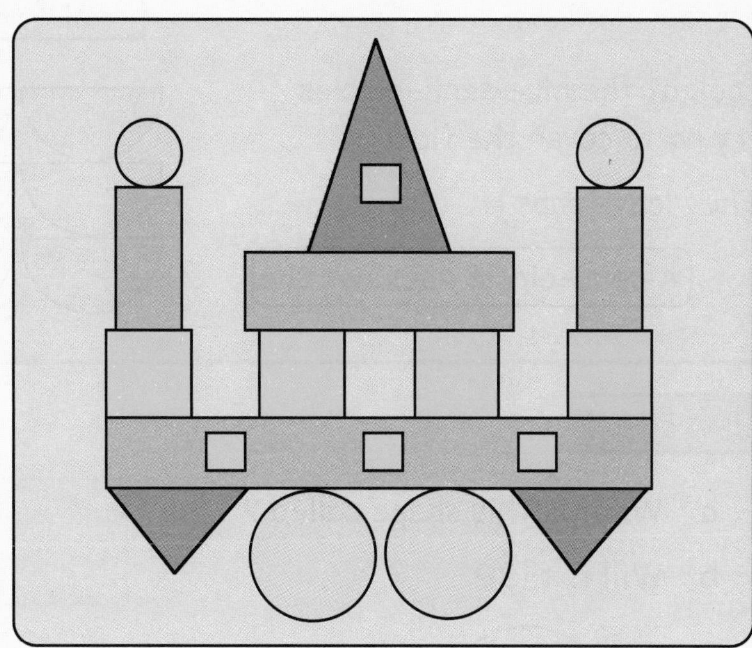

3. How many :-

a angles are in a triangle
b sides are in a circle
c angles are in a square
d corners are in a circle
e sides are in a triangle
f corners are in a triangle
g corners are in a square
h sides are in a rectangle
i corners are in a rectangle
j sides are in a square
k angles are in a rectangle
l angles are in a circle ?

4. Write down at least 3 ways in which :-

a a square is different from a triangle
b a circle is different from a rectangle.

Coloured Pencils will be needed

2 Dimensions

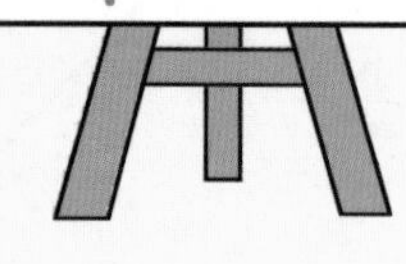

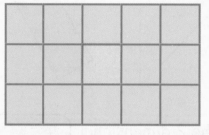

Be able to decide if a shape will tile

You can use **shapes** to cover a floor, leaving **no gaps**.

This is called **tiling**.

The shape which will cover the floor shown here is a yellow **square**.

A square can tile

Look at the blue **semi-circles** trying to cover the floor.

They leave gaps !

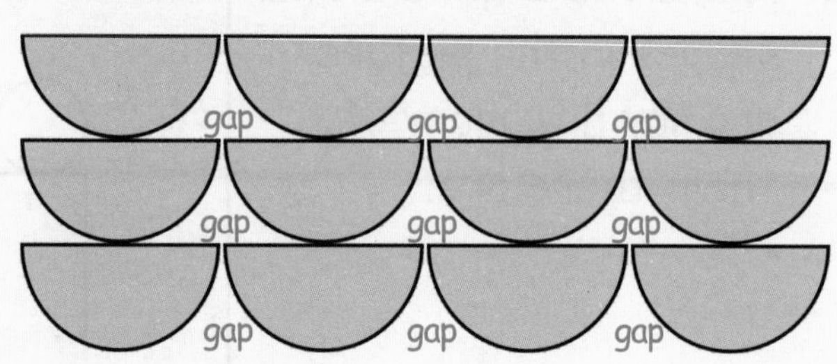

A semi-circle does not tile

Exercise 1

1. a What is this shape called ?

   b Will it tile ?

2. a What is the name of this shape ?

   b Will it tile ?

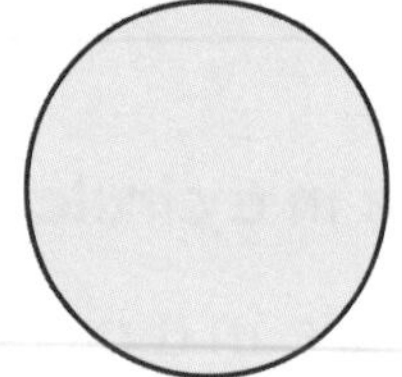

3. a What is this shape called ?

   b Will it tile ?

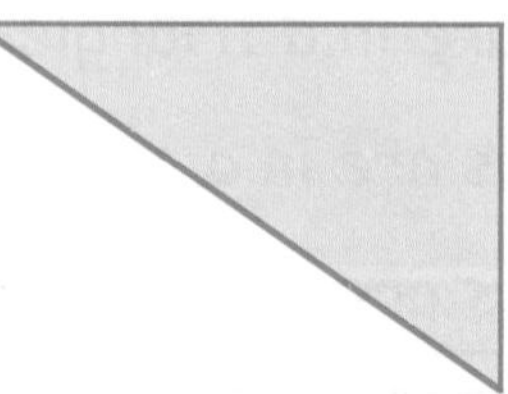

4. Do these shapes tile ? (Answer **yes** or **no**)

a 

b 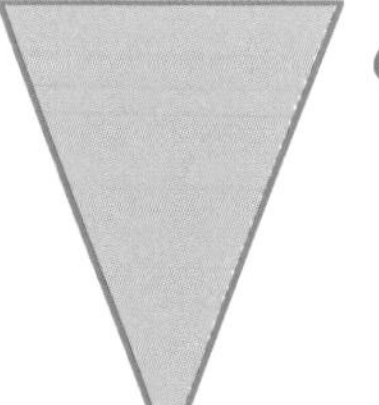

c 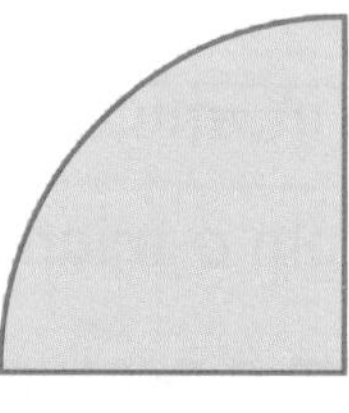

d 

e 

You will need **1 centimetre squared paper.**

Worksheet 9·1

5. Copy this **square** onto your squared paper and colour it in.

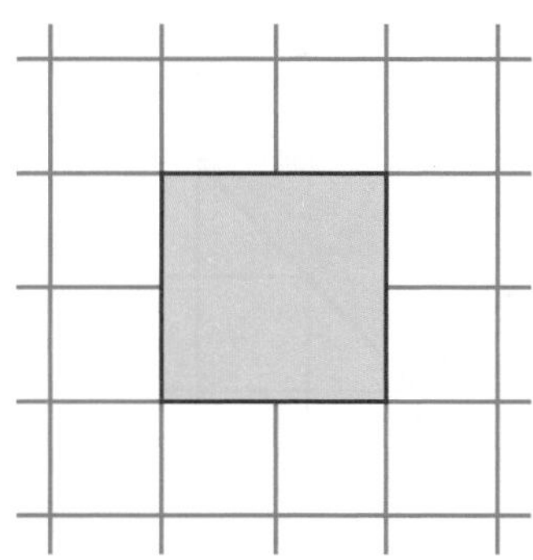

Draw **8** more squares around it to show how the **square tiles.**

6. Copy this **rectangle** onto the squared paper and colour it in.

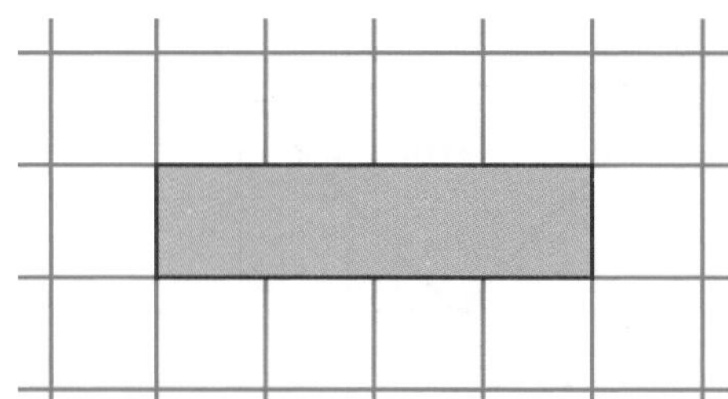

Draw **8** more rectangles around it to show how the **rectangle tiles.**

7. Copy the **triangle** onto the squared paper and colour it in.

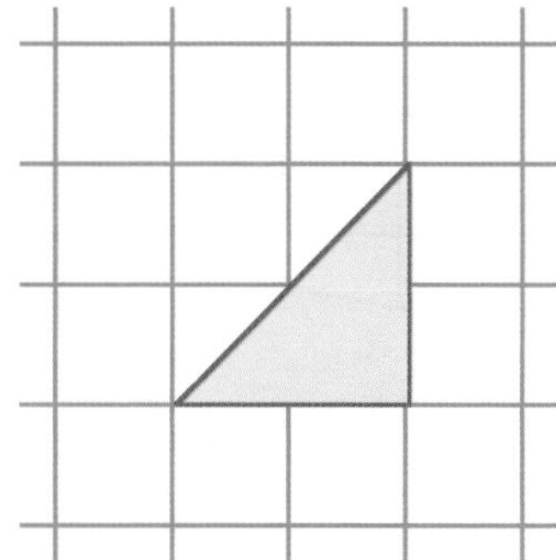

Draw **a few more** triangles around this one to show how the **triangle tiles.**

8. Copy this **square** onto squared paper and colour it in.

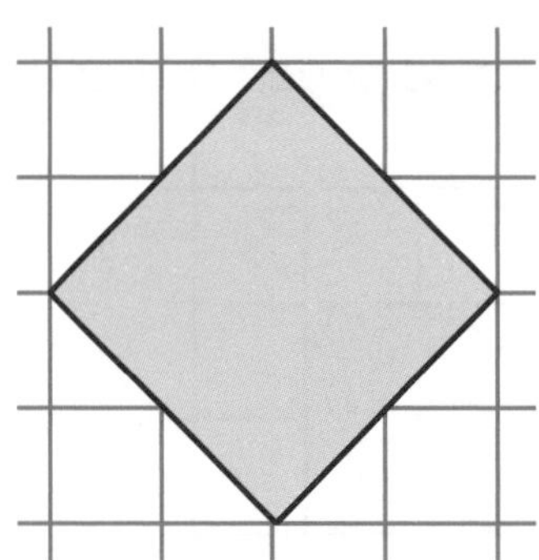

Draw **a few more** squares around it to show how this **square tiles**.

9. Copy this **triangle** onto squared paper and colour it in.

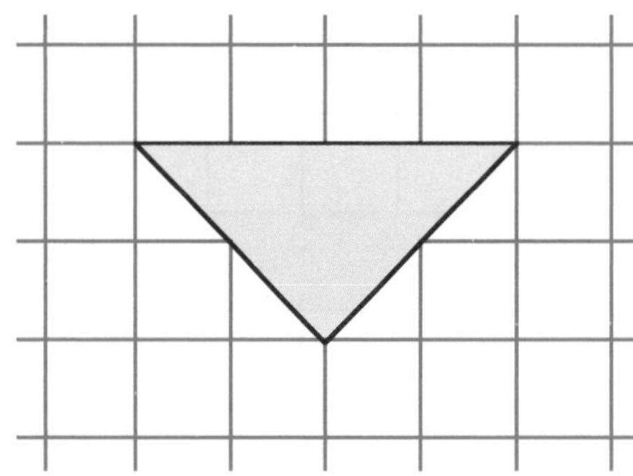

Draw **some more** triangles around this one to show how this **triangle tiles**.

10. Copy this **triangle** onto squared paper and colour it in.

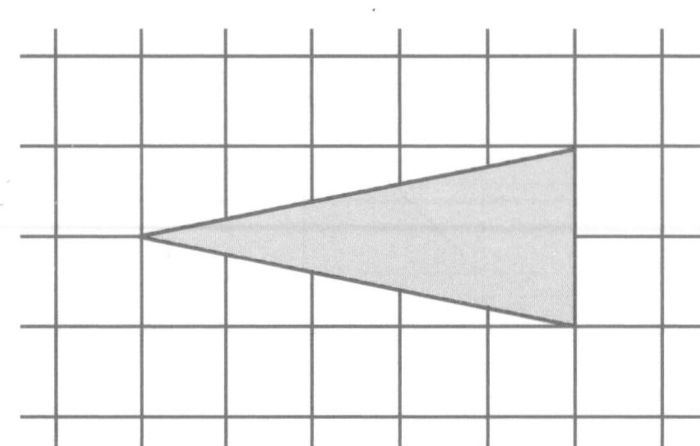

Draw **some more** triangles around this one to show how this **triangle tiles**.

You will need $\frac{1}{2}$ cm **squared paper** for the next few questions.

11. a On your squared paper, draw a **square** 4 boxes by 4 boxes and colour it in.

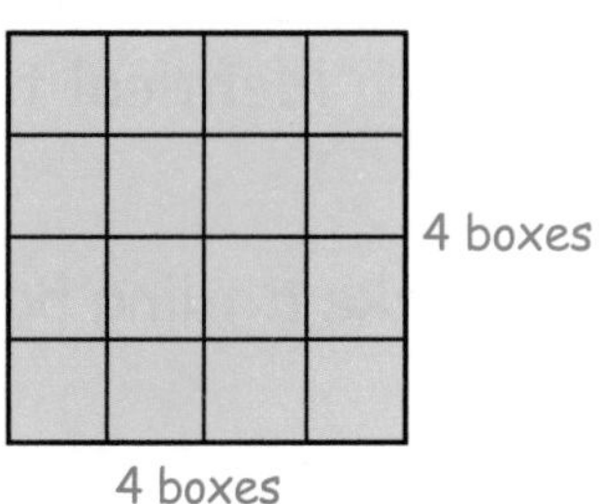

b Draw 8 or more squares of the same size around it to show how it "**tiles**".

c Use different colours for these squares.

12. a On your squared paper, draw a **rectangle** 4 boxes by 3 boxes and colour it in.

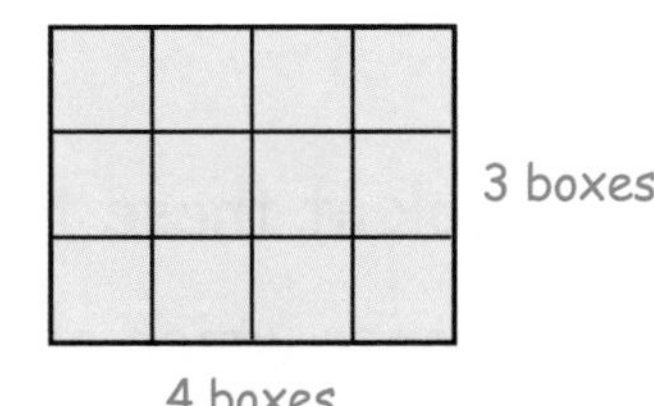

b Surround your rectangle with rectangles of the same size to show how it "**tiles**".

c Use different colours for these rectangles.

13.

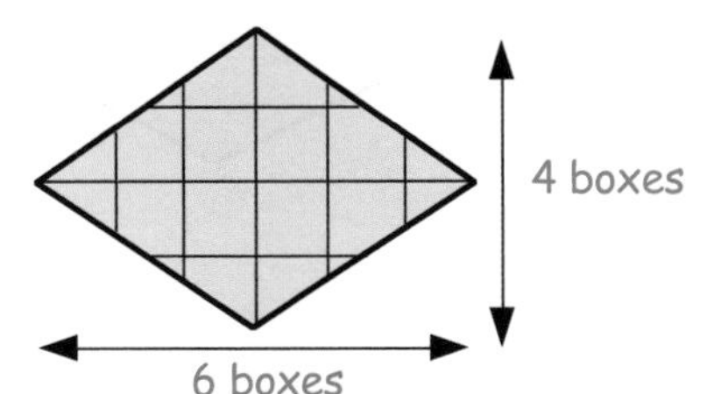

a What is this shape called ? A R...........

b Copy this diamond shape onto squared paper and colour it in.

c Show how to "tile" the paper by surrounding it with identical diamonds.

d Colour these in to create a nice pattern.

14. a Draw a **triangle** 2 boxes by 5 boxes and colour it in.

b Surround your triangle with triangles of the same size to show how it "**tiles**". (*Some will have to be turned upside down*).

c Use different colours for these triangles.

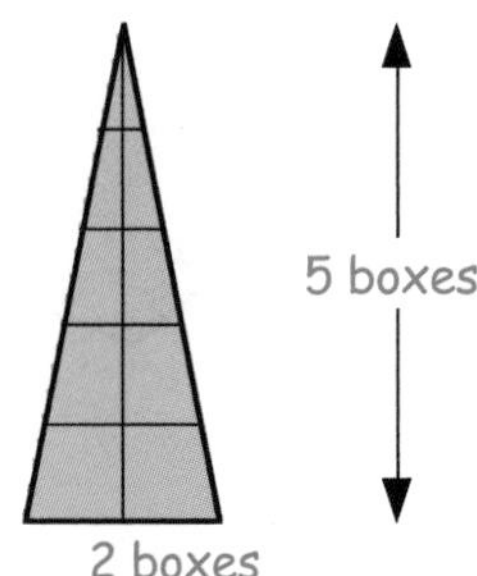

15. This shape is harder to tile.

a Make a neat copy of the shape and colour it in.

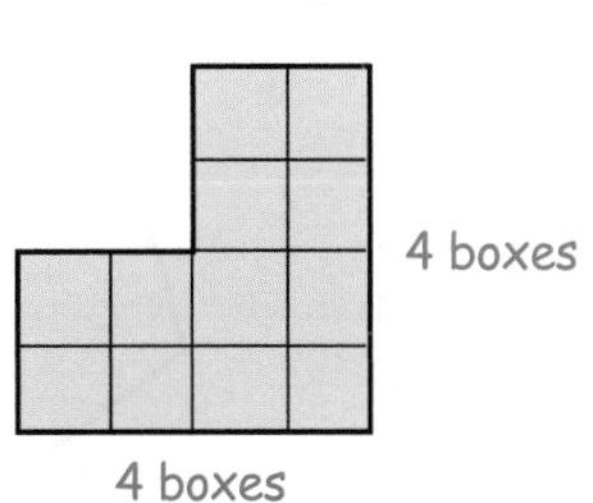

b Show how the shape can "**tile**" the paper completely by surrounding it with identical tiles (tiles of the same shape and size).

16. Draw this tile and show how to tile the page by completely surrounding it with identical tiles.

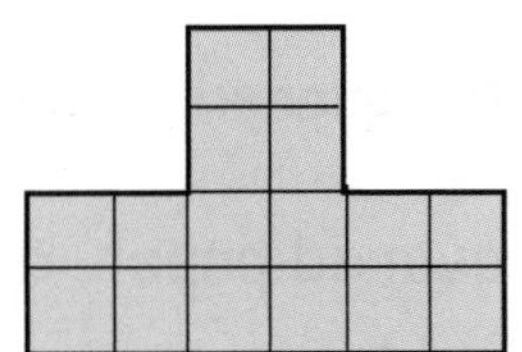

17. Make a tiling pattern with these tiles :-

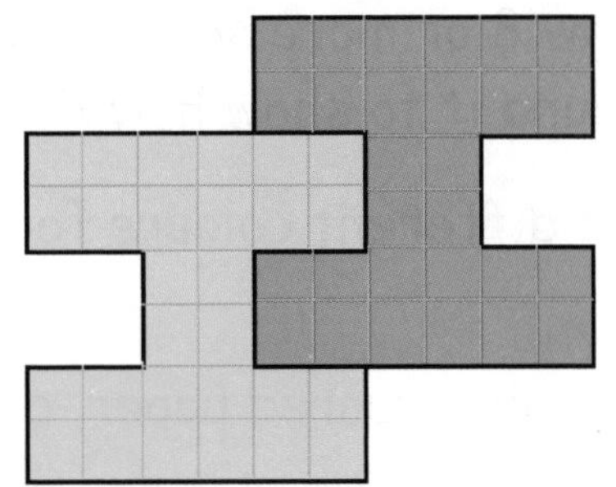

18. Look at these tiles :-

Choose which ones you think would make **good tiles**. (Answer **yes** or **no**).

a

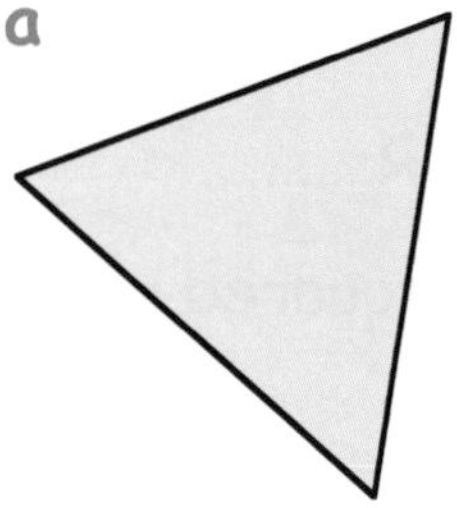

b

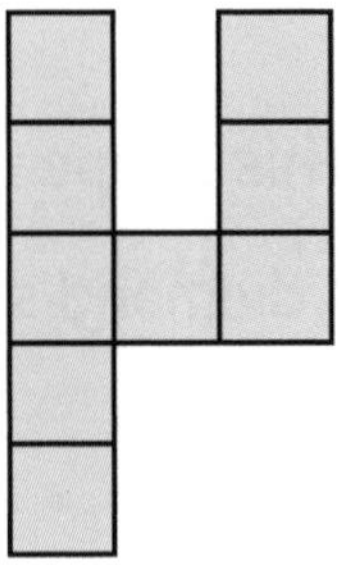

c

d

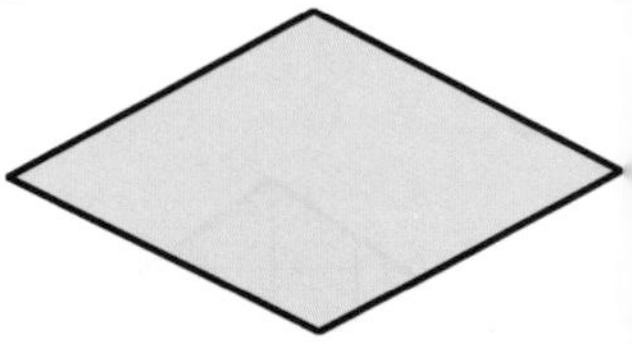

e

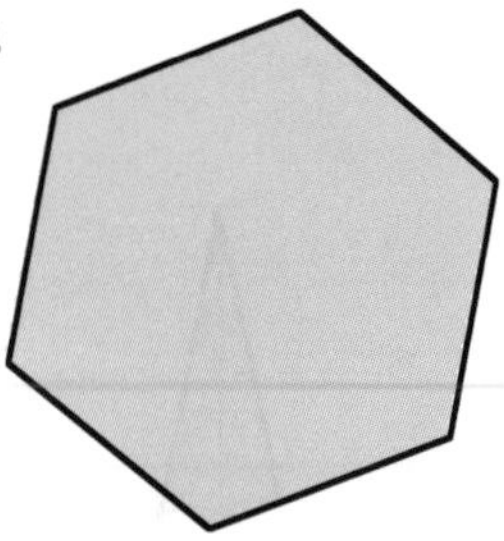

f

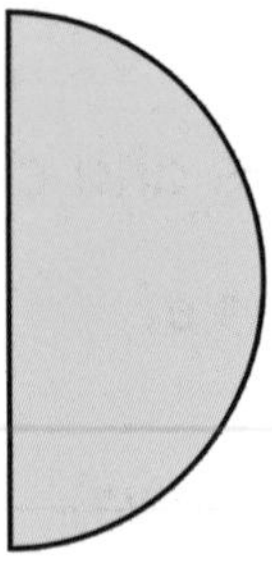

g

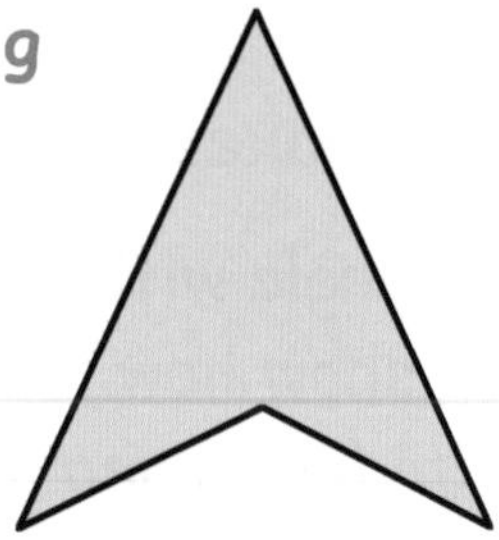

h

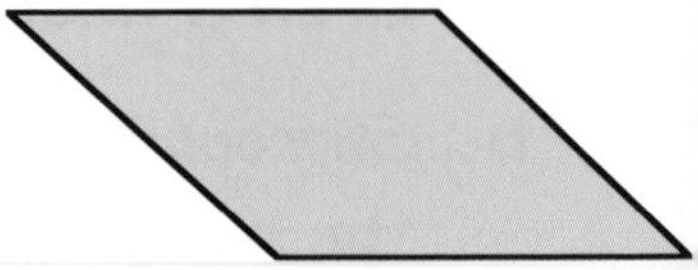

i

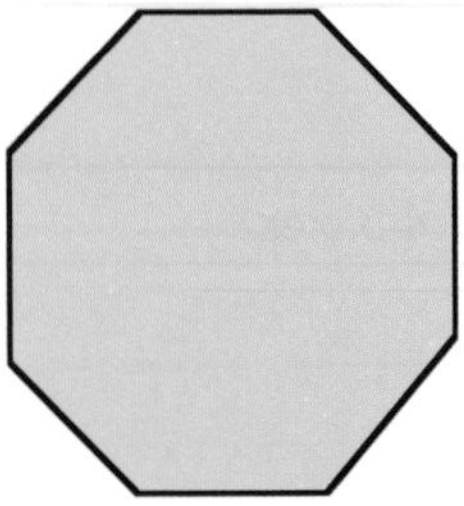

j

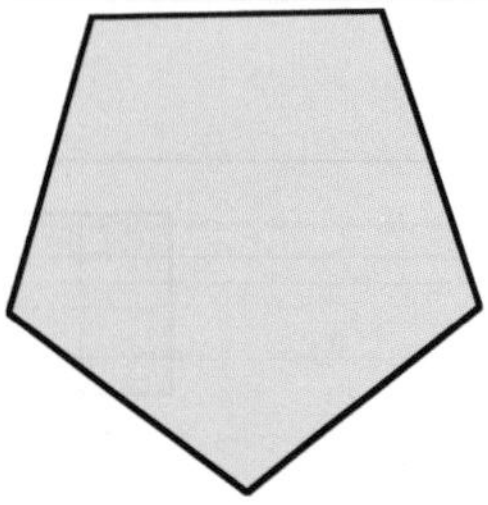

k

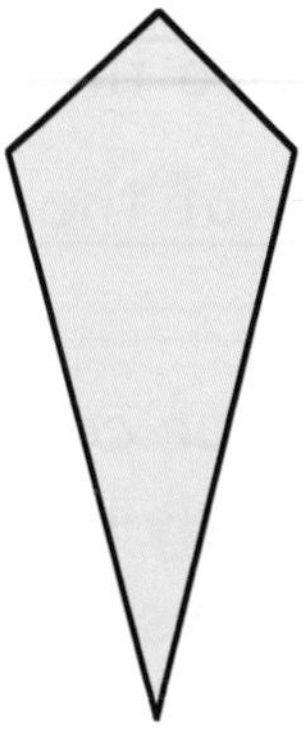

l

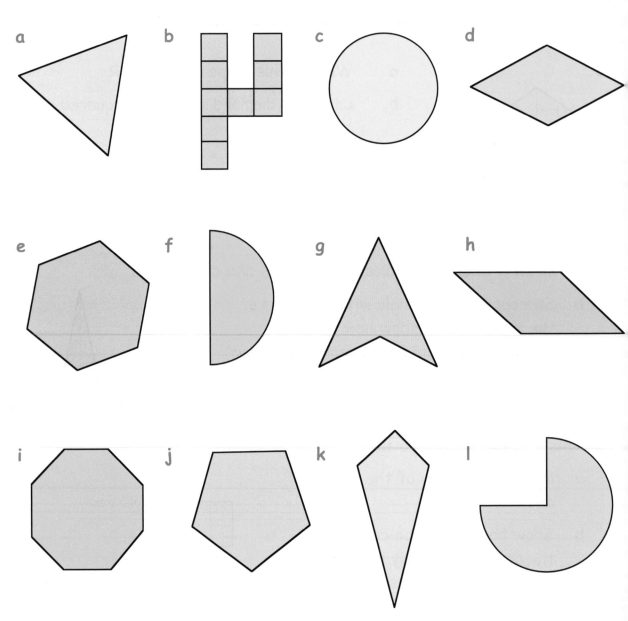

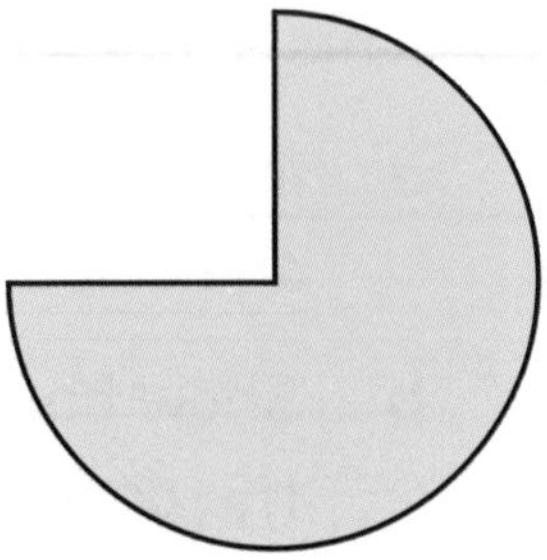

Revisit - Review - Revise

1. Which of these shapes would **not** make good tiles ?

a 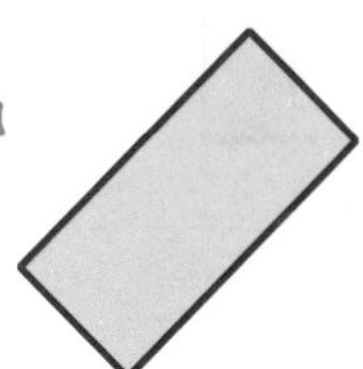 b 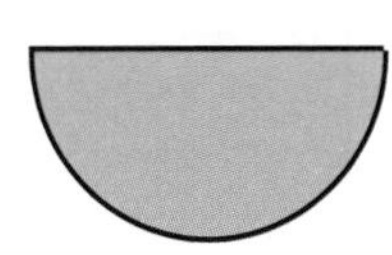 c  d 

2. Why would the tiles you chose in question 1 **not** make good tiles ?

   Write down at least one reason.

3. On squared paper, in the centre of the page, draw this square and colour it in.

   Now surround it with similar squares to show how it tiles.

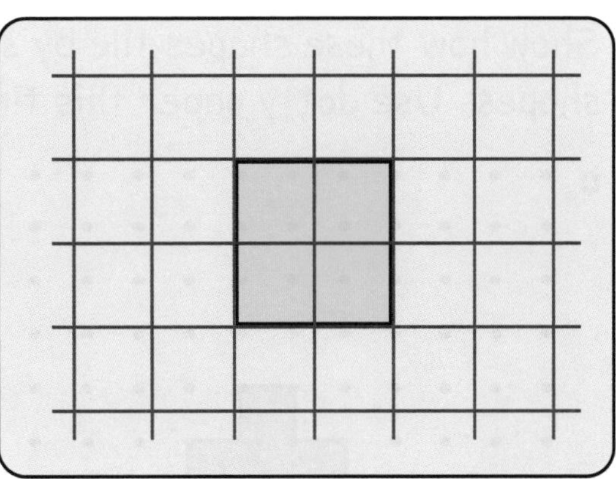

4. Draw the following shapes and surround each with similar shapes to show how they tile.

a 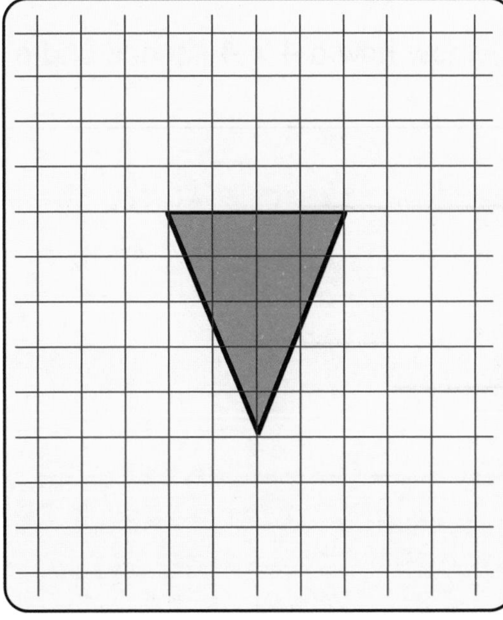

b 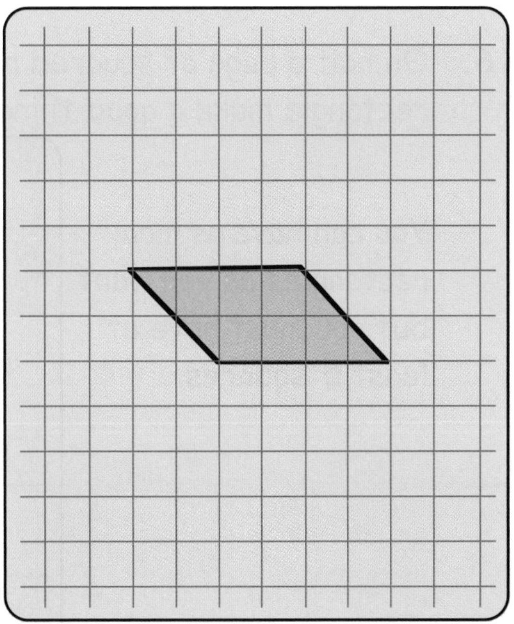

4. c

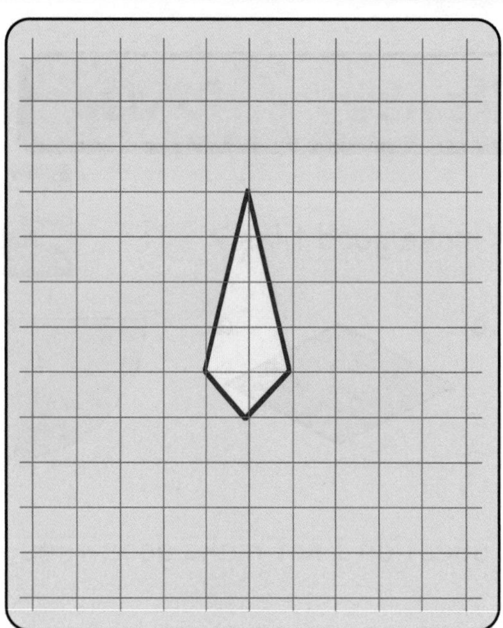

d

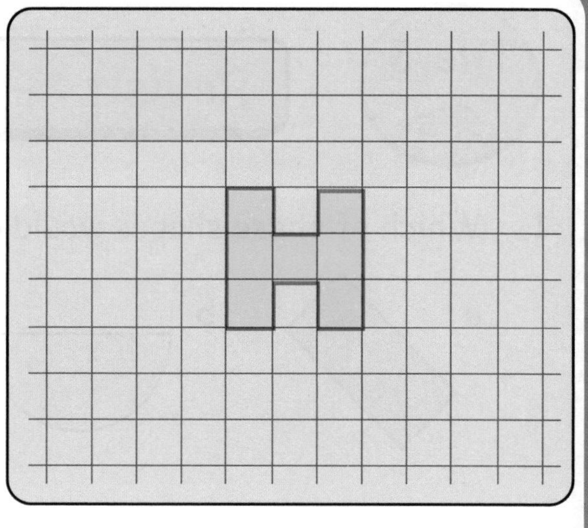

5. Show how these shapes tile by surrounding each one by **8 identical** shapes. Use dotty paper this time.

a

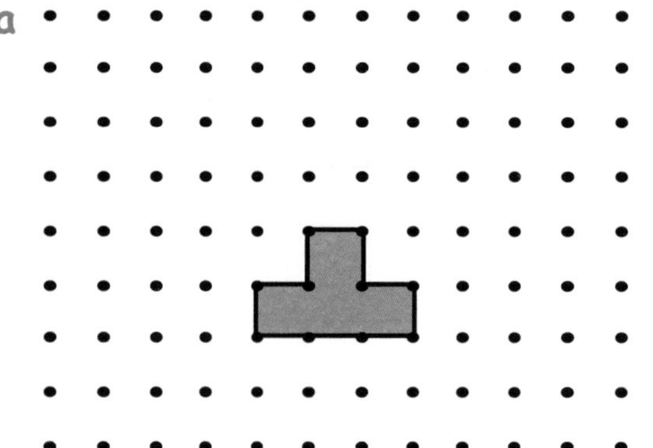

b

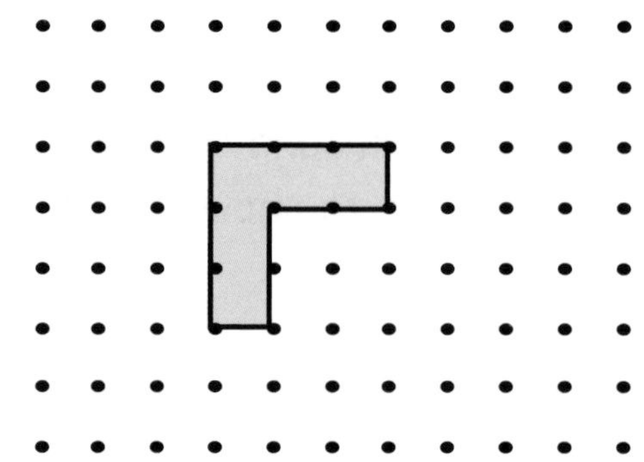

6. On half a page of squared paper, show how a 4 x 4 square and a 3 x 2 rectangle make a good tiling.

You can have as many rectangles as you want, but you must have at least **5 squares**.

Revision of Whole Numbers

1. Copy and complete :-

a	3 x 9 =	b	5 x 5 =	c	4 x 0 =
d	2 x 7 =	e	10 x 6 =	f	8 x 5 =

2. What numbers are missing ?

a	2 x .... = 18	b	3 x .... = 21	c	4 x .... = 20
d	5 x .... = 40	e	10 x .... = 70	f	.... x 10 = 400.

3. Copy and complete :-

a	26 x 5	b	67 x 3	c	38 x 2
d	80 x 4	e	95 x 2	f	87 x 5
g	94 x 3	h	67 x 4	i	178 x 5
j	296 x 4	k	324 x 5	l	819 x 3

4. Find :-

a	71 x 10	b	86 x 3	c	99 x 2
d	138 x 5	e	209 x 4	f	618 x 3
g	300 x 10	h	525 x 5	i	876 x 2.

5. When a tour bus pulled up outside a fish and chip shop 58 people got off and bought fish suppers, costing £4 each.

   How much money did the shop make from the tour bus ?

6. 

   145 people go to the church hall for a cuppa.

   If they each have 2 cups of tea, how many is this altogether ?

7. Charlie travels to and from work 3 days per week.

   If the return journey is 256 km, how far does he travel in total over these days ?

8. 

   A shopkeeper arranged chews into bags of 10.

   She had enough to fill 63 bags and have 2 chews left over.

   How many chews did she have to begin with ?

9. Murray went out one morning to find his hut covered in spiders' webs.

   He counted 109 webs, each with exactly 5 spiders !

   How many spiders altogether ?

10. 

    At the village fete, 59 children each received 3 balloons.

    How many balloons were handed out ?

11. Jon bought cans of diet cola at the Cash & Carry.

    He filled 5 trollies, each trolley with

    4 boxes containing 10 cans each.

    How many cans of cola did Jon buy ?

Whole Numbers 4

6 times table

Be able to multiply by 6 and learn.

You should now know the :-

2 times table, the
3 times table, the
4 times table, the
5 times table and the
10 times table.

The 6 times tables can be found in a similar way.

Use **Worksheet 10·1** to complete the 6 times table.

6 sets of 0 = 0	6 x 0 = 0
6 sets of 1 = 6	6 x 1 = 6
6 sets of 2 = 12	6 x 2 = 12
6 sets of 3 = 18	6 x 3 = 18
6 sets of 4 = 24	6 x 4 = 24
6 sets of 5 = ...	6 x 5 = 30
6 sets of 6 = ...	6 x 6 = ...
6 sets of .. = ...	6 x 7 = ...
6 sets of .. = ...	6 x .. = ...
6 sets of .. = ...	6 x .. = ...
6 sets of .. = ...	6 .. .. = ...

Exercise 1

1. Copy and complete :-

a 6 x 3 = b 6 x 5 = c 6 x 2 =
d 6 x 4 = e 6 x 6 = f 6 x 7 =
g 6 x 10 = h 6 x 8 = i 6 x 9 =

2. What numbers are **missing** ?

a 6 x .... = 12 b 6 x .... = 24 c 6 x .... = 36
d 6 x .... = 54 e 6 x .... = 0 f 6 x .... = 42
g 6 x .... = 48 h 6 x .... = 30 i 6 x .... = 60.

3. a Martha's mum hands her a few coins.

When she looks, she has **six 2 pence** coins.

How much money does Martha have ?

b 

Heather makes a **6** kilometre round trip to the gym each day.

How far does she travel in a week (**7** days) ?

c Colin gets **5** texts each hour from his girlfriend.

How many texts does he receive from **1 pm** until **7 pm** ?

d 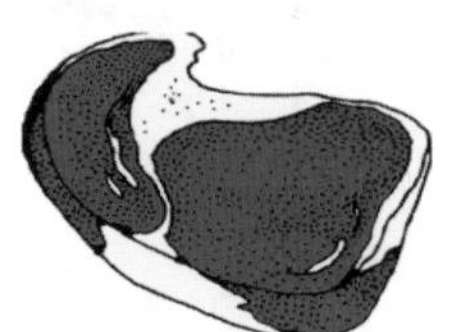

This steak costs **£4** in the butcher's.

Mrs Arnold bought **6** steaks.

How much did they cost her ?

e Up in the sky, I can see **6** groups of clouds.

Each group contains **3** clouds.

How many clouds can I see altogether ?

f 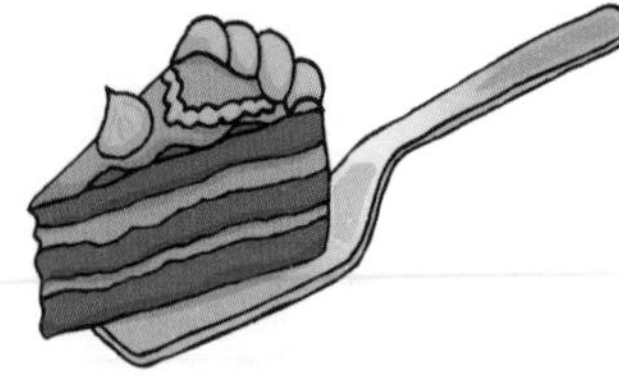

To get a large slice, George cuts a cake into **6** pieces.

How many pieces would he get from **6** cakes ?

g Each glass door in my house has **9** panes.

If I have **6** glass doors, how many panes in total ?

h 

Marlyn works from **9** am until **5** pm, Monday to Saturday inclusive.

How many hours does she work in the week ?

Multiplying by 6

Multiplying a 2 digit number by 6

Example 1 What is 91 x 6 ?

Example 2 Find 47 x 6

Exercise 2

1. Copy and complete :-

a. 14 x 6 b. 53 x 6 c. 67 x 6

d. 29 x 6 e. 43 x 6 f. 37 x 6

g. 62 x 6 h. 73 x 6 i. 81 x 6

j. 75 x 6 k. 86 x 6 l. 97 x 6

2. Find :-

a. 41 x 6 b. 58 x 6 c. 63 x 6

d. 38 x 6 e. 44 x 6 f. 65 x 6

g. 6 x 71 h. 6 x 82 i. 6 x 49

j. 6 x 96 k. 6 x 85 l. 6 x 99.

3. A beaver eats through **13** mm of wood in one minute.

How much will it get through in **6** minutes ?

4. 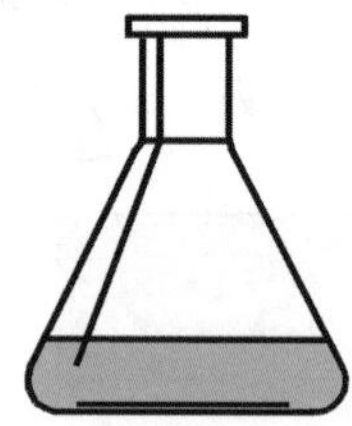

This beaker holds **45** ml of liquid.

How many ml in **6** beakers ?

5. Ken has scored **27** each time he has thrown a dart for the past **6** darts.

What is his total score for these darts ?

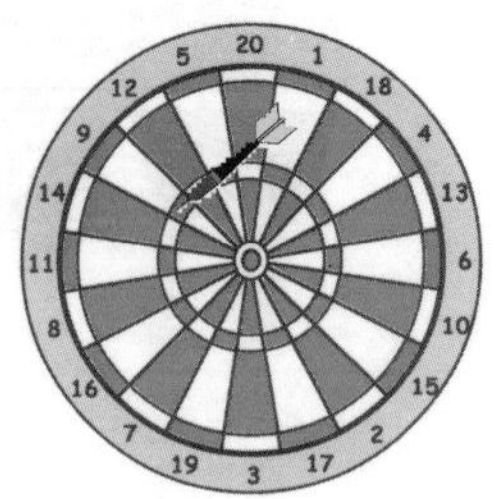

6. 

A packet of rollos weighs **39** grams.

What's the weight of **6** packets ?

7. An orange grower plants **70** trees in a row.

How many trees in **6** rows ?

8. 

A set of car mats costs **£6**.

A car rental company put these mats in each of its **68** cars.

What did this cost the company ?

9. There are **52** weeks in a year.

How many weeks in **6** years ?

10. 

An ant has **6** legs.

I counted **84** ants in my porch.

If I had counted their legs, how many should I have got ?

7 times table

Be able to multiply by 7 and learn.

You should now know the :-

2 times table, the
3 times table, the
4 times table, the
5 times table, the
6 times table and the
10 times table.

The 7 times tables can be found in a similar way.

Use **Worksheet 10·2** to complete the 7 times table.

7 sets of 0 = 0		7 x 0 = 0
7 sets of 1 = 7		7 x 1 = 7
7 sets of 2 = 14		7 x 2 = 14
7 sets of 3 = 21		7 x 3 = 21
7 sets of 4 = 28		7 x 4 = 28
7 sets of 5 = ...		7 x 5 = 35
7 sets of 6 = ...		7 x 6 = ...
7 sets of .. = ...		7 x 7 = ...
7 sets of .. = ...		7 x .. = ...
7 sets of .. = ...		7 x .. = ...
7 sets of .. = ...		7 .. .. = ...

Exercise 3

1. **Copy** and **complete** :-

a	7 x 4 =	b	7 x 2 =	c	7 x 6 =
d	7 x 3 =	e	7 x 5 =	f	7 x 10 =
g	7 x 9 =	h	7 x 7 =	i	7 x 8 =

2. What numbers are **missing** ?

a	7 x .... = 28	b	7 x .... = 14	c	7 x .... = 35
d	7 x .... = 21	e	7 x .... = 49	f	7 x .... = 56
g	7 x .... = 63	h	7 x .... = 70	i	7 x .... = 42.

3. a Thomas took a **7** at each of the first **3** holes on the putting green.

What was his total score for these holes ?

b

For every 1 step big Wullie takes, wee Davie takes **2** !

When Wullie has taken **7** steps, how many has Davie taken ?

c The temperature in Dunblane one day last spring was **6°** Celsius.

On the same day in Cyprus, it was **7** times hotter.

What was the temperature in Cyprus ?

d

The local shop charges **10p** per copy on its photocopying machine.

Jenna makes **7** copies of a one page document.

How much did she have to pay ?

e Mr Flannigan hired **7** taxis to take guests to his daughter's wedding.

If each taxi had **5** people in it, how many people in total were taken to the wedding in these taxis ?

f

Nine times last year Miss Baines won **£7** at the bingo.

How much were her total winnings ?

g To make doorstops, Joe cut **8** pieces of wood, each **7 cm** long from a plank.

What was the total length of wood cut ?

Multiplying by 7

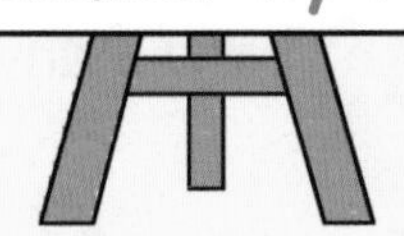

Example 1 What is **71 x 7** ?

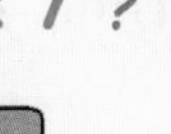

Example 2 Find **64 x 7**

Exercise 4

1. Copy and complete :-

a	12 x 7	b	54 x 7	c	63 x 7
d	28 x 7	e	45 x 7	f	76 x 7
g	17 x 7	h	34 x 7	i	26 x 7
j	69 x 7	k	88 x 7	l	96 x 7

2. Find :-

a	43 x 7	b	56 x 7	c	62 x 7
d	37 x 7	e	41 x 7	f	68 x 7
g	74 x 7	h	83 x 7	i	49 x 7
j	7 x 95	k	7 x 86	l	99 x 7.

3. Claire has bought **15** DVD's every month for the past **7** months.

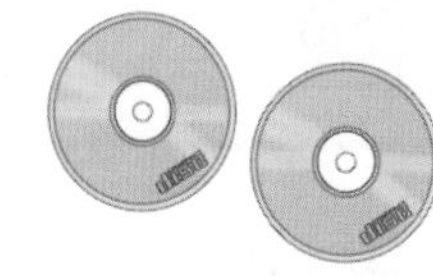

How many DVD's has she bought in that time ?

4. 

It costs **£7** to sign a visitor into the leisure club.

If you take **30** visitors over the year, how much will it cost ?

5. The Rovers were given **26** yellow cards last season.

This season, they have had **7** times that !

How many yellow cards have they had this time ?

6. 

There are **59** signals between Cotton Road Station and Queen's Cross.

Donald the train driver travels this route **7** times per day.

How many signals does he pass in total ?

7. A car park has **7** levels.

Each level can take **97** cars.

How many cars altogether can the car park take ?

8. 

Molly noticed that the **68** bulbs she planted in the spring were each beginning to produce **7** flower heads.

How many flowers will she have in total ?

9. It costs Mrs Wright **£97** each year to get her car serviced.

She has had her present car serviced each year for the past **7** years.

How much has this cost her altogether ?

Multiplying 3 digits

Multiplying a 3 digit number by 6 or 7.

Example 1 354 x 6

Example 2 429 x 7

Exercise 5

. Copy and complete :-

a 108 x 6 b 204 x 7 c 361 x 6

d 481 x 7 e 537 x 6 f 549 x 7

. Set down as in Question 1 and work out the answers :-

a 198 x 7 b 187 x 6 c 462 x 7

d 535 x 6 e 996 x 7 f 769 x 6.

. A barrel of apples holds **235** apples.
How many apples would there be in **7** barrels ?

. R-Mobile offer **374** free text messages every month.
How many should I get in my **6** month contract ?

. A lightbulb company sells **679** bulbs per hour on the internet.
One day, the internet went down for **7** hours.
How many lightbulb sales did the company lose that day ?

Mixed Exercise

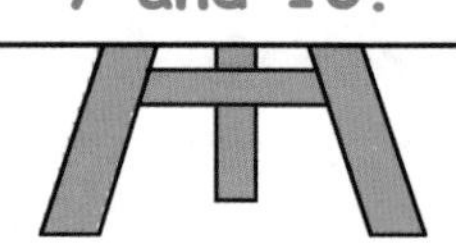

Exercise 6

1. Copy and complete each calculation :-

a	9 × 2	b	7 × 3	c	8 × 4	d	5 × 5
e	4 × 6	f	9 × 7	g	19 × 2	h	26 × 3
i	35 × 4	j	47 × 5	k	52 × 6	l	61 × 7
m	124 × 5	n	657 × 2	o	239 × 6	p	548 × 3
q	263 × 4	r	175 × 6	s	382 × 7	t	296 × 5

2. Set down as shown above and find the answer to these money examples :-

a	2 x 8p =	b	3 x 6p =	c	4 x 7p =	d	5 x 8p =
e	6 x 9p =	f	7 x 5p =	g	10 x 9p =	h	25 x 2p =
i	76 x 3p =	j	29 x 4p =	k	62 x 5p =	l	12 x 6p =
m	77 x 7p =	n	93 x 10p =	o	6 x £237 =	p	3 x £419 =
q	7 x £153 =	r	6 x £592 =	s	4 x £916 =	t	10 x £500 =

3. A tin of soup is on sale at **79** pence.

What is the cost of **5** tins ?

4. 

Mr Chapman has a computing class of **28** pupils.

He bought a **£3** memory stick for each of them.

What did it cost him ?

5. Gerry the joiner has just sealed a contract in which he is to be paid **£895** per week for a period of **4** weeks.

How much will he earn altogether ?

6. 

A bar of chocolate weighs **128** grams.

What is the weight of **7** bars ?

7. A syndicate of **6** factory workers won **£519** each in the Lotto.

How much was their total winnings ?

8. 

Five adults paid **£476** each to stay in the Glen Falcon Country Club over the weekend.

What was their total bill ?

9. The Butler family bought **3** slices of cherry pie at **86p** per slice and **4** slices of lemon tart at **50p** per slice.

How much change did they get from **£5** (500p) ?

10. 

One half of all the people who attended a football match were supporting the away team.

There were **945** away supporters.

How many people in total were at the match ?

The 3 Я's

Revisit - Review - Revise

1. **Copy** and **complete** :-

   a $6 \times 7 =$ b $4 \times 6 =$ c $3 \times 9 =$

   d $5 \times 5 =$ e $7 \times 7 =$ f $6 \times 9 =$.

2. What numbers are missing ?

   a 7 x .... = 56 b 10 x .... = 370 c 6 x .... = 48

   d 4 x .... = 28 e 3 x .... = 18 f 5 x .... = 45.

3. **Copy** and **complete** these multiplications :-

   a $\begin{array}{r} 75 \\ \times\ 6 \\ \hline \end{array}$ b $\begin{array}{r} 89 \\ \times\ 7 \\ \hline \end{array}$ c $\begin{array}{r} 293 \\ \times\ 4 \\ \hline \end{array}$

   d $\begin{array}{r} 619 \\ \times\ 3 \\ \hline \end{array}$ e $\begin{array}{r} 183 \\ \times\ 6 \\ \hline \end{array}$ f $\begin{array}{r} 429 \\ \times\ 7 \\ \hline \end{array}$

4. Daisy can play 76 notes per minute on her piano.

   How many notes can she play in a 6 minute practice ?

5. 

   Joseph has 764 five pence coins.

   How many pence does he have altogether ?

6. George cycled 67 kilometres each day for a period of 4 days.

   How far did he travel ?

7. 

   A box contains 24 cans of cola.

   6 shelves in a storeroom each have 7 boxes sitting on them.

   How many cans of cola are there in the room ?

Coordinates

Be able to identify the position of an object on a coordinate grid

Reading Coordinate Grids

The position of an object can be described by using a :-

COORDINATE GRID

The position can be given by showing which **square** the object is sitting in.

The position of the **dog** is **Bd**.

The **cat** is at **Eb**. The **mouse** is at **Cc**.

Always go **along** first, then **up**.

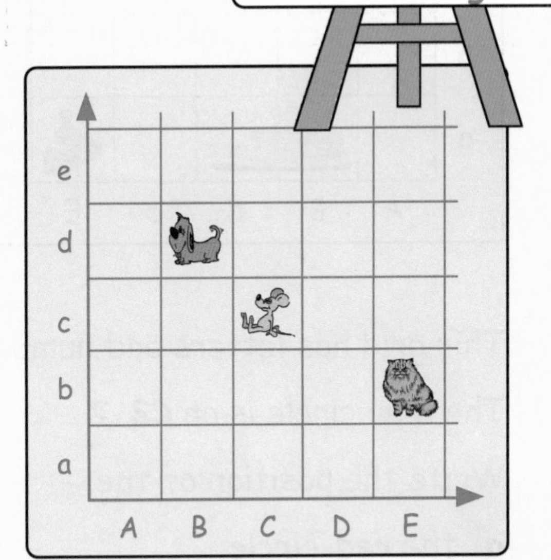

Exercise 1

1. Look at the grid shown.

   Write the position of :-

   a the **elephant** b the **panda**

   c the **tiger** d the **giraffe**

   e the **monkey** f the **lion**.

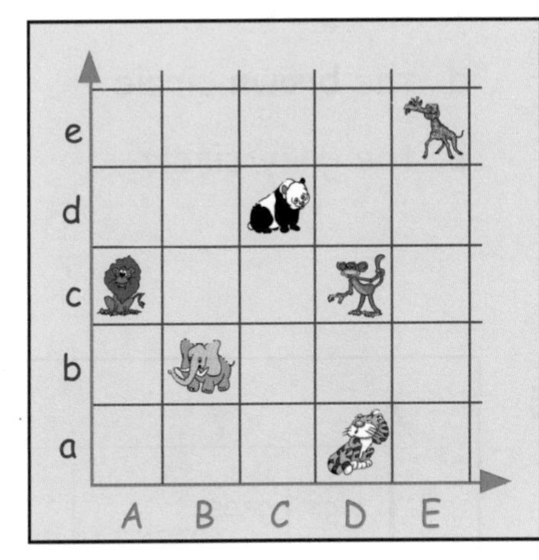

2. 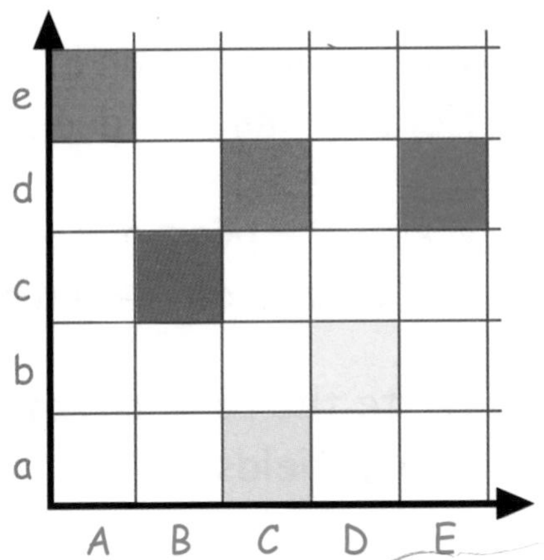

   Look at the grid shown.

   Write the position of the :-

   a **blue** square b **green** square

   c **red** square d **brown** square

   e **pink** square f **grey** square.

3.

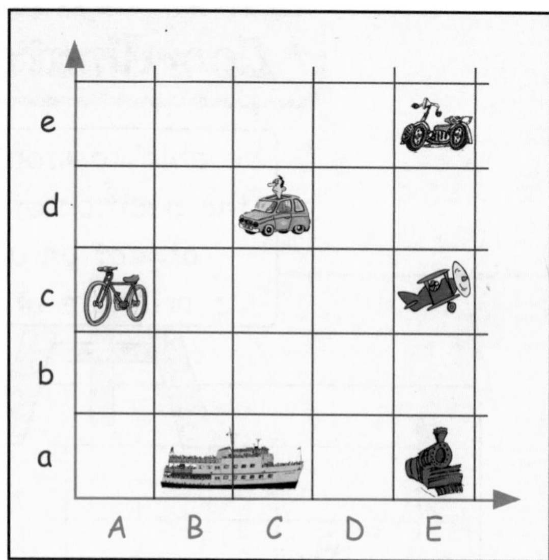

a What is at position **Cd** ?

b What is at **Ac** ?

c What is at **Ec** ?

d What is at **Ba** and **Ca** ?

e What is at **Ea** ?

f What is at **Ee** ?

4. This grid has letters and numbers.

The **blue** circle is on **C2** ?

Write the position of the :-

a the **red** circle

b the **pink** circle

c the **green** circle

d the **brown** circle

e the **grey** circle.

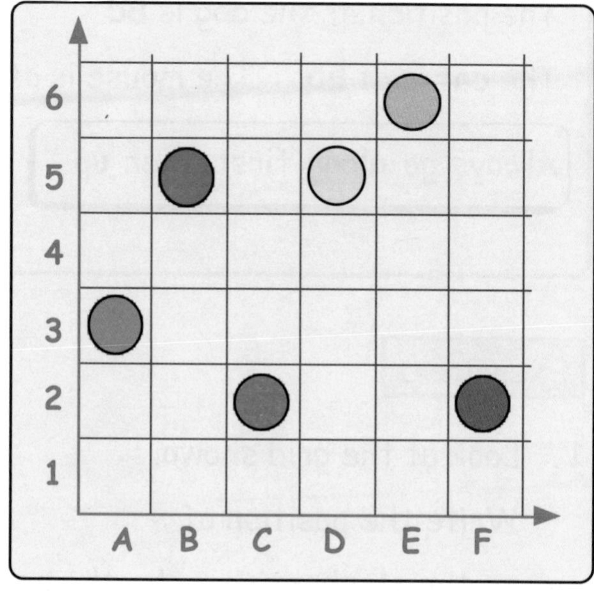

5.

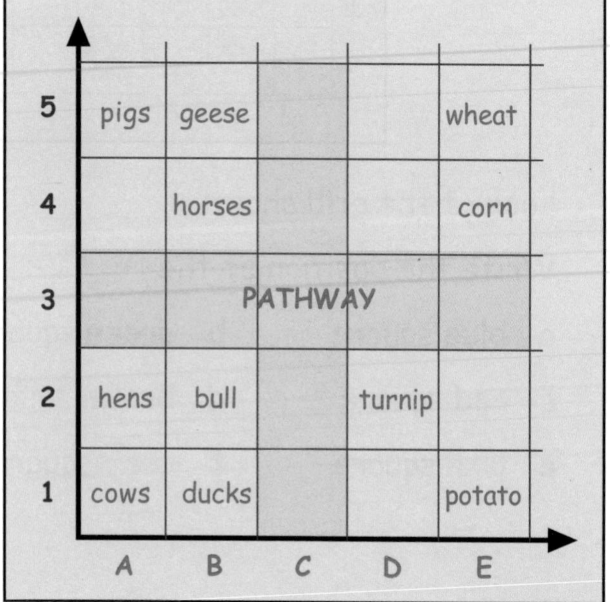

This grid shows fields on a farm where the farmer keeps his crops and his animals.

a Write the position of **each field** (*example* : ducks - B1)

b Write the positions of **each pink** square of the **pathway**.

c Write the positions of the **empty fields**.

6. 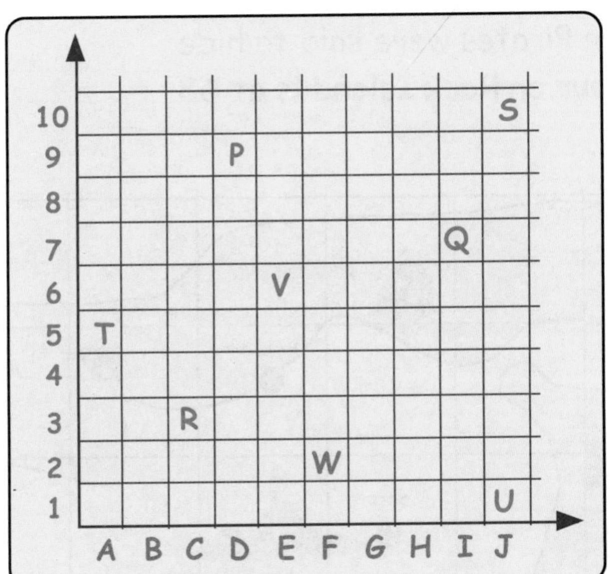

The letter P is in position **D9**.

Write down the positions of the other capital letters :-

Q, **R**, **S**, **T**, **U**, **V** and **W**.

Draw grids for **questions 7 to 9**, or use **Worksheet 11·1** if available.

7. Look at grid 1 on the worksheet.

   a Colour **B2 red**

   b Colour these squares **blue**

   A2, **D5**, **E1**.

   c Colour ***C1***, ***C4*** and **E3 brown**.

   d Colour ***A4*** and **B5 pink**.

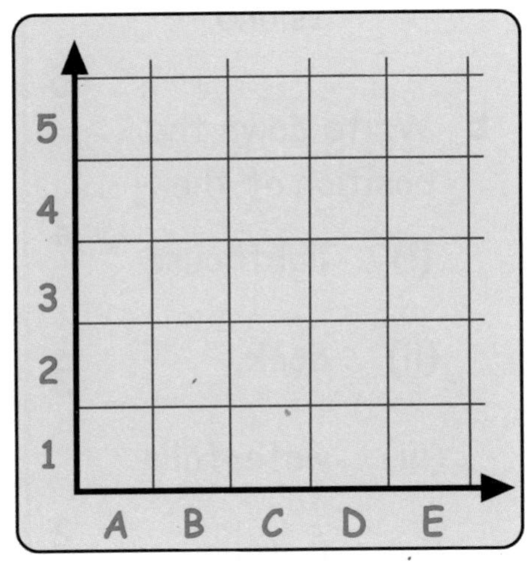

8. 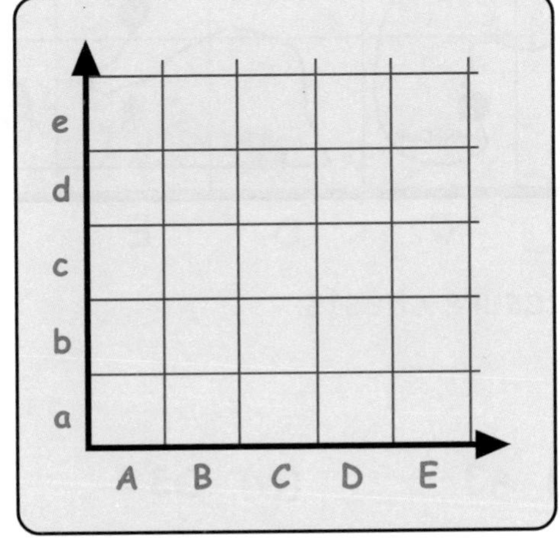

Look at grid 2 on the worksheet.

a Colour these squares **blue** :-

Bb, **De**, **Ea** and **Ae**.

b Colour these squares **red** :-

Ce, ***Cc***, **Aa** and **Ec**.

9. Look at grid 3 on the worksheet or draw your own.

   a This time, make a pattern of your own, using colours.

   b For each square you coloured in, write down its colour and its grid position. (***Example*** : **red - B2**).

10. Shown is a group of islands where Pirates were said to hide treasure. Notice that the **Harbour** on **Rock Island** is at **D8**.

a Write down the position of the Harbour on :-

(i) Marsh Island

(ii) Volcano Island

(iii) Palm tree Island

(iv) Waterfall Island.

b Write down the position of the :-

(i) lighthouse

(ii) dock

(iii) waterfalls

(iv) icebergs

(v) palm trees.

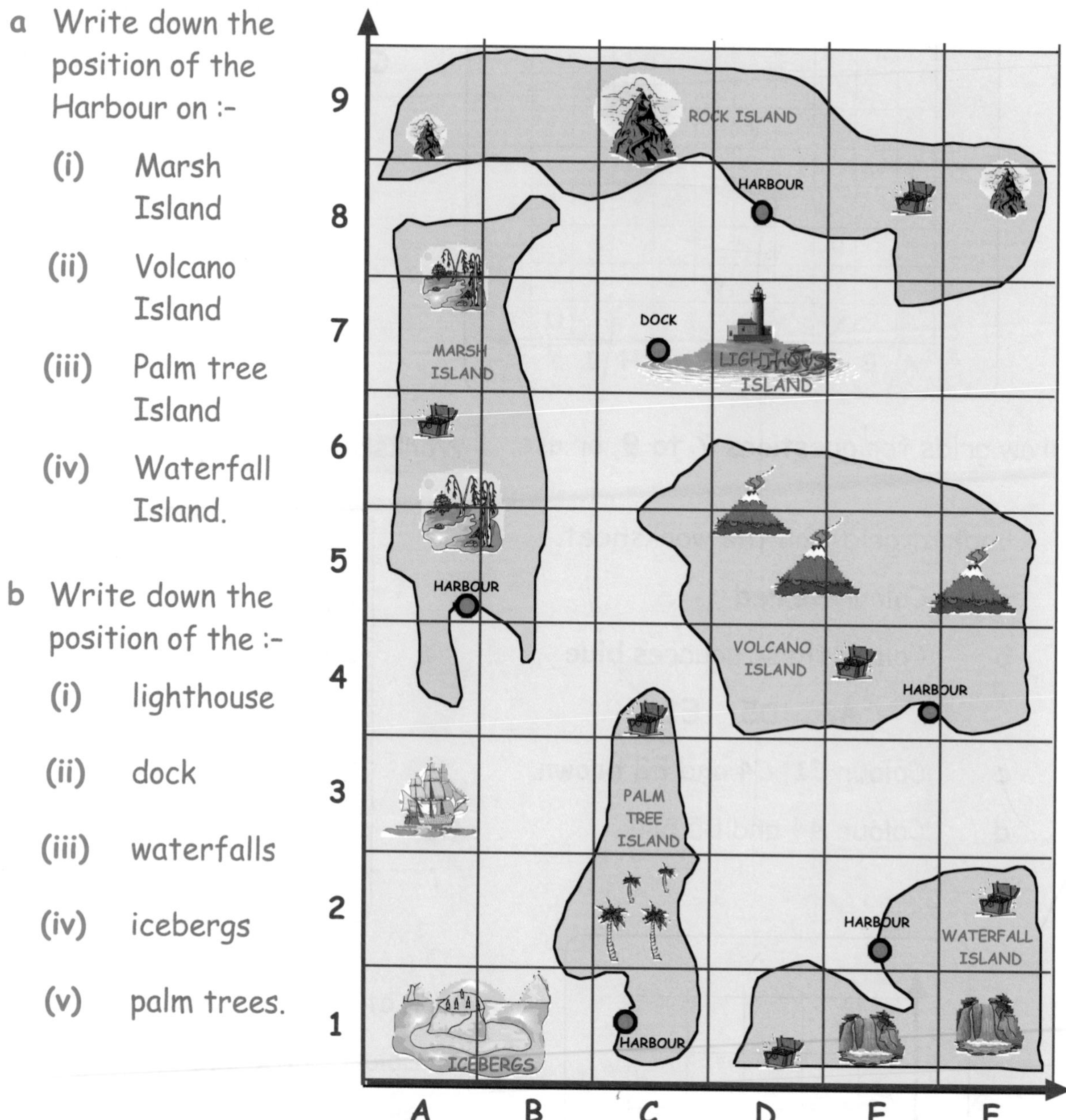

c Write down the position of all six treasure chests.

d What island is on :-

(i) **C9** (ii) **F5** (iii) **A3** (iv) **D3** ?

e A pirate ship sails from the harbour on Waterfall Island to the Harbour on Rock Island.

Describe the ship's journey using the grid references it must have passed through.

11. Write down the grid references of each of these towns :-

a Oban
b Peterhead
c Inverness
d Ayr
e Stranraer
f Glasgow
g Edinburgh
h Aberdeen
i Wick
j Belfast
k St. Andrews
l Perth
m Ullapool
n Elgin.

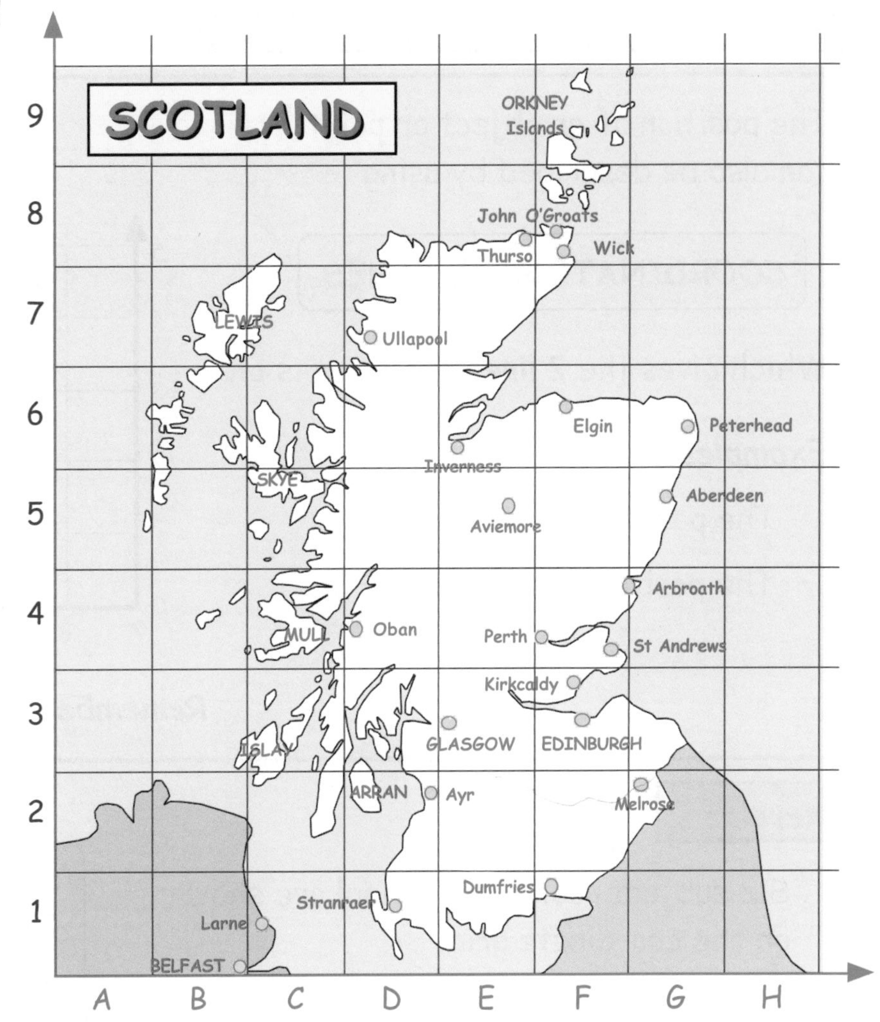

12. Write down all the grid references for :-

a Mull b Orkney Islands c Arran d Lewis.

13. A man cycles directly from Ayr to Melrose.

Write down all the grid references he might have cycled through.

14. 

A boat sails from Stranraer to Skye.

Write down all the grid references that the boat might sail through.

15. Investigate other maps or grids, like a map of the area around your school.

Reading Coordinates on Grid Lines

Be able to identify the position of an object on coordinate grid lines

The position of an object or point can also be described by using :-

COORDINATE GRID LINES.

Which gives the **2 lines** the point is on.

Examples

- The position of the dog **C5**.
- The position of the cat is **F3**.

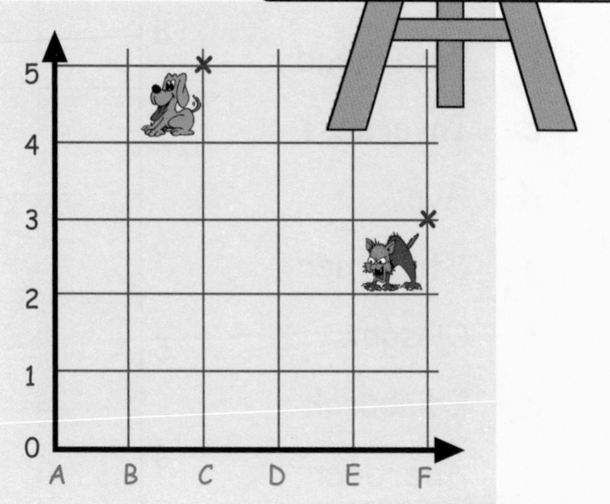

Remember :- **along** first then **up**.

Exercise 2

1. Six subject rooms in a school are shown on the coordinate grid.

   Write down the position of :-

   a Mathematics **M**   b English **E**

   c Geography **G**   d History **H**

   e Art **A**   f Computing **C**.

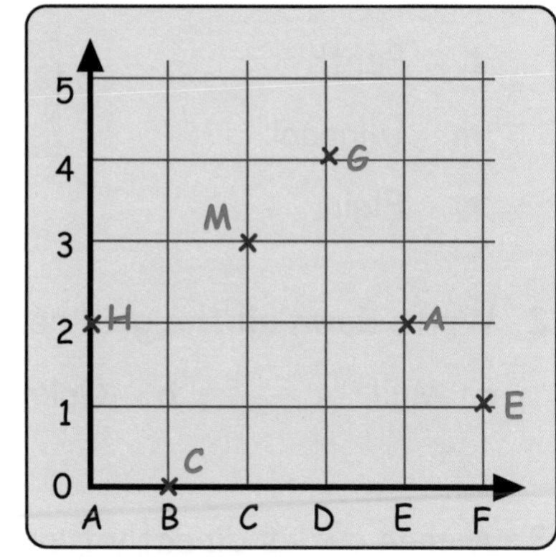

2.

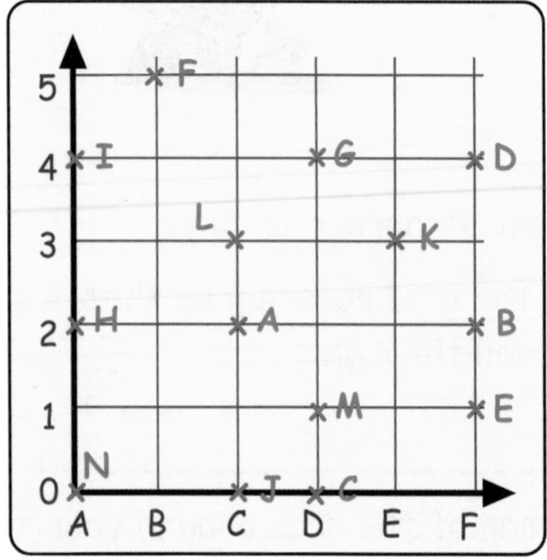

a Write down the grid coordinates of each letter in this grid. (eg. **A** is at **C2**).

b From point A, what letter is :-

(i) one along and 2 up

(ii) three along and one down ?

c Name the letters along gridline **D**.

d Name the letters along gridline **2**.

3. Eight soldiers are out on a training exercise in a field.

Name the soldier who is in position :-

a	D 2	b	B 4
c	A 9	d	J 3
e	K 6	f	F 5
g	I 10	h	G 0.

4. At the school fayre, Joyce was in charge of a stall where you could win cash prizes.

You had to push a pin through a hole on a piece of card.

Some of the holes had no prizes !

For example :-

- if you land on **B1**, you win £1,
- if you land on **C0**, you lose.

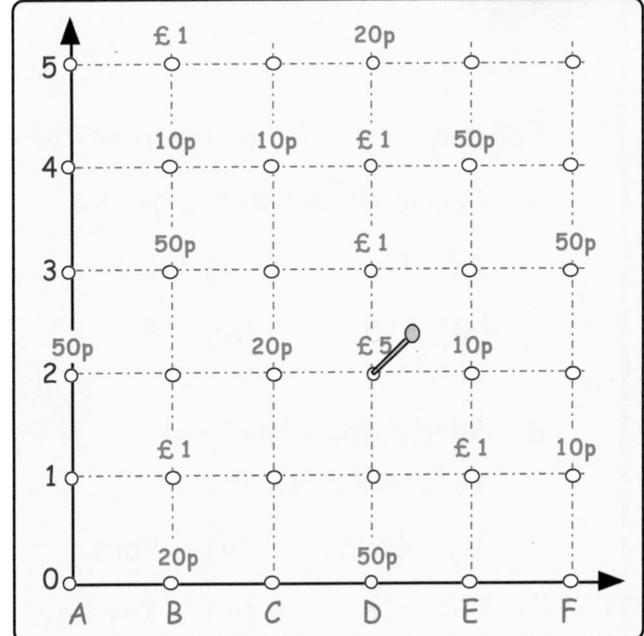

a What did you win if you pushed the pin through position :-

(i) **D3** (ii) **E4** (iii) **B2**

(iv) **F3** (v) **D5** (vi) **A0** ?

b Which positions give a **10p** prize ? (List all of them).

c What was the top prize and what was its position ?

5. Why do you think that using coordinate **grid lines** is better than using coordinate **boxes** ?

The 3 Я's

Revisit - Review - Revise

1. A 10p coin rolling board has the prizes as shown.

   If you roll a coin and it lands inside D 2 you win **£3**.

   a What would you win if your 10p coin landed on :-

   (i) B 1 (ii) E 3
   (iii) A 5 (iv) E 4 ?

   b List 5 other grid references where you would **NOT** win a prize.

   c Where would you win :- (i) 20p (ii) 1p (iii) £2 ?

2. Fantasy Island is as shown on the grid.

   a Write down what is at :-

   (i) B d (ii) B e
   (iii) D d (iv) E a.

   b Write down the grid reference for the :-

   (i) Caves (ii) Port
   (iii) City (iv) Koy Bay.

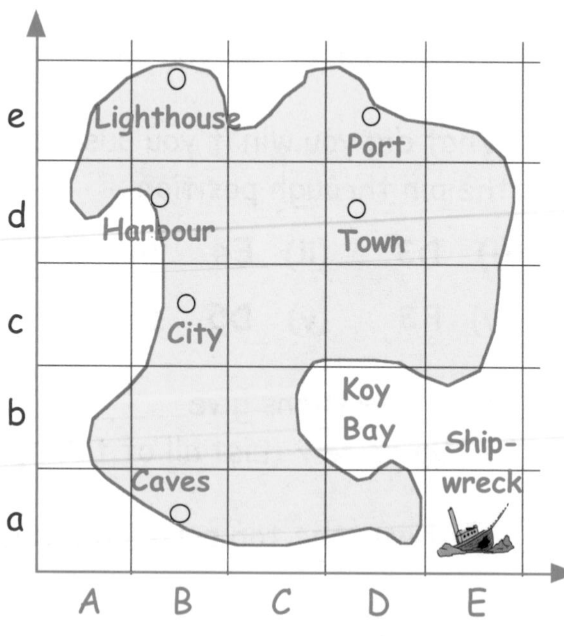

   There are rocks in the sea just **North** of the lighthouse.

   c Write down the grid reference for the rocks.

Revision of Whole Numbers

1. Copy and complete :-

a 5 x 9 = b 6 x 5 = c 4 x 8 =

d 3 x 8 = e 10 x 4 = f 7 x 9 =

2. What numbers are missing ?

a 2 x .... = 20 b 3 x .... = 18 c 4 x .... = 28

d 5 x .... = 45 e 7 x .... = 49 f .... x 10 = 350.

3. Copy and complete :-

a $\begin{array}{r} 35 \\ \times 6 \\ \hline \end{array}$ b $\begin{array}{r} 27 \\ \times 3 \\ \hline \end{array}$ c $\begin{array}{r} 36 \\ \times 4 \\ \hline \end{array}$

d $\begin{array}{r} 47 \\ \times 2 \\ \hline \end{array}$ e $\begin{array}{r} 19 \\ \times 7 \\ \hline \end{array}$ f $\begin{array}{r} 24 \\ \times 5 \\ \hline \end{array}$

g $\begin{array}{r} 83 \\ \times 4 \\ \hline \end{array}$ h $\begin{array}{r} 97 \\ \times 3 \\ \hline \end{array}$ i $\begin{array}{r} 254 \\ \times 5 \\ \hline \end{array}$

j $\begin{array}{r} 118 \\ \times 7 \\ \hline \end{array}$ k $\begin{array}{r} 467 \\ \times 3 \\ \hline \end{array}$ l $\begin{array}{r} 738 \\ \times 6 \\ \hline \end{array}$

4. Find :-

a 75 x 2 b 64 x 3 c 72 x 4

d 228 x 5 e 407 x 6 f 318 x 7

g 610 x 10 h 324 x 7 i 859 x 6.

5. This jacket is on sale in supermarkets at **£47**.

£47

There are **4** of them left for sale.

How much money will the supermarket take in when all four are sold ?

6. 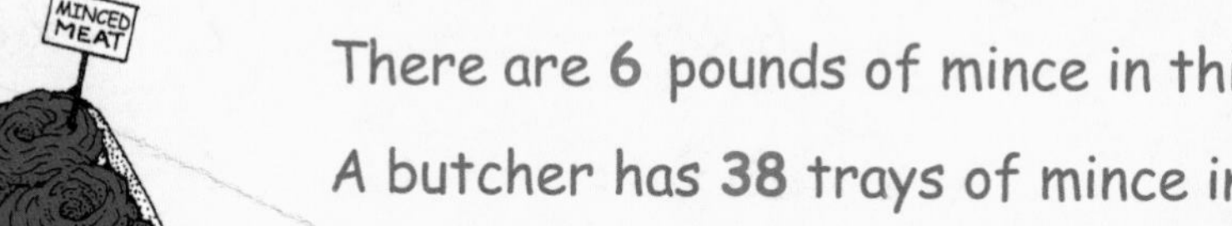

There are **6** pounds of mince in this tray.

A butcher has **38** trays of mince in his freezer.

How many pounds of mince does he have altogether ?

7. A roll of patterned linoleum is **7** metres long.

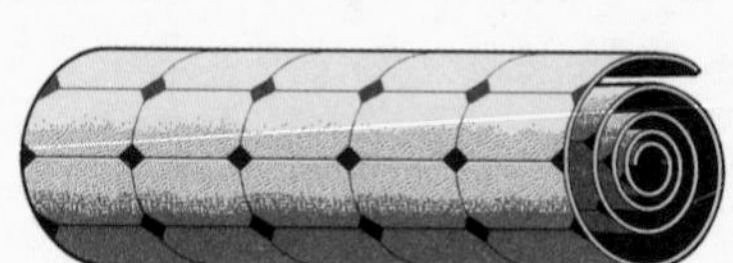

A carpet store has **39** rolls in stock.

What is the **total** length of linoleum that the store has.

8. 

Houses in a new estate are to be painted in groups of **5**, each being a different colour.

If there are **92** groups, how many houses are in the estate ?

9. These drums of oil each hold **180** litres.

How many litres in total does the **6** of them hold ?

10. 

An adult panda can eat **143** pounds of bamboo each day.

How many pounds of bamboo can it eat in a **week** ?

11. There are **138** metres of sellotape in a roll.

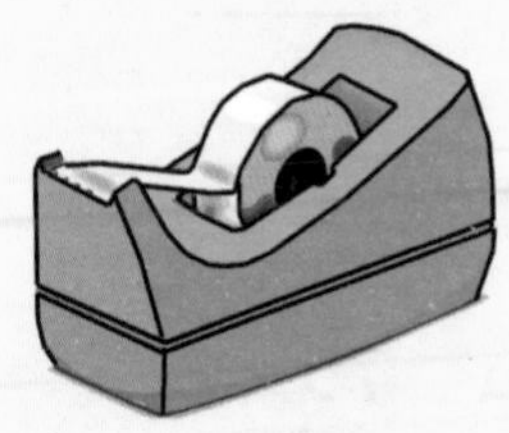

How many metres of tape would you have if you bought **9** rolls ?

12. 

There are 100 centilitres (cl) in a litre

A bottle of juice contains **75** centilitres of liquid.

a How many centilitres are in **3** bottles ?

b If I can fill **4** glasses from each bottle, what's the **total** number of glasses I can fill ?

8 times table

Be able to multiply by 8 and learn.

You should now know the :-

2 times table, the
3 times table, the
4 times table, the
5 times table, the
6 times table, the
7 times table and the
10 times table.

The 8 times tables can be found in a similar way.

Use **Worksheet 12·1** to complete the 8 times table.

8 sets of 0 = 0	8 x 0 = 0
8 sets of 1 = 8	8 x 1 = 8
8 sets of 2 = 16	8 x 2 = 16
8 sets of 3 = 24	8 x 3 = 24
8 sets of 4 = 32	8 x 4 = 32
8 sets of 5 = ...	8 x 5 = 40
8 sets of 6 = ...	8 x 6 = ...
8 sets of .. = ...	8 x 7 = ...
8 sets of .. = ...	8 x .. = ...
8 sets of .. = ...	8 x .. = ...
8 sets of .. = ...	8 .. .. = ...

Exercise 1

1. Copy and complete :-

a 8 x 4 =	b 8 x 2 =	c 8 x 6 =
d 8 x 5 =	e 8 x 0 =	f 8 x 8 =
g 8 x 10 =	h 8 x 9 =	i 8 x 7 =

2. What numbers are missing ?

a 8 x .... = 8	b 8 x .... = 24	c 8 x .... = 40
d 8 x .... = 16	e 8 x .... = 32	f 8 x .... = 48
g 8 x .... = 56	h 8 x .... = 72	i 8 x .... = 80.

3. a To returf his lawn, a gardener needs to know how many turf squares to lay.

To do this, he multiplies the two numbers.

How many turf squares does he need ?

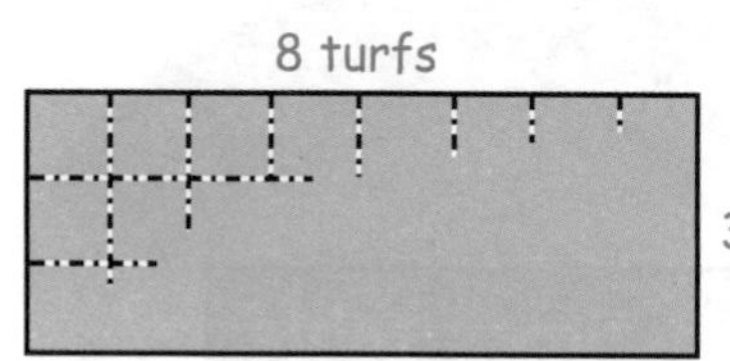
8 turfs
3 turfs

b  

Sally's grandfather is **8** times her age.

If Sally is **7** years old, how old is grandfather ?

c A lift takes **5** seconds to go from one level to the next.

How long will it take to go from the ground floor to level **8** ?

d 
NEWS
Joshua wins music prize at 9 months

George gets **£8** every week for his paper round.

How much does he earn in a month (**4** weeks) ?

e Evelyn practices on her piano **8** hours a week.

Her concert is in **8** weeks time.

How many hours of practice will she have put in by then ?

f 

This tidy holds a maximum of **10** items.

If there is one tidy on each of the **8** tables in a classroom what is the maximum number of items they can hold altogether ?

g Donald bought pencils costing **8** pence each.

How much did he pay for a box of **6** ?

h 

Choc ice lollies come in boxes of **nine**.

Mr Magnum has **8** boxes in his freezer.

How many choc ices is that in total ?

Multiplying by 8

Multiplying a 2 digit number by 8

Example 1 Find 51 x 8

Example 2 Work out 8 x 67

Exercise 2

1. Copy and complete :-

a 17 x 8	b 32 x 8	c 45 x 8
d 26 x 8	e 53 x 8	f 64 x 8
g 71 x 8	h 78 x 8	i 85 x 8
j 92 x 8	k 97 x 8	l 60 x 8

2. Find :-

a 13 x 8	b 25 x 8	c 37 x 8
d 44 x 8	e 52 x 8	f 68 x 8
g 8 x 79	h 8 x 86	i 8 x 19
j 8 x 90	k 8 x 94	l 8 x 99.

3. **8** children manage to get **30** sweets each from a large tin of toffees.

   How many toffees in total were in the tin ?

4. 

   Football tops are priced **£42**.

   Mrs Jones ruins **8** tops in her tumble drier and pops out to buy replacements.

   How much will she have to pay ?

5. It costs an ice cream seller **8p** for each flake he puts in a 99 cone.

   If he buys in enough flakes for **75** cones, how much will it cost him ?

6. 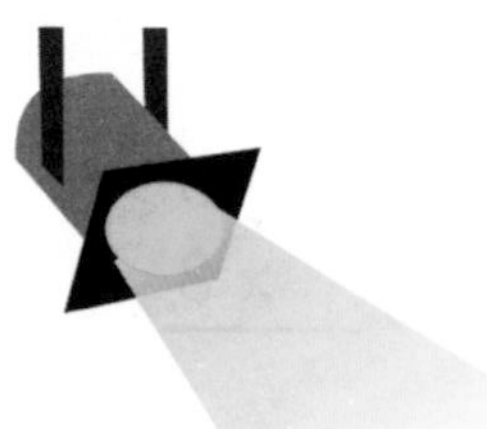

   The council decide to install **8** new lights in each of its **69** underpasses in the area.

   How many lights will be needed ?

7. Each of the houses round where I live were built with **8** light sockets in them.

   How many sockets were needed for the **88** houses ?

8. 

   There are **8** seats in each row of an aircraft.

   How many seats will there be in such a plane with **43** rows ?

9. There are **36** tall ships in the harbour.

   I notice that each ship is displaying **8** flags.

   How many flags in total ?

10. 

    An air freshener is set to puff out scent eight times in a day.

    If it lasts 57 days, how many times altogether will it have let out scent ?

9 times table

Be able to multiply by 9 and learn.

You should now know the :-

2 times table, the
3 times table, the
4 times table, the
5 times table, the
6 times table, the
7 times table, the
8 times table and the
10 times table.

The 9 times tables can be found in a similar way.

Use Worksheet 12·2 to complete the 9 times table.

9 sets of 0 = 0	9 x 0 = 0
9 sets of 1 = 9	9 x 1 = 9
9 sets of 2 = 18	9 x 2 = 18
9 sets of 3 = 27	9 x 3 = 27
9 sets of 4 = 36	9 x 4 = 36
9 sets of 5 = ...	9 x 5 = 45
9 sets of 6 = ...	9 x 6 = ...
9 sets of .. = ...	9 x 7 = ...
9 sets of .. = ...	9 x .. = ...
9 sets of .. = ...	9 x .. = ...
9 sets of .. = ...	9 .. .. = ...

Exercise 3

1. Copy and complete :-

a 9 x 3 =	b 9 x 2 =	c 9 x 6 =
d 9 x 4 =	e 9 x 7 =	f 9 x 5 =
g 9 x 8 =	h 9 x 10 =	i 9 x 9 =

2. What numbers are missing ?

a 9 x .... = 0	b 9 x .... = 45	c 9 x .... = 9
d 9 x .... = 63	e 9 x .... = 81	f 9 x .... = 27
g 9 x .... = 90	h 9 x .... = 72	i 9 x .... = 54.

3. This packet contains 9 chicken drumsticks.

Mrs Roache buys 2 packets.

How many drumsticks in total ?

4.

This handbag was in a sale priced £5.

Henry bought 9 of them for his nieces.

How much did he spend ?

5. Toilet rolls come in packs of 6.

Marjory bought 9 packs.

How many toilet rolls did she have ?

6.

There are 4 aces in a pack of playing cards.

How many should there be in 9 packs of cards ?

7. Beryl can get 8 good sized slices from this fruit loaf.

She has baked 9 loaves.

How many good sized slices will she get altogether ?

8.

Janet drinks 9 cups of coffee every day.

How many cups of coffee will she have had over 7 days ?

9. I costs Billy £10 to attend a football match.

How much will it cost him in total to get into the first 9 games of the season ?

10.

A new fizzy drink can be bought in packs of 9.

Jak stocks up by buying 9 packs.

How many cans has Jak bought ?

Multiplying by 9

Multiplying a 2 digit number by 9

Example 1 Work out 61 x 9

Example 2 Find 73 x 9

Exercise 4

1. Copy and complete :-

a	15 x 9	b	24 x 9	c	36 x 9
d	47 x 9	e	51 x 9	f	63 x 9
g	89 x 9	h	72 x 9	i	76 x 9
j	84 x 9	k	88 x 9	l	97 x 9

2. Find :-

a	19 x 9	b	21 x 9	c	56 x 9
d	28 x 9	e	75 x 9	f	42 x 9
g	82 x 9	h	33 x 9	i	95 x 9
j	69 x 9	k	77 x 9	l	87 x 9.

3. Noreen used her washing machine **9** times per week over **28** weeks last winter.

How many times was that altogether ?

4. 

Rexall Stores took on **9** new employees in each of its **46** stores.

How many people in total did the company take on ?

5. Old Jock plays golf on **72** days of the year.

He only plays **9** holes each time.

How many holes does he play in the year ?

6. 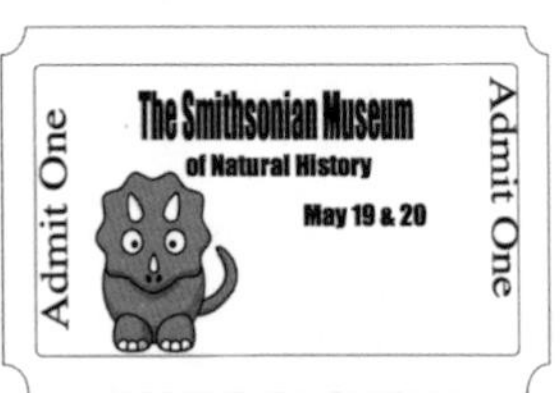

A group of historians bought **35** tickets for an event at **£9** each.

What was the total cost ?

7. A lawyer produces a **nine** page document which she sends to **69** fellow lawyers.

How many pages did she have to run off ?

8. 

Mary Baker always put **9** large bits of chocolate chip into her chocolate chip muffins.

How many bits does she use when she makes **50** muffins ?

9. A shop has **63** boxes of luxury chocolates on display.

They cost **£9** per box.

How much is this display worth ?

10. 

Over his time as a judge he reckons that he has given a **9** month sentence to **99** criminals.

How many months is that in total ?

Multiplying 3 digits

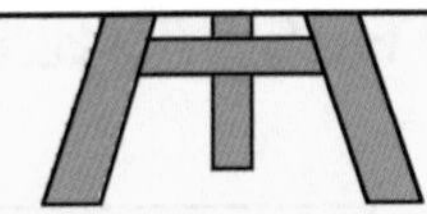

Example 1 276 x 8

Example 2 359 x 9

Exercise 5

1. **Copy** and **complete** :-

a) 213 x 8

b) 174 x 9

c) 385 x 8

d) 462 x 9

e) 519 x 8

f) 678 x 9

2. **Set down** as in Question 1 and work out the answers :-

a) 107 x 9 b) 265 x 8 c) 389 x 9

d) 613 x 8 e) 884 x 9 f) 963 x 8.

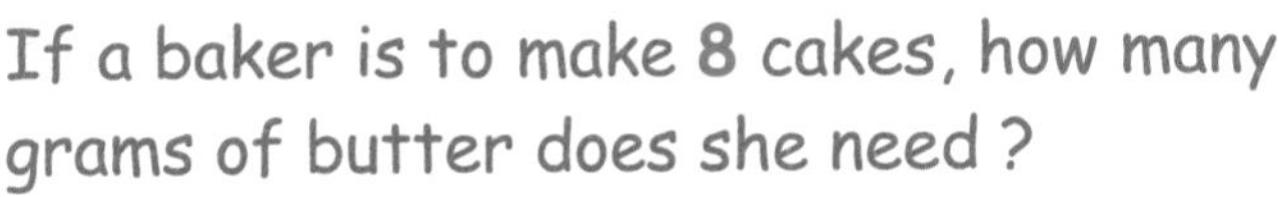

3. A recipe states that **146** grams of butter is needed to make a cake.

   If a baker is to make **8** cakes, how many grams of butter does she need ?

4. 

   A restaurant held an eat-all-you-can-eat buffet for **£9** per person.

   How much money did the restaurant take in on a day when **239** customers came in ?

Mixed Exercise

Multiplying by 2, 3, 4, 5, 6, 7, 8, 9 and 10.

THESE TABLES MUST BE LEARNED !

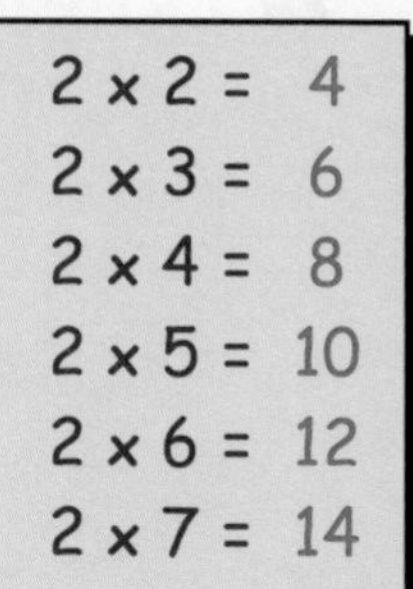

2 x 2 = 4	3 x 2 = 6	4 x 2 = 8	5 x 2 = 10
2 x 3 = 6	3 x 3 = 9	4 x 3 = 12	5 x 3 = 15
2 x 4 = 8	3 x 4 = 12	4 x 4 = 16	5 x 4 = 20
2 x 5 = 10	3 x 5 = 15	4 x 5 = 20	5 x 5 = 25
2 x 6 = 12	3 x 6 = 18	4 x 6 = 24	5 x 6 = 30
2 x 7 = 14	3 x 7 = 21	4 x 7 = 28	5 x 7 = 35
2 x 8 = 16	3 x 8 = 24	4 x 8 = 32	5 x 8 = 40
2 x 9 = 18	3 x 9 = 27	4 x 9 = 36	5 x 9 = 45

6 x 2 = 12	7 x 2 = 14	8 x 2 = 16	9 x 2 = 18
6 x 3 = 18	7 x 3 = 21	8 x 3 = 24	9 x 3 = 27
6 x 4 = 24	7 x 4 = 28	8 x 4 = 32	9 x 4 = 36
6 x 5 = 30	7 x 5 = 35	8 x 5 = 40	9 x 5 = 45
6 x 6 = 36	7 x 6 = 42	8 x 6 = 48	9 x 6 = 54
6 x 7 = 42	7 x 7 = 49	8 x 7 = 56	9 x 7 = 63
6 x 8 = 48	7 x 8 = 56	8 x 8 = 64	9 x 8 = 72
6 x 9 = 54	7 x 9 = 63	8 x 9 = 72	9 x 9 = 81

* To multiply by 10, simply put a 0 on to the end of the number. e.g. 57 x 10 = 570

Exercise 6

1. **Copy** and **complete** each calculation :-

a 86 x 2	b 74 x 3	c 39 x 4	d 85 x 5
e 62 x 6	f 93 x 7	g 81 x 8	h 57 x 9
i 276 x 4	j 145 x 9	k 897 x 2	l 319 x 8

2. Set down the following as in Question 1 and work them out :-

a	£249 x 2 =	b	84p x 3 =	c	£257 x 4 =	d	£73 x 5 =
e	117 x 6p =	f	£428 x 7 =	g	103 x 8p =	h	15 x 9p =
i	10p x 63 =	j	£308 x 4 =	k	762 x 3p =	l	£95 x 5 =
m	£234 x 9 =	n	54 x 8p =	o	72p x 7 =	p	£403 x 6 =
q	530 x 7p =	r	£28 x 10 =	s	420 x 8p =	t	718 x 9p =

3. A hotel serves **3** rashers of bacon on each breakfast plate.
67 people turn up for breakfast.
How many rashers of bacon are needed ?

4. 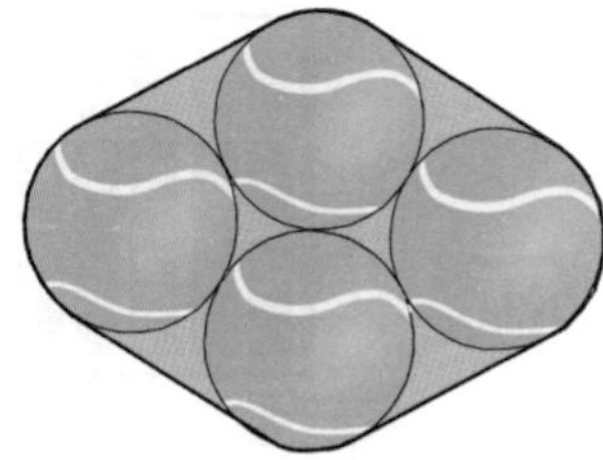

A ticket for the circus costs **£5**.
If **94** tickets are sold one evening, how much money did the circus make ?

5. A school bought in **68** packets of pencils.
Each packet had **6** pencils in it.
How many pencils did the school buy in total ?

6. These tennis balls come in packs of **4**.
A tennis club bought **17** packs.
How many balls in total is that ?

7. Sandy usually pays **£49** per month for his car insurance, but the insurance company gave him **2** months free.
How much of a saving was that ?

8. Each pot of flowers contains **9** marigolds.

How many marigolds has a garden centre with **45** pots ?

9. 

A baker's shop has only **7** cup cakes left for sale.

Mary buys them all at **98p** each.

What did it cost her ?

10. A piece of cake has **389** calories in it.

How many calories are there in **6** pieces of this cake ?

11. 

There are **4** shelves of cereal in a supermarket.

Each shelf has **237** packets on it.

How many packets of cereal in total ?

12. A jet can travel **569** miles in an hour.

How many miles can it travel in **5** hours ?

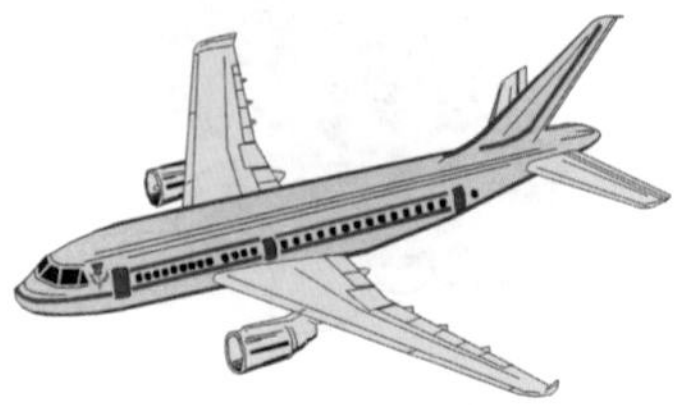

13. 

There are **382** dimples on a golf ball.

How many dimples will there be on **6** golf balls ?

14. A supermarket has **259** boxes of candles on sale.

Each box has **8** candles in it.

How many candles altogether does the supermarket have ?

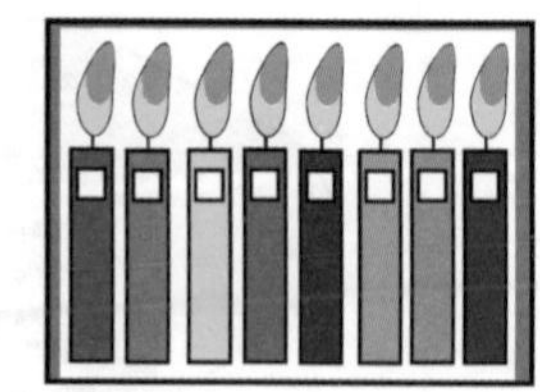

15. 

225 ml of fresh orange is needed to make up 1 litre of a cocktail.

How much would be needed to make **10** litres of the cocktail ?

Multiplying with a Calculator

Multiplying up to 3 digits using a calculator

Find these buttons on your **calculator** :-

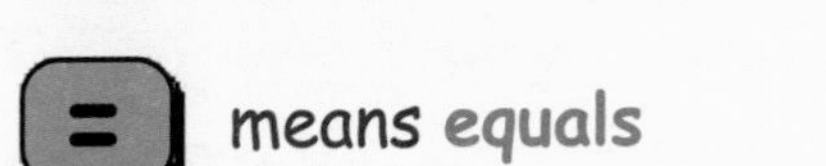

$\boxed{\times}$ means **multiply**

$\boxed{=}$ means **equals**

Examples

Press 389 $\boxed{\times}$ 4 $\boxed{=}$ → The answer is **1556**.

6 $\boxed{\times}$ 268 $\boxed{=}$ → The answer is **1608**.

Exercise 7

1. a Press 438 $\boxed{\times}$ 7 $\boxed{=}$. Write down your answer.

   b Press 9 $\boxed{\times}$ 385 $\boxed{=}$. Write down your answer.

2. Find :-

a	286 x 2	b	394 x 3	c	417 x 4	d	329 x 5
e	6 x 428	f	7 x 536	g	8 x 249	h	9 x 197.

3. Trees are planted in a forest in rows of **245**.
   There are **9** rows.
   How many trees are in the forest ?

4. 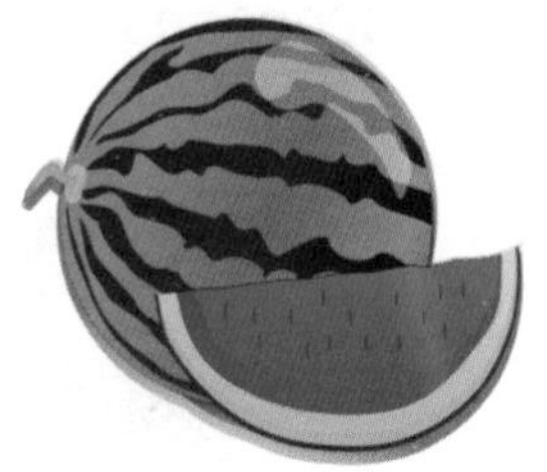

   A crate holds **214** watermelons.
   They are each cut into **8** slices.
   How many slices are there altogether ?

The 3 Я's

Revisit - Review - Revise

1. **Copy** and **complete** :-

   a 7 x 6 = b 9 x 5 = c 8 x 7 =

   d 6 x 9 = e 4 x 8 = f 10 x 9 = .

2. What numbers are missing ?

   a 5 x .... = 35 b 10 x .... = 4600 c 8 x .... = 64

   d 7 x .... = 63 e 6 x .... = 480 f 9 x .... = 630.

3. **Copy** and **complete** these multiplications :-

   a $\begin{array}{r} 187 \\ \times 4 \\ \hline \end{array}$ b $\begin{array}{r} 209 \\ \times 6 \\ \hline \end{array}$ c $\begin{array}{r} 165 \\ \times 7 \\ \hline \end{array}$

   d $\begin{array}{r} 269 \\ \times 8 \\ \hline \end{array}$ e $\begin{array}{r} 748 \\ \times 3 \\ \hline \end{array}$ f $\begin{array}{r} 163 \\ \times 9 \\ \hline \end{array}$

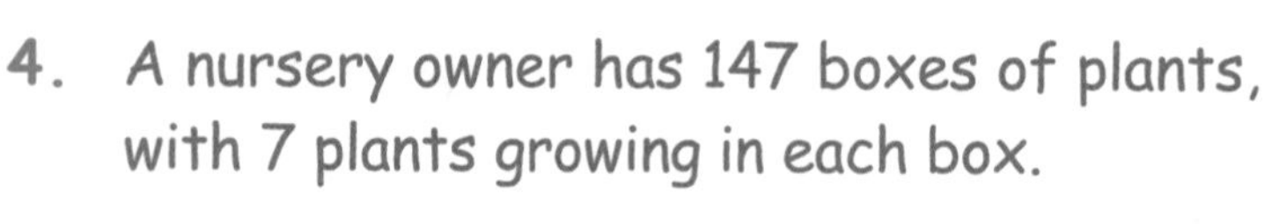

4. A nursery owner has 147 boxes of plants, with 7 plants growing in each box.

   How many plants altogether is he growing ?

5. A zoo has 85 tanks of tropical fish.

   There are 9 fish in each tank.

   How many tropical fish does the zoo have in total ?

6. These boxes of chocolates contain 24 chocolate macaroons.

   There are 8 shelves of them on display in a chain of 10 supermarkets.

   How many single macaroons are on display ?

Revision of Patterns

1. What colours should be used in the next three cubes for the pattern to continue ?

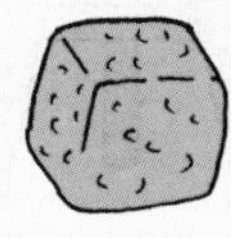  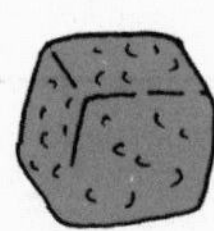  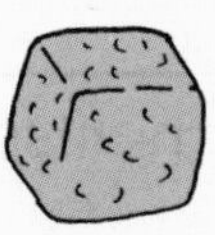    

2. Draw the next three shapes in this pattern :-

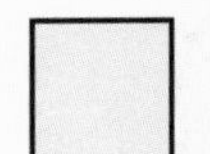 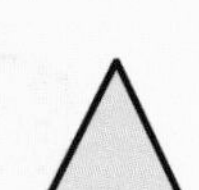       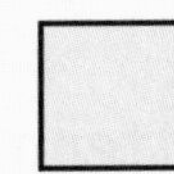 ....

3. Draw 2 more shapes in each of these patterns :-

a  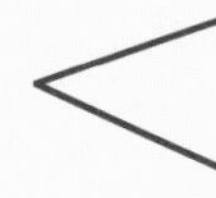  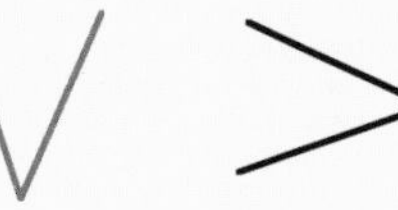   ....

b 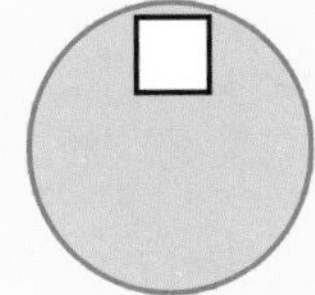 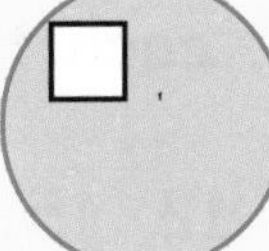 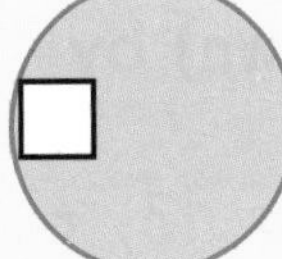 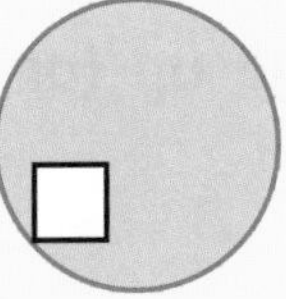 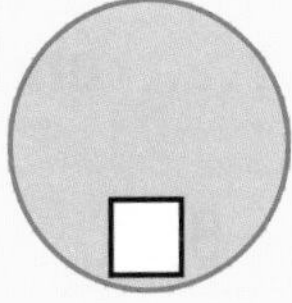 ....

c 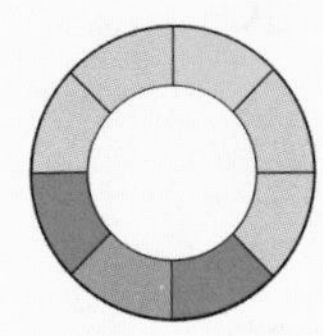 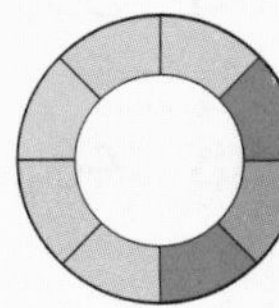 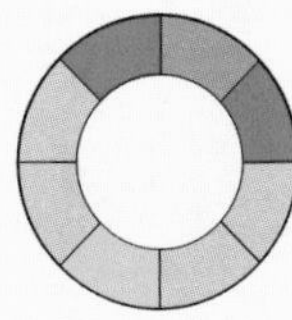 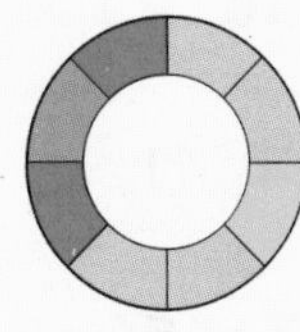 ....

4. Write down the next 2 numbers or letters in each pattern :-

a 6, 8, 10, 12, ...

b 2, 7, 12, 17, ...

c a, d, g, j, m, ...

d S, R, Q, P, ...

e 100, 80, 60, 40, ...

f 10, 22, 34, 46, ...

g efg, fgh, ghi, hij, ...

h $\frac{1}{2}, \frac{2}{3}, \frac{3}{4}, \frac{4}{5}$, ...

Patterns

Describing Number Patterns

To describe a **number pattern** :-

- write the **starting number**, then say ....
- by how much the numbers are **going up** or **coming down**.

Example

Describe the pattern 2, 7, 12, 17, 22, ...,

Start at 2 and go up by 5 each time.

Exercise 1

1. Describe each of the following patterns by writing :-
   "Start at ...... and go up (or down) by ..... each time".

   a 2, 4, 6, 8, ...
   b 3, 6, 9, 12, 15, ...
   c 1, 6, 11, 16, 21, ...
   d 70, 60, 50, 40, 30, ...
   e 20, 17, 14, 11, ...
   f 30, 38, 46, 54, ...
   g 21, 19, 17, 15, ...
   h 50, 100, 150, 200, ...
   i 200, 180, 160, 140, ...
   j 40, 100, 160, 220, ...
   k 18, 25, 32, 39, ...
   l 66, 55, 44, 33, ...
   m 650, 540, 430, 320, ...
   n 1, 13, 25, 37, ...
   o £1·50, £2, £2·50, £3, ...
   p £2·50, £5·50, £8·50, £11·50, ...

2. Write down the **next number** in each of the patterns in **question 1**.

3. Write down the **next number** in each pattern :-

a 9, 11, 13, 15, ...

b 40, 50, 60, 70, ...

c 6, 8, 10, 12, 14, ...

d 25, 30, 35, 40, 45, ...

e 4, 8, 12, 16, 20, ...

f 3, 7, 11, 15, 19, ...

g 5, 12, 19, 26, 33, ...

h 7, 15, 23, 31, 39, ...

i 36, 33, 30, 27, ...

j 50, 48, 46, 44, ...

k 50, 44, 38, 32, ...

l 80, 70, 60, 50, ...

m 60, 52, 44, 36, ...

n 2, 11, 20, 29, ...

o 34, 64, 94, 124, ...

p 230, 210, 190, 170, ...

4. Copy each number pattern and fill in all missing numbers :-

a 13, 15, ... 19, 21, ...

b 4, ... 10, 13, 16, ...

c 68, 58, 48, 38, ...

d 12, ... 22, ... 32, 37

e 77, 66, ... 44, 33, ...

f 3, 9, ... 27, 33, ...

g ... ... 18, 15, 12, ...

h ... 60, ... 50, 45, 40, ...

i ... 350, 300, ... 200, ...

j ... 40, ... 120, 160, ...

5. Write down the **next two** numbers for these patterns :-

a 32, 16, 8, 4, 2, ..., ...

b 4, 8, 16, 32, ..., ...

c 3, 4, 6, 9, 13, ..., ...

d 480, 240, 120, 60, ..., ...

e 676, 565, 454, 343, ...

f 1 x 3, 2 x 4, 3 x 5, 4 x 6, ...

g 1, 1, 2, 3, 5, 8, 13, ..., ...

Linking Patterns with Tables

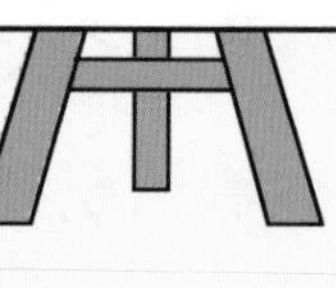

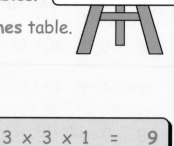

Connections can be found between some of the **times tables**.

Here is the **3 times** table linking with part of the **9 times** table.

3 x 1 = 3			
3 x 2 = 6			
3 x 3 = 9 →	9 x 1 = 9	or	3 x 3 x 1 = 9
3 x 4 = 12			
3 x 5 = 15			
3 x 6 = 18 →	9 x 2 = 18	or	3 x 3 x 2 = 18
3 x 7 = 21			
3 x 8 = 24			
3 x 9 = 27 →	9 x 3 = 27	or	3 x 3 x 3 = 27
3 x 10 = 30			

Exercise 2

1. Look at this multiplication chart.

   The line shaded **brown** shows the answers to the **2 times table**.

   a What times table does the **green** line show the answers to ?

   b Describe the number pattern for the :-

   (i) blue line

   (ii) red line

   (iii) pink line

   (iv) purple line.

X	1	2	3	4	5	6	7	8	9
1	1	2	3	4	5	6	7	8	9
2	2	4	6	8	10	12	14	16	18
3	3	6	9	12	15	18	21	24	27
4	4	8	12	16	20	24	28	32	36
5	5	10	15	20	25	30	35	40	45
6	6	12	18	24	30	36	42	48	54
7	7	14	21	28	35	42	49	56	63
8	8	16	24	32	40	48	56	64	72
9	9	18	27	36	45	54	63	72	81

2. a Make a copy of the multiplication chart shown in question 1 and mark on it with coloured pencils any other number patterns that you can find.

b Describe each of the number patterns you have found.

3. a **Copy** and **complete** the **2 times** table and the **4 times** table shown below.

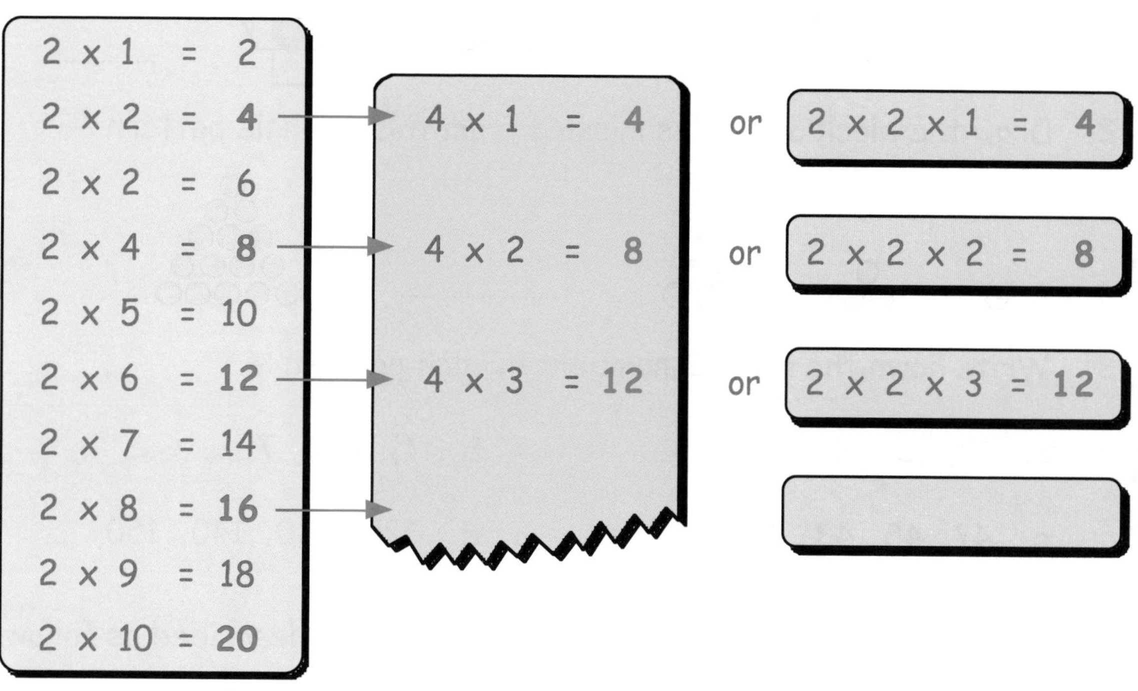

b Copy and fill in the yellow box for **2 x 2 x 4 = 16**.

c Now draw a box for **2 x 2 x 5 = ?** and complete it.

d Can you see a link between the **2 and 4 times** tables ?

Explain this link.

4. a Write out the **4 and the 8 times** tables.

b Explain the link between these two tables.

5. a Show a link between the **5 and the 10 times** tables.

b Show a link between the **2 and the 8 times** tables.

c Show a link between the **2 and the 10 times** tables.

6. Can you show other times table links ? - **INVESTIGATE**

The 3 Я's

Revisit - Review - Revise

1. Draw the **next** shape in this pattern :-

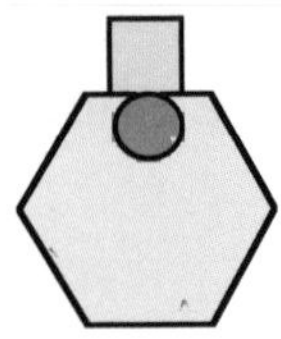 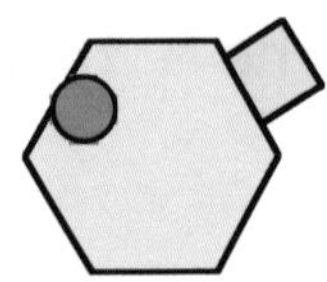 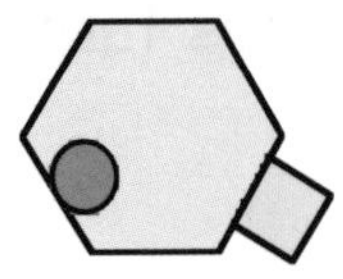 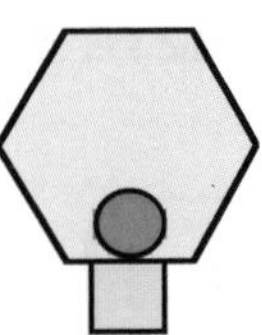 ....

2. Draw the block of circles missing from this triangle pattern :-

  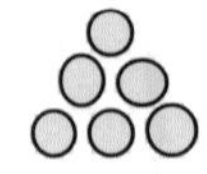  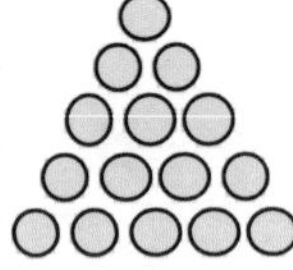

3. Write down the **next 2 numbers** in each pattern :-

   a 12, 13, 14, 15, ...
   b 1, 3, 5, 7, ...
   c 47, 45, 43, 41, ...
   d 120, 130, 140, 150, ...

4. The number pattern 3, 8, 13, 18, ..., can be described as follows :-

   "start at **3** and **add on 5** each time".

   Describe the following number patterns **in a similar way** :-

   a 10, 13, 16, 19, ...
   b 30, 25, 20, 15, ...

5. Write down the **next 2 numbers** in each pattern :-

   a 1, 5, 9, 13, ...
   b 5, 11, 17, 23, ...
   c 75, 80, 85, 90, ...
   d 800, 750, 700, 650, ...

6. **COPY** each number pattern and enter in **all the missing numbers** :-

   a 9, 12, ..., 18, 21, ...
   b ...., 7, 11, 15, ..., 23
   c 99, 88, 77, ..., 55, ...
   d 100, ..., 140, 160, ..., 200.

7. What is the **next number** in this pattern :- 5, 6, 8, 11, 15, ... ?

Revision of Whole Numbers

1. Find :-

a $12 \div 2 = \ldots$ b $21 \div 3 = \ldots$ c $36 \div 4 = \ldots$ d $30 \div 5 = \ldots$

e $80 \div 10 = \ldots$ f $33 \div 3 = \ldots$ g $48 \div 4 = \ldots$ h $780 \div 10 = \ldots$

i $2\overline{)46}$ j $3\overline{)93}$ k $4\overline{)84}$ l $5\overline{)55}$

m $4\overline{)72}$ n $2\overline{)38}$ o $5\overline{)95}$ p $3\overline{)78}$

q $2\overline{)602}$ r $3\overline{)963}$ s $4\overline{)804}$ t $5\overline{)505}$

u $3\overline{)807}$ v $2\overline{)514}$ w $5\overline{)875}$ x $4\overline{)980}$.

2. **Show all of your working** in each of these problems :-

a **32** people are on a Ferris Wheel.

If each carriage holds **4** people, how many carriages are there ?

b

Darren counts **56** legs on a group of spiders.

There are **7** spiders.

How many legs does a spider have ?

c **38** pins are used to display pictures.

If **2** pins are used for each picture, how many pictures are there ?

My maths workbook has **90** sums in it.

If I do **10** sums every night, how many nights will the book last ?

3. **Again, show all of your working** in these problems :-

a A lolly costs **4p**.

How lollies can I buy with **68p** ?

b 

A baker knows **5** kg of flour is needed to make a cake.

How many cakes can she make with **70** kg of flour ?

c A piece of wood measures **87** cm.

Harry has to cut it into **3** equal pieces.

How long is each piece ?

d 

Janine went to the baths and swam **4** lengths.

The distance she covered was **212** metres.

What was the length of the pool in the baths ?

e I have **240** beads to sew onto **10** tops.

An equal number is to be sewn onto each top.

How many beads can go on each top ?

f 

In a fairground, there are usually **5** times as many children as there are adults.

Today, **835** children went through the entrance gates.

How many adults ?

g A snail travels **3** mm in **5** minutes.

How far will it travel in **50** minutes ?

Whole Numbers 6

Dividing by 6

Dividing by 6 with no remainder.

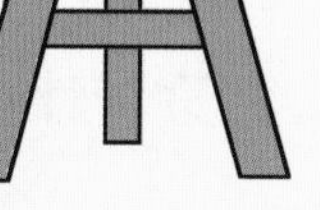

Remember your 6 times table ?

6 x 1 = 6	6 x 2 = 12	6 x 3 = 18	6 x 4 = 24	6 x 5 = 30
6 x 6 = 36	6 x 7 = 42	6 x 8 = 48	6 x 9 = 54	6 x 10 = 60

Example 1 18 ÷ 6

18 ÷ 6 = 3
from knowing 6 x table.

Example 2 72 ÷ 6

Example 3 894 ÷ 6

Exercise 1

1. Copy each of these and complete :-

a	18 ÷ 6 = ...	b	12 ÷ 6 = ...	c	30 ÷ 6 = ...
d	24 ÷ 6 = ...	e	42 ÷ 6 = ...	f	36 ÷ 6 = ...
g	48 ÷ 6 = ...	h	54 ÷ 6 = ...	i	60 ÷ 6 = ...

2. Find the missing numbers :-

a	● ÷ 6 = 0	b	● ÷ 6 = 7	c	● ÷ 6 = 1
d	● ÷ 6 = 8	e	● ÷ 6 = 4	f	● ÷ 6 = 9.

3. Copy and complete :-

a	6 ⟌78	b	6 ⟌96	c	6 ⟌90	d	6 ⟌102
e	6 ⟌108	f	6 ⟌114	g	6 ⟌222	h	6 ⟌324
i	6 ⟌408	j	6 ⟌528	k	6 ⟌606	l	6 ⟌810.

4. **Set these down** like Question 3 and find the answers :-

a $72 \div 6 = ...$ b $84 \div 6 = ...$ c $96 \div 6 = ...$

d $600 \div 6 = ...$ e $390 \div 6 = ...$ f $534 \div 6 = ...$

5. Try these questions **mentally**.

a I have just eaten **6** packets of sweets.

30 sweets altogether.

How many sweets were in a packet ?

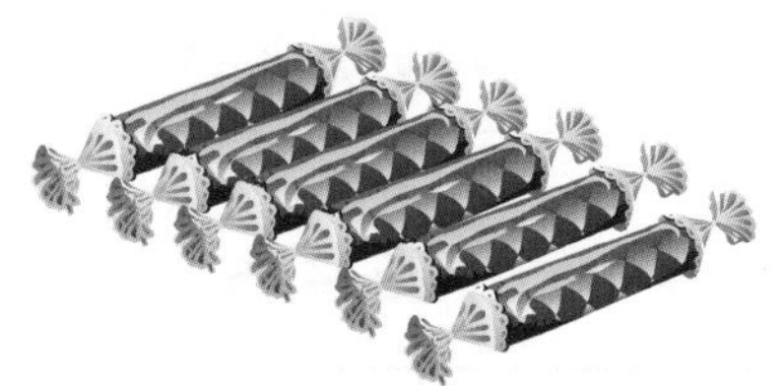

b 

Young Eck has **42** bricks.

How many towers of **6** can he make ?

c Mrs Young takes **36** books out of a box and divides them into sets of **6**.

How many sets ?

d 

24 pupils turn up to play basketball.

They are split into teams of **6**.

How many teams are made ?

e Tickets for a concert are priced **£6**.

How many can be bought for **£48** ?

f 

54 birds are spread out evenly over **6** branches.

How many birds on each branch ?

g Ryan has been collecting comics for **6** weeks and now has **60** in his collection.

He collected the same number each week.

How many did he collect each week ?

Set down these questions as division sums and work them out.

6. An elephant is allowed **6** bags of hay each day.

   How many days would it take the elephant to munch through **72** bags ?

7. 

   90 tins of paint are laid out on **6** shelves.

   How many tins are on each shelf ?

8. Emma shared out **84** strawberry chunks between **herself** and **five** pals.

   How many did they each get ?

9. 

   There are **126** snakes in the reptile house, spread out equally over **6** glass enclosures.

   How many snakes in each enclosure ?

10. James gets paid **£114** for **6** hours work.

    How much does he get paid per hour ?

11. 

    Sally paid **£288** to hire a car for **6** days.

    How much was that per day ?

12. **6** men go to a football match and pay **£210** in total to get in.

    How much did it cost for each of them ?

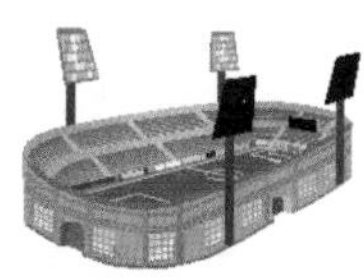

13. 

    6 farmers buy **378** cows and share them equally.

    How many cows do each of them get ?

14. There are **510** pieces of cutlery in a restaurant.

    At a function, everyone needs **6** pieces of cutlery.

    How many people are attending the function ?

Dividing by 6 - Remainders

Dividing by 6 with a remainder.

Example 1

69 ÷ 6 = ...

can be written as :-

$$\begin{array}{r} 1\ 1\ \text{r}\ 3 \\ 6 \overline{)\ 6\ 9} \end{array}$$

How many 6's are in 6 ? ans **1**

How many 6's are in **9** ? ans **1 r 3**.

Example 2

84 ÷ 6 = ...

can be written as :-

$$\begin{array}{r} 1\ 4 \\ 6 \overline{)\ 8\ {}^{2}4} \end{array}$$

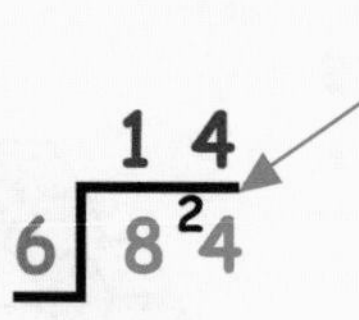

remainder **2** is carried

How many 6's are in **8** ? ans **1 r 2**

How many 6's are in **24** ? ans **4**

Example 3

236 ÷ 6 = ...

can be written as :-

$$\begin{array}{r} 0\ 3\ 9\ \text{r}\ 2 \\ 6 \overline{)\ 2\ {}^{2}3\ {}^{5}6} \end{array}$$

remainder **2** is carried

remainder **5** is carried and still another remainder appears

How many 6's are in **2** ? ans **0 r 2**

How many 6's are in **23** ? ans **3 r 5**

How many 6's are in **56** ? ans **9 r 2**

Exercise 2

1. **Copy and complete** :-

a 14 ÷ 6 = ... b 27 ÷ 6 = ... c 34 ÷ 6 = ...

d 40 ÷ 6 = ... e 43 ÷ 6 = ... f 52 ÷ 6 = ...

g 5 ÷ 6 = ... h 57 ÷ 6 = ... i 28 ÷ 6 = ...

2. **Set down and work out** :-

a $6\overline{)62}$ b $6\overline{)57}$ c $6\overline{)68}$ d $6\overline{)76}$

e $6\overline{)80}$ f $6\overline{)88}$ g $6\overline{)47}$ h $6\overline{)79}$

i $6\overline{)91}$ j $6\overline{)96}$ k $6\overline{)83}$ l $6\overline{)99}$.

3. **Copy** and **complete** :-

a $6\overline{)105}$ b $6\overline{)149}$ c $6\overline{)214}$ d $6\overline{)289}$

e $6\overline{)302}$ f $6\overline{)447}$ g $6\overline{)508}$ h $6\overline{)853}$

4. **Set these down** like Question 3 and find the answers :-

a $38 \div 6 =$ .... b $78 \div 6 =$ .... c $94 \div 6 =$ ....

d $606 \div 6 =$ .... e $570 \div 6 =$ .... f $725 \div 6 =$ ....

Set down these questions as division sums and work them out.

5. There are **75** fish to be put in equal numbers into **6** tanks.

How many fish go in each tank and how many will need to go in an extra tank ?

6. 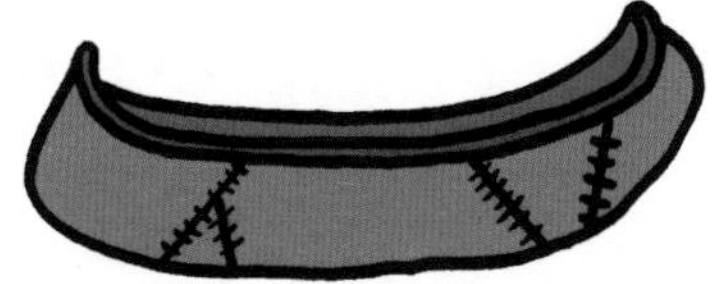

You can get **6** people into a canoe.

How many canoes will be needed for **100** people and how many have to do without ?

7. **179** apples are shared amongst **6** horses.

How many does each horse get and how many are left over ?

8. 

A cash and carry warehouse packs **260** packets of soap powder into **6** boxes.

How many go in each box and how many are left over ?

9. A watering can holds **6** litres of water.

If I worked out that I used **461** litres of water during the summer months to water my garden, how many times have I filled the watering can and how many litres of water were in the can for the final watering ?

Dividing by 7

Dividing by 7 with no remainder.

Remember your 7 times table ?

7 x 1 = 7	7 x 2 = 14	7 x 3 = 21	7 x 4 = 28	7 x 5 = 35
7 x 6 = 42	7 x 7 = 49	7 x 8 = 56	7 x 9 = 63	7 x 10 = 70

Example 1

35 ÷ 7

35 ÷ 7 = **5**
from knowing 7 x table.

Example 2

91 ÷ 7

$$\begin{array}{r} 1\ 3 \\ 7\,\overline{)\,9\,{}^{2}1} \end{array}$$

Example 3

868 ÷ 7

Exercise 3

1. **Copy** each of these and **complete** :-

a 21 ÷ 7 = ...	b 14 ÷ 7 = ...	c 35 ÷ 7 = ...
d 49 ÷ 7 = ...	e 28 ÷ 7 = ...	f 42 ÷ 7 = ...
g 56 ÷ 7 = ...	h 70 ÷ 7 = ...	i 63 ÷ 7 = ...

2. Find the missing numbers :-

a ◯ ÷ 7 = 7	b ◯ ÷ 7 = 0	c ◯ ÷ 7 = 6
d ◯ ÷ 7 = 1	e ◯ ÷ 7 = 8	f ◯ ÷ 7 = 10

3. **Copy** and **complete** :-

a $7\overline{)77}$	b $7\overline{)84}$	c $7\overline{)98}$	d $7\overline{)105}$
e $7\overline{)126}$	f $7\overline{)175}$	g $7\overline{)266}$	h $7\overline{)343}$
i $7\overline{)434}$	j $7\overline{)539}$	k $7\overline{)623}$	l $7\overline{)917}$.

4. **Set these down** like Question 3 and find the answers :-

a $91 \div 7 = ...$ b $112 \div 7 = ...$ c $413 \div 7 = ...$

d $700 \div 7 = ...$ e $518 \div 7 = ...$ f $896 \div 7 = ...$

5. Try these questions **mentally**.

a Charlotte has saved **£35** over the past **7** months.

If she saved the same amount each month, how much was that ?

b  

My skirt was **7** times dearer than my top.

My skirt cost **£56**.

What did I pay for my top ?

c Joe has **21** bananas which he shares between **himself** and **six** friends.

How many do they each get ?

d 

Scarves are on sale at **£7** each.

How many can be bought for **£42** ?

e In the oven there are **56** buns being made.

The buns are sitting on **7** small trays.

How many buns are on each tray ?

f 

There are **63** stamps on each page of a stamp book.

Each page has **7** columns of stamps.

How many stamps in each column ?

g Amy has a piece of ribbon **28** cm long.

If she cuts it into **7** pieces, how long is each piece ?

Set down these questions as division sums and work them out.

6. A caterer has **91** packets of tea which she empties into **7** containers.

   How many containers does she fill ?

7. 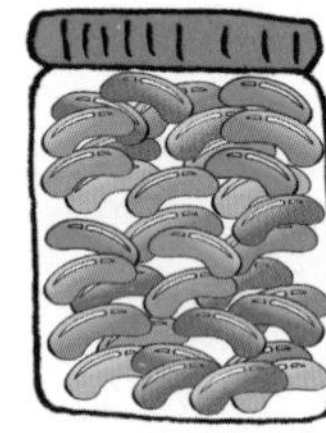

   A teacher has a jar with **210** jelly beans in it.

   If she gives each of her pupils **7** jelly beans each, how many pupils must there be in her class ?

8. **175** seniors turn up to play **seven**-a-side rugby.

   How many teams can be formed ?

9. 

   There are **322** seats on **7** coaches.

   How many seats on each coach ?

10. There are **7** days in a week.

    Old Simon was on his winter holiday for **168** days.

    For how many weeks was he away ?

11. 

    A cruise ship has **7** levels with **903** passengers spread out evenly throughout each level.

    How many people are on each level ?

12. Lipsticks are in a sale at **£7** for **TWO**.

    How many can you buy with **£84** ?

13. 

    Sugar mice are priced **7** pence each in a shop.

    The shop takes in £8·68 (**868** pence) from the sale of sugar mice.

    How many must it have sold ?

Dividing by 7 - Remainders

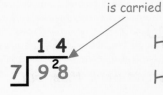

Dividing by 7 with a remainder.

Example 1

74 ÷ 7 = ...

can be written as :-

$$\begin{array}{r} 1\ 0\ \text{r}\ 4 \\ 7\overline{)\,7\ 4} \end{array}$$

How many 7's are in 7 ? ans **1**

How many 7's are in 4 ? ans **0 r 4**

Example 2

98 ÷ 7 = ...

can be written as :-

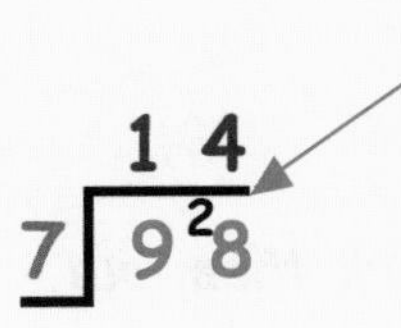

remainder 2 is carried

How many 7's are in 9 ? ans **1 r 2**

How many 7's are in 28 ? ans **4**

Example 3

251 ÷ 7 = ...

can be written as :-

remainder 2 is carried

remainder 4 is carried and still another remainder appears

$$\begin{array}{r} 0\ 3\ 5\ \text{r}\ 6 \\ 7\overline{)\,2\ {}^{2}5\ {}^{4}1} \end{array}$$

How many 7's are in 2 ? ans **0 r 2**

How many 7's are in 25 ? ans **3 r 4**

How many 7's are in 41 ? ans **5 r 6**

Exercise 4

. Copy and complete :-

a 17 ÷ 7 = ... b 26 ÷ 7 = ... c 37 ÷ 7 = ...

d 46 ÷ 7 = ... e 40 ÷ 7 = ... f 50 ÷ 7 = ...

g 55 ÷ 7 = ... h 59 ÷ 7 = ... i 65 ÷ 7 = ...

. **Set down and work out :-**

a $7\overline{)73}$ b $7\overline{)69}$ c $7\overline{)46}$ d $7\overline{)53}$

e $7\overline{)71}$ f $7\overline{)79}$ g $7\overline{)82}$ h $7\overline{)90}$

i $7\overline{)96}$ j $7\overline{)88}$ k $7\overline{)99}$ l $7\overline{)103}$.

3. **Copy and complete** :-

a $7\overline{)106}$ b $7\overline{)383}$ c $7\overline{)254}$ d $7\overline{)536}$

e $7\overline{)456}$ f $7\overline{)715}$ g $7\overline{)804}$ h $7\overline{)901}$.

4. **Set these down** like Question 3 and find the answers :-

a $47 \div 7 =$ .... b $98 \div 7 =$ .... c $87 \div 7 =$ ....

d $414 \div 7 =$ .... e $510 \div 7 =$ .... f $746 \div 7 =$ ....

Set down these questions as division sums and work them out.

5. Buses are lined up in the garage in rows of **7**.

   How many rows will there be when there are **89** buses in the garage and how many will be in a row of their own ?

6. 

   Gherkins are put into jars, **7** in each jar.

   If there are **128** gherkins, how many jars will be needed and how many extra gherkins will there be ?

7. Blank CD's come in packs of **7**.

   If I bought **185** CD's how many packs did I have and how many loose ones were there ?

8. 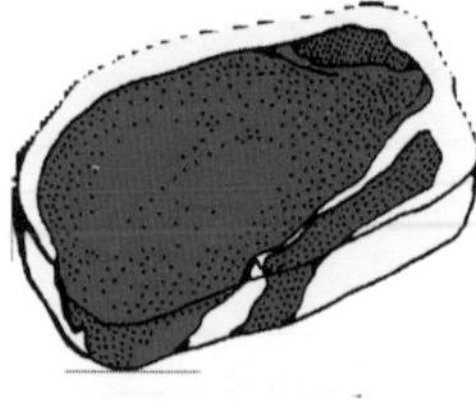

   Steaks cost **£7** each.

   A hotel paid its supplier **£576** for steaks.

   How many steaks were sent and how much change ?

9. Penguins are allowed **7** fish per feed.

   A zoo has a stock of **887** fish.

   How many feeds will this last and how many fish left over ?

Dividing by 8

Dividing by 8 with no remainder.

Remember your 8 times table ?

8 x 1 = 8	8 x 2 = 16	8 x 3 = 24	8 x 4 = 32	8 x 5 = 40
8 x 6 = 48	8 x 7 = 56	8 x 8 = 64	8 x 9 = 72	8 x 10 = 80

Example 1

40 ÷ 8

40 ÷ 8 = **5**
from knowing 8 x table.

Example 2

96 ÷ 8

Example 3

928 ÷ 8

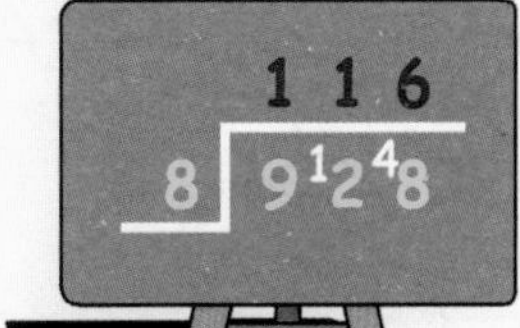

Exercise 5

1. Copy each of these and **complete** :-

   a 8 ÷ 8 = ... b 32 ÷ 8 = ... c 16 ÷ 8 = ...

   d 56 ÷ 8 = ... e 24 ÷ 8 = ... f 64 ÷ 8 = ...

   g 48 ÷ 8 = ... h 72 ÷ 8 = ... i 80 ÷ 8 = ...

2. Find the missing numbers :-

   a ◯ ÷ 8 = 8 b ◯ ÷ 8 = 2 c ◯ ÷ 8 = 4

   d ◯ ÷ 8 = 7 e ◯ ÷ 8 = 9 f ◯ ÷ 8 = 5.

3. Copy and **complete** :-

   a 8 | 48 b 8 | 88 c 8 | 96 d 8 | 104

   e 8 | 136 f 8 | 240 g 8 | 368 h 8 | 408

   i 8 | 544 j 8 | 632 k 8 | 704 l 8 | 904 .

4. **Set these down** like Question 3 and find the answers :-

a $72 \div 8 =$ ....
b $112 \div 8 =$ ....
c $312 \div 8 =$ ....
d $400 \div 8 =$ ....
e $736 \div 8 =$ ....
f $944 \div 8 =$ ....

5. Try these questions **mentally**.

a Zak's dad can remain underwater for **48** seconds.
This is **8** times longer than Zak.
For how long can Zak stay underwater ?

b 

32 sheep were split equally into **8** pens.
How many in each pen ?

c Holfords sold **56** bicycles over a period of **8** hours.
How many bicycles per hour is that ?

d 

The butcher was selling these hams for **£8** each.
He took in **£72** for selling a few.
How many did he actually sell ?

e At a business meeting there are **80** sales executives spread equally around **8** tables.
How many are sitting round each table ?

f 

Fiona works a **40** hour week.
If she works **8** hours a day, how many days does she work per week ?

g Tommy went on holiday for **8** days.
It was so hot, he spent **£64** in total on soft drinks alone.
What did that work out at per day ?

Set down these questions as division sums and work them out.

6. A rowing competition requires teams of **8** in each boat.

   How many teams can be made from **96** people ?

7. Jessie bought **8** cushions from Debnim Stores for a total price of **£136**.

   What was the price of each cushion ?

8. Car vacuums are on sale at **£8** each.

   A garage chain buys **£200** worth.

   How many did they buy ?

9. A company buys **544** pairs of trousers and gives them to a seamstress for alterations.

   If she alters **8** pairs an hour, how many hours will the whole job take ?

10. Kate has been saving **£8** per week.

    How many weeks has she been saving if she now has **£416** altogether ?

11. **Eight** people pay **£952** in total for a city break.

    How much did each of them have to pay ?

12. The **616** queuing in an airport departure lounge are separated into **8** equal rows to speed up checking in.

    How many are in each row ?

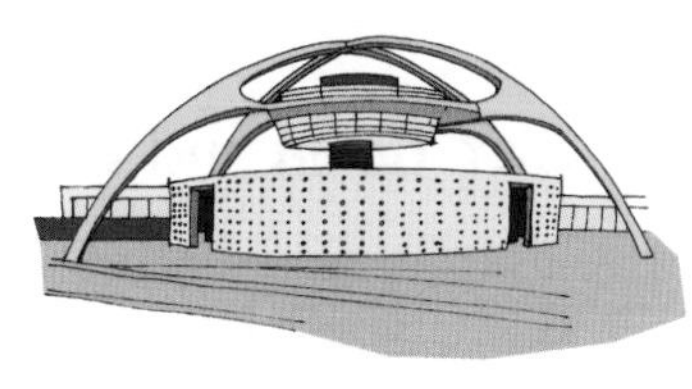

13. Paper clips are made from **8** cm of wire.

    How many can be made from **776** cm of wire ?

Dividing by 8 - Remainders

Dividing by 8 with a remainder.

Example 1

89 ÷ 8 = ...

can be written as :-

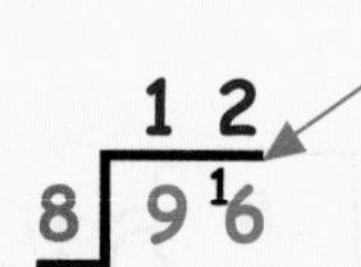

How many 8's are in 8 ? ans **1**

How many 8's are in 9 ? ans **1 r 1**

Example 2

96 ÷ 8 = ...

can be written as :-

remainder 1 is carried

How many 8's are in 9 ? ans **1 r 1**

How many 8's are in 16 ? ans **2**

Example 3

363 ÷ 8 = ...

can be written as :-

remainder 3 is carried

remainder 4 is carried and still another remainder appears

0 4 5 r 3

8 ⟌ 3 ³6 ⁴3

How many 8's are in 3 ? ans **0 r 3**

How many 8's are in 36 ? ans **4 r 4**

How many 8's are in 43 ? ans **5 r 3**

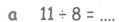

Exercise 6

1. Copy and **complete** :-

a	11 ÷ 8 = ...	b	34 ÷ 8 = ...	c	44 ÷ 8 = ...
d	52 ÷ 8 = ...	e	55 ÷ 8 = ...	f	62 ÷ 8 = ...
g	65 ÷ 8 = ...	h	76 ÷ 8 = ...	i	86 ÷ 8 = ...

2. **Set down** and **work out** :-

a	8⟌50	b	8⟌73	c	8⟌30	d	8⟌51
e	8⟌85	f	8⟌71	g	8⟌81	h	8⟌76
i	8⟌63	j	8⟌94	k	8⟌99	l	8⟌109 .

3. Copy and complete :-

a $8\overline{)172}$ b $8\overline{)437}$ c $8\overline{)363}$ d $8\overline{)535}$

e $8\overline{)608}$ f $8\overline{)705}$ g $8\overline{)857}$ h $8\overline{)902}$.

4. **Set these down** like Question 3 and find the answers :-

a $51 \div 8 =$ .... b $69 \div 8 =$ .... c $104 \div 8 =$ ....

d $368 \div 8 =$ .... e $551 \div 8 =$ .... f $806 \div 8 =$ ....

Set down these questions as division sums and work them out.

5. Chocolate bites are on sale for **8p** each.

How many will I get for **90p** and how much money will I have left ?

6. 

A chemist shop has **205** bottles of talcum powder to be lined up along **8** shelves.

How many bottles are on each shelf and how many can not go on display yet ?

7. A zoo has ordered **230** bananas to feed its **8** large monkeys over a period of time.

How many will each monkey get and how many will be left for the staff to eat ?

8. 

There are **379** frogs in a pond with **8** giant lilies in it.

If they spread themselves evenly over the lilies, how many will be on each and how many will not get on ?

9. An ice cream shop ordered **900** kg of ice cream from the factory.

If the ice cream comes in **8** kg tubs, how many tubs arrived and how many kg was in the extra small tub which made up the amount ordered ?

Dividing by 9

Dividing by 9 with no remainder.

Remember your 9 times table ?

9 x 1 = 9	9 x 2 = 18	9 x 3 = 27	9 x 4 = 36	9 x 5 = 45
9 x 6 = 54	9 x 7 = 63	9 x 8 = 72	9 x 9 = 81	9 x 10 = 90

Example 1

36 ÷ 9

36 ÷ 9 = 4
from knowing 9 x table.

Example 2

117 ÷ 9

$$9\overline{)1\ 1\ {}^{2}7}$$ = 1 3

Example 3

954 ÷ 6

Exercise 7

1. Copy each of these and complete :-

a 27 ÷ 9 = ... b 18 ÷ 9 = ... c 9 ÷ 9 = ...

d 54 ÷ 9 = ... e 45 ÷ 9 = ... f 63 ÷ 9 = ...

g 81 ÷ 9 = ... h 72 ÷ 9 = ... i 90 ÷ 9 = ...

2. Find the missing numbers :-

a ◯ ÷ 9 = 6 b ◯ ÷ 9 = 4 c ◯ ÷ 9 = 8

d ◯ ÷ 9 = 3 e ◯ ÷ 9 = 7 f ◯ ÷ 9 = 9.

3. Copy and complete :-

a $9\overline{)36}$ b $9\overline{)54}$ c $9\overline{)99}$ d $9\overline{)108}$

e $9\overline{)171}$ f $9\overline{)234}$ g $9\overline{)342}$ h $9\overline{)414}$

i $9\overline{)585}$ j $9\overline{)702}$ k $9\overline{)792}$ l $9\overline{)963}$.

4. Set these down like Question 3 and find the answers :-

a $81 \div 9 = ...$ b $126 \div 9 = ...$ c $315 \div 9 = ...$

d $414 \div 9 = ...$ e $783 \div 9 = ...$ f $801 \div 9 = ...$

5. Try these questions mentally.

a Auntie Ida spent £45 on her nieces at Christmas.

She gave each of them a £9 voucher for HVM Stores.

How many nieces does she have ?

b

A small ferry makes 9 trips across the river every hour.

In that hour, 72 cars altogether can be taken across.

How many cars can the ferry hold ?

c When building houses in a cul-de-sac Johnston Homes ordered in 90 windows.

If each house had 9 windows, how many houses did they build ?

d

Ian spent a total of £36 buying 9 magazines.

How much were they each ?

e These jars can hold 9 large cookies and keep them fresh.

Donna has made 63 large cookies.

How many jars will she need ?

f $\frac{18}{81}$

To simplify a fraction, divide the top and bottom number by the same number.

Simplify the fraction shown by dividing both numbers by 9.

Set down these questions as division sums and work them out.

6. One evening, Jenny knocked down **9** skittles and got **9** points each time she bowled.

   If she scored **108** points altogether, how many times did she roll a bowl ?

7. Alistair paid the **£621** he owed on his car in equal payments over a period of **9** months.

   What did he pay each month ?

8. At a scout camp **126** tents were set up in circular fashion around **9** campfires.

   How many tents were around each fire ?

9. 

   A farmer positioned **9** scarecrows in each of his fields.

   If he put up **252** scarecrows altogether, how many fields must he have covered ?

10. Each newspaper contains **9** pages of sport.

    If a company runs off **945** pages of sport, how many newspapers will it have run off ?

11. 

    A company director paid **£324** in total for **9** of his customers to have a day's golf.

    How much did he pay for each of them ?

12. Airport luggage handlers load **756** pieces of luggage onto an aircraft.

    They divide them equally into **9** crates.

    How many pieces of luggage are in each crate ?

13. 

    Cement is on special offer at **£9** for **packs of three**.

    How many packs will I get for **£162** ?

Dividing by 9 - Remainders

Dividing by 9 with a remainder.

Example 1

67 ÷ 9 = ...
can be written as :-

remainder 6 is carried

$$\begin{array}{r} 0\,7\text{ r }4 \\ 9\,\overline{)\,6\,{}^{6}7} \end{array}$$

How many 9's are in 6 ? ans **0 r 6**

How many 9's are in 67 ? ans **7 r 4**

Example 2

124 ÷ 9 = ...
can be written as :-

remainder 1 is carried

remainder 3 is carried

$$\begin{array}{r} 0\,1\,3\text{ r }7 \\ 9\,\overline{)\,1\,{}^{1}2\,{}^{3}4} \end{array}$$

How many 9's are in 1 ? ans **0 r 1**

How many 9's are in 12 ? ans **1 r 3**

How many 9's are in 34 ? ans **3 r 7**

Example 3

976 ÷ 9 = ...
can be written as :-

remainder 7 is carried and still another remainder appears

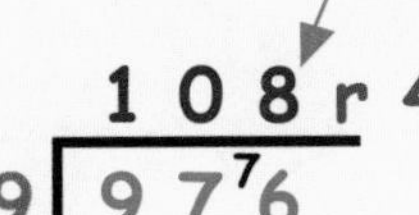

$$\begin{array}{r} 1\,0\,8\text{ r }4 \\ 9\,\overline{)\,9\,7\,{}^{7}6} \end{array}$$

How many 9's are in 9 ? ans **1**

How many 9's are in 7 ? ans **0 r 7**

How many 9's are in 76 ? ans **8 r 4**

Exercise 8

1. **Copy** and **complete** :-

a	19 ÷ 9 = ...	**b**	30 ÷ 9 = ...	**c**	38 ÷ 9 = ...
d	50 ÷ 9 = ...	**e**	58 ÷ 9 = ...	**f**	70 ÷ 9 = ...
g	78 ÷ 9 = ...	**h**	89 ÷ 9 = ...	**i**	100 ÷ 9 = ...

2. **Set down** and **work out** :-

a	$9\overline{)48}$	**b**	$9\overline{)24}$	**c**	$9\overline{)88}$	**d**	$9\overline{)44}$
e	$9\overline{)75}$	**f**	$9\overline{)68}$	**g**	$9\overline{)97}$	**h**	$9\overline{)71}$
i	$9\overline{)103}$	**j**	$9\overline{)116}$	**k**	$9\overline{)136}$	**l**	$9\overline{)141}$.

3. **Copy and complete** :-

a $9\overline{)146}$ b $9\overline{)229}$ c $9\overline{)406}$ d $9\overline{)527}$

e $9\overline{)608}$ f $9\overline{)778}$ g $9\overline{)809}$ h $9\overline{)916}$.

4. **Set these down** like Question 3 and find the answers :-

a $67 \div 9 =$ .... b $79 \div 9 =$ .... c $108 \div 9 =$ ....

d $383 \div 9 =$ .... e $684 \div 9 =$ .... f $790 \div 9 =$ ....

Set down these questions as division sums and work them out.

5. A football club orders **100** second hand footballs online for use in training.

If it has **9** teams, from under 10's to seniors, how many balls will each team get if they get the same amount and how many balls will not be used yet ?

6. 

Recipe books are on sale at **£9** each.

If a catering school has **£292** left to spend, how many of these books can it order and how much money will the school be left with ?

7. **Nine** fishermen agreed to share their catch.

Altogether they caught **240** fish.

How many did they each get and how many were given to the gulls ?

8. 

A paper hankie manufacturer splits **680** hankies amongst **9** boxes.

How many are in each box and how many are left over ?

9. Timothy moves **525** books from the store to a classroom.

If he could only manage **9** books at a time, how many trips did he have to make and how many books did he carry on his last trip ?

Mixed Exercise

Exercise 9

Be able to divide any 3 digit number by 2, 3, 4, 5, 6, 7, 8, 9 or 10

1. Copy and complete :-

a 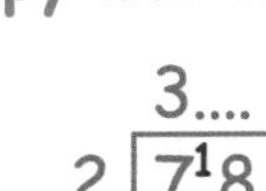 $\overset{3....}{2\overline{)7^18}}$ b $3\overline{)54}$ c $4\overline{)68}$ d $5\overline{)75}$

e $6\overline{)66}$ f $7\overline{)98}$ g $8\overline{)96}$ h $9\overline{)99}$

i $5\overline{)620}$ j $6\overline{)258}$ k $3\overline{)636}$ l $2\overline{)512}$

m $7\overline{)329}$ n $4\overline{)168}$ o $9\overline{)252}$ p $8\overline{)280}$

q $6\overline{)672}$ r $3\overline{)744}$ s $7\overline{)476}$ t $8\overline{)408}$.

There are several ways of asking how to divide 91 by 7.

Here they are :-

91 divided by 7 $7\overline{)91}$ 7 into 91 $91 \div 7$ $\frac{91}{7}$

2. Write the following in the form $3\overline{)78}$ and then work out the answer :-

a $78 \div 3$ b $7\overline{)133}$ c $\frac{96}{6}$

d 104 divided by 8   e 4 into 516   f $225 \div 5$

g $\frac{288}{9}$ h $2\overline{)778}$ i 6 into 768

j 608 divided by 4   k $\frac{252}{7}$ l $904 \div 8$.

3. **Show all of your working** in each of these problems :-

a There are **85** people waiting at a taxi rank.

If a taxi can hold **5** people, how many taxis are needed ?

b 

Coco the clown shared out **90** balloons to children.

How many children got **6** balloons each ?

c Mrs Moyer paid **£528** for **3** identical single beds for her children.

What was the price of each bed ?

d Grandpa gave out **72** sweets to be shared amongst his **4** grandchildren.

How many sweets did they get each ?

e A crisp company has **238** packets of crisps to be put into jumbo packs with **7** packets in each.

How many jumbo packs can be made up ?

f 

I read **342** pages of my book over **9** days reading the same number of pages each day.

How many pages was that ?

g A toy store took in **£232** selling **8** games consoles.

How many consoles were sold ?

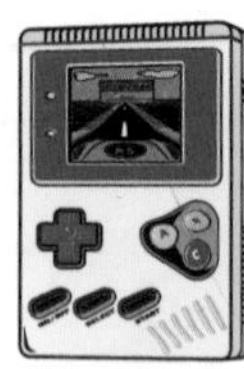

h 

A prize of **£427** was split amongst **10** young ladies.

How many £'s did each get and how much had to be changed into pennies ?

i Molly Bun baked **732** pancakes for a jamboree.

She gave **half** to the scouts and **half** to the cubs.

How many pancakes did the cubs get ?

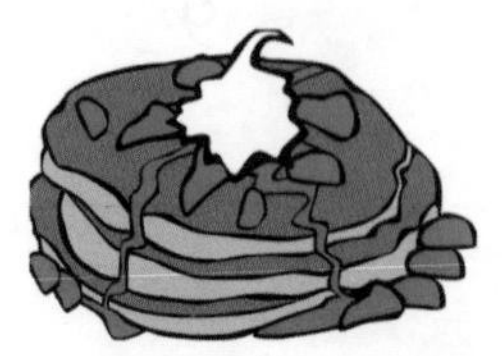

Mixed Problems Using +, −, x and ÷

Be able to add, subtract, multiply or divide by 2, 3, 4, 5, 6, 7, 8, 9 and 10

In the following exercise, you have to decide whether the problem involves **adding, subtracting, multiplying** or **dividing.**

When you have decided, carry on and solve the problem.

Show all of
your working

Exercise 10

1. A primary school has **58** pupils in the Primary 1 and **65** pupils in Primary 2.

   What is the **total** number of pupils in these stages of school ?

2. There are **91** pupils in primary 7.

   72 of them are going on a school trip to York in May.

   How many does that leave at school, slaving away at work ?

3. Tony sneezes **6** times a day.

   How many times did he sneeze in January ? (It has **31** days).

4. A multi-storey car park has **7** levels, each taking the same number of cars. When full, it holds **266** cars.

   How many cars can park on each level ?

5. The **£765** raised at a jumble sale was split equally between **9** charities.

   How much did each charity get ?

6. There are **8** roller coasters at Pleasureland Park.

   Children from Anniesland Primary had spread themselves in groups of **15** over these rides.

   How many children from Anniesland Primary were there ?

7. Davie bought **150** chews. He ate **88** and gave **20** away.

   How many chews did he have left ?

More Problems Involving +, −, x and ÷

Be able to add, subtract, multiply or divide by any number using a calculator

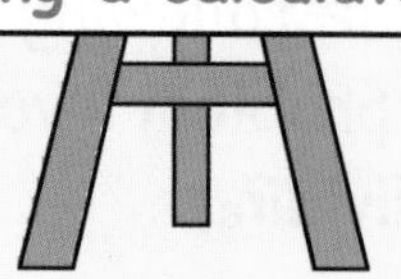

Same as the previous exercise.

Decide whether to **add**, **subtract**, **multiply** or **divide**.

Then solve each problem, this time using a **CALCULATOR** to help you. But .... you still must **show all of your working** !

Exercise 11

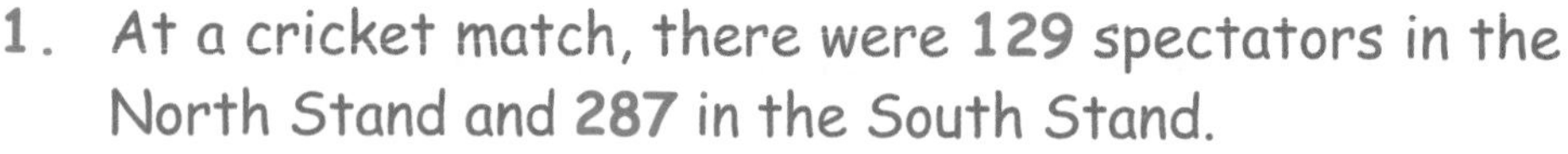

1. At a cricket match, there were **129** spectators in the North Stand and **287** in the South Stand.

   How many people **in total** were watching from the stands ?

2. **72** people in a rock choir are rehearsing.

   9 of them go to the toilet and **28** of them are sent home unwell.

   How many does that leave in the choir ?

3. Karen spends 4 days of her holidays stuck at home because of rain.

   She has nothing to do but watch cars passing by all day long.

   She counts **656** cars in **4** days.

   How many cars does that average out at each day ?

4. A city has **8** hotels. In each hotel there are **145** workers.

   How many hotel workers are there in that city ?

5. Three trains left Glasgow central just after 10 am.

   The Ayr train left with **158** passengers on board.

   The Gourock train had **172** and the train to Motherwell carried **97**.

   How many passengers **altogether** were on these three trains ?

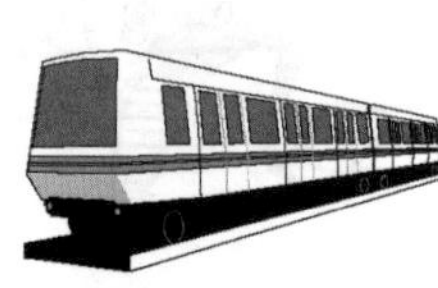

. Jo has **2** books of **100** stickers, **3** books of **10** stickers and **4** single stickers.

How many stickers does she have altogether ?

. A farmer had **250** mother pigs.

In summer **120** of them had **8** piglets each, while the rest each had **6** piglets.

How many piglets were born that summer ?

. A flock of **nine** swallows flew **168** miles south to escape the cold.

After resting for a day, they flew another **200** miles towards the coast.

a How many miles did each swallow fly ?

b How many miles did the nine of them fly **altogether** ?

. **Six** apes ate **30** bananas each day for a **week**.

How many bananas were eaten over the week ?

0. **5** children were swimming in the sea with **24** octopi.

How many **limbs** (arms and legs) were there altogether ?

1. **324** chickens laid **5** eggs each.

A fox ate **half** of the eggs in the first week, but the rest of the eggs hatched after a few weeks.

How many new chicks were born ?

2. Three restaurants are busy with bookings for christmas dinner.

Holton's have taken bookings for **252** people.

Latella's have **126** booked.

Spice Rack expect **84** people.

a What is the **total** number of people booked at these restaurants ?

b How many **more** at Holton's than at Spice Rack ?

The 3 Я's

Revisit - Review - Revise

1. Set these down and work them out :-

a
$$\begin{array}{r} 33 \\ +\ 8 \\ \hline \end{array}$$

b
$$\begin{array}{r} 490 \\ +\ 70 \\ \hline \end{array}$$

c
$$\begin{array}{r} 40 \\ 380 \\ +\ 90 \\ \hline \end{array}$$

d 76 + 19

e 85 + 27

f 330 + 50 + 70

g
$$\begin{array}{r} 67 \\ -\ 9 \\ \hline \end{array}$$

h
$$\begin{array}{r} 450 \\ -\ 80 \\ \hline \end{array}$$

2. Maurice has 86p and buys a chew for 9p.

   He then discovers he has another 7p in his holdall.

   How much does Maurice have now ?

3. Bob earns £26 per week in a snack bar.

   Mandy sells cosmetics and gets £4 more than Bob.

   Dave gets £7 less than Bob for delivering leaflets.

   a What does Mandy get paid ?

   b What does Dave earn ?

   c How much more than Dave does Mandy get ?

4. Find the missing number, shown by a * in these sums :-

a
$$\begin{array}{r} 3\,* \\ +\ 9 \\ \hline 4\,6 \end{array}$$

b
$$\begin{array}{r} 3\,6\,0 \\ +\ *\,0 \\ \hline 4\,3\,0 \end{array}$$

c
$$\begin{array}{r} 8\,* \\ -\ 6 \\ \hline 7\,5 \end{array}$$

d
$$\begin{array}{r} 6\,2\,0 \\ -\ *\,0 \\ \hline 5\,1\,0 \end{array}$$

5. A farmer has funny looking sheep and cows in one field.

   Of the 400 farm animals in the field 275 are cows.

   How many sheep are there ?

6. Set down and work out :-

a $\begin{array}{r} 41 \\ \times\ 8 \\ \hline \end{array}$ b $\begin{array}{r} 63 \\ \times\ 7 \\ \hline \end{array}$ c $\begin{array}{r} 183 \\ \times\ 9 \\ \hline \end{array}$ d 520 x 6

e 630 x 5   f $3\overline{)63}$ g $4\overline{)76}$ h $5\overline{)540}$

i 72 ÷ 6   j 9 into 981   k $\frac{237}{3}$ l 112 ÷ 7.

7. Jamie bought 9 CD's for £126. How much were they each ?

8. 

It costs £27 for a child to get into an amusement park.

What was the cost in total for Sally and her 7 friends ?

9. The train fare for a group of 7 adults came to £525.

What was the cost per person ?

10. 

A banana costs 18p and a pineapple costs 86p.

What is the total cost of 4 bananas and 5 pineapples ?

11. Write the answer to :-

a 76 x 10   b 280 x 10   c 490 ÷ 10   d 3100 ÷ 10.

12. Jean buys a box of 10 out of date doughnuts for 140p.

How much is that per doughnut ?

13. 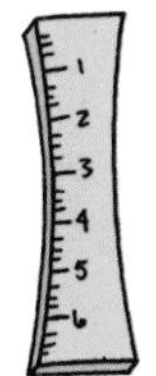

There are 10 millimetres in a centimetre.

a How many millimetres in 48 centimetres ?

b How many centimetres in 1500 millimetres ?.

14. Anne spent £260 on her jacket. Mary only spent £70 on hers.

a What did the two of them spend altogether ?

b How much more than Mary did Anne spend ?

Revision of Length

1. Write down the lengths of each of the lines drawn below :-

   a ________________

   b __________________________

   c _________________________________

   d ____

   e _____________

   f ____

   g _______________________

2. What you would use (a **ruler** or a **metre strip**) to measure :-

   a the length of this room

   b the distance from Stranraer to Inverness on a map

   c the length of a toy dinosaur

   d the length of a real dinosaur ?

3. Write down how many centimetres there are in two metres.

4. a Draw a **rectangle** with length 8 cm and breadth 3 cm.

   b Draw a **square** with side length 7 cm.

   c Draw a **rectangle** with length 5 cm and breadth $2\frac{1}{2}$ cm.

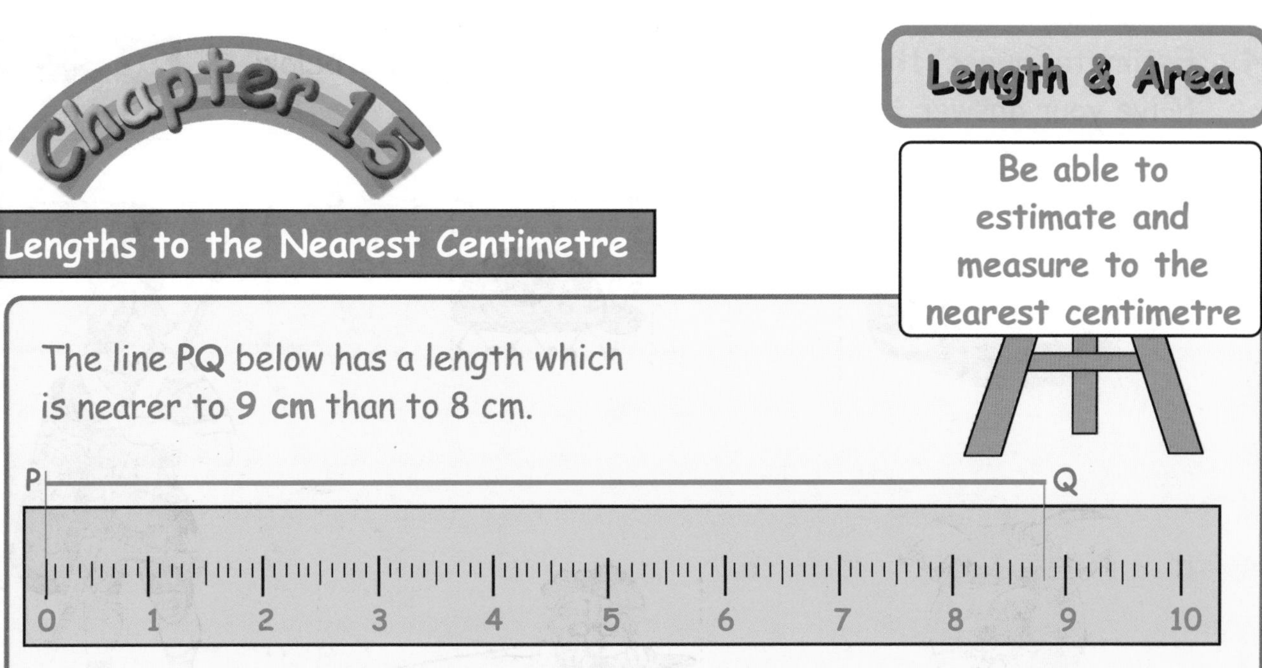

Chapter 15

Length & Area

Be able to estimate and measure to the nearest centimetre

Lengths to the Nearest Centimetre

The line PQ below has a length which is nearer to 9 cm than to 8 cm.

Line PQ is *approximately* 9 cm, **or** PQ is 9 cm (*to the nearest cm*).

Exercise 1

Worksheet 15·1

1. **Estimate** (guess) the length of each line below.
   Give your answer to **the nearest centimetre**.

   a A

   b B

   c C

   d D

   e E

   f F

2. Use your ruler to measure each of the lines in question 1.
   (Give your answer **to the nearest centimetre**).

3. a Write down the lines in order with the **longest** line first.

   b Find the **difference** between the shortest and longest lines.

4. Estimate (guess) the dimension shown in each picture below.
(Give your answer to the **nearest centimetre**).

a

b

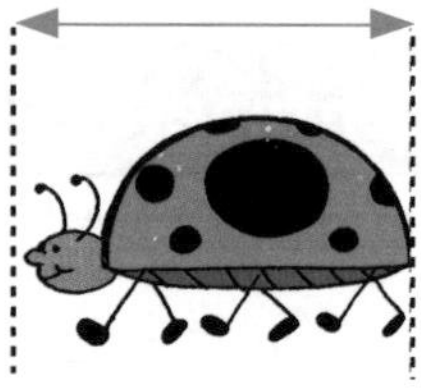

c

d

e

f

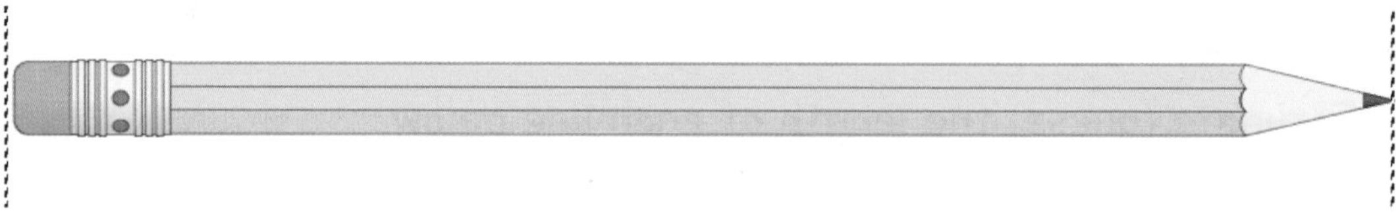

5. Use your ruler to measure each of the lines in question 4.
(Give your answer to the **nearest centimetre**).

6. a Measure each side of this shape to the **nearest centimetre**.

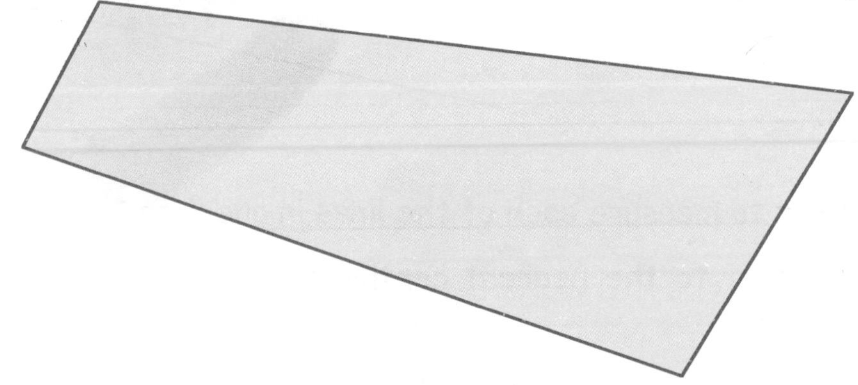

b Calculate the difference between the **longest** and the **shortest** side.

Units of Measurement

Be able to choose an appropriate unit of measure

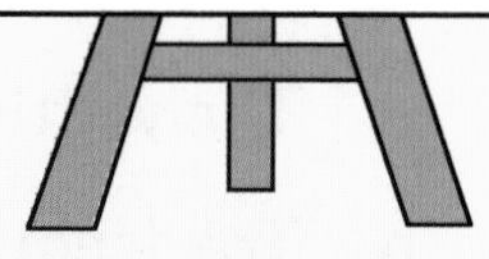

Centimetres (cm) and Millimetres (mm)

A **ruler** is used to measure **centimetres** or **millimetres**.

Centimetres are used to measure **small** lengths.

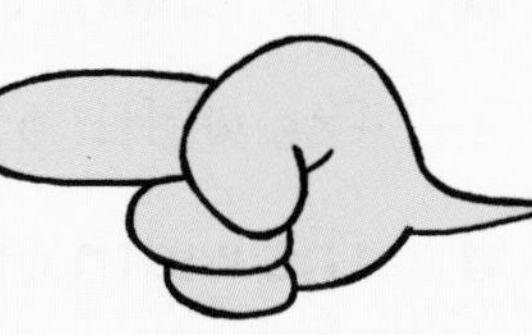

Examples
- The length of your finger
- The width of this page.

1 cm = 10 mm

A **centimetre** can be split into ***10 equal parts.***

Each part is called a **millimetre**.

1 mm
0 1
cm

Millimetres (mm)

Millimetres are used to measure **very small** lengths.

Examples
- The wire used in a paperclip is about 1 mm.
- The width of your fingernail is about 6 mm.

Metres (m)

A **metre stick** or **tape** or **trundle wheel** is used to measure metres.

Metres are used to measure longer lengths.

1 metre = 100 cm

Examples
- The length of the classroom
- The height of a building.

Kilometres (km)

1 km = 1000 metres

An **odometer** on a car is used to measure kilometres.

Kilometres are used to measure much longer distances.

Examples
- The length of a river.
- The distance from Ayr to Glasgow.

Exercise 2

1. Write down which unit of measurement you would use to measure :-
   (Choose between **millimetres, centimetres, metres & kilometres**)

   a The width of this page

   b The length of Scotland

   c The width of the school corridor

   d The width of a pencil

   e The length of a pencil

   f The thickness of a bank card

   g The distance from London to Paris

   h The height of a flagpole.

2. What measuring device would you use to measure something in :-

   a millimetres (**mm**) b centimetres (**cm**)

   c metres (**m**) d kilometres (**km**).

3. Write down a list of things that I might measure using :-

   a millimetres (**mm**) b centimetres (**cm**)

   c metres (**m**) d kilometres (**km**).

4. Jack measures the distance from his house to the school using a ruler.

   His sister Jill measures the same route with a trundle wheel.

   Write a few sentences about their methods of measuring.

5. Investigate different distances from one country to another.

6. Find the distance if you flew all the way round the world :-

   a from pole to pole b around the equator.

   Discuss your findings.

Area

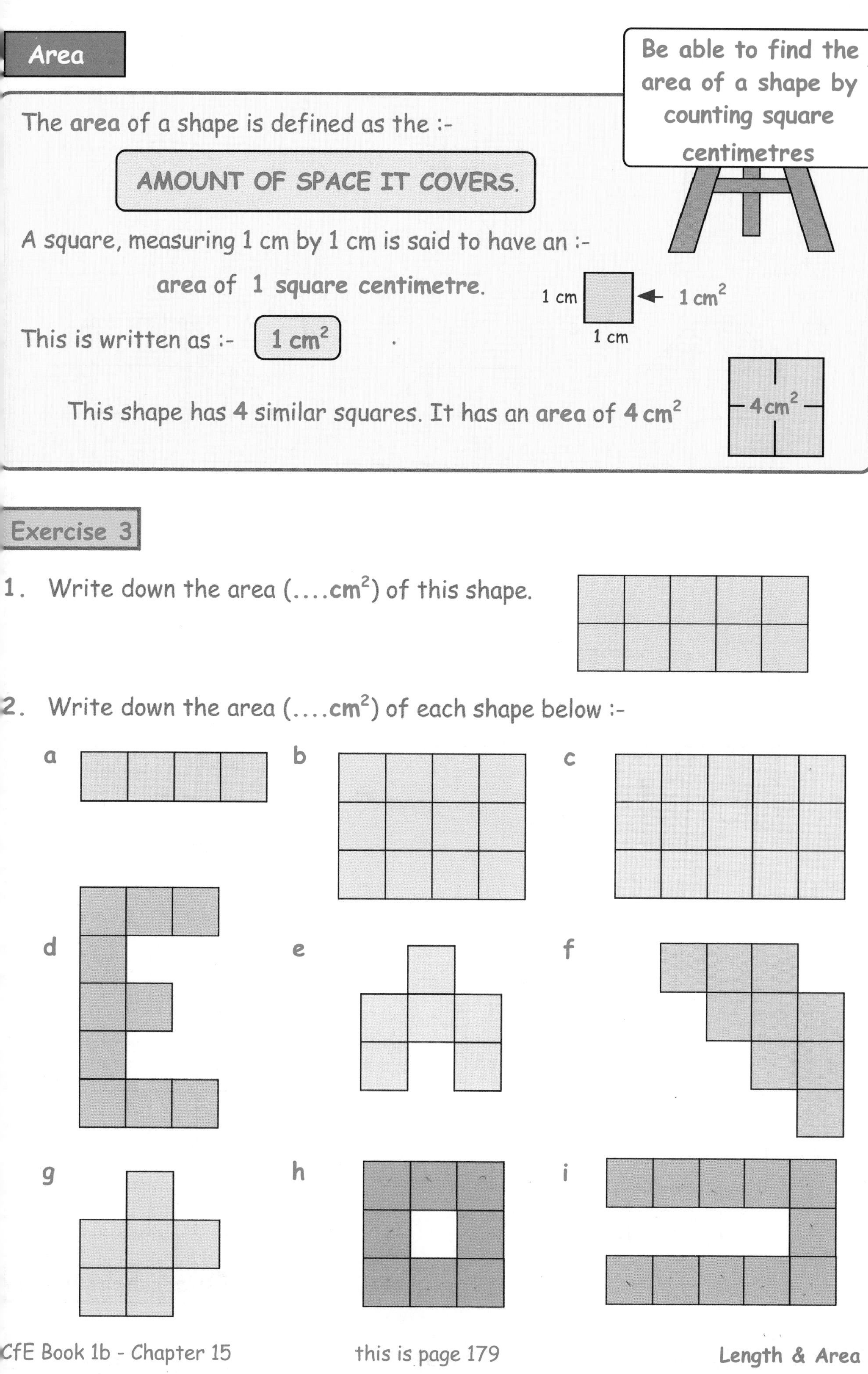

Be able to find the area of a shape by counting square centimetres

The area of a shape is defined as the :-

AMOUNT OF SPACE IT COVERS.

A square, measuring 1 cm by 1 cm is said to have an :-

area of 1 square centimetre.

This is written as :- 1 cm^2 .

This shape has 4 similar squares. It has an area of 4 cm^2

Exercise 3

1. Write down the area (....cm^2) of this shape.

2. Write down the area (....cm^2) of each shape below :-

3. Write down the area (....cm^2) of each shape below :-

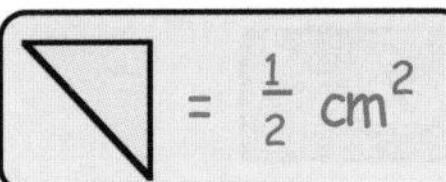

a

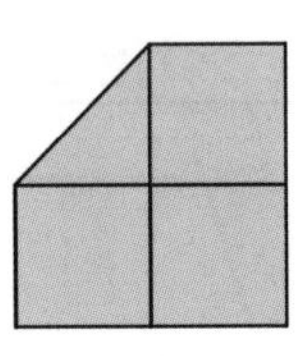

b

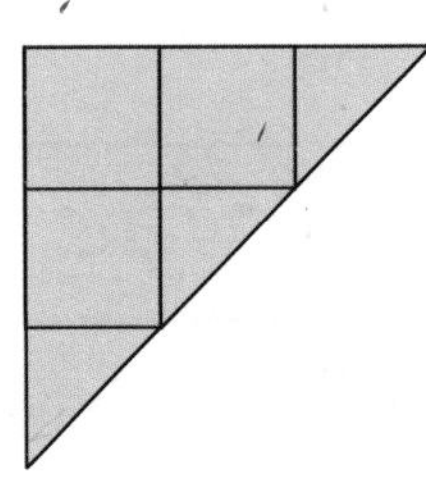

c

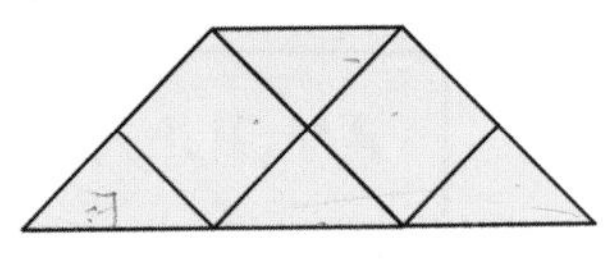

d

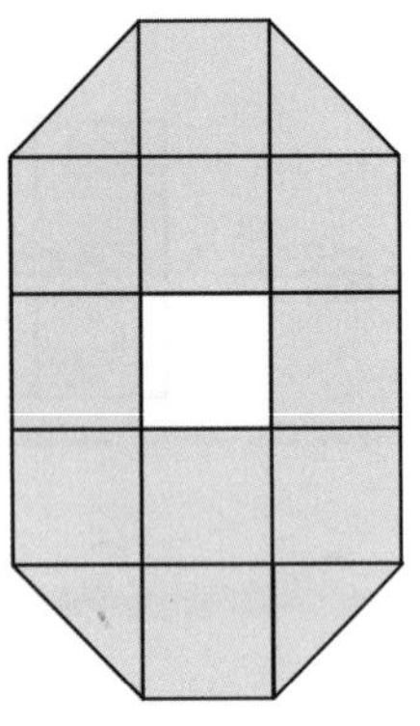

e

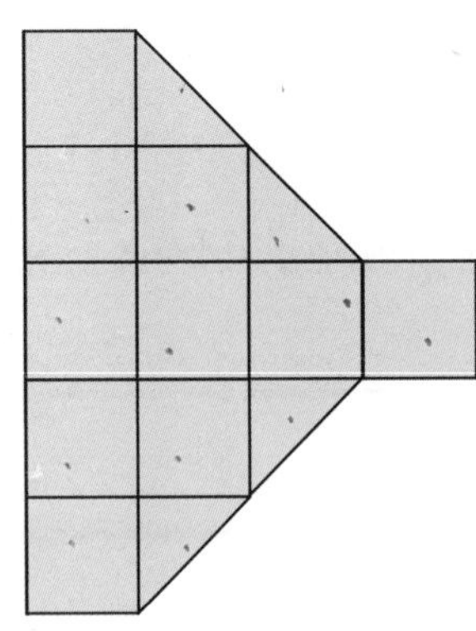

f

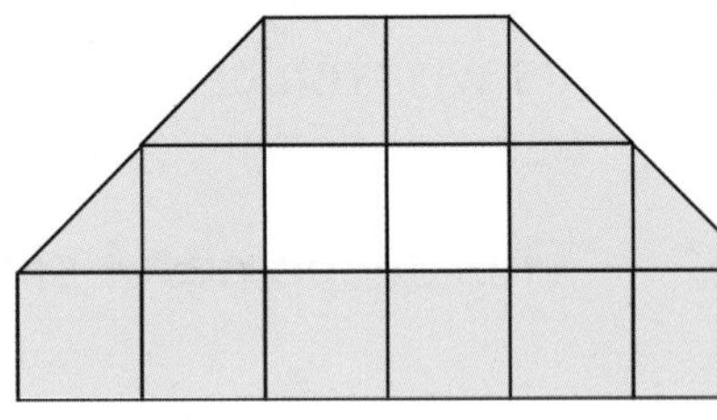

g

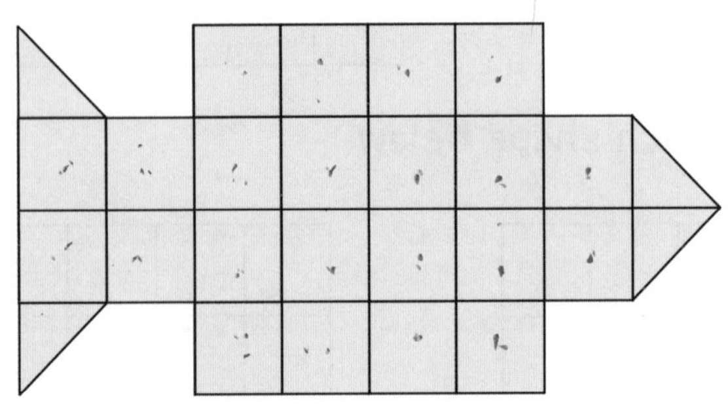

h

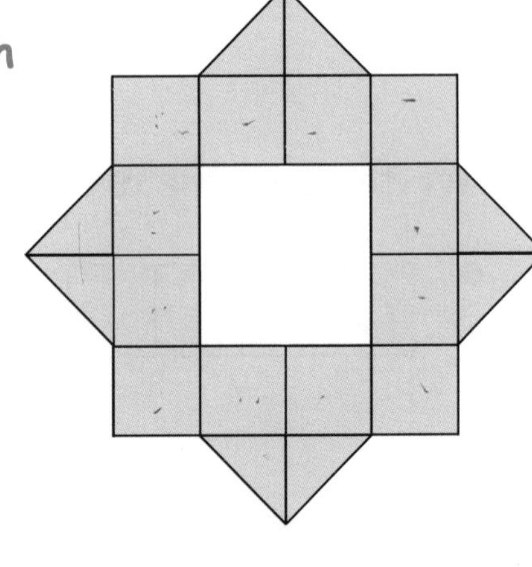

i

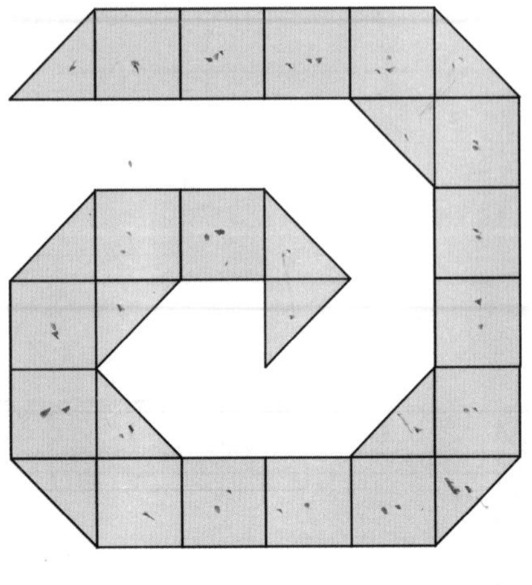

j

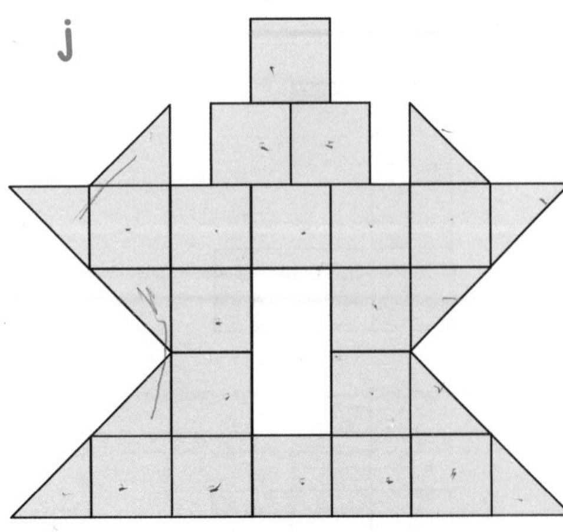

Worksheet 15·3

Estimating Area

Be able to estimate the area of a shape by counting square centimetres

It is possible to **estimate** the area of a shape which is not made of squares and half squares.

Example :- To find the **area** of this blue shape :-

- Begin by counting all the **whole squares**.
- Add on any bits that are **more than** $\frac{1}{2}$ covered.
- **Ignore** any bits that are **less than** $\frac{1}{2}$ covered.

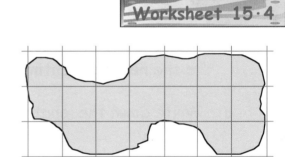

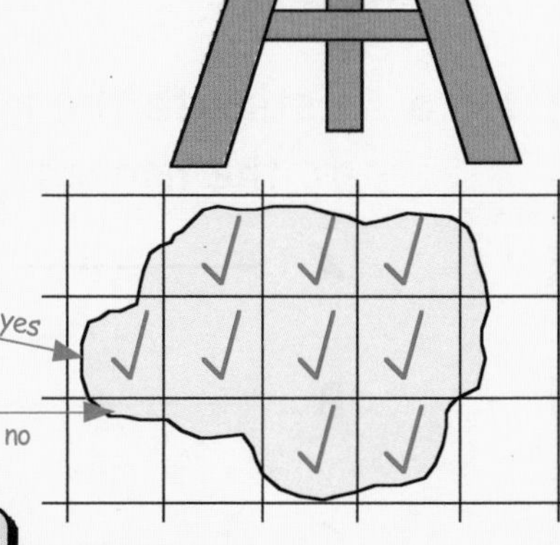

An **estimate** for the **area** of this shape is **9 cm²**.

Exercise 4

Worksheet 15·4

1. **Estimate** the area (....cm²) of the shape opposite :-

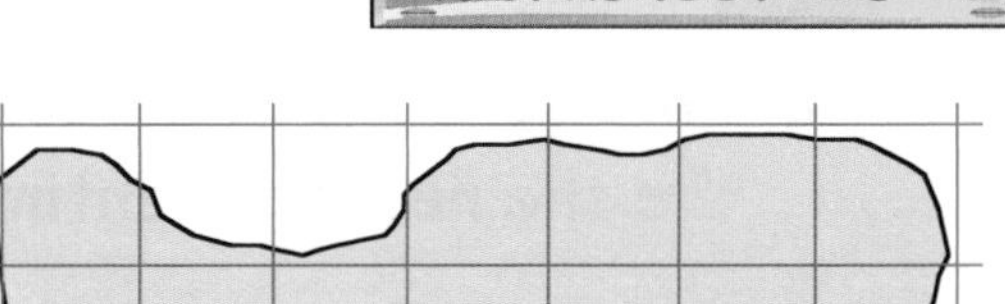

2. **Estimate** the area of each of these :-

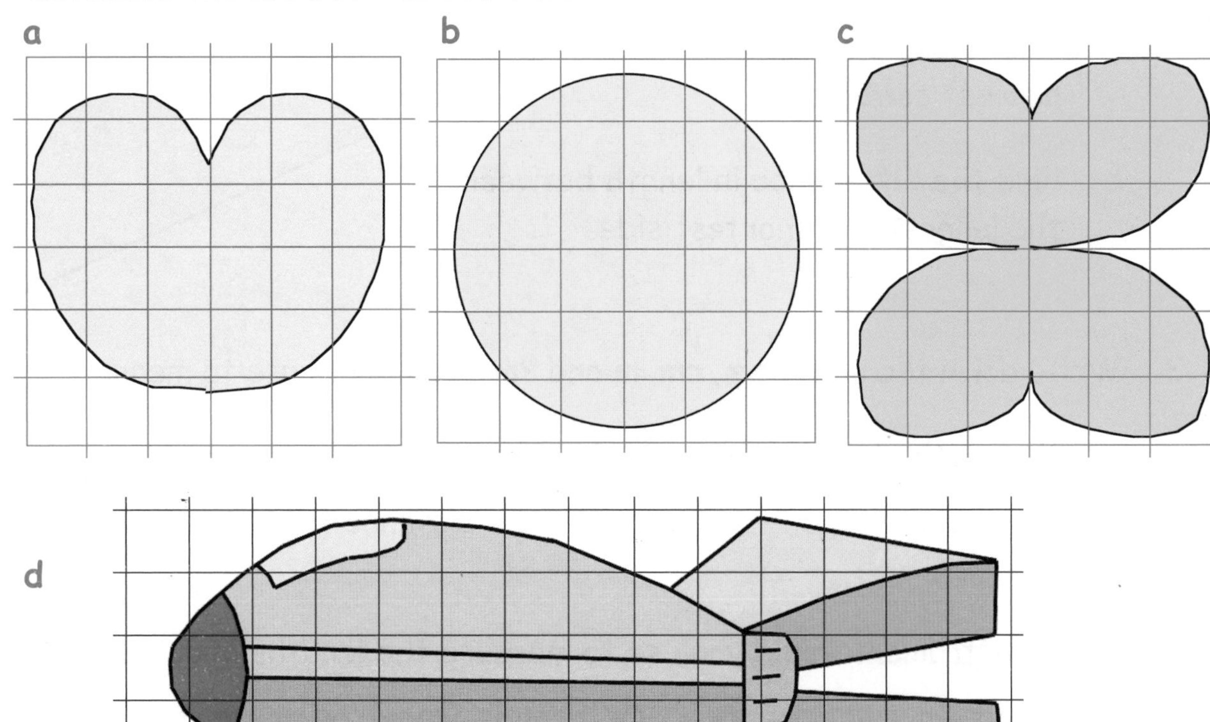

The 3 R's

Revisit - Review - Revise

1. a Estimate the length of each line below to the **nearest centimetre** :-

A

B

C

D

b Measure and write down the length of each line above to the **nearest centimetre**.

c Write down the length of the lines in order - **shortest** first.

2. a Measure each side of this triangle to the nearest centimetre.

b Find the **difference** in length between the longest and shortest side.

3. Write down the unit, (**mm**, **cm**, **m** and **km**), you would use to measure :-

a the width of the playground b the width of your pencil

c your height d the distance from Ayr to Glasgow.

4. What instrument would you use to measure the lengths in question 3 ? (Choose from **ruler**, **metre stick**, **trundle wheel**, **odometer**)

5. Which has a smaller area :-

a this page or a stamp

b the floor or the window ?

6. Write down the area of each shape in cm^2 :-

a

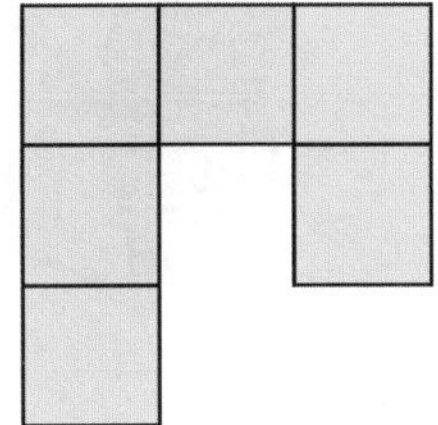

b

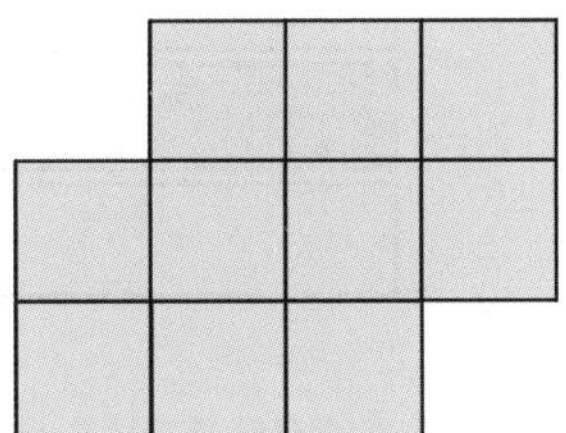

c

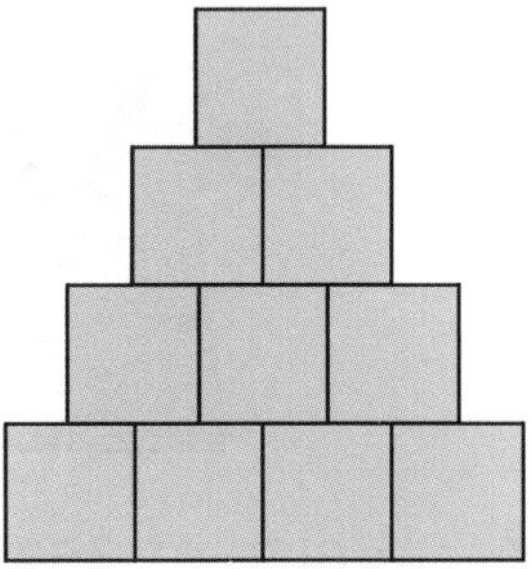

d

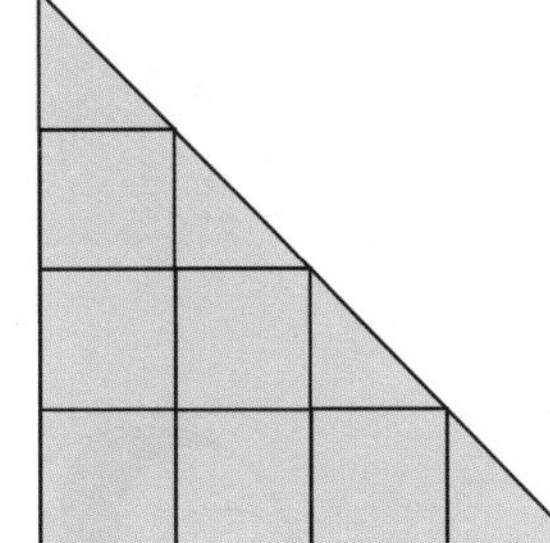

e

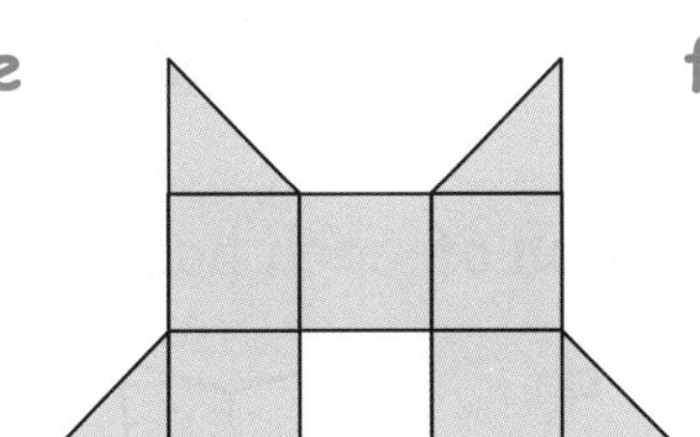

f

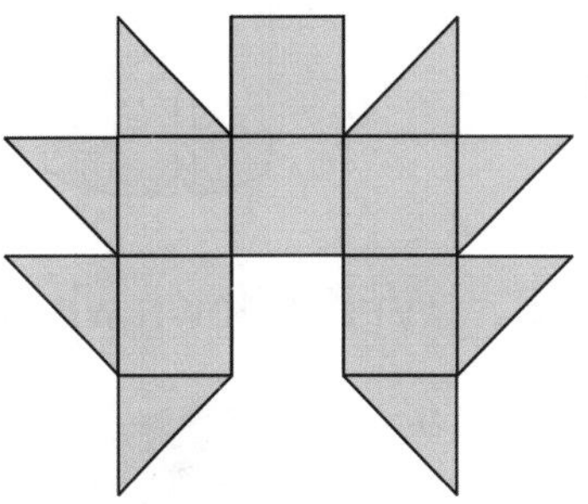

7. Estimate the area of each shape below :-

If more than $\frac{1}{2}$ a box is covered → count it as 1 cm^2

If less than $\frac{1}{2}$ a box is covered → do not count it at all.

a

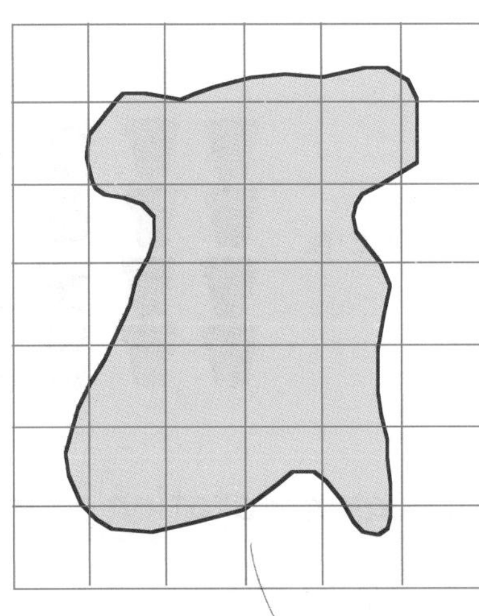

b

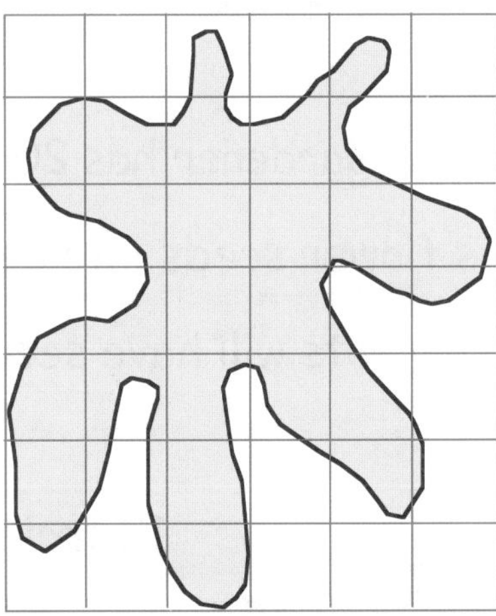

Revision of Fractions

1. Which of these shapes have been split in **half** ?

a  b  c 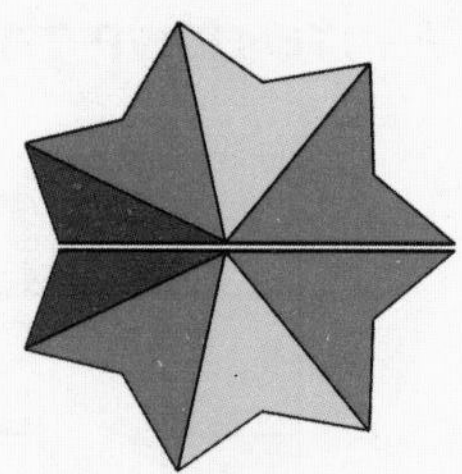

2. Which of these shapes have been split into **quarters** ?

a 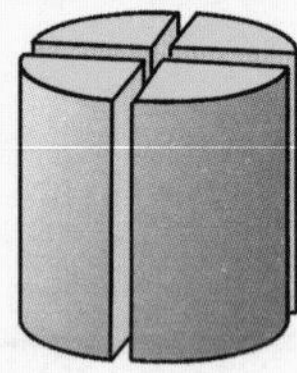 b  c 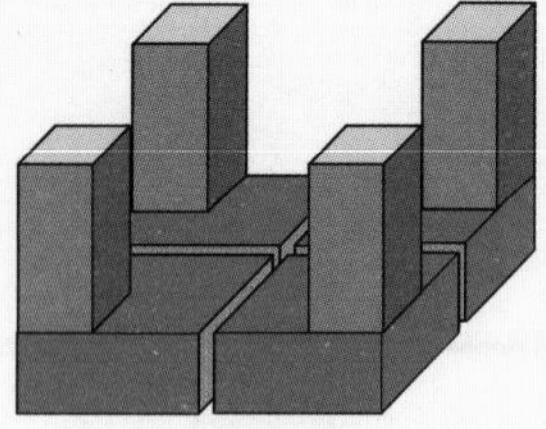

3. Write down what **fraction** of each has been coloured.

a  b 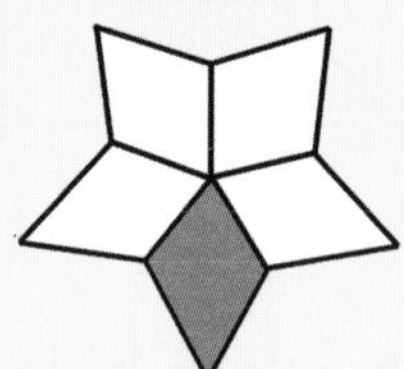 c 

4. 

There are 12 pies left in the baker shop.

Mrs Bolland buys **half** of them.

How many pies are left ?

5. George the gardener has 20 empty pots.

He puts flower seeds into a **quarter** of them.

How many pots will have seeds in them ?

6. 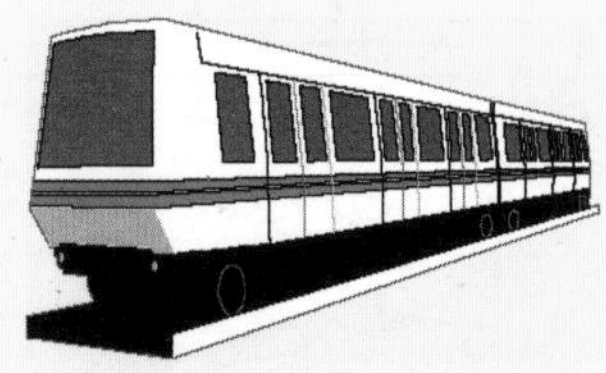

12 trains pass through my station every hour.

Only $\frac{1}{3}$ of them actually stop.

How many of them go straight through ?

Fractions

Be able to find a basic fraction of a quantity

Fraction of a Quantity

To find a fraction (like a $\frac{1}{2}$) of something - you **divide**.

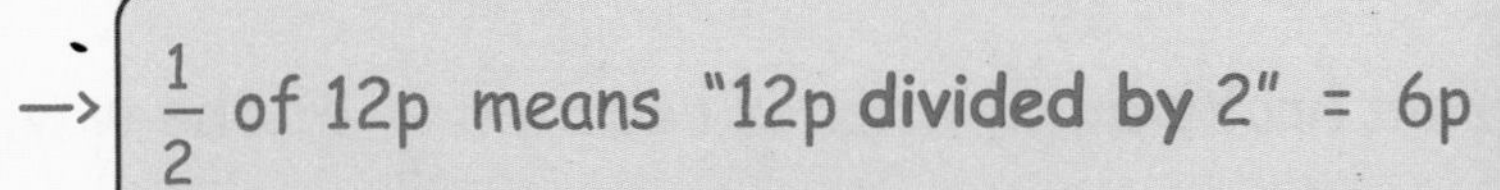

→ $\frac{1}{2}$ of 12p means "12p **divided by 2**" = 6p

→ $\frac{1}{3}$ of 21p means "21p **divided by 3**" = 7p

→ $\frac{1}{8}$ of 40p means "40p **divided by 8**" = 5p

Exercise 1

1. **Copy** and complete :-

   "$\frac{1}{2}$ of 20p means "20p **divided by 2**" = ... **p**".

2. **Copy** and complete :-

   "$\frac{1}{4}$ of 36 cm means "36 cm **divided by ...**" = ... **cm**"

3. Find :-

a	$\frac{1}{2}$ of 60p	b	$\frac{1}{3}$ of 18 metres	c	$\frac{1}{5}$ of 35 grams
d	$\frac{1}{10}$ of £80	e	$\frac{1}{4}$ of 32 litres	f	$\frac{1}{6}$ of £66
g	$\frac{1}{8}$ of 48 cm	h	$\frac{1}{7}$ of 63p	i	$\frac{1}{3}$ of 93p.

4. 27 children are in a classroom. $\frac{1}{3}$ of them are girls.

a How many girls are in the classroom ?

b How many boys are there ?

5.

It is 36 miles from my home town to Glasgow by train.

The train broke down when it reached $\frac{1}{4}$ of the way.

a How far had I travelled ?

b How far was I then from Glasgow ?

6. Lucy got 30 birthday cards on her birthday.

$\frac{1}{5}$ of them had money in them.

How many cards had money in them ?

7.

Most cats sleep for about $\frac{1}{3}$ of each day.

How many hours is this ?

8. Draw this rectangle (24 squares) on squared paper.

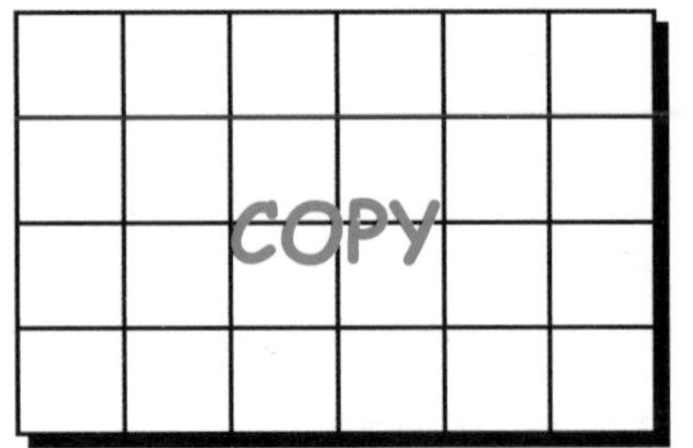

a What is $\frac{1}{6}$ of 24 ?

b **Colour** $\frac{1}{6}$ of the rectangle red.

c **Colour** $\frac{1}{8}$ of it blue and $\frac{1}{4}$ of it yellow.

d How many of the 24 squares are **not** coloured at all ?

9. Draw the same rectangle again.

Colour :- • one half red • **one quarter blue** • one eighth green.

How many squares are **not** coloured ?

10. a How many days are there in June ?

b It rained on $\frac{1}{6}$ of these days.

How many days was this ?

c 

I was on holiday for $\frac{1}{3}$ of **June**.

For how long was I on holiday ?

d Alice went on holiday for **half** of July and August.

How many days was Alice on holiday ?

e Billy was in bed ill all of last Friday.

What fraction of the week was Billy in bed ill ?

f What fraction of an hour is one minute ?

g What fraction of a day is one hour ?

11. I had some money in my pocket, I spent $\frac{1}{6}$ of it on sweets.

The sweets cost 9 pence.

a How much money must I have had to begin with ?

b How much money did I have left ?

12. 

Bob's dad went on a tour of duty with the army in **March**, **April** and **May**.

What fraction of the year was his dad on his tour of duty ?

13. a Draw the rectangle shown.

b Colour one half red, one quarter blue and one eighth orange.

c What fraction of the rectangle is not coloured ?

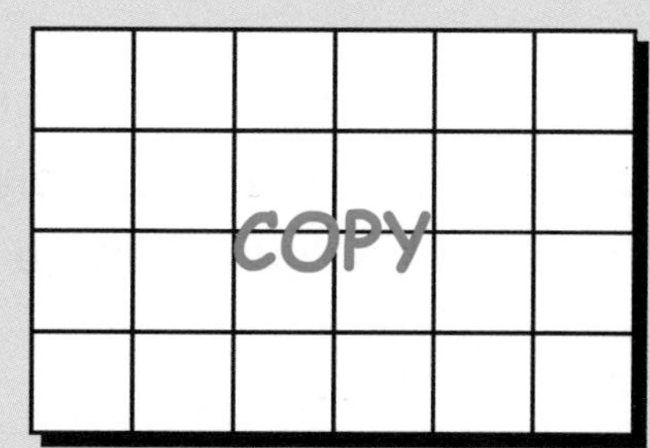

Equivalent Fractions

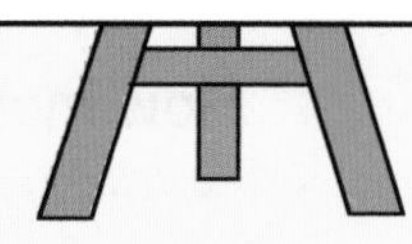

This rectangle has been divided up in **TWO** different ways :-

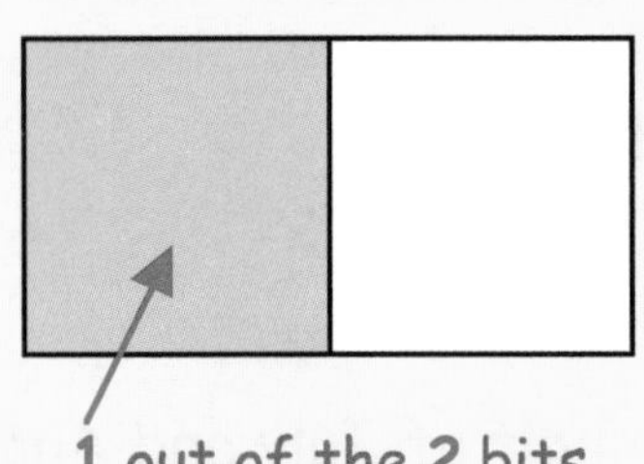

1 out of the 2 bits is shaded pink = 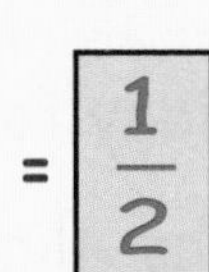

$\frac{1}{2}$

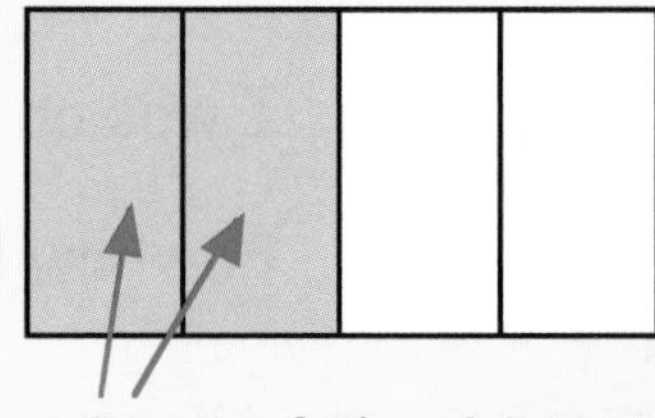

2 out of the 4 bits are shaded pink = 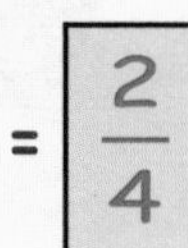

$\frac{2}{4}$

Can you see from the diagrams that the two fractions $\frac{1}{2}$ and $\frac{2}{4}$ are **the SAME** ?

$\frac{2}{4} = \frac{1}{2}$

These are called **equivalent** fractions.

Exercise 2

1. This circle has been divided into 3 equal parts.

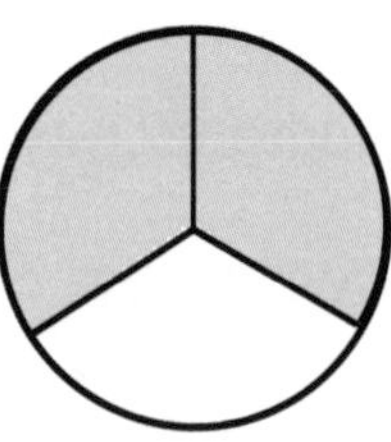

a What fraction of the circle is coloured blue ?

b 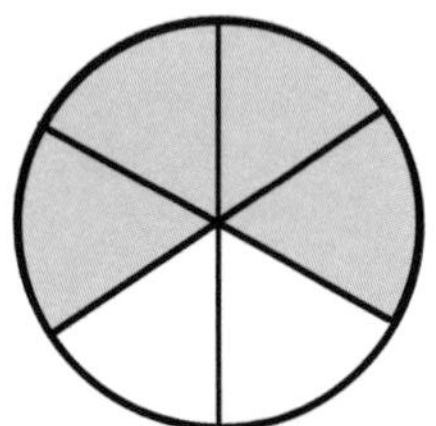

The same circle has been divided into 6 parts this time.

What fraction this time is coloured blue ?

Can you see that the same amount has been coloured blue both times ?

c **Copy** this sentence and finish it :-

"The 2 diagrams show that the fractions  $\frac{2}{3} = \frac{...}{6}$ are **equivalent**".

2. Use the two drawings opposite to write down the 2 fractions that are shown to be **equivalent** to each other.

i.e. $\frac{3}{4}$ = ...

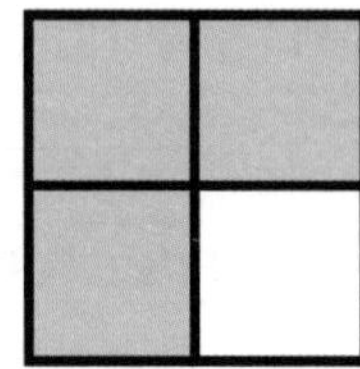

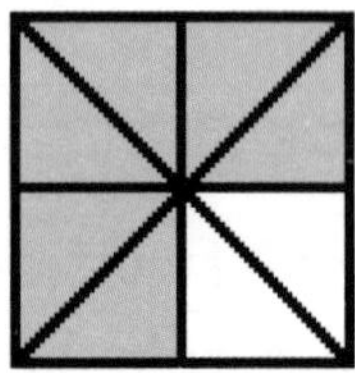

3. Use each pair of drawings below to write down the 2 fractions that are shown to be **equivalent** to each other.

a 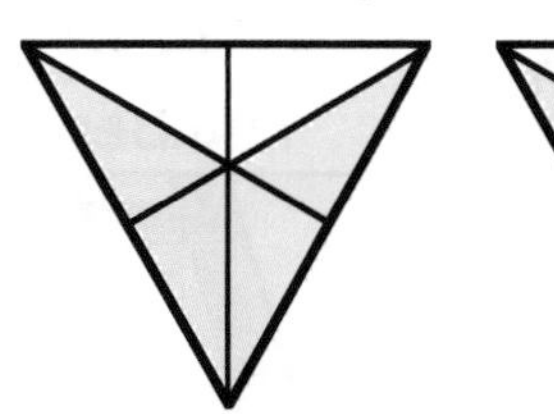

b 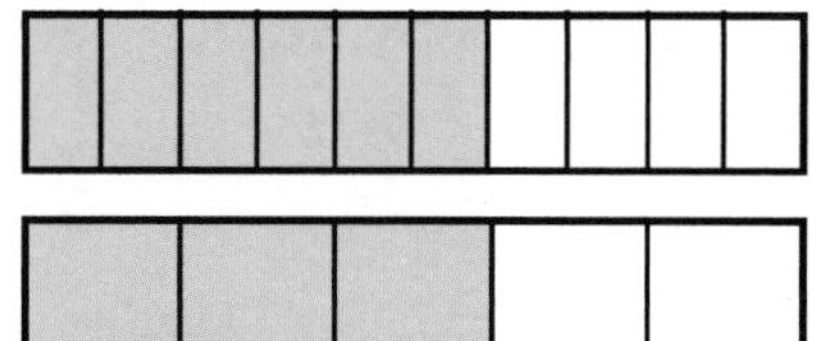

c 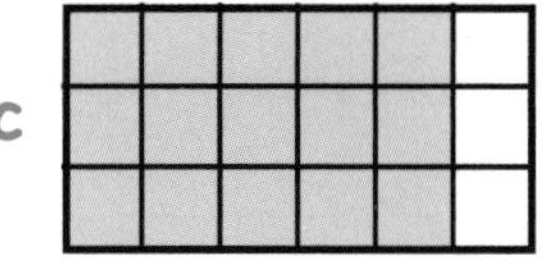 

d 

e 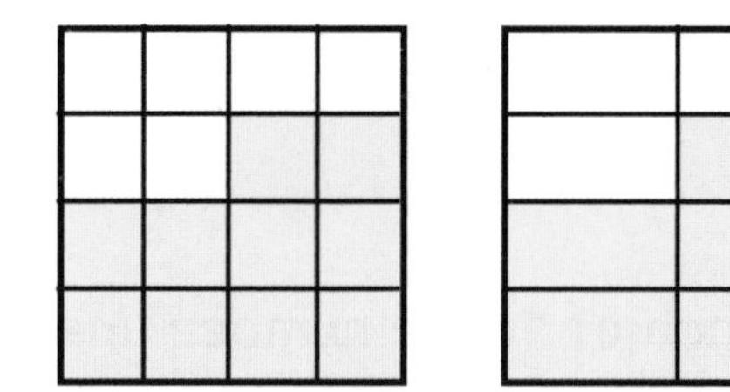

f 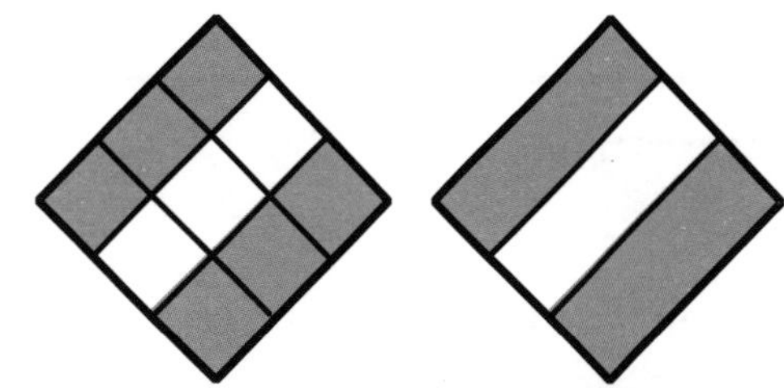

Worksheet 16·2

4. **Draw** or **trace** both of these squares.

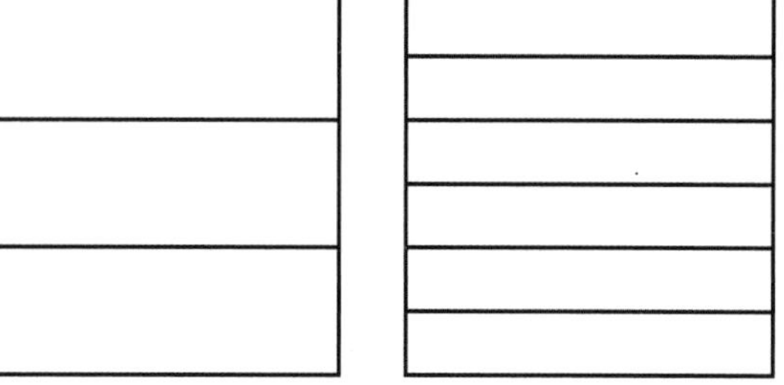

a In the first one, colour in 2 boxes.

b What **fraction** have you shaded ?

c Colour in the correct number of boxes in your 2nd square so that both look the same.

d Use your drawings to **complete** :- $\frac{...}{3} = \frac{?}{6}$.

5. **Draw** or **trace** both of these circles.

a In the first one, colour in **3 parts**.

b What **fraction** have you shaded ?

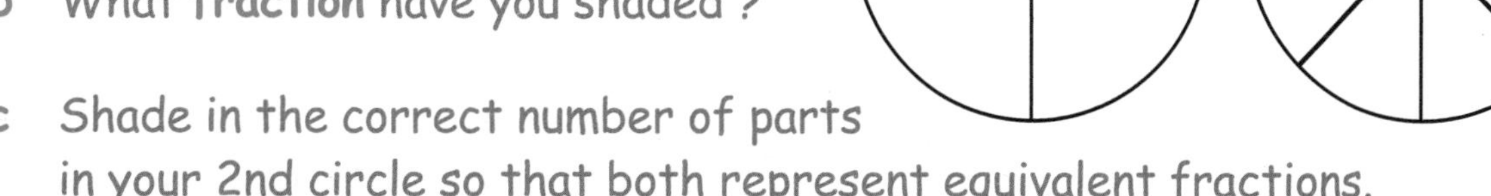

c Shade in the correct number of parts in your 2nd circle so that both represent equivalent fractions.

d Use your drawings to **complete** :- $\frac{?}{4} = \frac{6}{?}$.

Fractions on a Number Line

Identify where a basic fraction would be on a number line

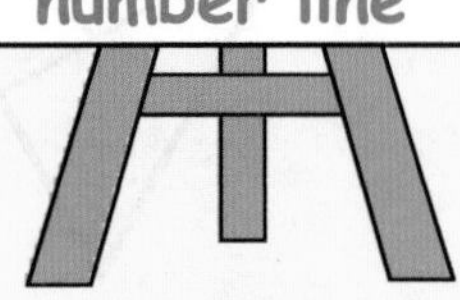

This number line has been split equally into 2 bits.

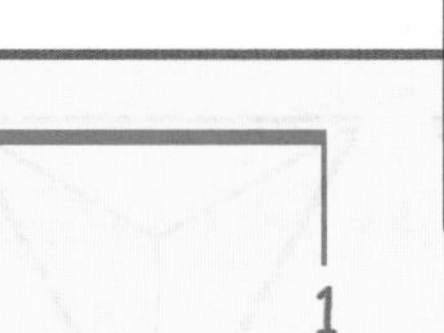

Each bit would be $\frac{1}{2}$.

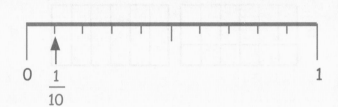

This number line has been split equally into 10 bits.

Each bit would be $\frac{1}{10}$.

Exercise 3

1. What fraction does each bit represent on each of these number lines :-

a

b

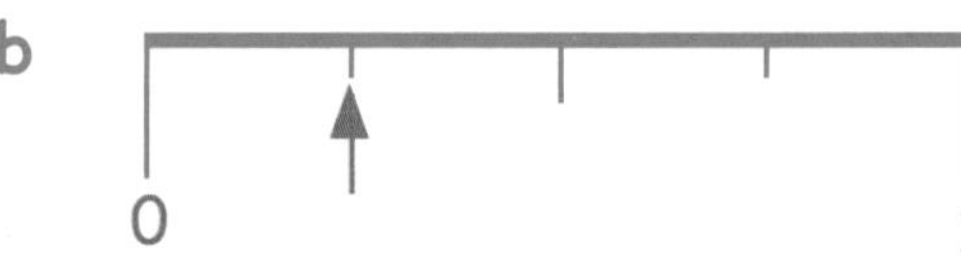

c

d

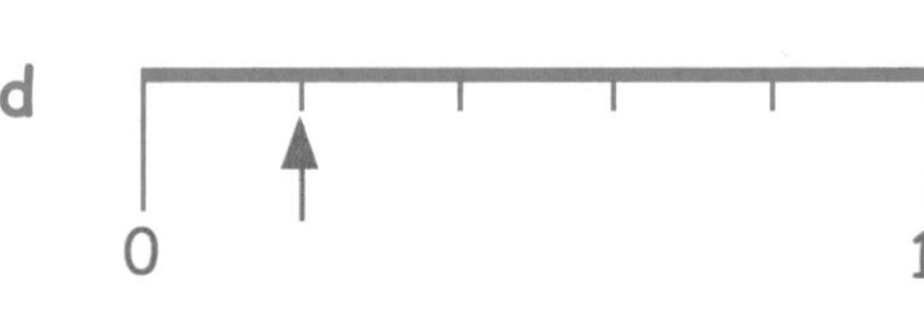

e

f

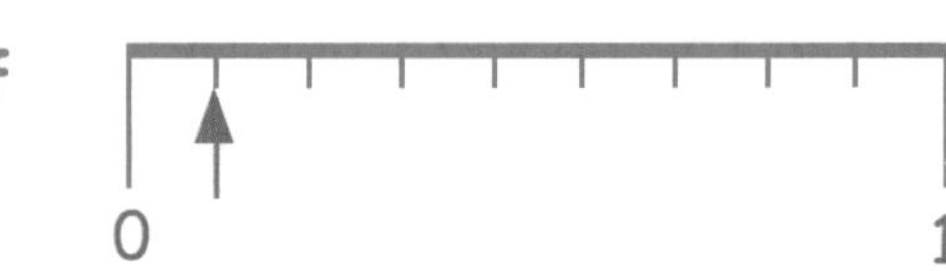

2. If you were *very* hungry, would you prefer :-

   a a half or a third of a pizza
   b a quarter or a third of a pizza
   c a fifth or a sixth of a pizza
   d an eighth or a ninth of a pizza ?

3. Put each of these lists of fractions in order (*largest* first) :-

   a $\frac{1}{5}, \frac{1}{2}, \frac{1}{9}$
   b $\frac{1}{5}, \frac{1}{4}, \frac{1}{10}, \frac{1}{7}, \frac{1}{100}$
   c $\frac{1}{3}, \frac{1}{13}, \frac{1}{6}, \frac{1}{5}, \frac{1}{11}$
   d a tenth, a third, an eighth, a fifth.

This number line is split into quarters.

The arrow is pointing to **3 and a three quarters.** ($3\frac{3}{4}$).

4. What number is each arrow pointing to :-

a

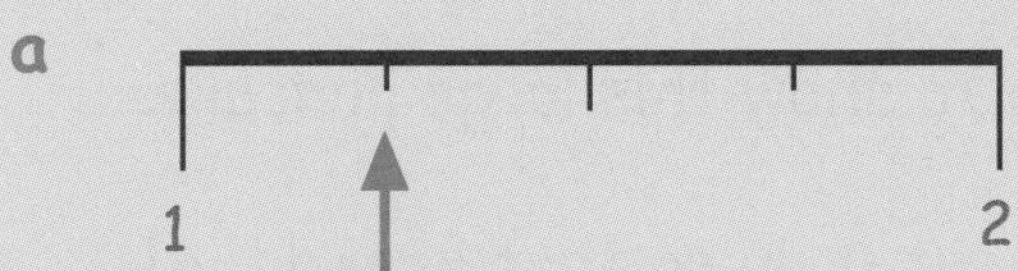

b

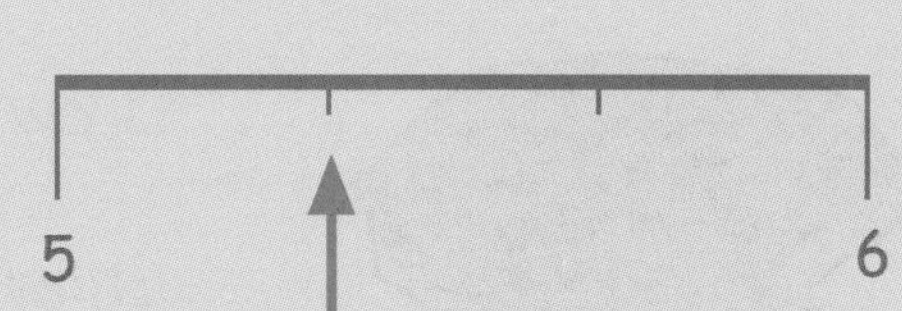

c

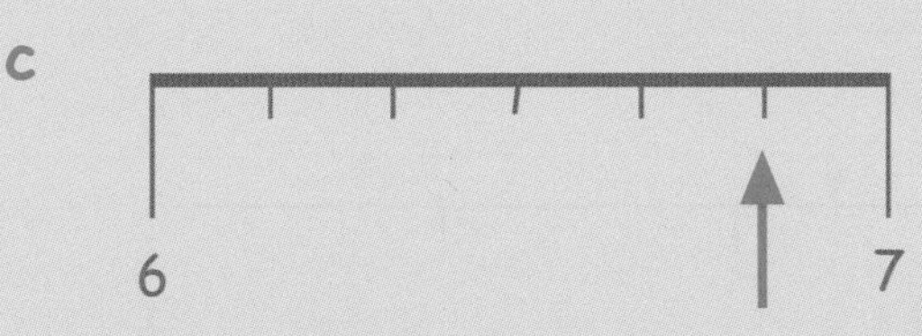

d

e

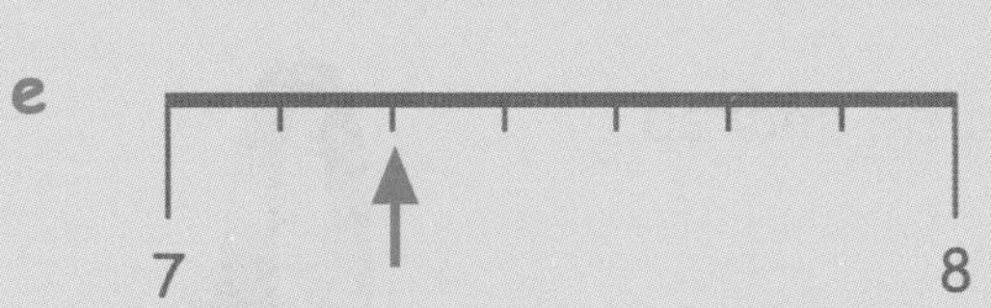

f

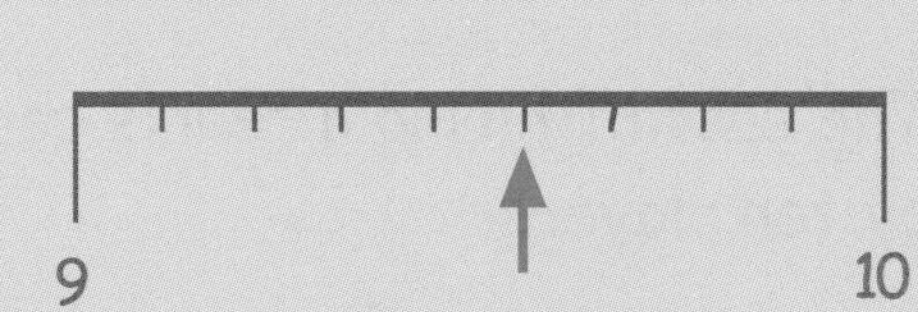

5. Draw number line diagrams to show each of the following fractions :-

a $6\frac{1}{2}$ b $2\frac{2}{3}$ c $2\frac{1}{5}$ d $3\frac{1}{6}$

e $5\frac{3}{4}$ f $1\frac{3}{5}$ g $3\frac{5}{6}$ h $4\frac{2}{5}$.

6. Make a fraction line along the classroom wall or corridor.
(You could make a very big fraction line in the playground with chalk.)

7. a Investigate where fractions are used in everyday life.

b Make a poster to show your findings.

The 3 Я's

Revisit - Review - Revise

1. What **fraction** of this jam roll has been cut off ?

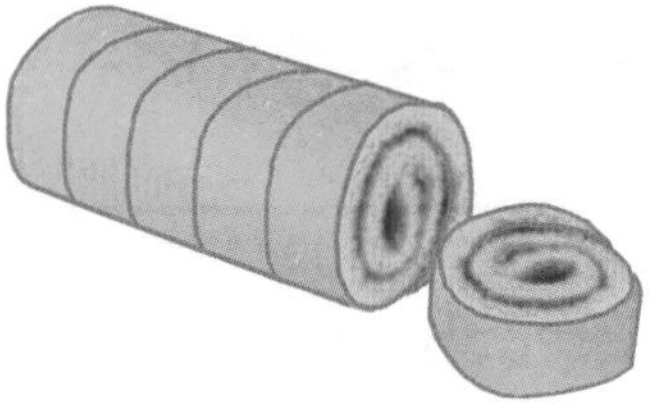

2. 

Draw a **circle** to show this large pancake.

Show how to cut it up so that Brenda, Alex and Tara get an **equal** share of the pancake.

3. What fraction is represented on this number line ?

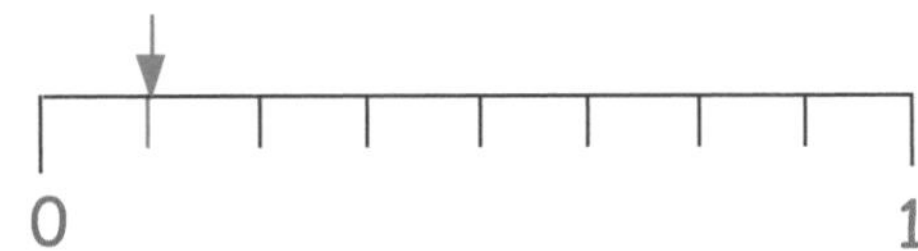

4. The cost of hiring a tennis court is to be shared by ten players.

What **fraction** of the cost has each person to pay ?

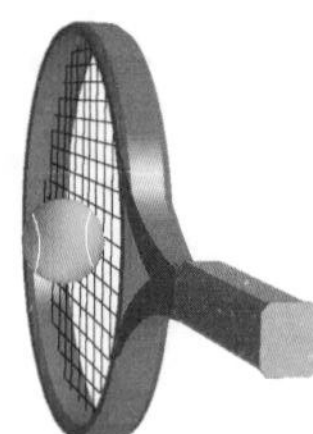

5. What **fraction** of each shape has been coloured here ?

a 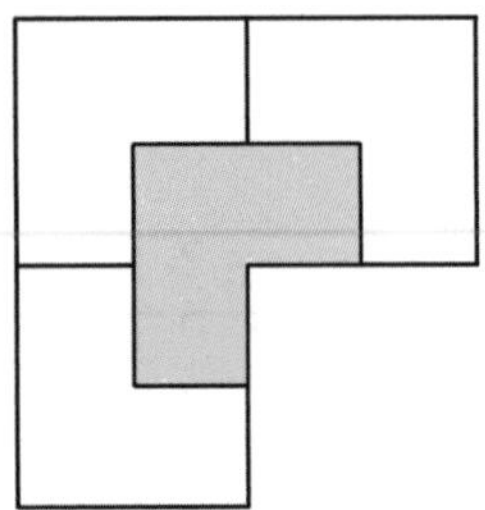

b 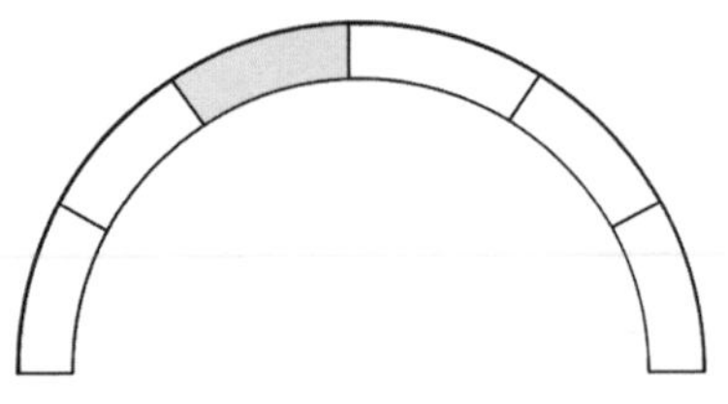

c 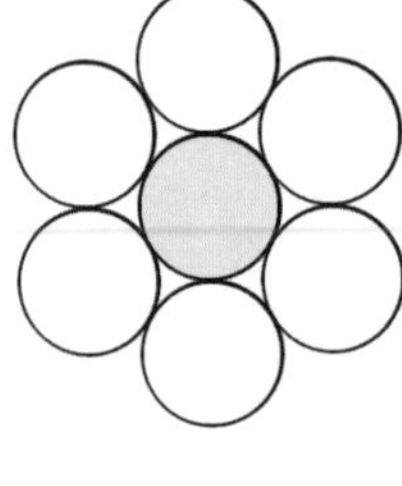

6. This jar was full of water. Terry drank some of it.

Estimate what **fraction** of the water Terry drank.

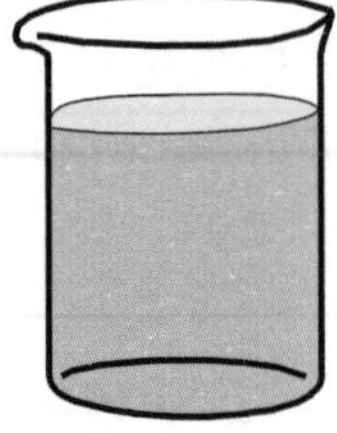

7. What is :-

a $\frac{1}{2}$ of 60p   b $\frac{1}{5}$ of 30 cards   c $\frac{1}{9}$ of £450 ?

8. Teodor had a collection of 240 comics.

He sold $\frac{1}{3}$ of them to his friend Marek.

How many comics did he sell to Marek ?

9. 

To raise funds for charity, Danny took 200 shots at a basketball net.

He scored with $\frac{1}{4}$ of his shots.

a With how many shots did Danny score ?

b How many did he fail to score with ?

10. This diagram shows 2 **equivalent** fractions.

Copy and **complete** - $\frac{1}{4}$ is the same as $\frac{2}{\dots}$.

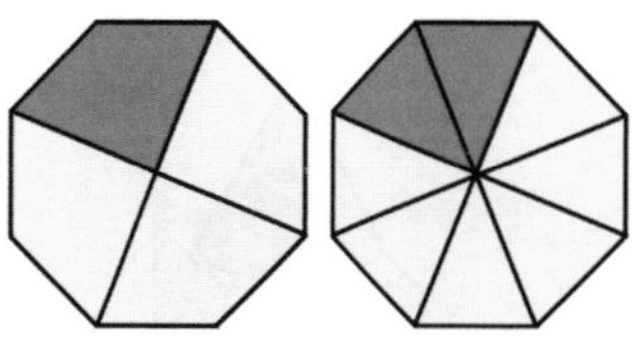

11. Each diagram below shows 2 fractions that are **equivalent**.

Write down what the fractions are.

a

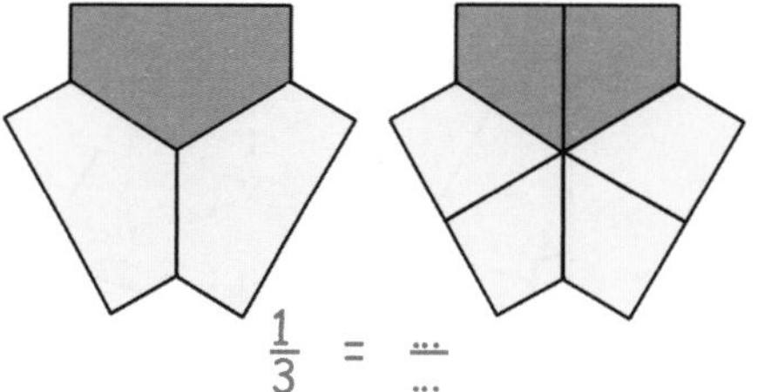

$\frac{1}{3} = \frac{\dots}{\dots}$

b

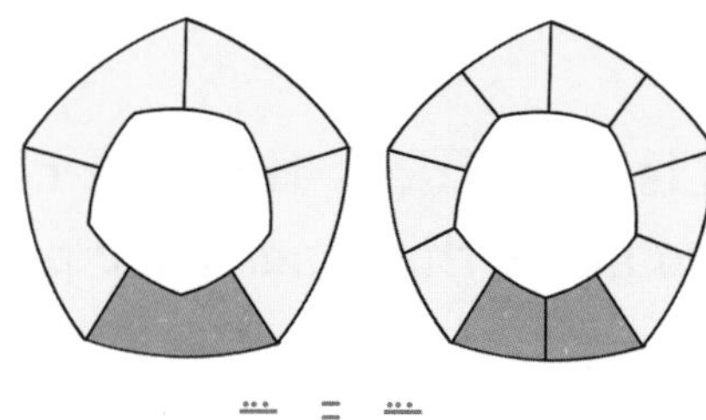

$\frac{\dots}{\dots} = \frac{\dots}{\dots}$

12. This chocolate cake was moulded into **12** sections.

Sara ate $\frac{1}{3}$ of the cake at her party.

How many **sections** must Sara have eaten ?

13. 

Henry and some of his friends were paid £35 for washing cars.

They shared the money equally.

Henry's share was £5.

How many friends must have helped him wash the cars ?

Revision of 3 Dimensions

1. Name the 3 dimensional shapes in the pictures :-

a 
b 
c 
d 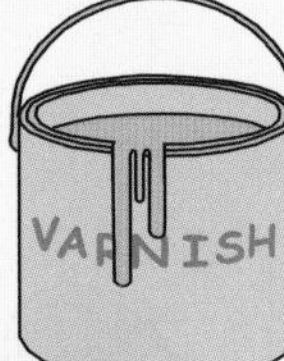

e 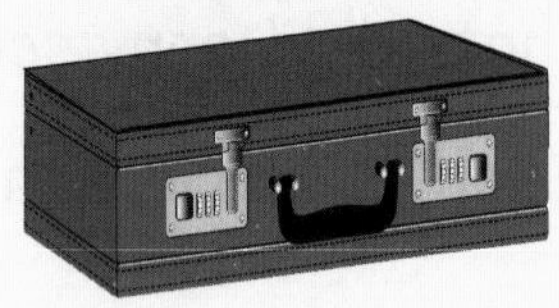
f 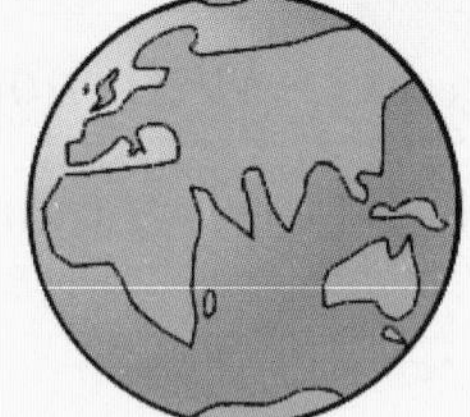
g 

2. 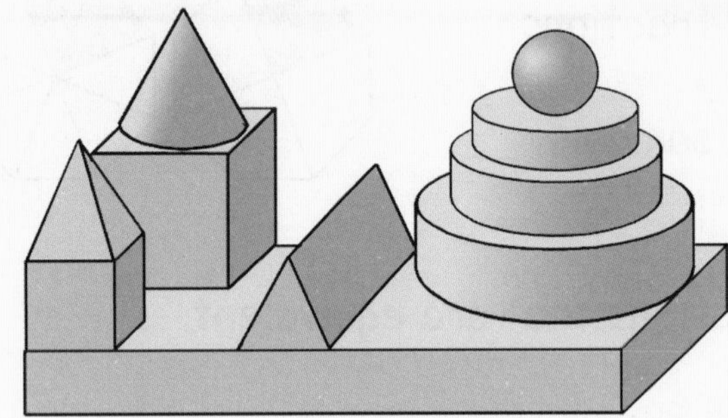

Name all the 3 dimensional shapes in the picture and say how many of them there are.

3. List the faces that are needed to make this triangular prism.

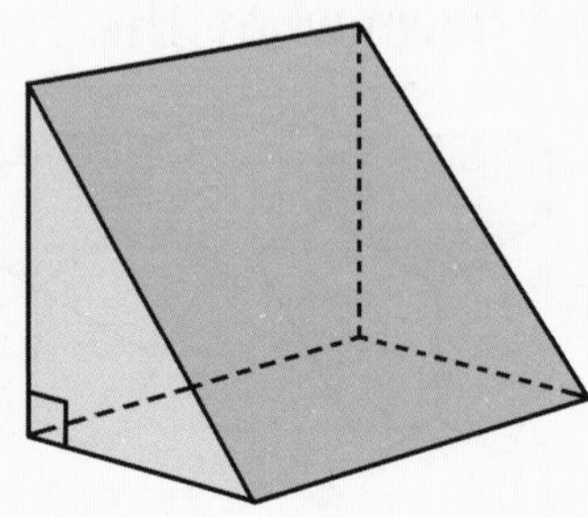

4. What 3 dimensional shape can be made up of :-

a 2 squares and 4 rectangles
b 2 circles and 1 rectangle
c 1 square and 4 triangles
d 2 triangles and 3 rectangles ?

5. How many :-

a edges has a cuboid
b corners has a sphere
c edges has a triangular prism
d corners has a cone ?

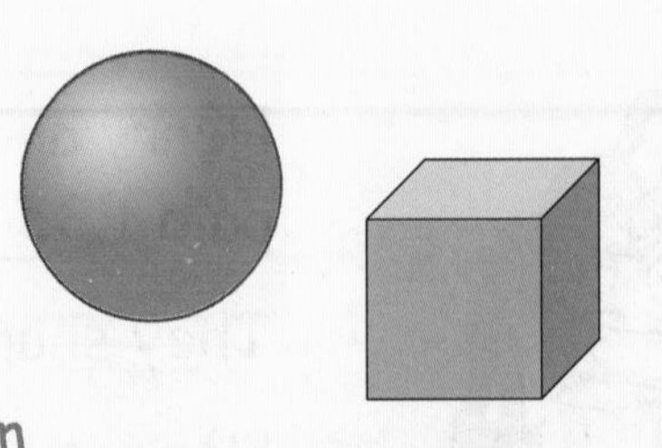
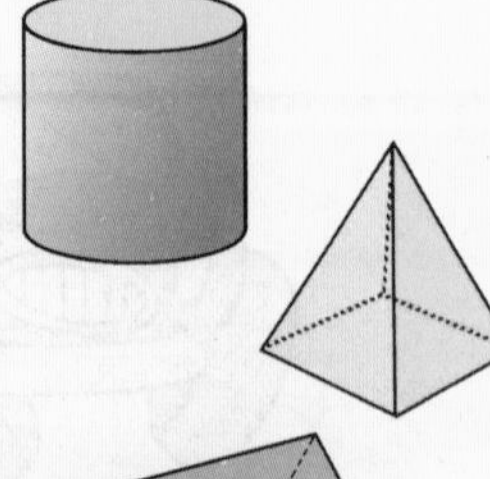
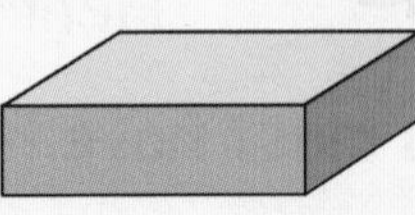

3 Dimensions

Discover how many faces, edges and corners a 3D shape has

Faces, Corners and Edges

All 3 dimensional shapes have **faces**, but whether or not they also have **corners** and **edges** will have to be looked at.

Let us examine the **cuboid**.

One **face** is coloured **green**, but there are more .

It has **corners** - an **arrow** points to **one**. There are more !
(corners are often referred to as vertices)

It also has **edges** - the one shown is a line coloured **red**.
There are more !

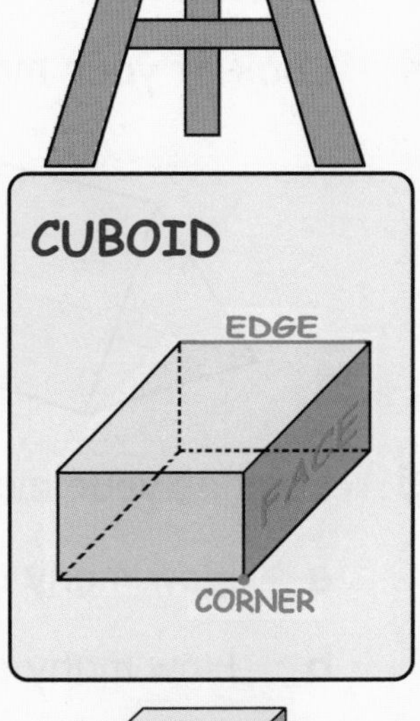

* Sometimes not all faces, corners and edges can be seen.
They are hiding round the back of the shape.

e.g. this cube has 3 faces showing,
but it really has more than 3 !

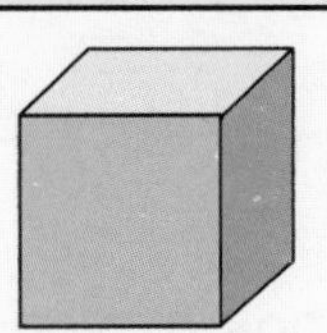

Exercise 1

For this exercise, you will need a model of a:-
cube; cuboid; square based pyramid;
triangular prism; cone; sphere and cylinder.

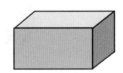

1. Pick up your model **cuboid**.
   - a Slide your finger along one of its **faces** and then the other faces.
     How many **faces** does it have ?
   - b Press your finger against one of its **corners** and then the others.
     How many **corners** does it have ?
   - c Run your finger along one of its **edges** and then the others.
     How many **edges** does it have ?

2. Look at your model **cube**.
   - a How many **faces** does it have ?
   - b How many **corners** does it have ?
   - c How many **edges** does it have ?

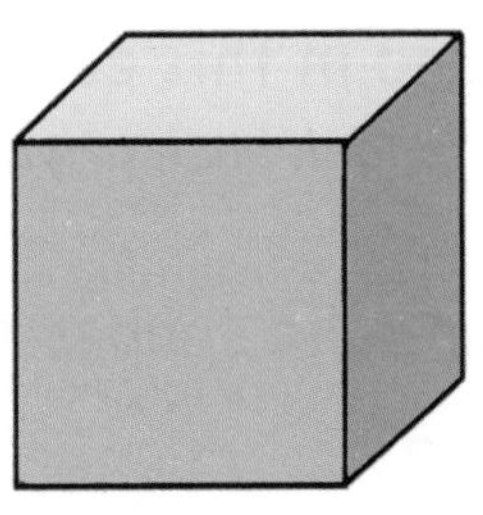

3. Look at your model **square based pyramid**.

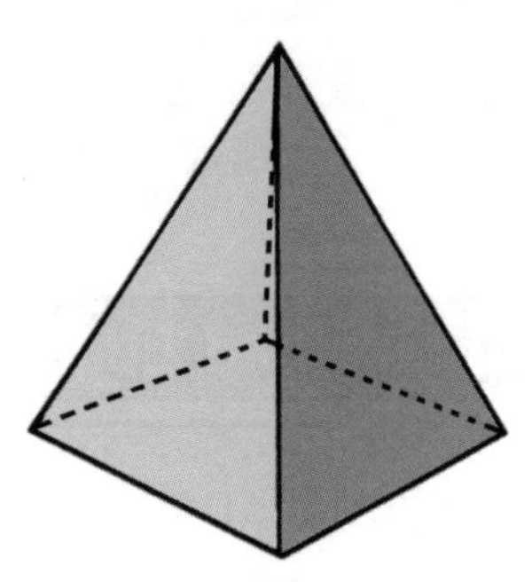

   a How many **corners** does it have ?

   b How many **faces** does it have ?

   c How many **edges** does it have ?

4. Look at your model **triangular prism**.

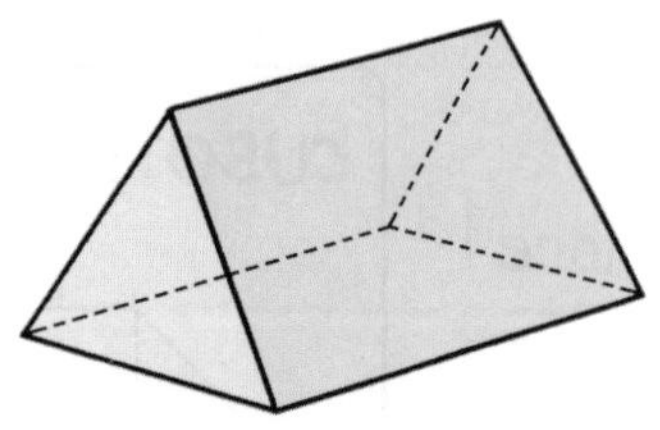

   a How many **edges** does it have ?

   b How many **corners** does it have ?

   c How many **faces** does it have ?

5. Look at your model **cone**.

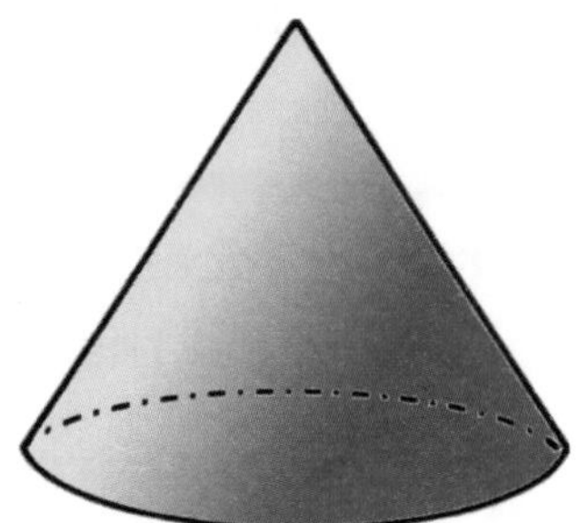

   a How many **corners** does it have ?

   b How many **edges** does it have ?

   c How many **faces** does it have ?

6. Look at your model **sphere**.

   a How many **faces** does it have ?

   b How many **corners** does it have ?

   c How many **edges** does it have ?

7. Look at your model **cylinder**.

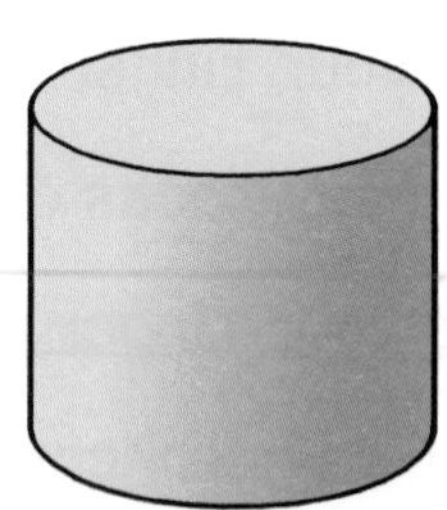

   a How many **corners** does it have ?

   b How many **edges** does it have ?

   c How many **faces** does it have ?

8. **Copy** and **fill in** this table to display all the results you have found in this exercise.
   (*Try not to look back at your answers*).

	FACES	CORNERS	EDGES
Cuboid	6		
Cube			
Pyramid		COPY	
Δ Prism			
Cone			
Sphere			
Cylinder			

9. 3 of your solid shapes can be **rolled**.

   Which 3 ?

The 3 Я's

Revisit - Review - Revise

1. The shapes below are 2 dimensional. Name them.

a 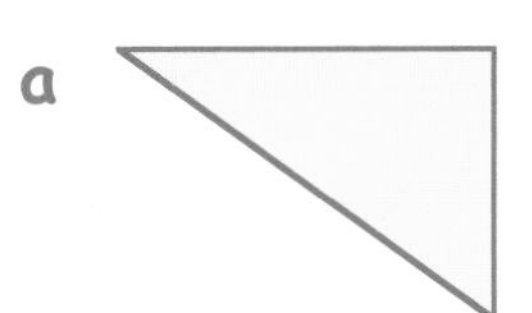 b  c  d 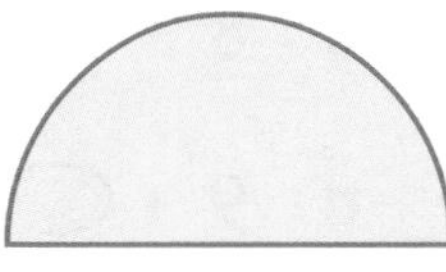

2. Make a list of all the 2D shapes used to make this picture and say how many of them there are.

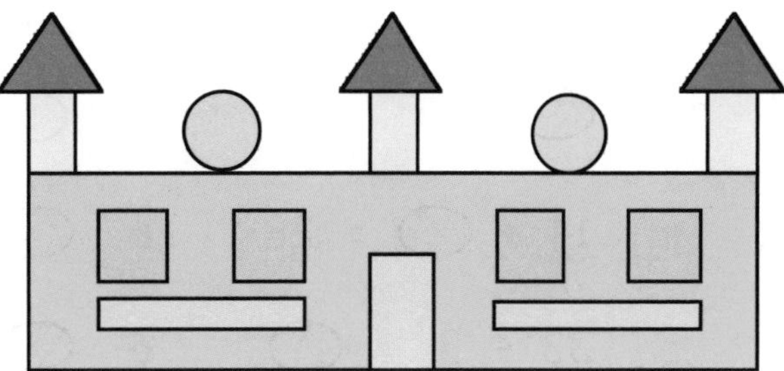

3. a How many sides has a **rectangle** ?

   b List a few ways in which a **square** is different from a **rectangle**.

4. The shapes below are 3 dimensional. Name them.

a  b 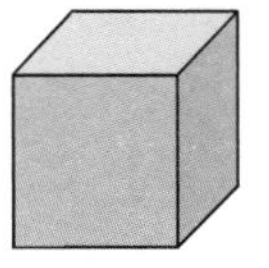 c  d 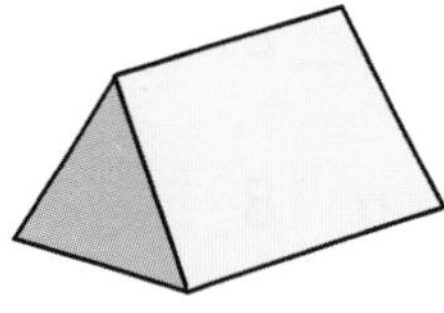

e  f 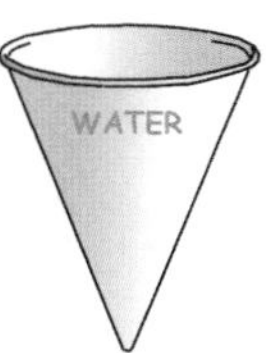

g 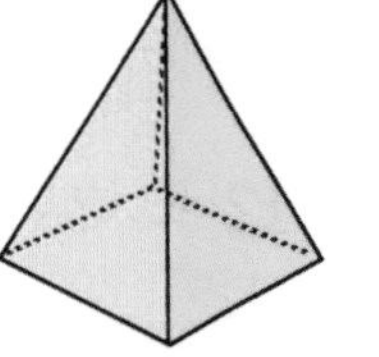

5. Some of the shapes in question 4 can be **rolled**. Which ones ?

6. How many faces has a :- a cuboid b triangular prism ?

7. How many corners has a :- a cube b square based pyramid ?

8. Here is a mixture of 2D and 3D shapes.

   Write down their names and say whether they are 2D or 3D.

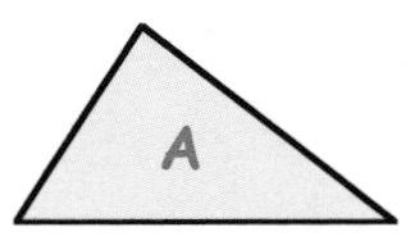

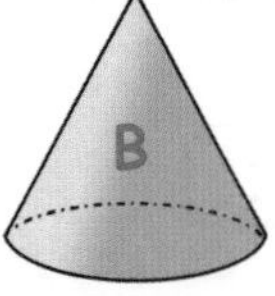

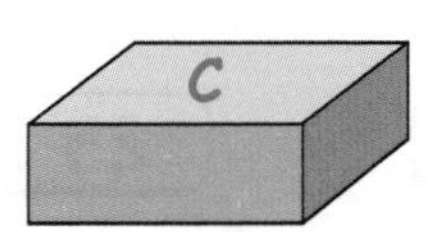

Revision of Algebra

1. What **number** does the ⬭ stand for in each of these equations :-

a 8 - ⬭ = 2	b 3 + ⬭ = 10	c 18 - ⬭ = 11
d 9 + ⬭ = 17	e 2 x ⬭ = 12	f 3 x ⬭ = 15
g ⬭ - 8 = 14	h ⬭ + 10 = 24	i ⬭ - 9 = 17
j ⬭ + 5 = 32	k ⬭ x 3 = 21	l ⬭ x 2 = 18
m 14 + ⬭ = 28	n ⬭ - 15 = 20	o ⬭ ÷ 2 = 7
p 33 ÷ 3 = ⬭	q ⬭ ÷ 3 = 9	r ⬭ ÷ 2 = 100.

2. **Copy** the following and put in a **+**, **–**, **x** or **÷** to make the equation true.

a 7 ... 6 = 1	b 4 ... 7 = 11	c 2 ... 7 = 14
d 27 ... 3 = 9	e 9 ... 18 = 27	f 23 ... 8 = 15
g 8 ... 2 = 16	h 7 ... 3 = 21	i 7 ... 7 = 1
j 20 ... 2 = 10	k 40 ... 13 = 53	l 40 ... 12 = 28
m 2 ... 12 = 24	n 30 ... 3 = 90	o 40 ... 2 = 20
p 60 ... 3 = 20	q 50 ... 19 = 69	r 60 ... 2 = 120.

3. Here are 10 calculations.

Match them into the correct **5 pairs** with an = sign between them.

8 x 3	**22 – 10**	**21 ÷ 3**	**18 ÷ 2**
27 ÷ 3	**18 – 11**	**15 + 9**	**26 + 24**
	6 x 2	**25 x 2**	

Algebra

Simple Equations with × and ÷

Solve simple equations involving multiplication & division.

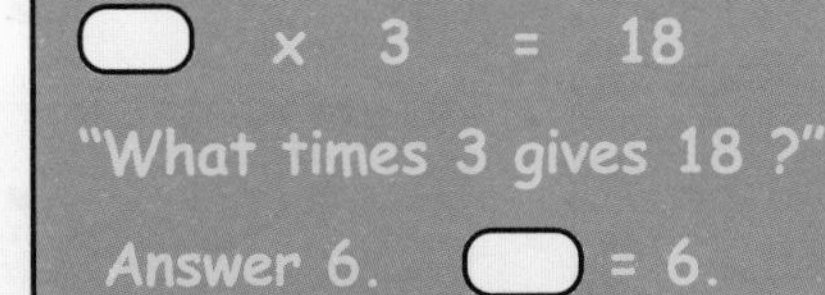

◯ × 3 = 18
"What times 3 gives 18 ?"
Answer 6. ◯ = 6.

▭ ÷ 4 = 7
"What divided by 4 gives 7 ?"
Answer 28. ▭ = 28.

Exercise 1

1. What **number** does ◯ stand for in each of these ?

a ◯ × 2 = 8	b ◯ × 3 = 21	c ◯ × 4 = 20
d ◯ × 5 = 40	e ◯ × 10 = 70	f ◯ × 2 = 16
g ◯ × 9 = 27	h ◯ × 8 = 72	i ◯ × 5 = 40
j ◯ ÷ 2 = 6	k ◯ ÷ 7 = 3	l ◯ ÷ 8 = 7
m ◯ ÷ 5 = 6	n ◯ ÷ 10 = 4	o ◯ ÷ 9 = 6.

2. Work out what **number** ▭ stands for in each of these :-

a 3 × ▭ = 6	b 5 × ▭ = 30	c 8 × ▭ = 48
d 16 ÷ ▭ = 4	e 7 ÷ ▭ = 1	f 45 ÷ ▭ = 5
g ▭ × 2 = 20	h ▭ × 10 = 100	i ▭ × 6 = 42
j ▭ ÷ 3 = 9	k ▭ ÷ 2 = 20	l ▭ ÷ 10 = 6
m 30 ÷ ▭ = 10	n 7 × ▭ = 35	o 56 ÷ ▭ = 8.

Which signs are missing ?

Be able to decide what symbol to use to make an expression correct

What mathematical sign has been covered up here ?

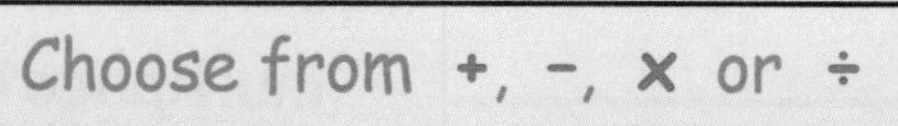

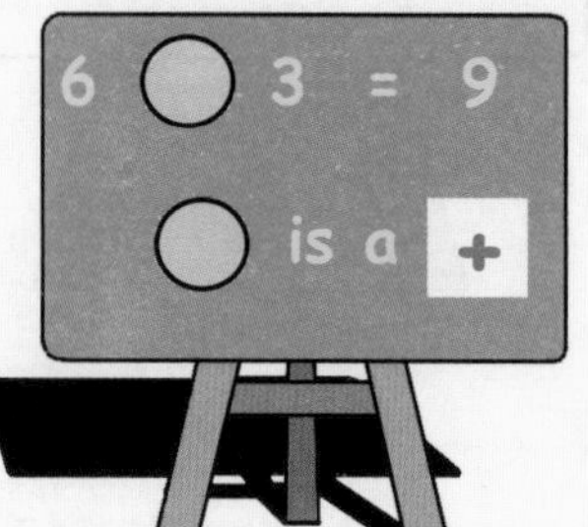

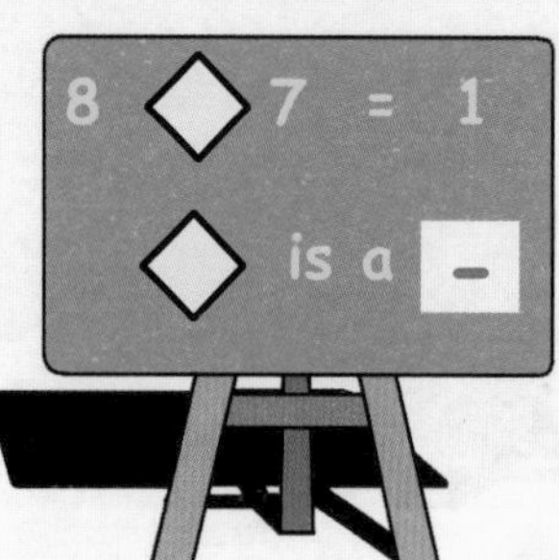

Exercise 2

1\. What **sign** does ○ stand for here ? Choose from +, −, x or ÷.

a 6 ○ 6 = 12	b 7 ○ 7 = 0	c 3 ○ 6 = 18
d 32 ○ 8 = 4	e 6 ○ 5 = 30	f 8 ○ 3 = 5
g 49 ○ 7 = 7	h 8 ○ 9 = 17	i 10 ○ 8 = 80
j 12 ○ 9 = 21	k 18 ○ 8 = 10	l 36 ○ 9 = 4
m 3 ○ 9 = 27	n 58 ○ 57 = 1	o 50 ○ 2 = 25.

2\. **Copy** the following and put in a +, −, x or ÷ to make the sum work.

a 6 ... 6 = 0	b 6 ... 5 = 11	c 4 ... 5 = 20
d 28 ... 4 = 7	e 40 ... 5 = 8	f 9 ... 10 = 19
g 6 ... 7 = 42	h 18 ... 11 = 7	i 8 ... 3 = 24
j 21 ... 9 = 12	k 7 ... 23 = 30	l 8 ... 8 = 64
m 50 ... 30 = 20	n 45 ... 9 = 5	o 9 ... 8 = 72.

Making up Equations with + or – *Extension*

Given a problem, make up an equation and find the answer.

Example 1

Amy bought **5** apples and was given some more by Ali.

Amy now has **8** apples.

How many did Ali give her ?

Make up an equation.

5 + ◯ = 8

◯ = **3**

Ali gave **3** apples.

Example 2

Make up an equation.

20 – ☆ = 5

☆ = **15**

Ball cost **15p**.

George had **20p**, but after buying a rubber ball he was left with **5p**.

What was the cost of the ball ?

Exercise 3

For each of the problems in this exercise, an **equation** has been given.

Use the **equation** to work out the answer.

1. **3** baby chicks hatched early in the morning.
   More hatched later on in the day.
   By evening, there were **10** new born chicks.
   How many chicks must have hatched later on ?

equation 3 + □ = 10

2. Billy's gran gave him **£2** pocket money.
   His dad also gave him money for being helpful.
   Billy then had a total of **£9**.
   How much must his dad have given him ?

equation 2 + △ = 9

3. Hazel lives **7** minutes away from the nursery.

Her friend Jenny takes a bit longer to get there.

Jenny takes **12** minutes.

How many minutes more does it take her ?

equation 7 + ◇ = 12

4. It takes Penny **11** minutes to cut the grass in spring

It takes her longer in summer.

It takes Penny **17** minutes to cut it in summer.

How much longer is that ?

equation 11 + ◇ = 17

5. Brian bought **12** orange cremes for his sister.

He ate some of them on the way home.

He ended up having only **4** left.

How many orange cremes did Brian eat ?

equation 12 – ....

6. A joiner was working on a **30 cm** piece of wood.

He sawed a piece off.

He was left with a piece **10 cm** long.

How long was the bit sawn off ?

equation 30 – ....

7. A vase had **14** tulips in it.

After a week some had rotted away.

This left only **5** in the vase.

How many tulips had rotted away ?

equation ....

8. 

A pet shop had some mice for sale.

After selling **8** mice, the owner of the shop still had **12** left.

How many did he have to begin with ?

equation ....

Recognise and understand other mathematical symbols

You have already come across the mathematical sign = (is equal to) many times. e.g. 5 + 3 = 8, 4 x 5 = 2 x 10.

Here are 3 more to be learned.

"**is NOT equal to**" can be shortened to the sign ≠.

"**is greater than**" can be shortened to the sign >.

"**is smaller than**" can be shortened to the sign <.

is smaller than is often written as "is less than"

Example 1

7 is greater than 3

7 > 3

Example 2

4 is smaller than 9

4 < 9

Example 3

1 + 7 is not equal to 9

1 + 7 ≠ 9

* *Note that the arrow > or < always points to the smaller number*

Example 4

3 x 9 ..... 4 x 6

3 x 9 > 4 x 6

(27) > (24)

Example 5

15 ÷ 3 ..... 35 ÷ 5

15 ÷ 3 < 35 ÷ 5

(5) < (7)

Exercise 4

1. **Copy** the following calculations and put the symbol = (equals) or ≠ (not equal to) between each calculation :-

a	6 + 4 ... 2 + 8	b	10 - 6 ... 14 - 11
c	5 x 6 ... 3 x 10	d	5 x 8 ... 2 x 20
e	20 ÷ 10 ... 18 ÷ 6	f	44 ÷ 4 ... 36 ÷ 3
g	2 x 4 x 5 ... 10 x 1 x 4	h	$\frac{1}{2}$ of 22 ..... $\frac{1}{3}$ of 27.

2. **Copy** each of the following and choose from these **words** to fill the space :-

is equal to	is smaller than	is greater than

a 4 ... 7

b 14 ... 12

c 108 ... 109

d 230 ... 219

e 2 x 9 ... 3 x 6

f 4 x 9 ... 5 x 7

g 24 ÷ 4 ... 48 ÷ 8

h 89 - 8 ... 98 - 9.

3. **Copy** and put in one **symbol** from ....

(= is equal to)	(< is smaller than)	(> is greater than)

to make these statements correct :-

a 45 ... 54

b 13 ... 12

c 8 x 7 ... 7 x 8

d 15 x 4 ... 14 x 5

e 80 ÷ 4 ... 60 ÷ 3

f 72 ÷ 8 ... 63 ÷ 9

g $\frac{1}{2}$ of 30 ..... 7 x 2

h $\frac{1}{4}$ of 28 ... 20 - 12.

4. Here are 10 calculations.

Match them up in pairs so that the symbol > is in ALL of your pairs.

23 - 4	12 + 10 + 4	5 x 9	8 + 9 - 5	99 ÷ 3
15 + 14	3 x 6	40 - 4	2 x 11	50 ÷ 2

Here is one pair to start you off :-

5 x 9 > 40 - 4

Number Machines

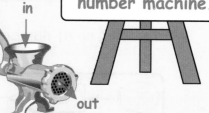

Be able to change one number into another using a number machine.

A **number machine** (or **function machine**) is the name for a mathematical rule which changes **one number** into **another**.

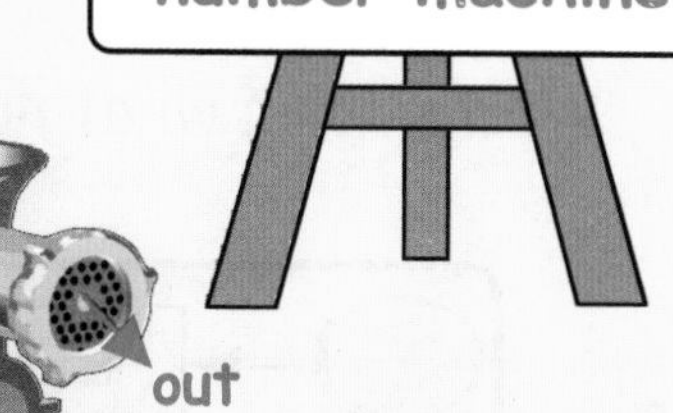

Example

The number machine shown below takes a number **IN** one side, **multiplies it by 4** and pushes it **OUT** the other side.

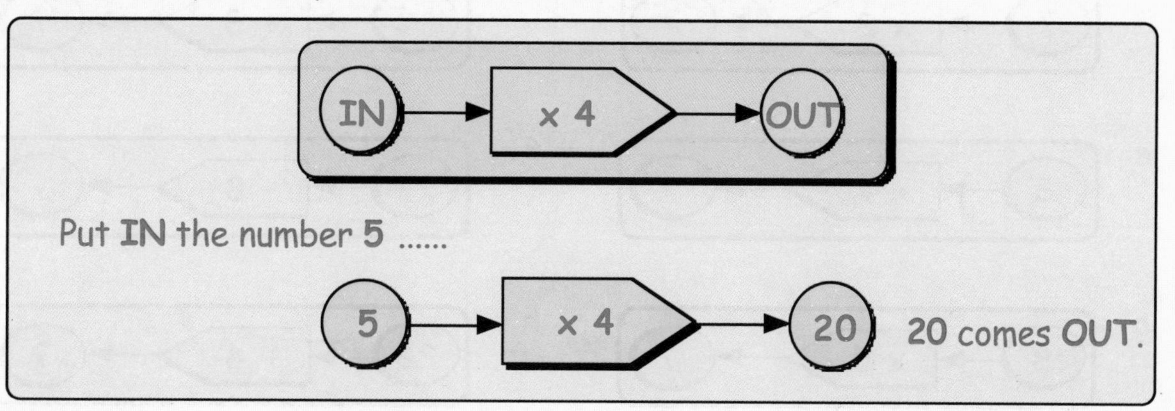

Exercise 5

1. Use the **x 4** number machine shown above to find :-

   a What comes **OUT** when you put in the number :-

   (i) 3 (ii) 8 (iii) 10 (iv) 25 ?

   b What number must have been put **IN** to get the answer :-

   (i) 16 (ii) 28 (iii) 44 (iv) 120 ?

2. Here is a new number machine :-

   a What comes **OUT** when you put in the number :-

   (i) 7 (ii) 13 (iii) 20 (iv) 25 ?

   b What number must have been put **IN** to get the answer :-

   (i) 2 (ii) 14 (iii) 29 (iv) 94 ?

3. Write down what number comes OUT of these number machines :-

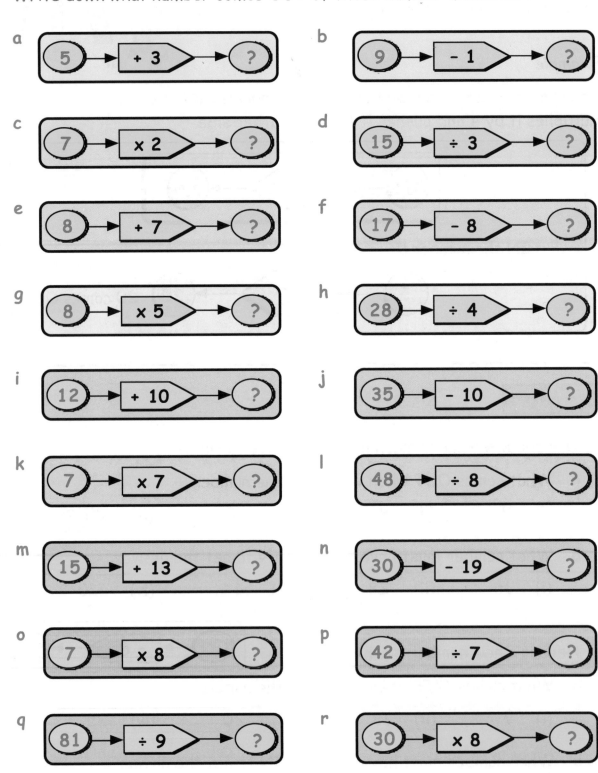

a 5 → + 3 → ?

b 9 → - 1 → ?

c 7 → x 2 → ?

d 15 → ÷ 3 → ?

e 8 → + 7 → ?

f 17 → - 8 → ?

g 8 → x 5 → ?

h 28 → ÷ 4 → ?

i 12 → + 10 → ?

j 35 → - 10 → ?

k 7 → x 7 → ?

l 48 → ÷ 8 → ?

m 15 → + 13 → ?

n 30 → - 19 → ?

o 7 → x 8 → ?

p 42 → ÷ 7 → ?

q 81 → ÷ 9 → ?

r 30 → x 8 → ?

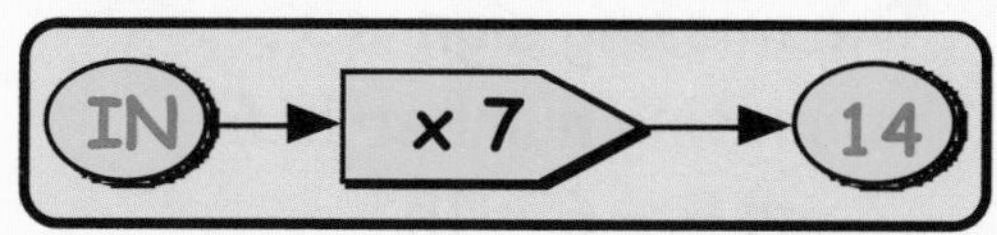

14 has come out .... 2 must have gone IN.

4. For these number machines, what number must have been put IN ?

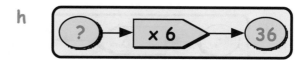

a 

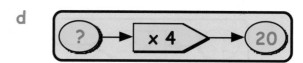

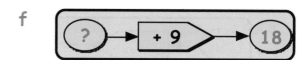

b ? → + 3 → 9

c 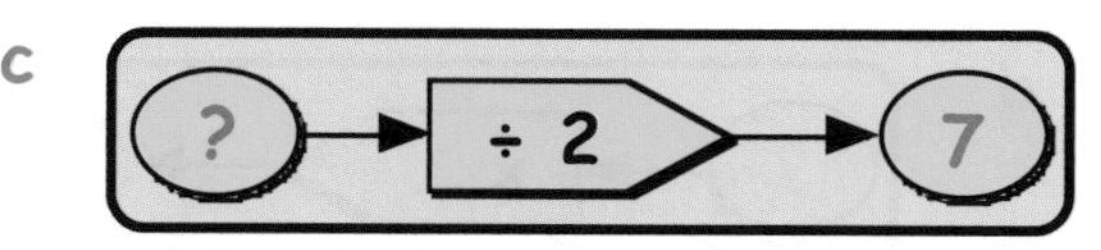

d ? → x 4 → 20

e 

f ? → + 9 → 18

g 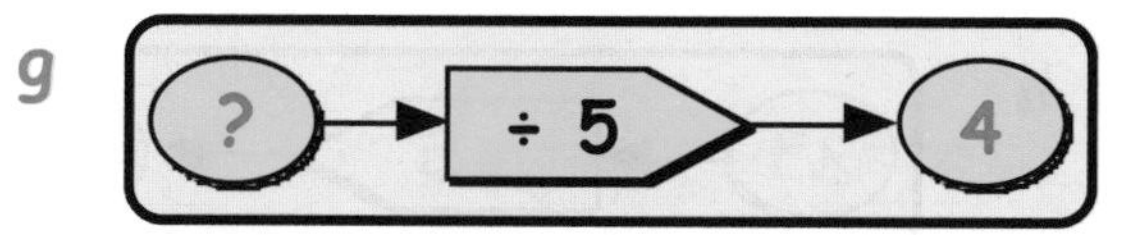

h ? → x 6 → 36

i 

j 

k 

l 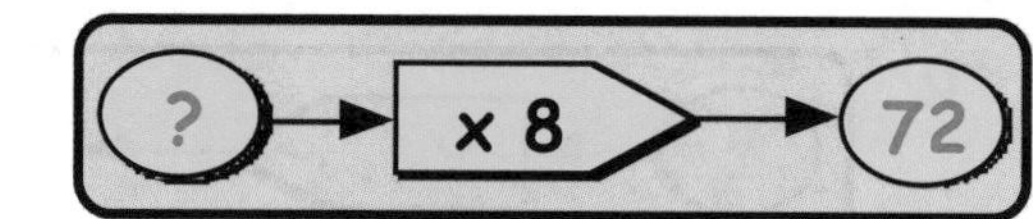

m 

n 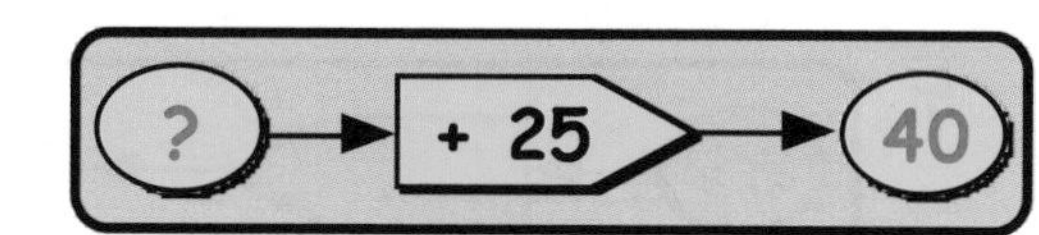

o 

p 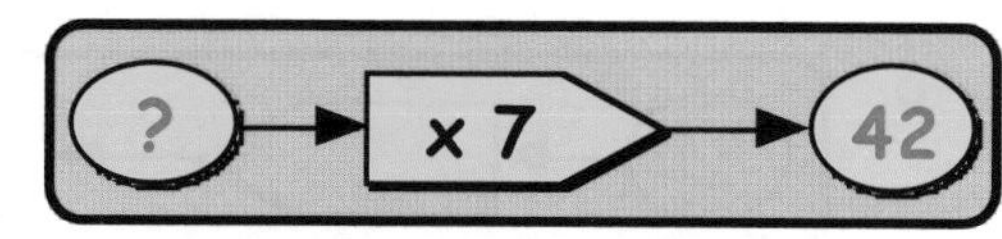

q ? → ÷ 9 → 7

r 

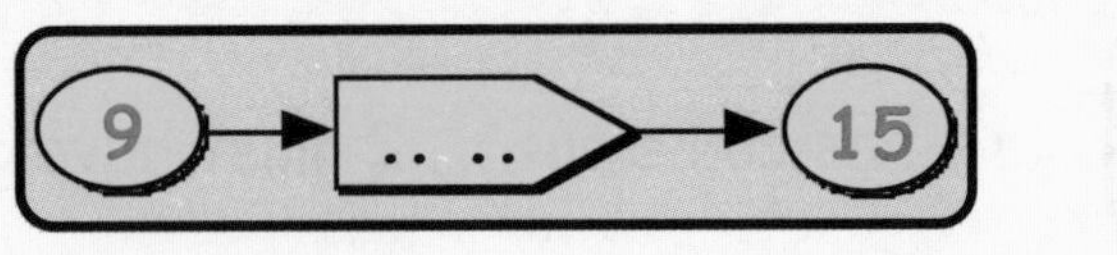

The missing **sign** is +,
the missing **number** is 6
as 9 + 6 = 15.

5. Write down the missing **sign** and **number** for each machine :-

a 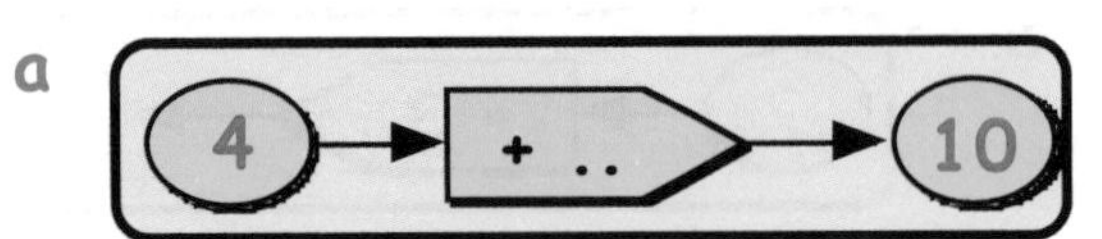

b 9 → − .. → 4

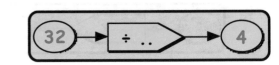

c 

d 3 → × .. → 27

e 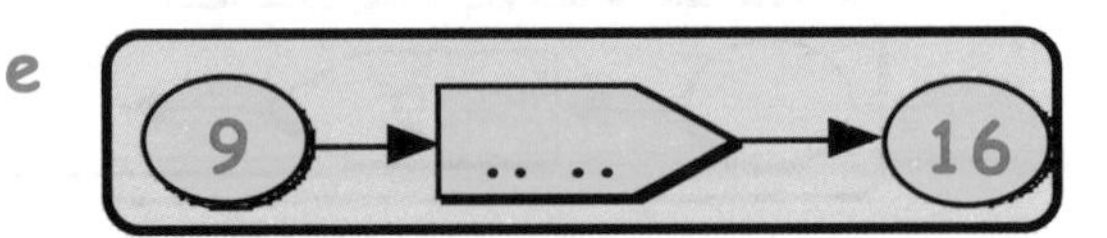

f 18 → .. .. → 12

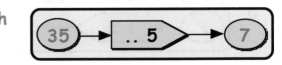

g 

h 35 → .. 5 → 7

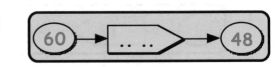

i 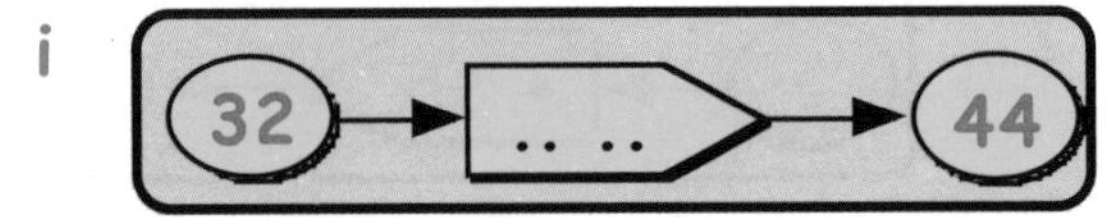

j 60 → .. .. → 48

k 

l 32 → ÷ .. → 4

m 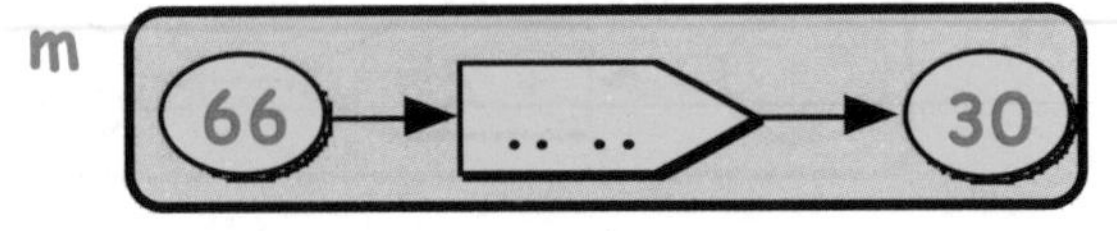

n 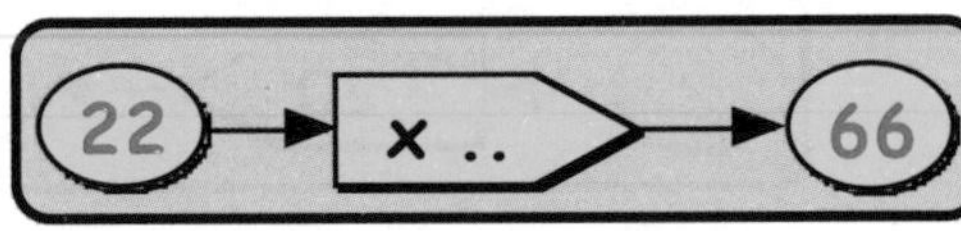

o 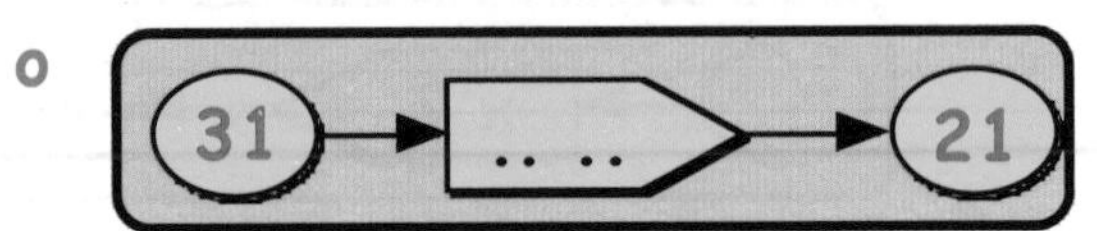

p 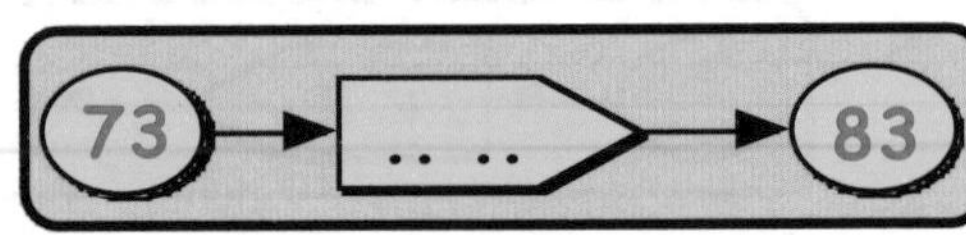

q 

r 

The 3 Я's

Revisit - Review - Revise

1. Put a +, −, x or ÷ in the circle to make the calculation correct.

a 14 ◯ 8 = 6 b 12 ◯ 9 = 21 c 56 ◯ 7 = 8

d 4 ◯ 9 = 36 e 60 ◯ 14 = 46 f 26 ◯ 5 = 130.

2. Here are 6 calculations.

Match them up in pairs, using the = sign.

7 x 3 = ...

7 x 3 | 40 ÷ 4 | 39 - 19 | 1 + 2 + 3 + 4 | 2 x 10 | 15 + 6

3. **Copy** each statement and fill in the space, choosing from the words :-

is equal to, is smaller than or is greater than to make it correct.

a 8 .... 12 b 32 .... 29 c 202 220

d 2 x 9 .... 3 x 6 e 54 ÷ 6 .... 72 ÷ 9 f 41 − 7 .... 44 − 9.

4. **Copy** each calculation and put the symbol = (equals) or ≠ (not equal to) into each of them to make them true :-

a 6 x 6 ..... 9 x 4 b 28 ÷ 7 ..... 30 ÷ 5 c $\frac{1}{2}$ of 22 ..... $\frac{1}{3}$ of 27.

5. There is something wrong with the balance on the scales. The banana seems to be the same weight as the feather.

Draw how you think the scales should really look.

6. **Copy** each statement and make it correct by choosing a **symbol** from :-

(= is equal to) (> is greater than) (< is less than)

a 24 ...... 42 b 18 ..... 17 c 6 x 7 ..... 7 x 6

d $\frac{1}{2}$ of 50 ..... 3 x 8 e 16 x 3 ..... 6 x 13 f $\frac{1}{4}$ of 32 ..... 37 − 29.

7. What number should come **OUT** of these number machines ?

a $7 \rightarrow + 9 \rightarrow$ OUT b $25 \rightarrow - 7 \rightarrow$ OUT

c $5 \rightarrow \times 9 \rightarrow$ OUT d $42 \rightarrow \div 6 \rightarrow$ OUT

e $57 \rightarrow - 8 \rightarrow$ OUT f $750 \rightarrow \div 10 \rightarrow$ OUT

8. What number must have gone **IN** to each of these number machines ?

a IN $\rightarrow - 4 \rightarrow 12$ b IN $\rightarrow + 18 \rightarrow 23$

c IN $\rightarrow \times 8 \rightarrow 56$ d IN $\rightarrow \div 3 \rightarrow 13$

9. Write the numbers that are missing from these number machines :-

a $11 \rightarrow - \dots \rightarrow 5$ b $19 \rightarrow + \dots \rightarrow 31$

c $45 \rightarrow \div \dots \rightarrow 9$ d $8 \rightarrow \times \dots \rightarrow 64$

10. Write down what number the letter X stands for in these equations :-

a $7 + X = 15$ b $14 - X = 11$ c $4 \times X = 28$

d $63 \div X = 9$ e $X - 10 = 15$ f $490 \div X = 49$.

11. **Copy** each of these equations and put in a number to make them work :-

a $6 \times \dots = 30$ b $31 - \dots = 23$ c $49 \div \dots = 7$

d $58 + \dots = 98$ e $\dots - 3 = 78$ f $\frac{1}{2}$ of $\dots = 25$

g $\dots - 5 = 195$ h $84 + \dots = 100$ i $\frac{1}{3}$ of $\dots = 30$.

Revision of Weight

1. a Which one is **heavier** ..... a calculator or a pencil sharpener ?

   b Which one is **lighter** ..... a rowing boat or a cruise ship ?

2. Put these in order. Start with the **lightest**.

horse **squirrel** **pigeon** **bison** **ladybird**

3. Which is **heavier** .....

   the red parcel or the blue parcel ?

4. Think of yourself being in a supermarket.

   Write down 3 items you could buy that are each :-

   a **lighter** than 1 kilogram

   b **heavier** than 1 kilogram.

5. Write down the weight on each of these scales :-

a

b

c

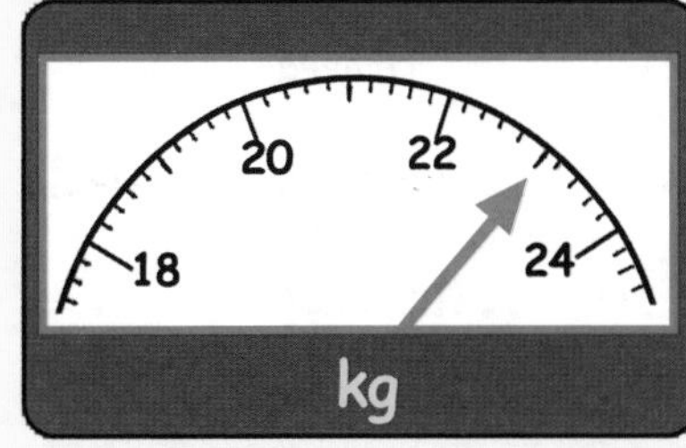

Calculators should NOT be used in this chapter

Weight and Volume

Kilograms and Grams

Be able to use kilograms and grams

Finding the **weight** of an object lets us know how heavy it is.

In Book 1a we compared heavy objects with light ones.

The weight of **heavier** items is measured in **kilograms** (kg).

The weight of **lighter** items is measured in **grams** (g).

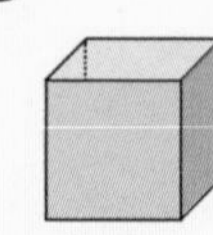

1 cm

A small hollow cube, 1 cm by 1 cm by 1 cm, when filled with water weighs 1 gram

A **kilogram** is made up of **1000 grams**.

Example 1

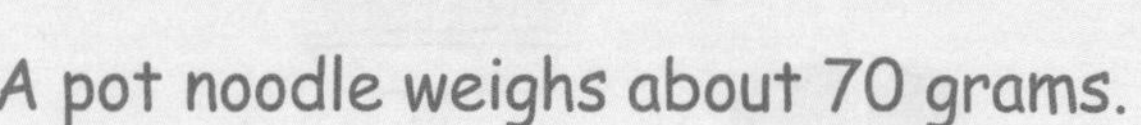

A sack of potatoes weighs about 12 kg.

A pot noodle weighs about 70 grams.

Example 2

a $\quad$ 2 kg = 2000 g $\qquad$ b $\quad 3\frac{1}{2}$ kg = 3500 g

c $\quad$ 1900 g + 100 g = 2000 g = 2 kg

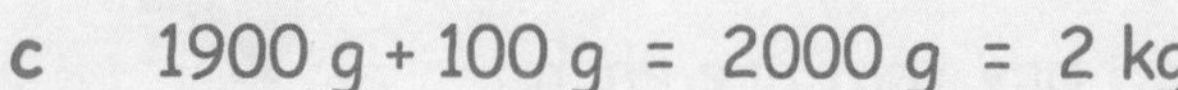

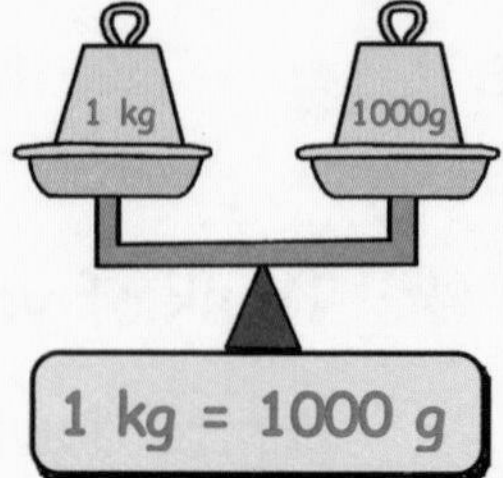

1 kg = 1000 g

Exercise 1

1. Put these items in order of weight, starting with the **lightest** :-

camera

iron

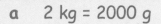

wafer biscuit

phone

2. State what unit these objects should be weighed in, **kilograms** or **grams** :-

a	computer	b	jar of coffee	c	dice
d	vacuum cleaner	e	bag of crisps	f	football top
g	caterpillar	h	sandwich	i	foot bath
j	boy	k	fruit scone	l	bag of cement.

A bag of sugar weights 1 **kilogram** or **1000 grams**.

If you use **half** the bag, you are left with a $\frac{1}{2}$ **kilogram** or **500 grams**.

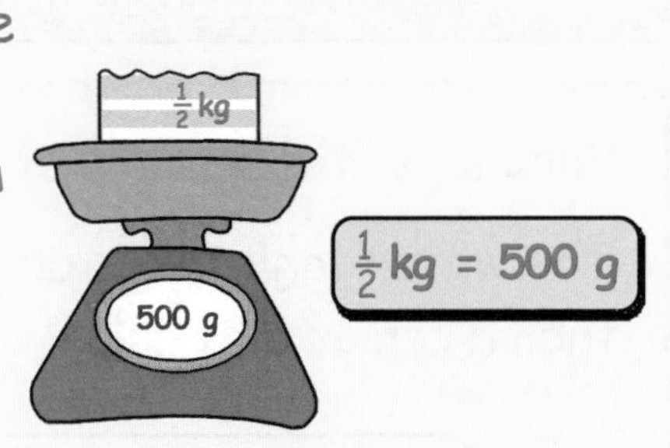

3. Change these kilograms to grams (remember 1 kg = 1000 g, $\frac{1}{2}$ kg = 500 g) :-

   a 3 kg b 5 kg c 9 kg d 10 kg

   e $4\frac{1}{2}$ kg f $6\frac{1}{2}$ kg g $8\frac{1}{2}$ kg h $12\frac{1}{2}$ kg.

4. These weights are given in grams. Change them into kilograms.

   a 2000 g b 4000 g c 7000 g d 6000 g

   e 1500 g f 5500 g g 8500 g h 9500 g.

5. Add or subtract these weights, giving your final answer in **kilograms**.

   a 1700 g + 300 g = ... g = ... kg b 2400 g + 600 g = ... g = ... kg

   c 4100 g – 100 g = ... g = ... kg d 6800 g – 300 g = ... g = ... kg.

6. Santa delivered 2 parcels - one for Pete and one for Ina.
   Pete's parcel weighed 2 kg 300 g and Ina's weighed 1 kg 700 g.
   What did the parcels weigh altogether (in kilograms) ?

7. Lesley bought 2 bottles of sauce, each weighing 750 g.
   What is their total weight :-

   a in grams b in kilograms ?

8. Harry bought 3 bags of potatoes, weighing 2 kg each.
   He used 500 grams to make baked potatoes.
   What weight (in grams) of potatoes did he have left ?

Volume - an Introduction

Be able to understand what "volume" is

Volume is "the amount of **space** an object takes up".

The water tank takes up more space than a can of diet cola.

=> The water tank has a **larger volume.**

The volume of a water tank or a can of cola is usually measured in **litres** or **millilitres**.

Exercise 2

1. Which of these objects holds **more** :-

   a a glass or a jug

   b a wheelie bin or a skip

   c an oil drum or a tin of beans

   d a wash hand basin or a bath

   e a chest freezer or a fridge

   f a holdall or a trunk ?

2. Which takes up **less** space -

   a crocodile or a lizard ?

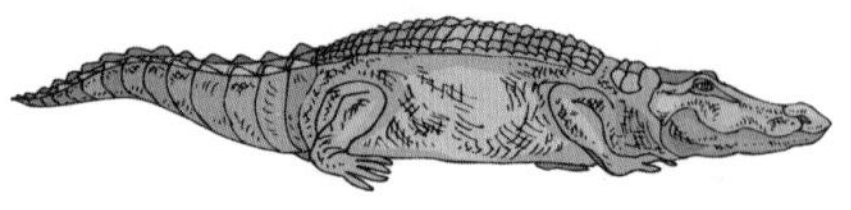

3. Put these animals in the correct order.

   Start with the one which you think takes up the **most** space.

cow

chick

elephant

hen

goat

4. What are the readings on the bottles (in litres) ?

a

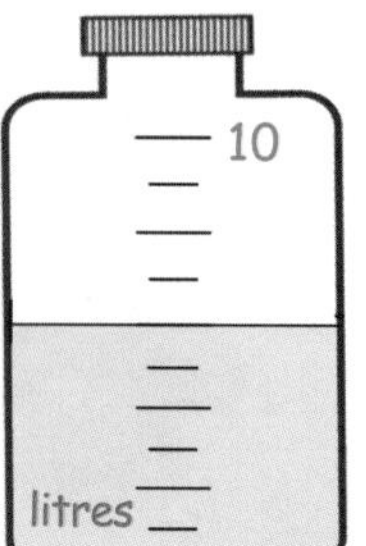

b

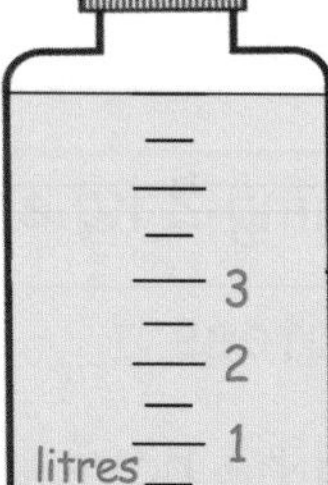

c

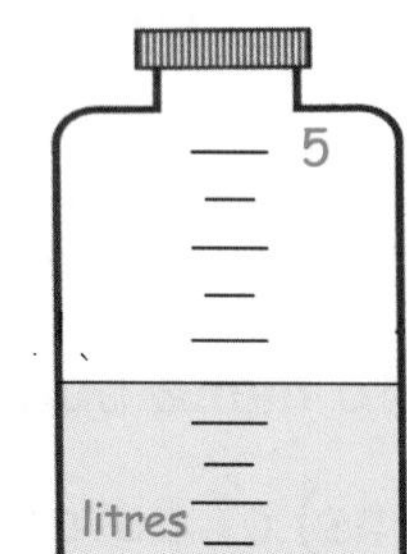

d

Litres and Millilitres

Be able to use litres and millilitres

Liquid volumes are usually measured in **litres** or **millilitres**.

The volume of **larger** containers are measured in **litres** (*L*).

The volume of **smaller** containers are measured in **millilitres** (*ml*).

A **litre** is made up of 1000 **millilitres**.

1 cm

A small hollow cube, 1 cm by 1 cm by 1 cm, when filled with water, holds 1 millilitre.

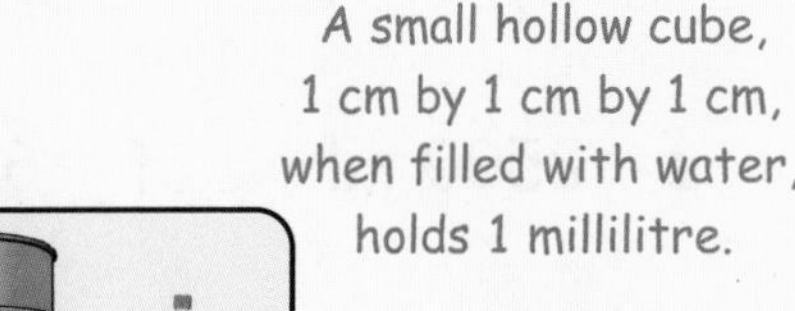

Example 1

This drum of oil holds 10 litres.

The small bottle of cola holds 250 millilitres.

OIL

10 litres

250 ml

Example 2

a 3 litres = 3000 ml b $4\frac{1}{2}$ litres = 4500 ml

c 2700 ml + 300 ml = 3000 ml = 3 litres

1 *L* = 1000 ml

Exercise 3

1. What unit of volume, **litres** or **millilitres**, should these be measured in :-

   a bath b tea spoon c basin

   d can of juice   e glass of wine f oil drum

   g washing machine h cough bottle i tin of paint

   j carton of milk k cup of tea l watering can ?

2. Change these litres to millilitres (remember 1 *L* = 1000 ml) :-

   a 2 *L* b 4 *L* c 7 *L* d 12 *L*.

3. The volumes below are given in millilitres. Change them into litres.

   a 3000 ml b 5000 ml c 9000 ml d 11000 ml.

This bottle holds **1 litre** or **1000 ml**.

If you use **half** the bottle, you are left with a $\frac{1}{2}$ **litre** or **500 ml**.

$\frac{1}{2}L$ = 500 ml

4. Change these volumes from litres to millilitres or millilitres back to litres.

a $3\frac{1}{2}$ *L* b $5\frac{1}{2}$ *L* c $9\frac{1}{2}$ *L* d $14\frac{1}{2}$ *L*.

e 2500 ml f 6500 ml g 8500 ml h 13500 ml.

5. Add or subtract these liquid volumes, giving your final answer in **litres**.

a 1500 ml + 500 ml = ... ml = ... *L* b 2800 ml + 200 ml = ... ml = ... *L*

c 5300 ml – 300 ml = ... ml = ... *L* d 4900 ml – 400 ml = ... ml = ... *L*

6. George has a sore tummy and has been given some medicine.

He has to take it as follows :-

one 5 ml spoonful, 3 times a day for 5 days.

How many ml of tummy medicine will George have taken by the end of the 5 days ?

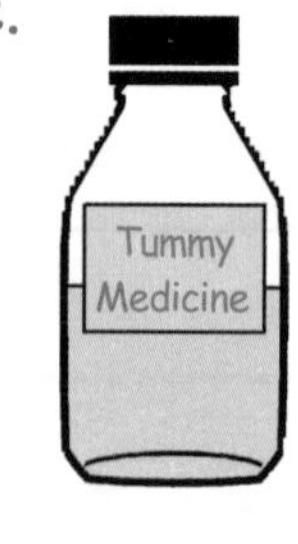

One 5 ml spoonful 3 times per day

7.

For her bad cough, Mabel has to take two 10 ml doses of cough mixture, 5 times per day.

a How many ml of medicine is that per day ?

b Her cough bottle contains 1 litre.

How many days will the bottle last ?

8. Jock has a 2 litre carton of apple juice.

He pours himself half a litre.

How many ml's are left in the carton ?

9. A glass for juice holds half a litre. How many glasses can be filled from :-

a a 1 litre bottle of lemonade b a 5 litre bottle of pineapple juice ?

Volumes by Counting Cubes

Be able to find the volume of a shape by counting cubes

One unit of volume used in measuring the volume of a **solid** shape such as a golf ball, is the **cubic centimetre**.

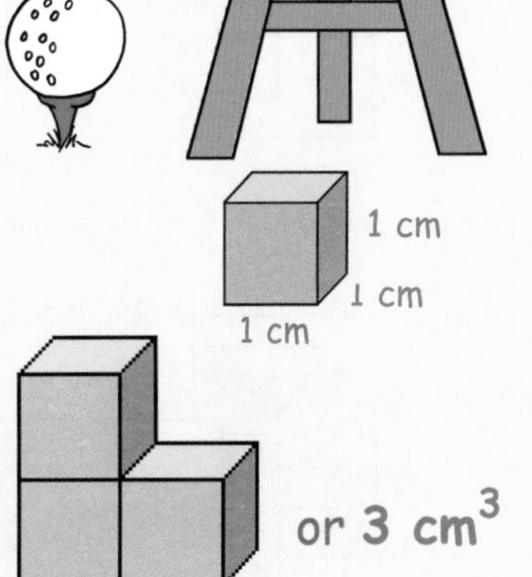

The small cube shown measures 1 cm by 1 cm by 1 cm.

It has a volume of 1 **cubic centimetre**.

This is written as **$1\ cm^3$**.

This solid has a volume of **3 cubic centimetres**. or **$3\ cm^3$**

Exercise 4

1. Count the number of **cubic centimetres** in each of these shapes :-

a 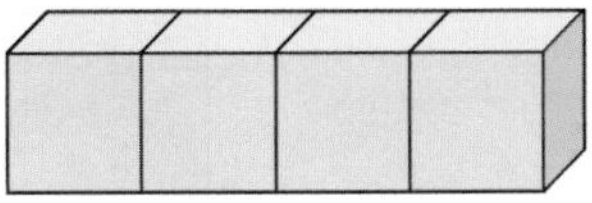 b 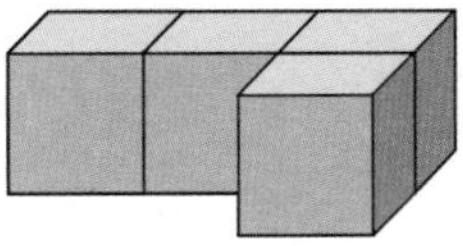 c

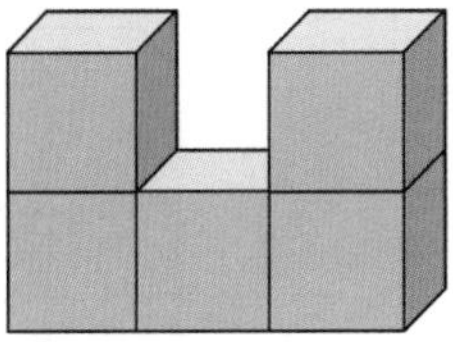

d 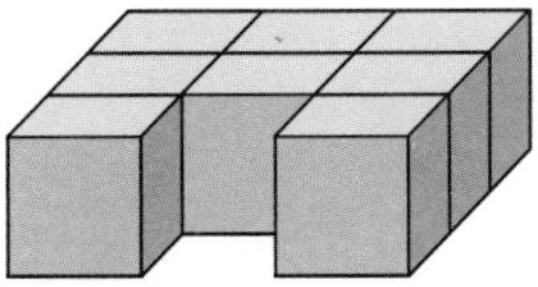 e 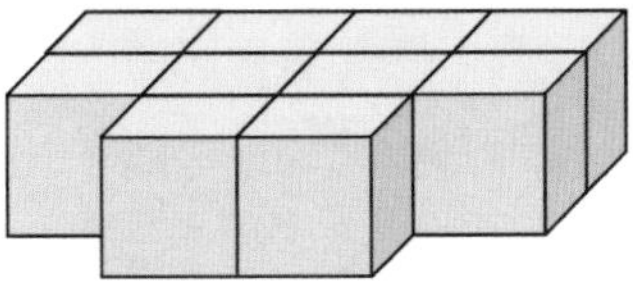 f

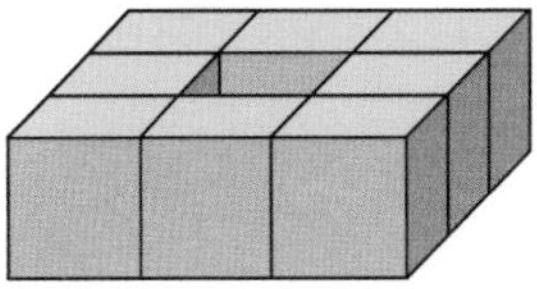

g 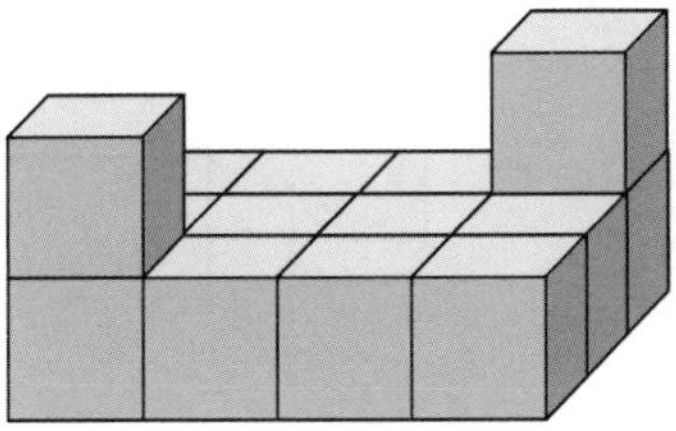 h 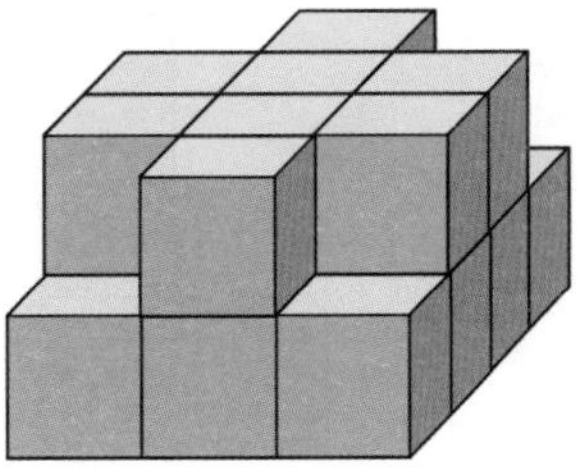 i

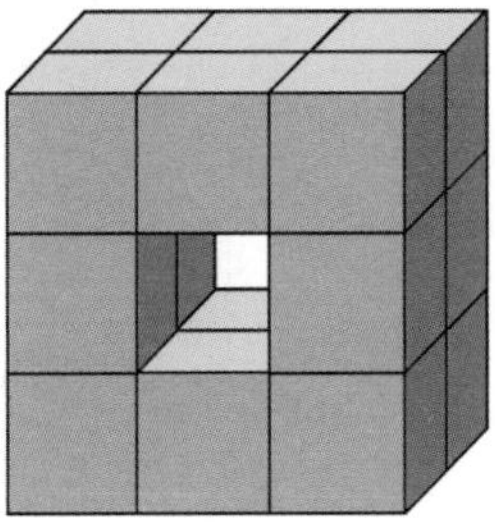

j 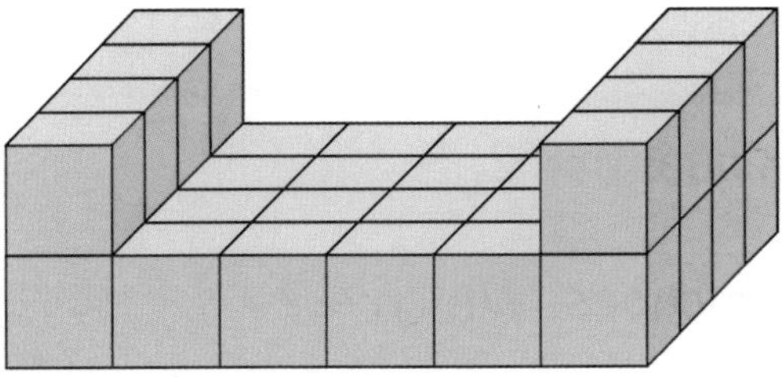 k 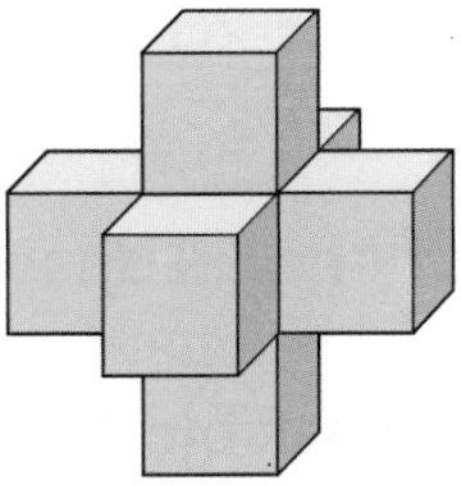 l

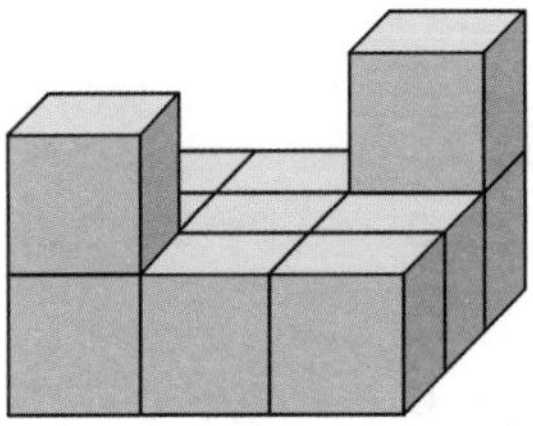

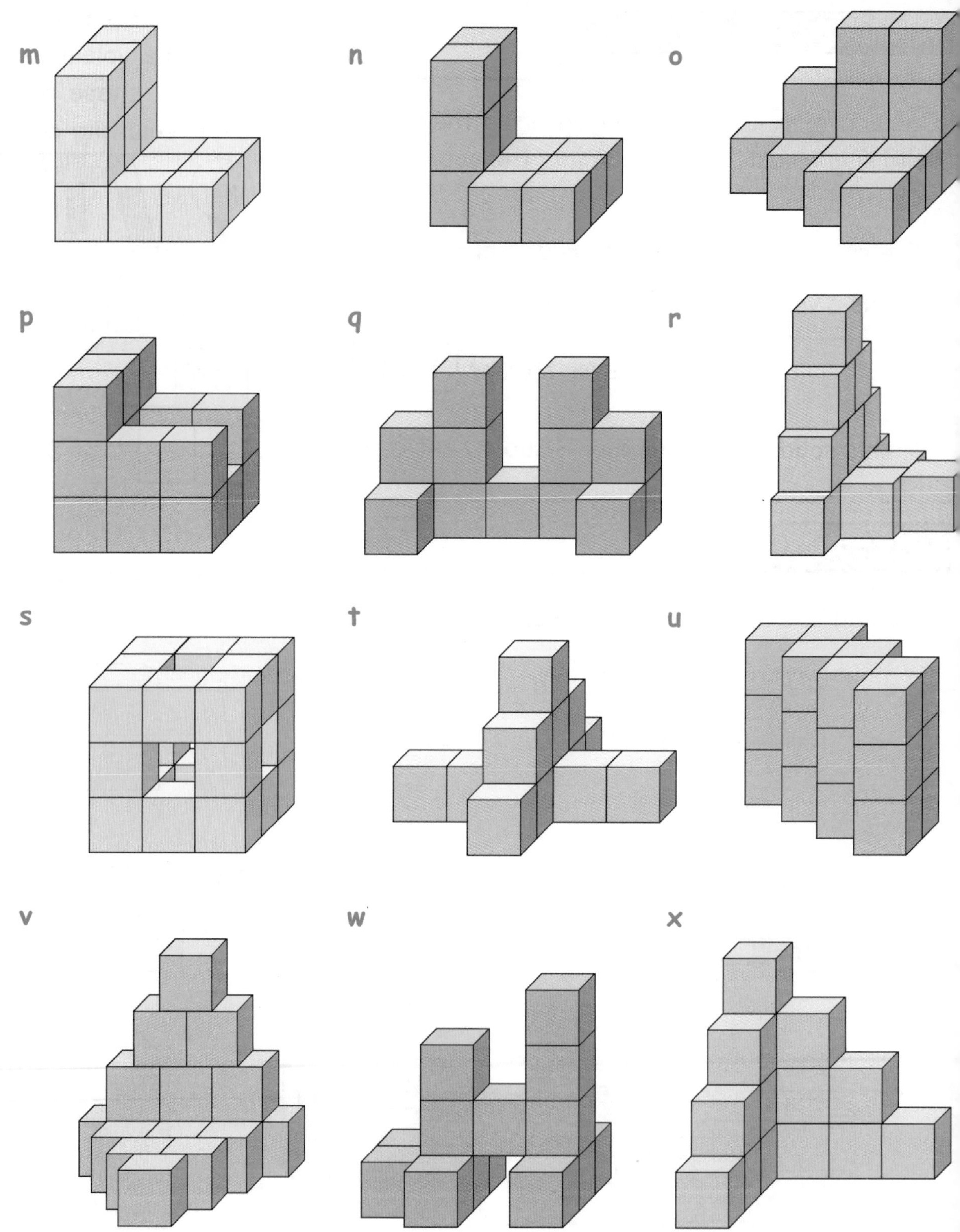

2. Ask your teacher for about 20 small wooden or plastic centimetre cubes. (Possibly work in pairs).

   a Try to build each of the 24 shapes from question 2.

   b **Four** of them are impossible to make with cubes. Which 4 ?

Revisit - Review - Revise

1. What instrument would you use to measure the length of :-

   a a caterpillar  b a leg of a pair of denims ? 

2. Measure and write down the length of this pencil, to the nearest cm.

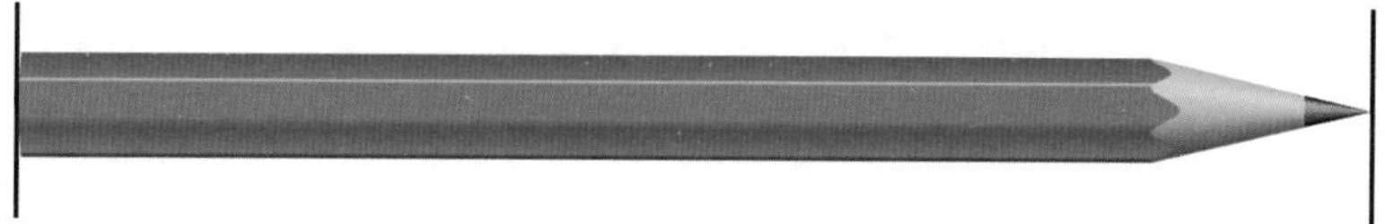

3. Would you use **millimetres**, **centimetres**, **metres** or **kilometres** to measure :-

   a the height of a bottle of brown sauce

   b the length of a corridor in the school building

   c the thickness of a bank card

   d the distance travelled on a holiday ?

4. Write down which one is **heavier** in each case :-

   a book or jotter b lion or hippo c lorry or car.

5. Which vegetable is **lighter** :-

   the carrot or the mushroom ?

6. Which of the 3 boxes is the **lightest** ?

7. What weight is shown on these scales ?

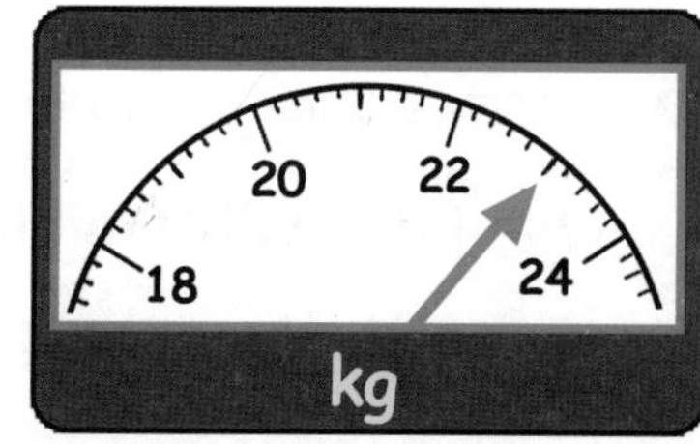

8. Write these objects in order with the **longest** first :-

steak knife, garden hose, mobile phone, sunbed.

9. 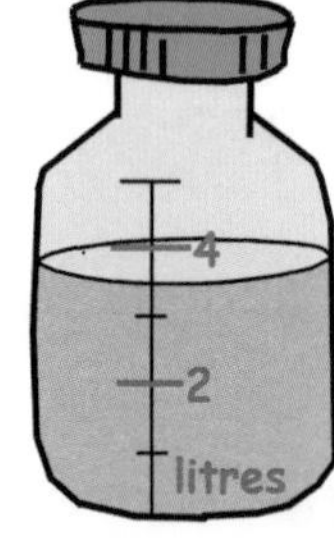

How many litres of blueberry juice are in this bottle ?

10. Jenny opened a $2\frac{1}{2}$ litre bottle of fizzy juice and poured it evenly into glasses which held $\frac{1}{2}$ a litre.

How many glasses did she fill ?

11. 

How many cubes were used to make this shape ?

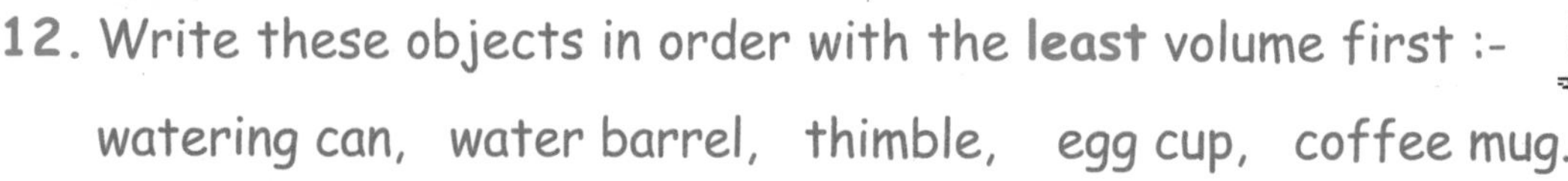

12. Write these objects in order with the **least** volume first :-

watering can, water barrel, thimble, egg cup, coffee mug.

13. Would you use **kilograms** or **grams** to measure the weight of :-

a an apple 

b a lawnmower ?

14. Would you use **millilitres** or **litres** to measure the volume of liquid in :-

a a salt dish 

b a paddling pool ?

15. Kerry bought two cartons of apple juice.

One held **1300 millilitres**, the other had **700 millilitres**.

What was the **total** volume of the two cartons in **litres** ?

Revision of Statistics

1. A group of cooks was asked what kind of soup they preferred. Their answers are shown in the bar graph.

   a Is the scale going up in 1's, 2's, 3's or 4's ?

   b How many cooks said Tomato ?

   d What is the **total** for Lentil and Leek ?

   e How many **more** preferred Pea and Ham to Tomato ?

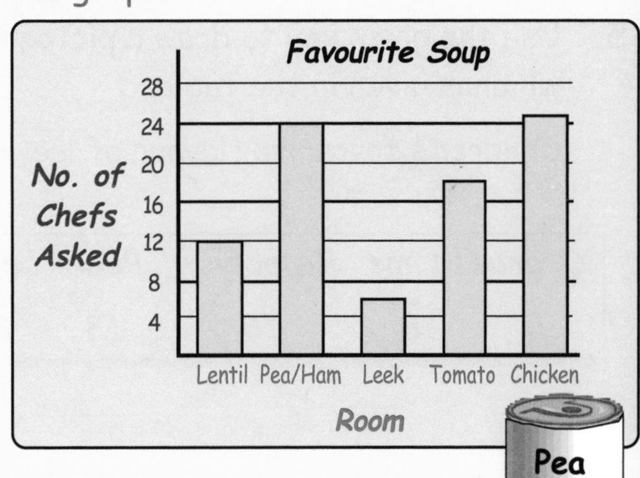

2. Mr Rice fancies one of these hotels for a few days holiday.

   a How much would it cost to stay at the Shore Hotel for 2 nights ?

   b How much dearer would it be to stay for 4 nights in the Park Hotel rather than in the Bay Hotel ?

   c How many nights stay would you get in the Shore Hotel for the same price as 2 nights in the Park Hotel ?

	1 night	2 nights	3 nights	4 nights
Bay Hotel	£40	£70	£85	£100
Shore Hotel	£50	£90	£120	£150
Park Hotel	£100	£150	£200	£250

3. The pictograph shows how many animals Farmer Baines has on his small farm.

   a How many cows ?

   b How many hens ?

   c How many more sheep than pigs ?

   d How many bulls ?

Pigs	
Cows	
Sheep	
Hens	
Bulls	

Key: stands for 4 farm animals.

4. 𝍸 represents the number **5**. Use tally marks to show :-

a 7 b 14 c 23 d 31.

5. Use the given **key** to draw a **pictograph** showing the information which is given in the table.

Children's favourite flavour of ice-lolly.

Orange	*Lime*	*Raspberry*	*Pear*	*Lemon*
5	*8*	*10*	*13*	*20*

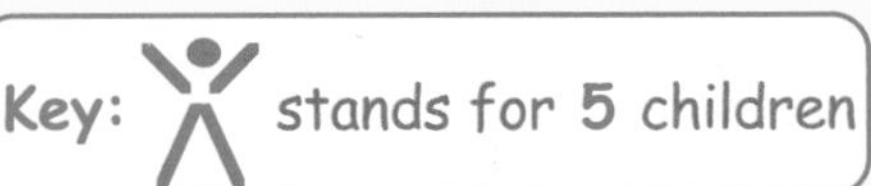

6. Some beauticians in Boon's the Chemist were asked to name the best dandruff shampoo.

Their answers are in the table.

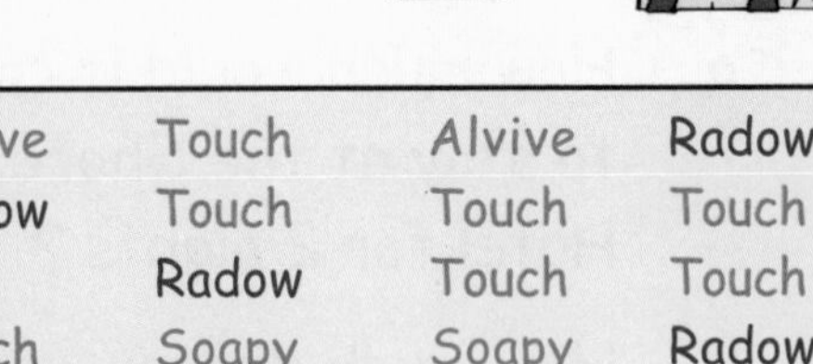

Alvive	Touch	Alvive	Radow
Radow	Touch	Touch	Touch
E62	Radow	Touch	Touch
Touch	Soapy	Soapy	Radow
Soapy	Soapy	Radow	Alvive
Touch	Touch	Soapy	Soapy

a Copy and complete the **tally table** to show these results.

Shampoo	Tally	Total
Alvive		
Radow		
E62		
Touch		
Soapy		

b How many beauticians gave the answer E62 ?

c What was the **most** popular answer ?

d How many beauticians were asked ?

e How many more votes did Soapy get compared to Alvive ?

f Draw a **bar chart** from the table. (remember the scale; title; headings; labels and bars)

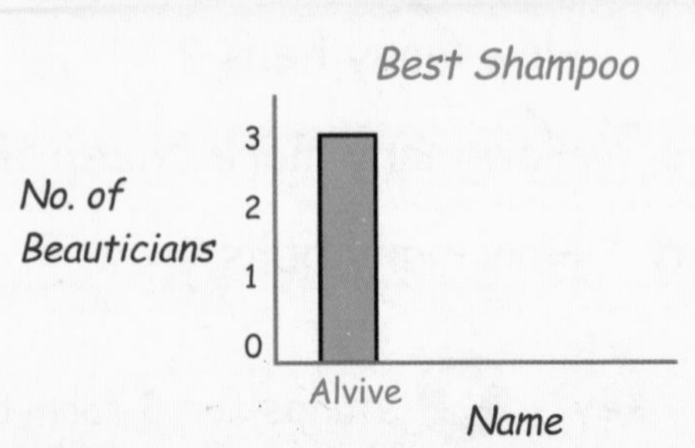

Statistics

Be able to carry out a simple survey and display results

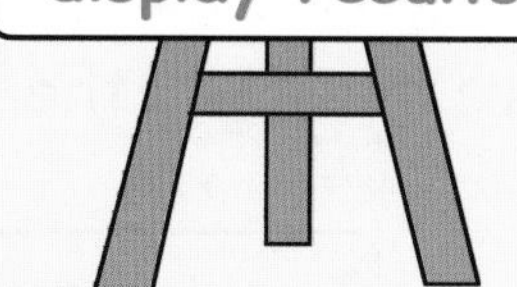

Carrying out a Survey

A survey is when you collect information about something, study the results of that information and display it.

There are various ways of collecting information. (*Discuss*).

When carrying out a survey you need to consider several points :-

- the type of questions you will ask.
- what the questionnaire will look like.
- who you will ask.
- how will you collect and organise your results.
- how will you display your results. and explain them.

You may wish to use a **tally table, pictograph, bar graph** or **line graph**.

Exercise 1

1. Choose **one** from the list below and carry out a survey.

   a The shoe sizes in your class.

   b Which month of the year were the members of your class born ?

   c Favourite class cartoon character.

   d Favourite international football team.

   e Favourite pop star.

   f Most popular breakfast.

   g How do you get to school ?

   h Number of words each member of your class can write in 30 seconds.

   i Heights of each pupil in your class.

2. Choose **another** from the list or do your own survey. Ask your teacher first.

   Make sure that this survey is different from your first.

   You could work in groups – Display your graphs and charts.

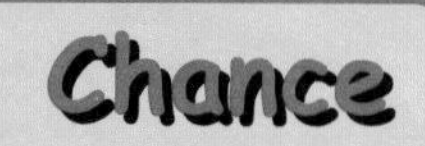

Calculators should NOT be used in this chapter.

Likely or Unlikely ?

Be able to find the likelihood of an event happening.

When we talk about the **Chance** of something happening, we mean whether it is **likely** or **unlikely** to happen.

It may be **certain**, **impossible** or somewhere **in between.**

This line is called a **Chance Line** :-

For example, we know that it is **likely** to snow sometime in December.

1. Use one of these words to say how likely it is for each of these to happen :-

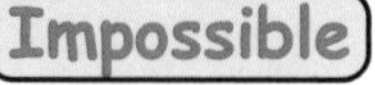

Not Likely **Even Chance** **Likely** **Certain**

a You will eat something today.

b You will go to bed before 7 o'clock on a Saturday night.

c You will ski to school tomorrow.

d You will go into a shop this week.

e You will run a mile on Sunday morning.

f You pick a card from a pack - it will be black.

g The roofs will get wet if it rains.

h You will eat sweets and your weight will not rise.

i You will have a birthday this year.

j You will find a slice of pear in an apple crumble.

k You pick a jelly bean from this jar - it will be red.

l The person checking your ticket on a train will be male.

2. Which label best fits each of these events ?

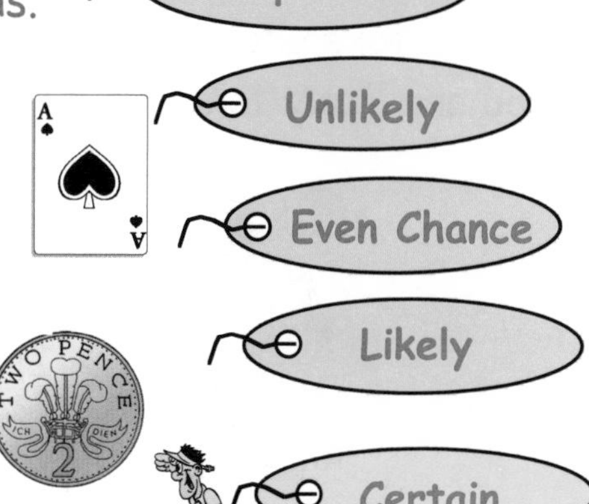

a Picking the ace of spades from a pack of cards.

b Getting an even number when you roll a dice.

c <u>You</u> will drive to school.

d It will not rain at all in January.

e If you drop a coin on the floor, it will land tails up.

f A domino will have at least one dot on it.

g You can play good golf in the dark with no light.

3. a Imagine you had a circular piece of card with a small pencil stuck through its middle to make a spinner.

Draw the circle in your jotter and use red and blue to colour it so that there is an **equal chance** that it will land on red or blue.

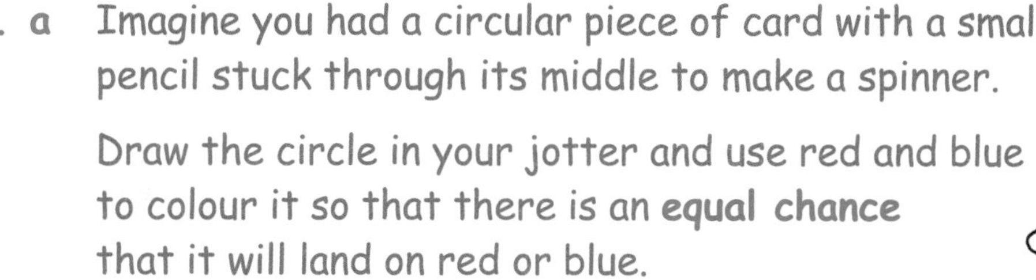

b Now draw and colour a circle that does **not** give an even chance.

4. a Write down 3 events that you think are **likely** to happen.

b Write down 3 events that you think are **unlikely** to happen.

Some events have an **equal chance** of happening and others do **not**.

5. Which of these gives an **evens chance** ? Answer **yes** or **no**.

a When tossing a coin you get heads or tails.

b When chosing a card from a pack, it will be a spade.

c When a baby was born, it arrived at the weekend.

6. Jenny has **10** chews.

Some of them are **blue** and the rest are orange.

When she puts them in a bag there is an **equal chance** of picking out a **blue** or an orange chew.

How many orange chews does she have ?

More Likely or Less Likely ?

Be able to predict how likely an event will happen.

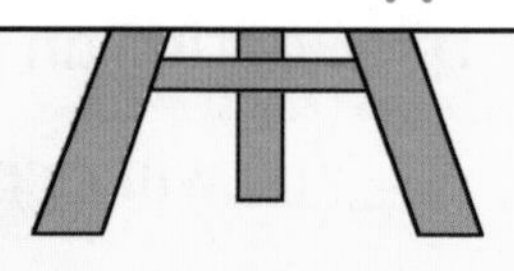

If you take enough shots with a ball at goal you are **likely** to score a goal at some point.

If you cover yourself with sun cream on a hot day you are **less likely** to get sunburned.

Exercise 2

1. Billy has 3 toffee apples in a bag. 2 of them are green and one is red. He cannot see them as he takes them out of the bag.

   Which colour of apple is he **more likely** to choose when he takes the first one from the bag ?

2. 

   Joan has 2 lemon T-shirts and 6 pink T-shirts in her drawer.

   If she takes one without looking to see the colour, which colour is she **more likely** to take ?

3. Trev has 9 pairs of socks in his drawer. 2 pairs are red and 7 pairs are white.

   Which colour is he **less likely** to choose ?

4. There are 11 coloured pencils in a packet. 7 of them are blunt or broken.

   If Toni choses one pencil, is it **more likely** or **less likely** to be a sharp one ?

5. John and Lesley have been asked to arrange 50 chairs in a hall for assembly. 40 of the chairs are blue. The rest are red.

   Is it **more likely** or **less likely** they will move a red chair first ?

6. You **win** if you can pick the red ball from this bag without looking.

a How many ways of winning are there ?

b How many ways of losing are there ?

c Which is more **likely**, winning or losing ?

7. Which of these three bags offers the best chance of **winning** ? (Choosing a red ball).

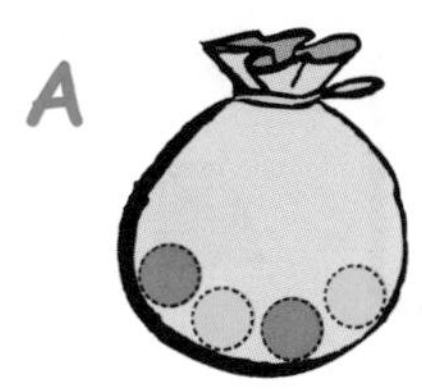

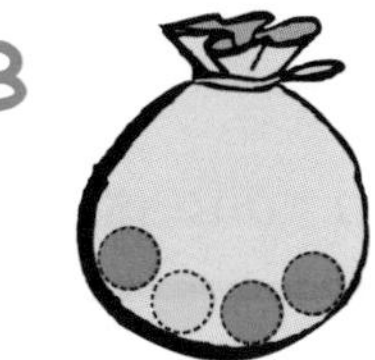

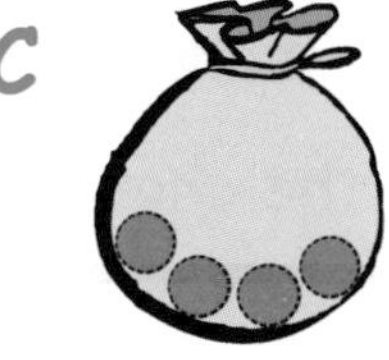

8. 100 raffle tickets are sold at a school show.

PRIZES

1st Prize - dinner for two

10 runner up prizes of cinema tickets for two

The board shows all the prizes to be won.
Alistair buys 1 ticket.

Is he **more likely** or **less likely** to be a prize winner ?

9. Jed, Bob and Mary are playing with this spinner.

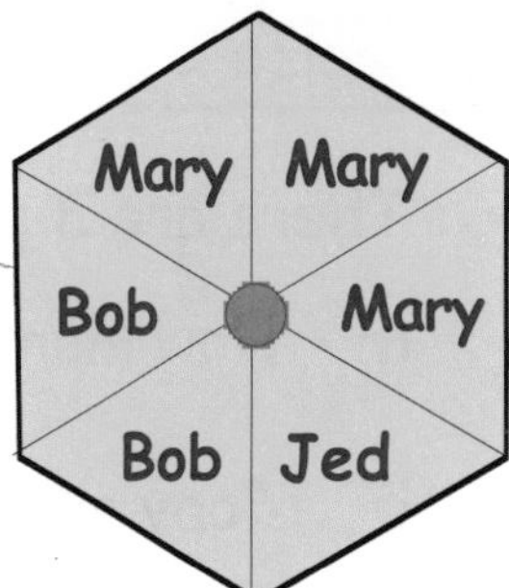

a Who gets the best deal from the spinner ?

b What would you change to make the spinner fairer ?

10. Answer :- **certain**, **likely**, **even chance**, **unlikely** or **no chance**.

When a dice is rolled, what is the chance that :-

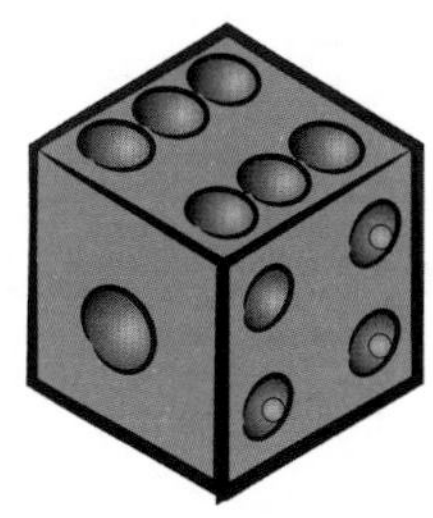

a the number 2 comes up

b 1, 2 or 3 comes up

c a number less than 6 comes up

d the number 7 comes up ?

11. 1 2 3 2 4 2

5 8 2 2

Both of these sets of number cards offer the **same chance** of picking the number **2** at random.

Explain why ?

Calculating Chance

Be able to work out the chance of an event happening.

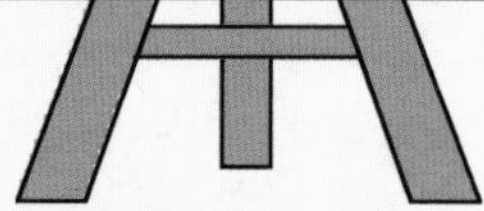

Example

There are 2 rollos and 5 strawberry chunks in a bag.

What is the chance that, with your eyes closed, you will choose a rollo ?

How many rollos ? **2**

How many sweets altogether ? **(2 + 5) = 7**

So the chance of choosing a rollo is :- **2 out of 7**.

We look at the number of items we **want** and compare it to the **total number** of items.

* Notice that the **chance** of choosing a strawberry chunk is **5 out of 7**.

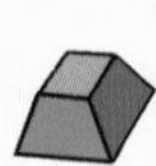

Exercise 3

1. There are 3 pink marbles and 1 blue marble in a jar.

   a How many marbles are in the jar ?

   b **Copy** and **complete** the sentence :-

   "The **chance** of me picking the blue marble out first is .... out of **4** ".

   c **Copy** and **complete** the sentence :-

   "The chance of me picking a pink marble out first is .... out of .... ".

2. There are 7 gold fish and 1 silver fish in a bowl.

   a How many fish are there in the bowl ?

   b **Copy** and **complete** the sentence :-

   "The chance of the silver fish being the fastest is .... out of .... ".

   c **Copy** and **complete** the sentence :-

   "The chance of a gold fish being the fastest is .... out of .... ".

3. Bill tosses a £2 coin in the air.

   a How many different ways can the coin land ?

   b What is the chance that it will land **heads** up ? (........ out of ....)

   c What is the chance that it will land **tails** up ? (........ out of ....)

4. 

   There are 5 choc ice lollies and 3 orange ice lollies in a mobile freezer.

   a How many ice lollies are in the freezer ?

   b When Frank reaches in to pick one out, what is the **chance** that it will be a choc ice ?

   c What is the **chance** it will be orange ?

5. There are 8 cars and 2 buses parked outside a theatre.

   a How many vehicles are parked ?

   b What is the **chance** that the first one to leave will be a bus ?

   c What is the **chance** that the first one to leave will be a car ?

   d What is the **chance** that the first one to leave will be a **yellow** car ?

6. 

   In a group of boys, 4 are right handed and 1 is left handed.

   a What is the **chance** of you correctly guessing which boy is left handed ?

   b What is the **chance** of you correctly guessing which boy is right handed ?

7. Benny has 20 oranges and 10 apples stacked on a shelf.

   a If they fall off the shelf, what is the **chance** that the first one to land on the ground will be an orange ?

   b What is the **chance** that it will be an apple ?

8. a When a dice is rolled, what is the **chance** that it will stop, showing a 6 on top ?

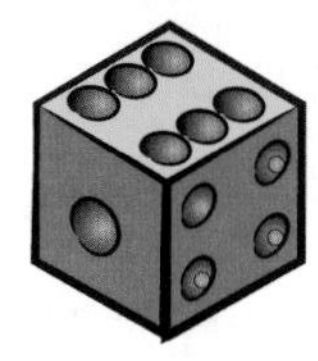

b What is the **chance** a 1, 2 or 3 will show at the top ?

9. George has **4** lettuces, **2** cabbages and **1** cauliflower left in his garden.

He spots a caterpillar crawling towards them !

a How many vegetables **altogether** does George have ?

b What is the **chance** that the caterpillar will head first for the cauliflower ?

c What is the **chance** that the caterpillar will head first for a cabbage ?

d What is the **chance** it will head towards the lettuce first ?

10. 

Cup cakes are kept on a shelf, high up in a baker's shop.

There are **3** with blue icing, **4** with pink and **5** with white icing.

a How many cup cakes does the shop have ?

b When a shop assistant reaches up, what is the **chance** that she will bring down a white cup cake ?

c What is the **chance** it will have blue icing ?

d What is the **chance** it will **not** have white icing ?

11. There are **20** light aircraft, **30** Thistle Airways planes and **50** Ryanjet planes heading for Glasgow Airport.

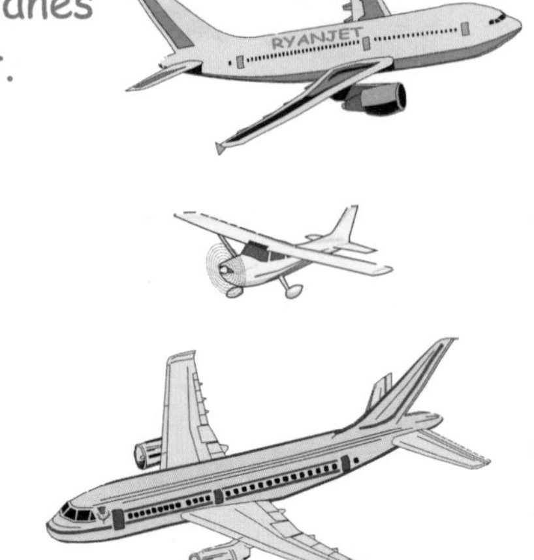

a What is the **chance** that the first plane to land will be a light aircraft ?

b What is the **chance** the first one to land will be a Ryanjet plane ?

c What is the **chance** the first plane down **not** be a Thistle Airways plane ?

Revisit - Review - Revise

Use the **probability line** shown below to answer question 1.

Example That I will see plants in a garden centre this summer is **certain**.

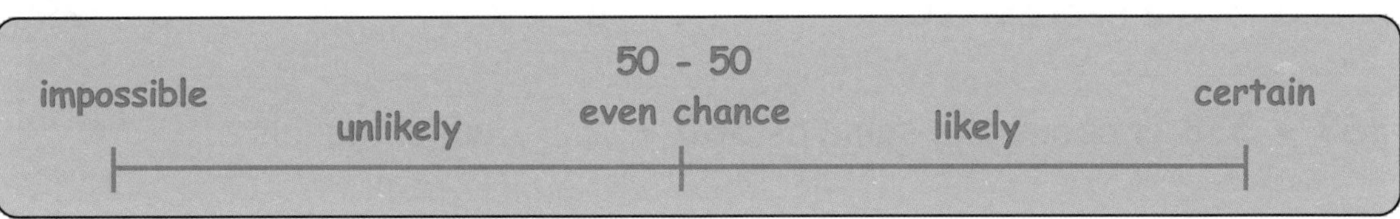

1. a I will drive a car when I am older.

   b I am nine years old today. This time last year, I was eight.

   c It will be cold in Iceland in winter.

   d Toss a coin and it will land tails up.

   e Choose a card from a pack of cards and get a green king of hearts.

   f East Stirling will win the football world cup.

   g It will be hot in the desert during the day.

   h There's 1 red apple and 1 green one in a bag. I will pick the red one.

   i When I go swimming, I will take a towel with me.

   j I will draw a square and it will have 5 sides.

   k There are 4 bananas and 1 orange in a bag. I will pick the orange.

   l When I roll a dice, it will show a 1, 2 or a 3.

   m There will be a news programme at some point on TV today.

2. Harry's bag has **1 blue**, **8 red** and **3 green** chewies.

   a What is the chance of Harry picking at random, a **blue** chewie ?

   b What is the chance of him picking at random, a **red** chewie ?

   c What is the chance of him picking at random, a **green** chewie ?

   d What is the chance of him picking at random, a **purple** chewie ?

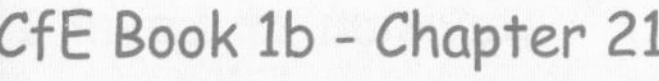

Revision of Level 1

Revise ALL the work covered in CfE Level 1

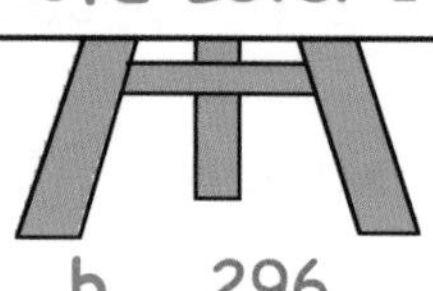

Do **NOT** use a calculator except where you see the this sign.

1. **Round to the nearest 10** :- a 74 b 296.

2. **363 + 538** is about the same as **360 +** .... , which equals ....

3. Write the number **six thousand and forty** using **digits**.

4. Write the number 9106 in **words**.

5. Write the number that comes :-

   a just **before** 850 b just **after** 509.

6. Find the following :-

   a $\begin{array}{r} 380 \\ +\ 60 \\ \hline \end{array}$ b 35 + 57 c $\begin{array}{r} 91 \\ -\ 8 \\ \hline \end{array}$ d 620 - 270

7. Tadsco ordered in 300 litres of milk.
   By lunchtime, they had sold 170 litres.
   How many litres remained at lunchtime ?

8. Find the following :-

   a $\begin{array}{r} 43 \\ \times\ 7 \\ \hline \end{array}$ b 320 x 8 c $5\overline{)87}$ d 840 ÷ 6.

9. Four car wheels weigh 144 kg in total.
   What is the weight of 1 wheel ?

10. What **fraction** of this shape has been removed ?

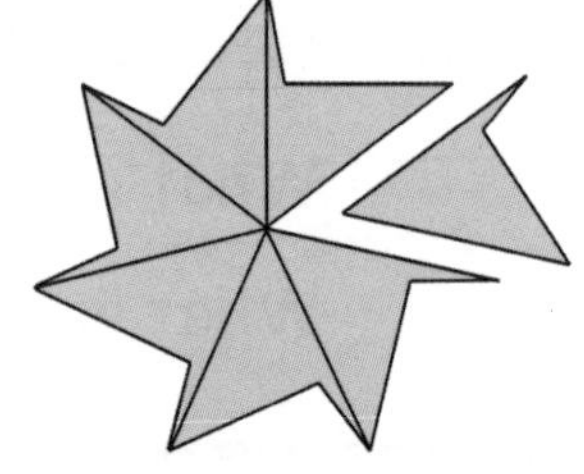

11. Draw or trace a circle like this and show how to divide it into $\frac{1}{3}$'s.

12. What is $\frac{1}{4}$ of £240 ?

13. This picture shows two **equivalent** fractions.

What number does the star (*) stand for ?

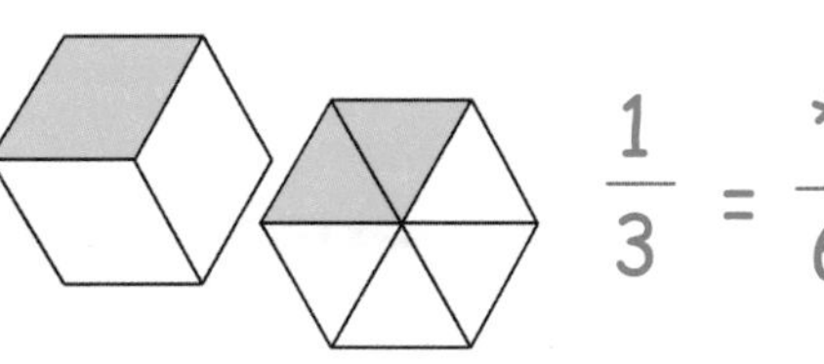

14. a *COPY* and *COMPLETE* this bill, and find the **total** cost.

6 tins of tomatoes at 60p each	= £
2 pizzas at £2·45 each	= £
1 bag of frozen chips at £2·55	= £
TOTAL	= £

b How much change would I get from a £20 note ?

15. Write the time on this clock face in **2 ways**.

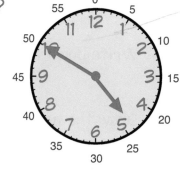

16. What is 11:45 pm in **24 hour** time ?

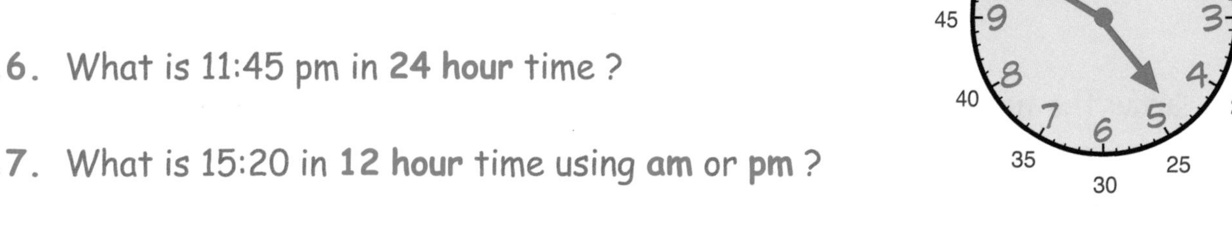

17. What is 15:20 in **12 hour** time using **am** or **pm** ?

18. What day is **2 days before** Saturday ?

19. How many days are there in November ?

20. Which **season** comes just **before** winter ?

21. I have a shower.

Which of these times gives the best **estimate** as to how long it took.

1 minutes | half an hour | 5 minutes | 10 seconds | 4 hours

22. How long is it from 7:45 pm till 8:10 pm ?

23. What instrument would you use to measure the length of a car ?

24. Which of these is the best **estimation** of the length of a car ?

50 cm, 1 metre, 3 metres, 1 kilometre

25. Measure the length of this paintbrush to the nearest centimetre ?

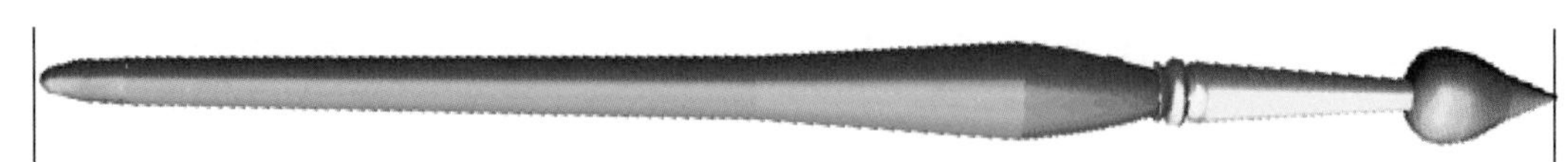

26. Write these objects in order with the **largest** volume first.

{tennis ball - milk carton - wheelie bin, - bucket}.

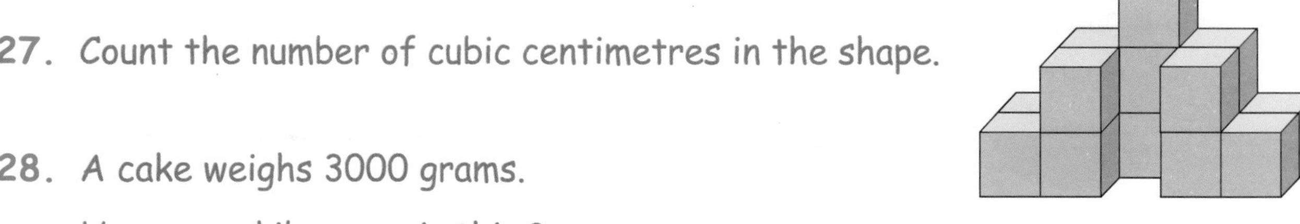

27. Count the number of cubic centimetres in the shape.

28. A cake weighs 3000 grams.

How many kilograms is this ?

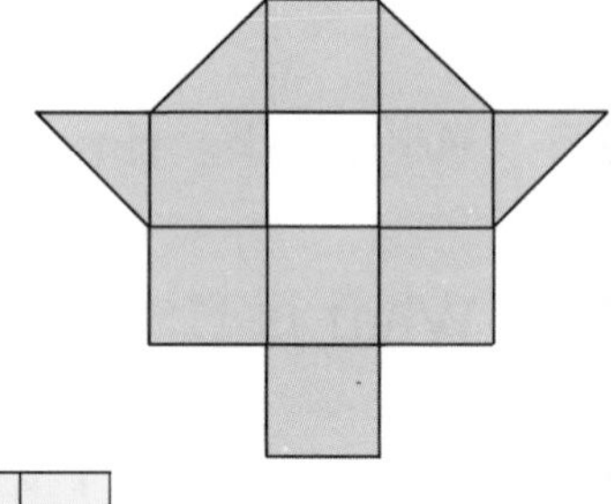

29. Write down the coloured area of this shape in **cm^2**.

30. Draw the next shape in this pattern :-

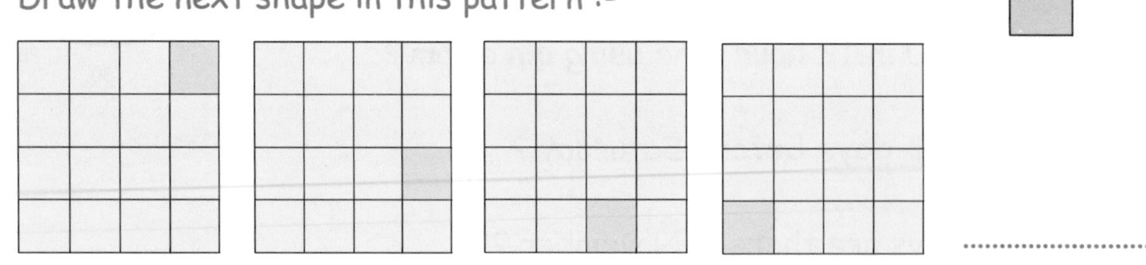

31. Write down the **next 2 numbers** or **letters** in each pattern :-

a 3, 6, 9, 12, 15, ..., ...

b 32, 36, 40, 44, 48, ..., ...

c 77, 72, 67, 62, 57, ..., ...

d B, E, H, K, N, ..., ...

32. Write these in order with the **largest** answer first.

8 x 5

8 + 9 + 10 + 11

82 ÷ 2

50 - 11

33. **Copy** each of these and write =, >, or < between each one to make the calculations correct.

a 23 ...... 32 b 4 + 5 + 6 ...... $\frac{1}{2}$ of 30 c 12 x 3 ...... 13 x 2.

34. What number comes **OUT** of this number machine ?

35. What number was put **IN** this number machine ?

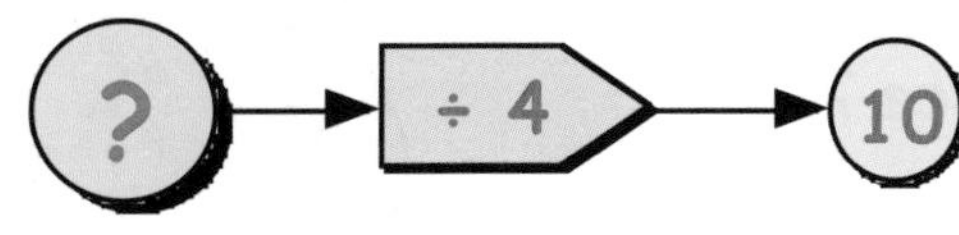

36. What number does each symbol stand for in these number statements :-

a 17 + □ = 20 b 4 x ◇ = 36 c 48 ÷ ▽ = 6 ?

37. What do these symbols stand for :- (*Answer +, -, x or ÷*)

a 6 ○ 6 = 12 b 6 ⬠ 6 = 36 c 6 ⏢ 6 = 1 ?

38. Name the following shapes :-

a 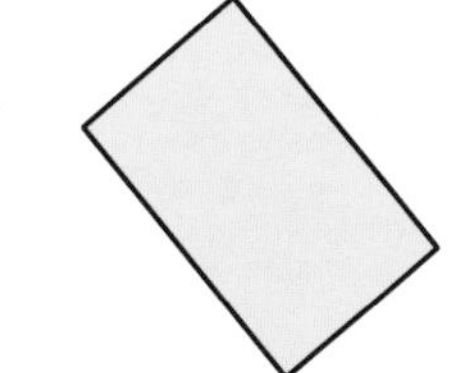 b  c 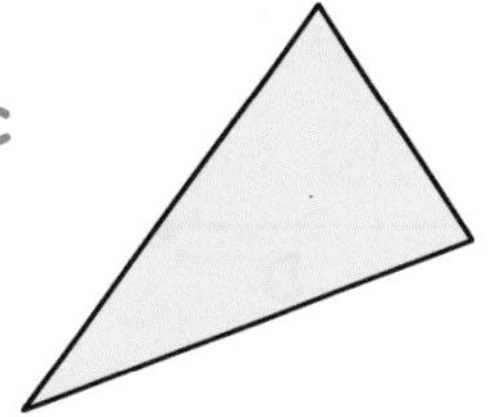 d 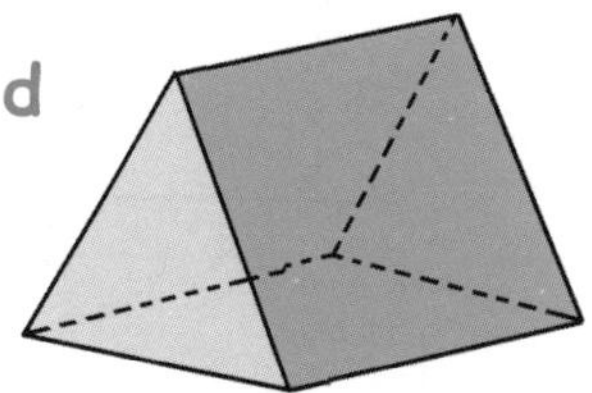

39. Name a **different 2D** shape from the two shown above.

40. Name a **different 3D** shape from the two shown above.

41. **COPY** this shape onto squared paper.

Surround it with similar shapes to show how it **tiles**.

(*About 8 tiles should do*).

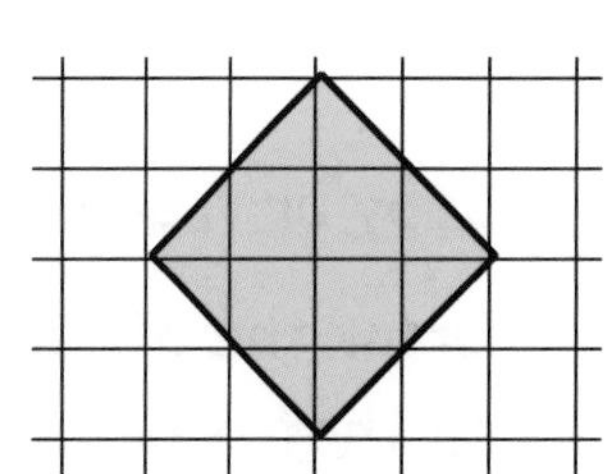

42. 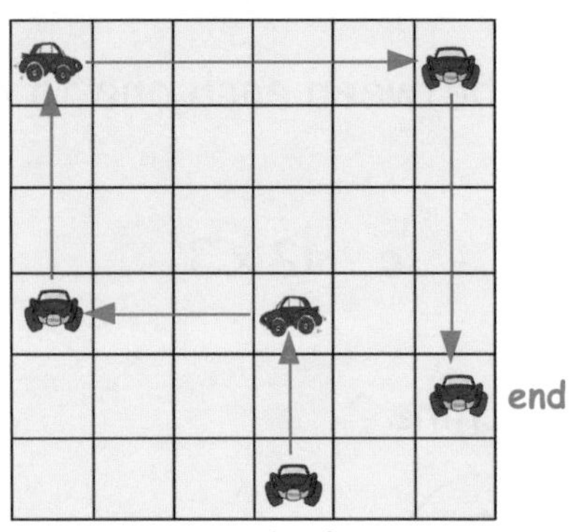

A remote controlled car is driven over some tiles on the kitchen floor.

Describe the journey the car makes.

(*Use turn left, turn right, forward*).

43. This map shows the lay-out of a mini-zoo.

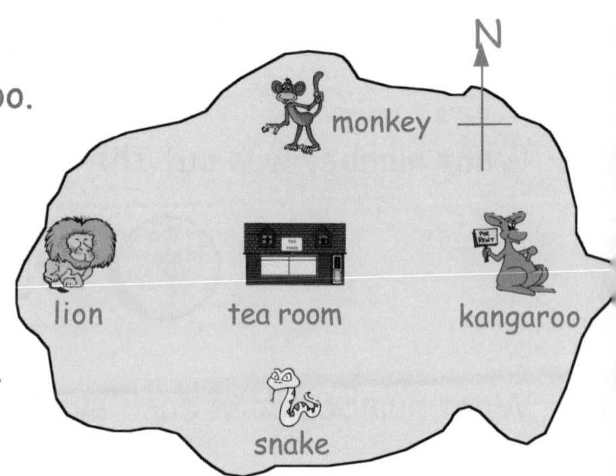

a From the **tea room** I look West.

Which animal do I see ?

b From the **tea room** I see the snake.

What direction am I facing ?

44. This grid shows where Zoe's toys are lying on the tiles of the bathroom floor.

a What toy is lying at **Cd** ?

b What is the position of the ball ?

45. Which of the shapes below are symmetrical ?

a

b

c

46. **Copy** or **trace** this shape.

Draw the other half of the figure so that it becomes **symmetrical**.

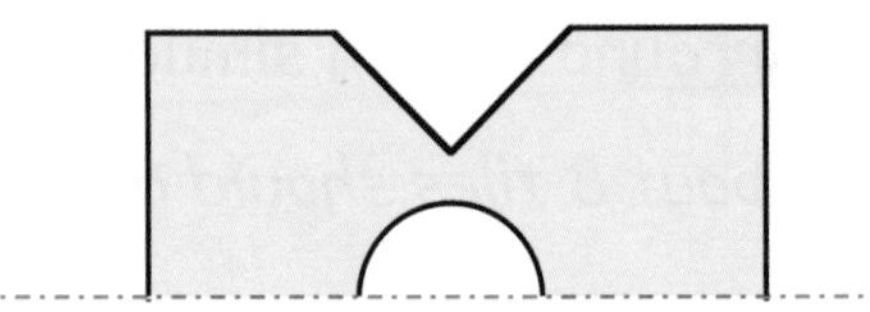

47. Children in Primary 4 are asked who their favourite teacher was.

The table shows their answers.

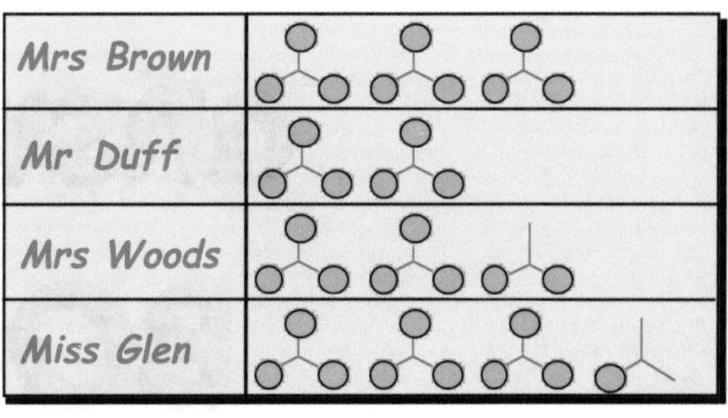

a Who was the **most** popular teacher?

b How many children said **Mrs Woods** was the best teacher ?

c How many **more** children chose **Miss Glen** than **Mr Duff** ?

48. **GROUPSON** offers cheap 3 course lunches and dinners as a special deal.

	Monday - Friday		Saturday/Sunday	
	Adult	Child	Adult	Child
3 course lunch	£6·50	£3·90	£8·50	£5·50
3 course dinner	£8·25	£5·00	£10·50	£7·25

a How much would it cost for one adult having a **3 course lunch** on **Monday** ?

b How much would it cost **in total** for Mr and Mrs Davies and their **two** children to go for a **3 course dinner** on **Saturday** ?

49. The arrow on this spinner is spun 24 times and the number is recorded.

The arrow pointed to these numbers :-.

4	3	2	4
3	4	3	1
4	1	4	2
3	2	3	4
4	3	4	3
2	4	2	4

Number	*Tally Marks*	*How Many*
1		
2		
3		
4		

COPY the table and use tally marks to **complete** it.

50. Choose from :- **Impossible** - **Unlikely** - **Even Chance** - **Likely** - **Certain** to answer these questions on probability :-

a The next child I meet will neither be a boy nor a girl.

b It will rain at some point in March.

c If I toss a coin it will end up showing a head.

answers to BOOK 1B

Answers to Ch 1 (page 1)

Ch 1 Consolidation Exercise (page 1)

1. a 75 b 489
2. a ninety six
   b two hundred and seven
   c eight hundred and forty six
   d three hundred and thirty three
3. 413, 381, 328, 319, 287, 278
4. a 49 b 406
5. a 240 b 398 c 593
6. 8 hundreds, 3 tens and 9 units
7. 756
8. a 4 and 1 b 36 and 5
   c 7 and 2 d 20 and 8
9. £7·98

Chapter 1 Exercise 1 (page 2)

1. a 3000 b 700 c 40 d 6 units
2. a 8000 b 80 c 8 d 800
3. a One thousand seven hundred and twenty
   b Three thousand five hundred and eighty six
   c two thousand nine hundred and eight
   d eight thousand and nine
   e nine hundred and thirty seven
   f six thousand three hundred and forty
   g nine thousand and eighty seven
   h nine thousand eight hundred and seventy six
4. a 444 b 906 c 3172 d 5207
   e 8466 f 7700 g 8399 h 9050
5. a 690 b 1200 c 910 d 1100
   e 4300 f 5300 g 8500 h 1300
   i 6000 j 5000
6. a 335, 380, 381, 397, 399, 400, 402, 410, 413
   b 2895, 2899, 2985, 3002, 3009, 3054, 3095, 3100
   c 8200, 8234, 8243, 8249, 8300, 8355, 8400, 8432
7. A = 48 B = 89 C = 101 D = 106
   E = 124 F = 740 G = 820 H = 850
   I = 920 J = 2500
   K = 3250 L = 4500
   M = 7000 N = 5300
   O = 5700 P = 1500
   Q = 2800 R = 4100
   S = 4500 T = 5400
   U = 6100
8. a 230 b 1000 c 2300
   d 5000 e 6000 f 5000

Chapter 1 Exercise 2 (page 4)

1. 73 lies between 70 and 80
   73 is closer to 70
   73 rounds to 70 to the nearest 10
2. 129 lies between 120 and 130
   129 is closer to 130
   129 rounds to 130
3. 24 lies between 20 and 30
   24 is closer to 20
   24 rounds to 20
4. a 87 is closer to 90
   b 133 is closer to 130
   c 458 is closer to 460
   d 902 is closer to 900
5. a 40 b 70 c 20 d 60
   e 160 f 140 g 320 h 530
   i 50 j 410 k 700 h 780
6. a 30 cm b 510 mph
   c £190 d 630

Chapter 1 Exercise 3 (page 6)

1. a 100 b 170 c 70 d 360
   e 120 f 50 g 250 h 360
   i 880 j 300 k 970 l 700
2. a 90 b 150 c 130 d 270
   e 40 f 70 g 150 h 400
3. £480

Answers to Ch 2 (page 9)

Ch 1 Consolidation Exercise (page 9)

1. a yes b yes c no
   d yes e no f yes
   g yes h no i yes
   j no k yes h no
2. various
3. see drawing

Chapter 2 Exercise 1 (page 10)

1. a yes b yes c yes
   d no e yes f yes
2.

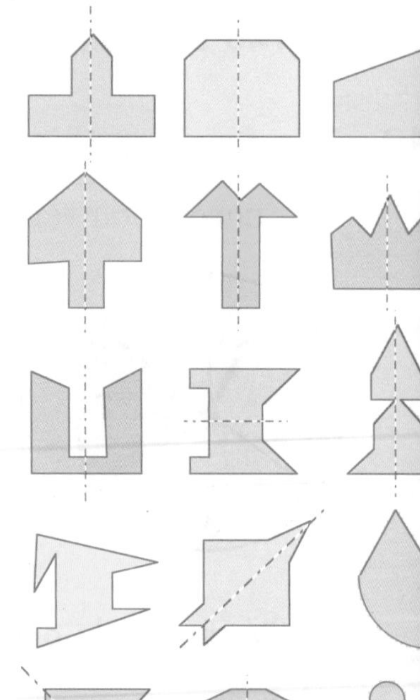

3. a 2 b 4 c 4
   d 6 e 2 f 2

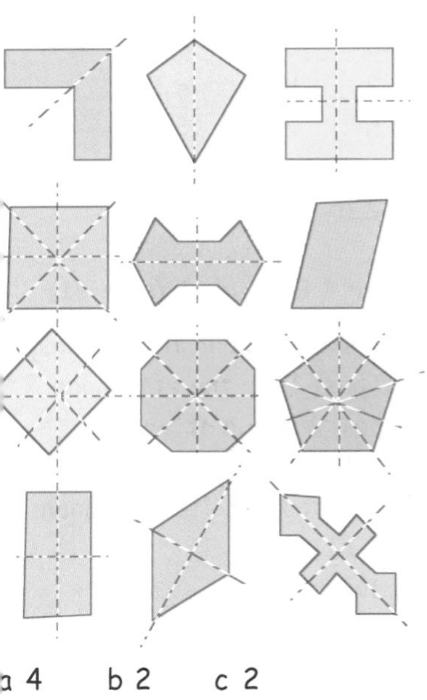

a 4 b 2 c 2
d 1 e 1 f 5
g 2 h 8 i 4
j 1 k 0 l 0

pter 2 Exercise 2 (page 15)

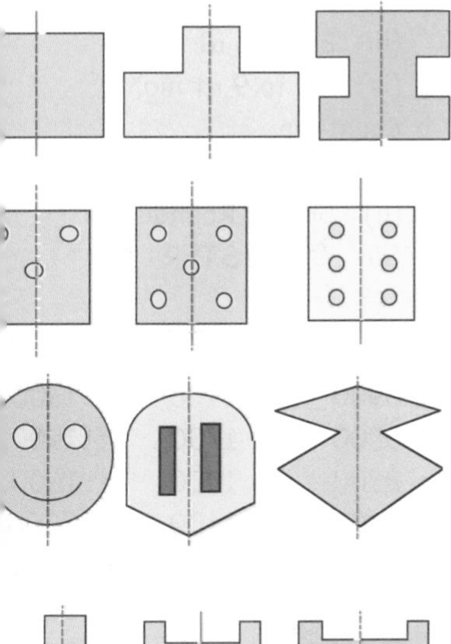

3.

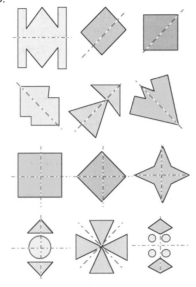

Answers to Ch 3 (page 19)

Ch 3 Consolidation Exercise (page 19)

1. a 36 b 89 c 824 d 983
   e 72 f 433 g 578 h 518
2. a 132 b 803 c 35 d 646
3. a 108 b 219 c 178 d 204
4. a 110 b 273 c 156 d 147
5. 81
6. 14
7. £93
8. 133 pies
9. £435
10. a 57 b 152
11. £84
12. £45·70

Chapter 3 Exercise 1 (page 21)

1. a 16 b 8 c 12
   d 24 e 20 f 40
   g 28 h 32 i 36
2. a 5 b 2 c 4
   d 7 e 3 f 9
   g 6 h 1 i 8
3. a 56 b 108 c 172
   d 208 e 340 f 152
   g 280 h 388 i 356
4. a 108 b 212 c 184
   d 296 e 324 f 372
   g 140 h 52 i 272
5. a 180 b 76 c 148

Chapter 3 Exercise 2 (page 23)

1. a 15 b 10 c 20
   d 50 e 30 f 25
   g 40 h 35 i 45
2. a 5 b 2 c 1
   d 3 e 7 f 9
   g 4 h 6 i 8
3. a 80 b 210 c 265
   d 370 e 175 f 435
   g 455 h 390 i 750
4. a 135 b 160 c 330
   d 220 e 405 f 365
   g 290 h 465 i 625
5. a 250 ml b 120 c 375p

Chapter 3 Exercise 3 (page 25)

1. a 0 b 20 c 50
   d 80 e 70 f 60
   g 100 h 90 i 30
2. a 5 b 2 c 8
   d 3 e 6 f 7
   g 9 h 4 i 10

Chapter 3 Exercise 4 (page 26)

1. a 190 b 470
   c 680 d 950
2. a 240 b 370
   c 560 e 820
3. a 12 b 50 c 100
4. a 130 b 720 c 470

Chapter 3 Exercise 5 (page 27)

1. a 208 b 609 c 844
   d 560 e 1528 f 1488
   g 2100 h 3335 i 1774
   j 2274 k 2396 l 4500
2. a 558 b 648 c 652
   d 885 e 1190 f 1842
   g 1792 h 3045 i 8150
3. 920
4. £975
5. £1352
6. £1830
7. £550
8. 582
9. 720 litres

Chapter 3 Exercise 6 (page 29)

1. a 12 b 21 c 32
   d 45 e 50 f 400
2. a 8 b 9 c 3
   d 7 e 8 f 21

3. a 36 b 138 c 116
d 300 e 172 f 291
g 300 h 240 i 1250
j 1257 k 1052 l 3600
4. a 90 b 252 c 272
d 720 h 240 f 1925
g 2864 h 2421 i 6370
5. 172p 6. 450
7. £152
8. £4300
9. £1300
10. 297
11. 2400

Chapter 3 Exercise 7 (page 31)

1. 16 b 30 c 68
d 134
2. 27 b 60 c 126
d 225
3. a 50 b 60
c 60 d 170
4. a 60 b 185 c 260

Answers to Ch 4 (page 33)

Ch 4 Consolidation Exercise (page 33)

1. a Wed b Thur c Oct
d April e May f 2.45pm
2. a 8 o'clock
b half past one
c quarter past ten
3. a quarter to four or 3.45 am
b ten past one or 1.10 pm
c ten to seven or 6.50 pm

Chapter 4 Exercise 1 (page 34)

1. a half past 4 b quarter past 5
c quarter to 2 d half past 8
e nine o'clock f quarter to 7
g half past 2 h quarter to 10
i quarter past 11
j half past 9 k quarter past 1
l quarter to 6
2. a 5:15 b 7:30 c 1:45
d 11:15 e 7:45 f 10:30
3. a 9:30 b 1:15 c 8:45
d 3:15 e 11:45 f 2:30
g 7:15 h 10:45 i 6:30
4. a 5:10 b 11:40 c 3:53
d 3:05 e 12:10 f 2:20
g 6:45 h 11:30 i 6:40
j 9:55 k 11:20 l 3:30
m 5:55 n 12:50 o 3:40
p 12:35 q 1:59 r 7:59
s 3:33

Chapter 4 Exercise 2 (page 37)

1. a 8 o'clock in the morning or 8.00 am
b half past 11 in the morning or 11.30 am
c quarter past 9 in the evening or 9.15 pm
d half past 3 in the afternoon 3.30 pm
e 20 past 6 in the morning or 6.20 am
f 5 past 7 at night or 7.05 pm
g 25 past 10 in the morning or 10.25 am
h quarter to 8 in the morning or 7.45 am
i 5 to 10 at night or 9.55 pm
j 10 to 7 at night or 6.50 pm
k 5 to 11 in the morning or 10.55 am
l quarter past 3 in the morning or 3.15 am
2. a 6.15 pm
b 7.45 pm and 10.30 pm
c 7.05 pm and 7.55 pm
d 1.10 pm and 3.15 pm
e 6.50 am and 7.55 am
f 3.20 pm and 3.35 pm
3. a half past 2 in the afternoon
b quarter to 10 in the morning
c 10 to 11 at night
d 8 minutes to 8 at night
e 10 past 6 in the morning
f 5 to 12 in the morning
g half past 11 in the morning
h 10 to 7 at night
i 25 to 9 in the morning
j 19 mins to 4 in the afternoon
k 17 mins to 6 in the morning
l 1 minute to 11 in the morning
m 28 mins past 10 at night
n 7 mins past 2 in the morning
o 12 mins to 11 in the morning
p 11 mins past 1 in the afternoon
q 27 mins past 7 in the morning
r 2 mins to 9 in the morning

Chapter 4 Exercise 3 (page 40)

1. a 3 b 5 c 3 d 6
2. a 2 b 5 c 5
d 5 e 5 f 5
3. a half past 1 b 15
c 2.15 d 3.00

Chapter 4 Exercise 4 (page 41)

1. 1 minute to 12 in the morning
20 past 12 in the afternoon
5 past 1 in the afternoon
2. a 5 to 10 in the morning
b 5 past 12 in the afternoon
c 3.10 pm
d twenty to six at night
e 6.50 pm
3. 5 minutes late
4. 20 to 12 in the morning
25 to 1 in the afternoon
5 past 1 in the afternoon
10 to 3 in the afternoon
20 past 3 in the afternoon
5. a (i) 10 to 4 in the afternoon
(ii) 25 past 5 at night
(iii) 25 to 8 at night
(iv) 10 to 9 at night
b Count-Up
c (i) Away and Home
(ii) Sports Roundup
(iii) Big SISTER

Chapter 4 Exercise 5 (page 43)

1. a 0900 b 0100 c 1300
d 0500 e 1700 f 1900
g 2300 h 1000 i 1600
j 2200 k 1400 l 0300
2. a 2 pm b 3 pm c 6 am
d 11 am e 6 pm f 2 am
g 9 pm h 11 pm i 1.30 p

Answers to Ch 5 (page 46)

Ch 5 Consolidation Exercise (page 4

1. a 14 b 13
c 17 r 1 d 16
e 21 r 1 f 35 r 1
g 49 h 25 r 2
2. a 19 r 1 b 17 r 2
c 15 r 1 d 25 r 1

e 17 f 34
g 44 r 1 h 29
14 metres
19 with 2 left over
41 and 42
a 17 r 1 b £102

hapter 5 Exercise 1 (page 47)

see tables
a 3 b 2 c 4
d 6 e 5 f 7
g 9 h 8 i 10
a 20 b 40 c 28
d 24 e 36 f 32
a 8 b 10 c 7
d 4 e 3 f £9
a 10 b 12 c 11
d 20 e 21 f 22
a 21 b £12
c 22 d 10

hapter 5 Exercise 2 (page 50)

a 4 r 1 b 2 r 3 c 3 r 2
d 5 r 3 e 2 r 1 f 1 r 3
g 4 r 2 h 3 r 3 i 4 r 3
a 10 r 2 b 10 r 3 c 11 r 2
d 12 r 1 e 20 r 1 f 20 r 2
g 21 r 1 h 21 r 3
a 4 and 1 b 10 and 1 c 22 r 1
d 3 e 63
a 7 b 8 c 10 d 13
e 14 f 17 g 16 h 15
i 18 j 19 k 23 l 24
a 9 b 12 c £21
d 19 e £17
a 15 r 2 b 13 r 3
c 18 r 1 d 14 r 2
e 17 r 3 f 23 r 1
g 18 r 2 h 23 r 3
i 24 r 3 j 6 r 2
k 9 r 3 l 25 r 2
a 15 r 3 b 17 r 2 c 16 r 1
d 24 r 1 e 9 - 3 f 13 r 2
a 6 r 3 b 7 r 1
c 8 r 2 d 9 r 1
e 11 f 12 r 3
g 14 r 1 h 15 r 1
i 16 r 2 j 18
k 19 r 3 l 21 r 2

Chapter 5 Exercise 3 (page 53)

1. see tables
2. a 3 b 6 c 10
   d 7 e 4 f 8
   g 5 h 9 i 11
3. a 15 b 35 c 50
   d 30 e 40 f 25
4. a 9 b 4 c 8
   d 10 e 7 f 5
   g 6 h 11 i 14p

Chapter 5 Exercise 4 (page 55)

1. a 2 r 2 b 1 r 2 c 3 r 3
   d 1 r 4 e 0 r 3 f 3 r 1
   g 3 r 4 h 2 r 3 i 3 r 2
2. a 10 r 1 b 10 r 3
   c 11 r 2 d 10 r 2
   e 11 r 3 f 10 r 4
   g 11 r 4 h 11 r 1
3. a 10 r 2 b 11 r 3
   c 1 head of state with no guards
4. a 10 b 16 c 12 d 14
   e 17 f 15 g 11 h 13
   i 18 j 19 k 20 l 21
5. a 15 b 16 c 18
6. a 7 r 4 b 8 r 2
   c 18 r 3 d 10 r 1
   e 17 r 2 f 12 r 4
   g 13 r 3 h 14 r 1
   i 18 r 4 j 17 r 3
   k 19 r 2 l 20 r 4
7. a 3 b 13 r 4
8. a 10 b 51
9. a 6 b 1 minute
10. a 12 r 2 b 14 r 4
   c 16 r 3 d 19 r 1
   e 17 f 15 r 4
   g 19 r 3 h 21 r 2

Chapter 5 Exercise 5 (page 58)

1. see tables
2. a 6 b 4 c 2
   d 7 e 1 f 9
3. a 30 b 50 c 90
   d 80 e 60 f 100
4. a (i) 7 (ii) 5 b 8
   c 6 d 3 e 14
5. a 8 b 4 c 10
   d 13 e 19 f 21
   g 25 h 32 i 36
   j 40 k 41 l 48

6. £100

Chapter 5 Exercise 6 (page 60)

1. a 134 b 123
   c 102 d 102
   e 159 r 1 f 186 r 2
   g 56 r 3 h 469 r 1
   i 89 r 1 j 148 r 4
   k 388 r 1 l 275 r 2
2. a 152 r 1 b 68 r 2 c 90 r 2
   d 120 e 30 f 180 r 1
   g 102 r 2 h 306 r 1 i 66 r 2
   j 220 r 1 k 167 r 4 l 225
   m 87 n 206 o 199 r 4
3. £86
4. 289 runs
5. 69 miles
6. £234
7. 232 r 1
8. 178 cm
9. 125 ml
10. 99
11. 30

Chapter 5 Exercise 7 (page 62)

1. a 32 b 48 c 114
   d 235 e 165 f 9
   g 429 h 234 i 442
   j 632 k 34 l 218
   m 821 n 2160 o 69
2. a 52 b 45 c 150
   d 120 e 120 f 291
   g 582 h 14 i 435
   j 581 k 923 l 840
   m 179 n 210 o 2900
   p 600 q 100 r 20
3. £141 4. 705
5. £123 6. £247
7. 152 litres 8. 16
9. 480 10. £483

Answers to Ch 6 (page 65)

Ch 6 Consolidation Exercise (page 65)

1. a 4 b 5 c 3
2. a yes b no c yes
3. 6
4. see drawing
5. a TV b table
6. move 4 forward, turn left,

move 6 forward, turn right,
move 4 forward, turn right,
move 9 forward, stop

7. Drive along Main Street.
Turn 2nd right onto Troggs Road.
Turn 1st left onto Allans Way.
Turn 1st left onto Tile Road.
School is on your left.
(*Various answers*).

Chapter 6 Exercise 1 (page 67)

1. a 90° b 90° c smaller
d bigger e 90° f smaller
2. a 9 b 7
3. smaller - a, b, e, i, j,
bigger - c, d, f, g, h, k
90° - l, m
4. a 3 b 2, 4 c 1, 5

Chapter 6 Exercise 2 (page 69)

1. a 90° b 180° c 360°
2. a 90° b 180° c 90°
d 180° e 270° f 360°
3. a 90° b 180° c 90°
d 270° e 90° f 360°
4. a 90° b 180° c 270°
d 90° e 270° f 90°
5. a 90° clockwise or 270 anticlockwise
b 180° clockwise - 180 anticlockwise
c 360°clockwise or 360anticlockwise
d 270° clockwise or 90 anticlockwise
e 270° clockwise or 90 anticlockwise
f 90° clockwise or 270 anticlockwise

Chapter 6 Exercise 3 (page 71)

1. See diagram
2. a 90° b 90° c 90°
d 270° e 180° f 270°
3. a South b East c West
d 270° e East
4. a (i) South (ii) West (iii) North
b West c (i) North (ii) South
d South

Answers to Ch 7 (page 75)

Ch 7 Consolidation Exercise (page 75)

1. a 50 b 15 c 9
2. 50p, 20p, 20p, 5p, 2p, 1p
3. a £0·37 b £0·08
c £2·41 d £0·90
4. a £0·90 b £2·67 c £10·14
d £2·49 e £7·08 f £0·89
5. a £1·95 b £1·40 c £7·07
6. a £5·00 b £1·87

Chapter 7 Exercise 1 (page 76)

1. a 10 b 15 c 15
d 8 e 11 f 19
2. a 4 b 3
c 4 d 4
3. a £9·73 b £13·98
c £15·45 d £18·80

4/5. various answers

6. a 88p
b 50p, 20p, 10p, 5p, 2p, 1p
7. a £3·21
b £2, £1, 20p, 1p
8. £10, £5, 20p, 5p
9. a £7·31
b £5, £2, 20p, 10p, 1p
10. a £6·73
b £5, £1, 50p, 20p, 2p, 1p
11. £10, £5, 50p, 20p, 10p, 5p
12. Incorrect - 20p short
13. £10, £5, £2, £1, 50p, 2p, 1p

Chapter 7 Exercise 2 (page 79)

1. a £5·79 b £9·77
c £12·81 d £11·56
e £4·32 f £6·80
g £7·95 h £11·28
i £11·21 j £11·15
k £2·46 l £9·84
m £18·40 n £16·51
o £13·93 p £3·99
2. a £9·79 b £2·31
c £19·03 d £8·88
e £19·42 f £12·83
g £12·98 h £3·02
i £19·90 j £1·01
k £19·93 l £5·69

Chapter 7 Exercise 3 (page 80)

1. £1·17
2. a 67p b £3·48 c £2·70
3. 10p
4. a £2·70 b 20p short
5. a £4·70 b £2, £2, 50p, 20p
6. a £27 b £6
7. a £3·75 b £6

Chapter 7 Exercise 4 (page 81)

1. a £5·35 b £8·20
c £10·80 d £10·01
e £18·11 f £15·10
g 7p h £54·10
2. £4·10
3. £6·10
4. a £3·85 b £4·85
c £4·60 d £9·80
e £1·40 f £5·70
g £2·85 h £3·05
5. a £13·72 b 28p
6. a £15·50 b £1·25
7. 4

Answers to Ch 8 (page 85)

Chapter 8 Exercise 1 (page 85)

1. a Jan b Dec c Sat
d Fri e Oct f Jan
2. a 31 b 28(29) c 30
d 30 e 31 f 31
g 30 h 31
3. a June b March
c October d August
4. a 23/02/14 b 19/04/13
c 22/07/14 d 18/08/17
e 07/06/09 f 03/03/21
g 10/12/07 h 01/01/16
i 04/02/16
5. a 14th January 2013
b 1st March 2014
c 11th November 2011
d 23rd April 2005
e 12th December 2012
f 7th August 2015
g 9th March 2020
h 31st June 2016
i 30th February 2010
6. Only 30 days in June and only 28 or 29 days in February
7. a 5 b Thursday
c 24th April d 31st March
8. a 9 b 4th June
c (i) 30th April 2015
(ii) 2nd July 2015
(iii) 1st July 2015
(iv) 5th June 2015
(v) 22nd May 2015
(vi) 1st June 2015

a 10 b 17 c 20
d 2 e 12
. various - depends on the year

apter 8 Exercise 2 (page 88)

a minutes b seconds c days
d hours e seconds f hours
g minutes h hours i minutes
j days
various
various
a 120 b 180 c 300
d 480 e 30 f 540
g 600 h 150
a 120 b 240 c 300
d 540 e 180 f 30
g 15 h 90
Read alphabet - fifteen seconds
Walk a mile - twenty minutes
A School afternoon - 2 hours
Watch a DVD - two hours
Grow a small plant - six days
Eat breakfast - ten minutes
Write your name - eight seconds
Cycle round Scotland - five weeks
a possibly Usain Bolt
b possibly Hicham El Guerrouj
c possibly Patrick Makau
various

apter 8 Exercise 3 (page 90)

Various 2/3. Practical

nswers to Ch 9 (page 93)

9 Consolidation Exercise (page 93)

a triangle b rectangle
c square d circle
rectangles - 4 squares - 8
triangles - 3 circles - 4
a 3 b 1 c 4 d 0
e 3 f 3 g 4 h 4
i 4 j 4 k 4 l 0
a 4 sides instead of 3
4 angles instead of 3
more (4) lines of symmetry
b only 1 side
no angles
lots of lines of symmetry

Chapter 9 Exercise 1 (page 94)

1. a rectangle b yes
2. a circle b no
3. a triangle b yes
4. a yes b yes c no
d no e yes
5. see tiling
6. see tiling
7. see tiling
8. see tiling
9. see tiling
10. see tiling
11. see tiling
12. see tiling
13. see tiling - rhombus
14. see tiling
15. see tiling
16. see tiling
17. see tiling
18. a yes b yes c no d yes
e yes f no g yes h yes
i no j no k yes l no

Answers to Ch 10 (page 101)

Ch 10 Consolidation Ex (page 101)

1. a 27 b 25 c 0
d 14 e 60 f 40
2. a 9 b 7 c 5
d 8 e 7 f 40
3. a 130 b 201 c 76
d 320 e 190 f 435
g 282 h 268 i 890
j 1184 k 1620 l 2457
4. a 710 b 258 c 198
d 690 e 836 e 1854
g 3000 h 2625 i 1752
5. £232
6. 290
7. 768 km
8. 632
9. 545
10. 177
11. 200

Chapter 10 Exercise 1 (page 103)

1. a 18 b 30 c 12
d 24 e 36 f 42
g 60 h 48 i 54
2. a 2 b 4 c 6
d 9 e 0 f 7
g 8 h 5 i 10
3. a 12p b 42 km c 30
d £24 e 18 f 36
g 54 h 48 hours

Chapter 10 Exercise 2 (page 105)

1. a 84 b 318 c 402
d 174 e 252 f 222
g 372 h 438 i 486
j 450 k 516 l 582
2. a 246 b 348 c 378
d 228 e 264 f 390
g 426 h 492 i 294
j 576 k 510 l 594
3. 78 mm 4. 270 ml
5. 162 6. 234
7. 420 8. £408
9. 312
10. 504 legs

Chapter 10 Exercise 3 (page 107)

1. a 28 b 14 c 42
d 21 e 35 f 70
g 63 h 49 i 56
2. a 4 b 2 c 5
d 3 e 7 f 8
g 9 h 10 i 6
3. a 21 b 14 c 42°
d 70p e 35 f £63
g 56 cm

Chapter 10 Exercise 4 (page 109)

1. a 84 b 378 c 441
d 196 e 315 f 532
g 119 h 238 i 182
j 483 k 616 l 672
2. a 301 b 392 c 434
d 259 e 287 f 476
g 518 h 581 i 343
j 665 k 602 l 693
3. 105
4. £210
5. 182
6. 413
7. 679
8. 476
9. £679

Chapter 10 Exercise 5 (page 111)

1. a 648 b 1428 c 2166
   d 3367 e 3222 f 3843
2. a 1386 b 1122 c 3234
   d 3210 e 6972 f 4614
3. 1645
4. 2244
5. 4753

Chapter 10 Exercise 6 (page 112)

1. a 18 b 21 c 32 d 25
   e 24 f 63 g 38 h 78
   i 140 j 235 k 312 l 427
   m 620 n 1314 o 1434 p 1644
   q 1052 r 1050 s 2674 t 1480
2. a 16p b 18p c 28p d 40p
   e 54p f 35p g 90p h 50p
   i £2·28 j £1·16
   k £3·10 l 72p
   m £5·39 n £9·30
   o £1422 p £1257
   q £1071 r £3552
   s £3664 t £5000
3. £3·95 4. £84
5. £3580 6. 896 grams
7. £3114
8. £2380
9. Cost = £4·58 - Change = 42p
10. 1890

Answers to Ch 11 (page 115)

Chapter 11 Exercise 5 (page 115)

1. a Bb b Cd c Da
   d Ee e Dc f Ac
2. a Db b Ca c Ae
   d Bc e Ed f Cd
3. a car b bike c plane
   d boat e train f scooter
4. a B5 b A3 c D5
   d F2 e E6
5. a cows - A1 hens - A2
   pigs - A5 ducks - B1
   bull - B2 horses - B4
   geese - B5 turnip - D2
   potato - E1 corn - E4
   wheat - E5
   b A3,B3,C1,C2,C3,C4,C5,D3,E3
   c A4, D1, D4, D5, E2
6. Q - I7, R - C3, S - J10, T - A5
   U - J1, V - E6, W - F2
7/8/9. see drawings
10. a (i) A5 (ii) E4 (iii) C1 (iv) E2
    b (i) D7 (ii) C7 (iii) E1/F1
    (iv) A1/B1 (v) C2
    c A6, C4, D1, E4, E8, F2
    d (i) mountain on Rock Island
    (ii) volcano on Volcano Island
    (iii) ship at sea (iv) water
    e E2 - D3 - C4 - C5 - C6 - C7- D8
11. a D4 b G6 c E6
    d D2 e D1 f E3
    g F3 h G5 i F8
    j B1 k F4 l F4
    m D7 n F6
12. a C4 b F8/F9
    c D2/D3 d B7/C7/C8
13. D2- E2 - F2 - G2
14. D1 - C2 - B2 - B3 -= B4 - C5

Chapter 11 Exercise 2 (page 120)

1. a C3 b F1 c D4
   d A2 e E2 f B0
2. a A - C2 B - F2 C - D0
   D - F4 E - F1 F - B5
   G - D4 H - A2 I - A4
   J - C0 K - E3 L - C3
   M - D1 N - A0
   b C, M, G d H, A, B
3. a Len b Fred c Jim
   d Kit e Don f Sid
   g Tom h Col
4. a (i) - £1 (ii) 50p (iii) 0
   (iv) 50p (v) 20p (vi) 0
   b B4, C4, E2, F1
   c £5 at D2
5. More accurate - you are plotting a single point instead of an area within a box.

Answers to Ch 12 (page 123)

Ch 12 Consolidation Ex (page 123)

1. a 45 b 30 c 32
   d 24 e 40 f 63
2. a 10 b 6 c 7
   d 9 e 7 f 35
3. a 210 b 81 c 144
   d 94 e 133 f 120
   g 332 h 291 i 1270
   j 826 k 1401 l 4428
4. a 150 b 192 c 288
   d 1140 e 2442 f 2226
   g 6100 h 2268 i 5154
5. £188
6. 228 pounds
7. 273 metres
8. 460
9. 1080 litres
10. 1001 pounds
11. 1242
12. a 225 b 12

Chapter 12 Exercise 1 (page 125)

1. a 32 b 16 c 48
   d 40 e 0 f 64
   g 80 h 72 i 56
2. a 1 b 3 c 5
   d 2 e 4 f 6
   g 7 h 9 i 10
3. a 24 b 56 c 40 sec
   d £32 e 64 hrs f 80
   g 48p h 72

Chapter 12 Exercise 2 (page 127)

1. a 136 b 256 c 360
   d 208 e 424 f 512
   g 568 h 624 i 680
   j 736 k 776 l 480
2. a 104 b 200 c 296
   d 352 e 416 f 544
   g 632 h 688 i 152
   j 720 k 752 l 792
3. 240 4. £336
5. £6
6. 552
7. 704
8. 344
9. 288
10. 456 times

Chapter 12 Exercise 3 (page 129)

1. a 27 b 18 c 54
   d 36 e 63 f 45
   g 72 h 90 i 81
2. a 0 b 5 c 1
   d 7 e 9 f 3
   g 10 h 8 i 6
3. 18 4. £45

54 6. 36
72 8. 63
£90 10. 81

apter 12 Exercise 4 (page 131)

a 135 b 216 c 324
d 423 e 459 f 567
g 801 h 648 i 684
j 756 k 792 l 873
a 171 b 189 c 504
d 252 e 675 f 378
g 738 h 297 i 855
j 621 k 693 l 783
252
414
648
£315
621
450
£567
. 891

apter 12 Exercise 5 (page 133)

a 1704 b 1566 c 3080
d 4158 e 4152 f 6102
a 963 b 2120 c 3501
d 4904 e 7956 f 7704
1168 grams
£2151

apter 12 Exercise 6 (page 134)

a 172 b 222 c 156
d 425 e 372 f 651
g 648 h 513 i 1104
j 1305 k 1794 l 2552
a £498 b £2·52 c £1028
d £365 e £7·02 f £2996
g £8·24 h £1·35 i £6·30
j £1232 k £22·86 l £475
m £2106 n £4·32 o £5·04
p £2418 q £37·10 r £280
s £33·60 t £64·62
201
£470
408
68
£98
405
£6·86
. 2334
. 948

12. 2845 miles
13. 2292
14. 2072
15. 2250 ml

Chapter 12 Exercise 7 (page 137)

1. a 3066 b 3465
2. a 572 b 1182 c 1668
   d 1645 e 2568 f 3752
   g 1992 h 1773
3. 2205 4. 1712

Answers to Ch 13 (page 139)

Ch 13 Consolidation Ex (page 139)

1. red - blue - orange.
2.

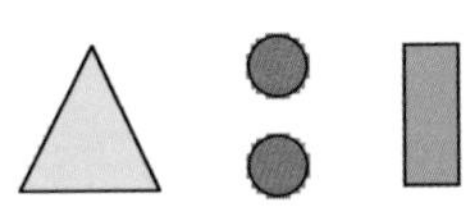

3. a

   b

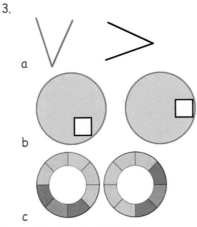

   c
4. a 14, 16 b 22, 27 c p, s
   d O, N e 20, 0 f 58, 70
   g ijk, jkl h $\frac{5}{6}, \frac{6}{7}$

Chapter 13 Exercise 1 (page 140)

1. a start at 2 and go up by 2
   b start at 3 and go up by 3
   c start at 1 and go up by 5
   d start at 70 and go down by 10
   e start at 20 and go down by 3
   f start at 30 and go up by 8
   g start at 21 and go down by 2
   h start at 50 and go up by 50
   i start at 200 go down by 20
   j start at 40 and go up by 60
   k start at 18 and go up by 7
   l start at 66 and go down by 11
   m start at 650 go down by 110
   n start at 1 and go up by 12
   o start at £1·50 go up by 50p
   p start at £2·50 go up by £3
2. a 10 b 18 c 26
   d 20 e 8 f 62
   g 13 h 250 i 120
   j 280 k 46 l 22
   m 210 n 49 o £3·50
   p £14·50
3. a 17 b 80 c 16
   d 50 e 24 f 23
   g 40 h 47 i 24
   j 42 k 26 l 40
   m 28 n 38 o 154
   p 150
4. a 17, 23 b 7, 19
   c 28, 18 d 17, 27
   e 55, 22 f 15, 21, 39
   g 24, 21, 9 h 65, 55, 35
   i 400,250,150 j 0, 80, 200, 240
5. a 1, $\frac{1}{2}$ b 64, 128
   c 18, 24 d 30, 15
   e 232, 121 f 5 x 7, 6 x 8
   g 21, 34

Chapter 13 Exercise 2 (page 142)

1. a 7
   b (i) the 5 times table
   (ii) the 9 times table
   (iii) start at 15 and go up by 5
   (iv) start at 6 and go up by 2
2. various
3. a see tables
   b 2 x 2 x 4 = 16
   c 2 x 2 x 5 = 20
   d 4 times table is double the 2 times table
4. a see tables
   b 8 times table is double the 4 times table
5. a 10 times table is double the 5 times table
   b 8 times table is 4 times the 2 times table
   c 10 times table is 5 times the 2 times table
6. various

Answers to Ch 14 (page 145)

Ch 14 Consolidation Ex (page 145)

1. a 6 b 7 c 9 d 6
e 8 f 11 g 12 h 78
i 23 j 31 k 21 l 11
m 18 n 19 o 19 p 26
q 301 r 321 s 201 t 101
u 269 v 257 w 175 x 245
2. a 8 b 8 c 19 d 9
3. a 17 b 14 c 29 cm d 53 m
e 24 f 167 g 30 mm

Chapter 14 Exercise 1 (page 147)

1. a 3 b 2 c 5
d 4 e 7 f 6
g 8 h 9 i 10
2. a 0 b 42 c 6
d 48 e 24 f 54
3. a 13 b 16 c 15
d 17 e 18 f 19
g 37 h 54 i 68
j 88 k 101 l 135
4. a 12 b 14 c 16
d 100 e 65 f 89
5 a 5 b 7 c 6
d 4 e 8 f 9
g 10
6. 12 7. 15
8. 14 9. 21
10. £19 11. £48
12. £35 13. 63
14. 85

Chapter 14 Exercise 2 (page 150)

1. a 2 r 2 b 4 r 3 c 5 r 4
d 6 r 4 e 7 r 1 f 8 r 4
g 0 r 5 h 9 r 3 i 4 r 4
2. a 10 r 2 b 9 r 3 c 11 r 2
d 12 r 4 e 13 r 2 f 14 r 4
g 7 r 5 h 13 r 1 i 15 r 1
j 16 k 13 r 5 l 16 r 3
3. a 17 r 3 b 24 r 5 c 35 r 4
d 48 r 1 e 50 r 2 f 74 r 3
g 84 r 4 h 142 r 1
4. a 6 r 2 b 13 c 15 r 4
d 101 e 95 f 120 r 5
5. 12 r 3 6. 16 r 4
7. 29 r 5 8. 43 r 2
9. 76 - 5 litres remaining

Chapter 14 Exercise 3 (page 152)

1. a 3 b 2 c 5
d 7 e 4 f 6
g 8 h 10 i 9
2. a 49 b 0 c 42
d 7 e 56 f 70
3. a 11 b 12 c 14
d 15 e 18 f 25
g 38 h 49 i 62
j 77 k 89 l 131
4. a 13 b 16 c 59
d 100 e 74 f 128
5. a £5 b £8 c 3
d 6 e 8 f 9
g 4 cm
6. 13
7. 30
8. 25
9. 46
10. 24
11. 129
12. 24
13. 124

Chapter 14 Exercise 4 (page 155)

1. a 2 r 3 b 3 r 5 c 5 r 2
d 6 r 4 e 5 r 5 f 7 r 1
g 7 r 6 h 8 r 3 i 9 r 2
2. a 10 r 3 b 9 r 6 c 6 r 4
d 7 r 4 e 10 r 1 f 11 r 2
g 11 r 5 h 12 r 6 i 13 r 5
j 12 r 4 k 14 r 1 l 14 r 5
3. a 15 r 1 b 54 r 5 c 36 r 2
d 76 r 4 e 65 r 1 f 102 r 1
g 114 r 6 h 128 r 5
4. a 6 r 5 b 14 c 12 r 3
d 59 r 1 e 72 r 6 f 106 r 4
5. 12 r 5
6. 18 r 2
7. 26 r 3
8. 82 and £2
9. 126 r 5

Chapter 14 Exercise 5 (page 157)

1. a 1 b 4 c 2
d 7 e 3 f 8
g 6 h 9 i 10
2. a 64 b 16 c 32
d 56 e 72 f 40
3. a 6 b 11 c 12
d 13 e 17 f 30
g 46 h 51 i 68
j 79 k 88 l 113
4. a 9 b 14 c 39
d 50 e 92 f 118
5. a 6 secs b 4 c 7
d 9 e 10 f 5
g £8
6. 12
7. £17
8. 25
9. 68
10. 52
11. £119
12. 77
13. 97

Chapter 14 Exercise 6 (page 160)

1. a 1 r 3 b 4 r 2 c 5 r 4
d 6 r 4 e 6 r 7 f 7 r 6
g 8 r 1 h 9 r 4 i 10 r 6
2. a 6 r 2 b 9 r 1 c 3 r 6
d 6 r 3 e 10 r 5 f 8 r 7
g 10 r 1 h 9 r 4 i 7 r 7
j 11 r 6 k 12 r 3 l 13 r 5
3. a 21 r 4 b 54 r 5 c 45 r 3
d 66 r 7 e 76 f 88 r 1
g 107 r 1 h 112 r 6
4. a 6 r 3 b 8 r 5 c 13
d 46 e 68 r 7 f 100 r
5. 11 and 2p left over
6. 25 r 5 7. 28 r 6
8. 47 r 3 9. 112 - 4 kg left ove

Chapter 14 Exercise 7 (page 162)

1. a 3 b 2 c 1
d 6 e 5 f 7
g 9 h 8 i 10
2. a 54 b 36 c 72
d 27 e 63 f 81
3. a 4 b 6 c 11
d 12 e 19 f 26
g 38 h 46 i 65
j 78 k 88 l 107
4. a 9 b 14 c 35
d 46 e 87 f 89
5. a 5 b 8 c 10
d £4 e 7 f $^2/_9$
6. 12 7. £69
8. 14 9. 28
10. 105 11. £36
12. 84 13. 54 (not 18)

apter 14 Exercise 8 (page 165)

a 2 r 1 b 3 r 3 c 4 r 2
d 5 r 5 e 6 r 4 f 7 r 7
g 8 r 6 h 9 r 8 i 11 r 1
a 5 r 3 b 2 r 6 c 9 r 7
d 4 r 8 e 8 r 3 f 7 r 5
g 10 r 7 h 7 r 8 i 11 r 4
j 12 r 8 k 15 r 1 l 15 r 6
a 16 r 2 b 25 r 4 c 45 r 1
d 58 r 5 e 67 r 5 f 86 r 4
g 89 r 8 h 101 r 7
a 7 r 4 b 8 r 7 c 12
d 42 r 5 e 76 f 87 r 7
11 r 1
32 and £4 left over
26 r 6
75 r 5
58 r 3

apter 14 Exercise 9 (page 167)

a 39 b 18 c 17
d 15 e 11 f 14
g 12 h 11 i 124
j 43 k 212 l 256
m 47 n 42 o 28
p 35 q 112 r 248
s 68 t 51
a 26 b 19 c 16
d 13 e 129 f 45
g 32 h 389 i 128
j 152 k 36 l 113
a 17 b 15 c £176
d 18 e 34 f 38
g 29 h £40-£7 i 366

apter 14 Exercise 10 (page 169)

123
19
186
38
£85
120
42

apter 14 Exercise 11 (page 170)

416
35
164
1160
427
234

7. 1740
8. a 368 m b 3312 miles
9. 1260
10. 212
11. 810
12. a 462 b 168

Answers to Ch 15 (page 174)

Ch 15 Consolidation Ex (page 174)

1. a 5 cm b 8 cm c 10 cm
   d 14 cm e 4 cm f 12 cm
   g 7 cm
2. a metre strip b ruler
   c ruler d metre strip
3. 200 cm
4. a rectangle 8 cm by 3 cm
   b square 7 cm by 7 cm
   c rectangle 5 cm by $2\frac{1}{2}$ cm

Chapter 15 Exercise 1 (page 175)

1. a 5 cm b 87 cm c 2 cm
   d 8 cm e 3 cm f 10 cm
2. a 5 cm b 8 cm c 2 cm
   d 8 cm e 3 cm f 10 cm
3. a F - D - B - A - E - C
   b 10 cm - 2 cm = 8 cm
4. a 4 cm b 3 cm c 7 cm
   d 3 cm e 5 cm f 14 cm
5. a 4 cm b 3 cm c 7 cm
   d 3 cm e 5 cm f 14 cm
6. a 10 cm, 4 cm, 10 cm and 2 cm
   b 10 cm - 2 cm = 8 cm

Chapter 15 Exercise 2 (page 178)

1. a cm b km c m
   d mm e cm f mm
   g km h m
2. a ruler b ruler
   c tape d car (odometer)
3. various
4. Jill's better, easier, more accurate, not so sore on knees
5. use of maps or internet
6. a about 40008 km
   b about 40075 km
   Its a bit longer because the Earth kind of "bulges" around the equator.

Chapter 15 Exercise 3 (page 179)

1. 10 cm^2
2. a 4 cm^2 b 12 cm^2 c 15 cm^2
   d 10 cm^2 e 6 cm^2 f 9 cm^2
   g 6 cm^2 h 8 cm^2 i 11 cm^2
3. a $3\frac{1}{2}$ cm^2 b $4\frac{1}{2}$ cm^2 c 4 cm^2
   d 12 cm^2 e 12 cm^2 f 12 cm^2
   g 24 cm^2 h 16 cm^2 i $21\frac{1}{2}$ cm^2
   j 22 cm^2

Chapter 15 Exercise 4 (page 181)

1. 16 cm^2
2. a 22 cm^2 b 24 cm^2 c 32 cm^2
   d 40-44 cm^2

Answers to Ch 16 (page 184)

Ch 16 Consolidation Ex (page 184)

1. a yes b no c yes
2. a yes b no c yes
3. a $\frac{1}{2}$ b $\frac{1}{5}$ c $\frac{1}{8}$
4. 6 5. 5 6. 8

Chapter 16 Exercise 1 (page 185)

1. 10p 2. 9 cm
3. a 30p b 6 m c 7 g
   d £8 e 8 l f £11
   g 6 cm h 9p i 31p
4. a 9 b 18
5. a 9 miles b 27 miles
6. 6 7. 8 hours
8. a 4
   b/c

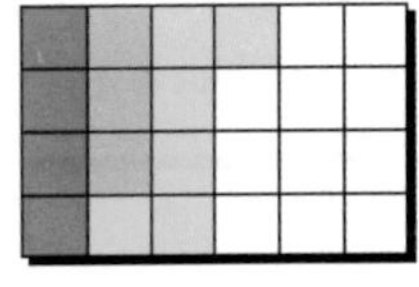

   d 11
9.

3 squares

10. a 30 b 5 c 10 days

d 31 e $\frac{1}{7}$ f $\frac{1}{60}$ g $\frac{1}{24}$

11. a 54p b 45p

12. $\frac{1}{4}$ (or $\frac{92}{365}$)

13. $\frac{1}{8}$

Chapter 16 Exercise 2 (page 188)

1. a $\frac{2}{3}$ b $\frac{4}{6}$ c $\frac{2}{3} = \frac{4}{6}$
2. $\frac{3}{4} = \frac{6}{8}$
3. a $\frac{4}{6} = \frac{2}{3}$ b $\frac{6}{10} = \frac{3}{5}$ c $\frac{15}{18} = \frac{5}{6}$

   d $\frac{2}{6} = \frac{1}{3}$ e $\frac{10}{16} = \frac{5}{8}$ f $\frac{6}{9} = \frac{2}{3}$
4. b $\frac{2}{3}$ c 4 boxes d $\frac{2}{3} = \frac{4}{6}$
5. a see drawings b $\frac{3}{4}$

   c 6 boxes d $\frac{3}{4} = \frac{6}{8}$

Chapter 16 Exercise 3 (page 190)

1. a $\frac{1}{3}$ b $\frac{1}{4}$ c $\frac{1}{6}$

   d $\frac{1}{5}$ e $\frac{1}{7}$ f $\frac{1}{9}$
2. a half b third
   c fifth d eighth
3. a $\frac{1}{2}, \frac{1}{5}, \frac{1}{9}$ b $\frac{1}{4}, \frac{1}{5}, \frac{1}{7}, \frac{1}{10}, \frac{1}{100}$

   c $\frac{1}{3}, \frac{1}{5}, \frac{1}{6}, \frac{1}{11}, \frac{1}{13}$

   d third, fifth, eighth, tenth
4. a $1\frac{1}{4}$ b $5\frac{1}{3}$ c $6\frac{5}{6}$

   d $3\frac{2}{5}$ e $7\frac{2}{7}$ f $9\frac{5}{9}$
5. see number lines like a :-

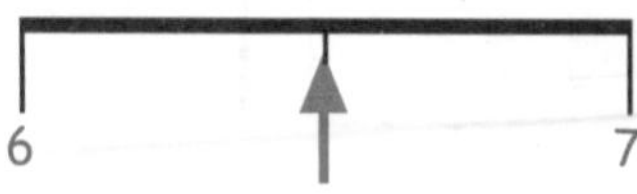

6. Practical
7. a/b Practical

Answers to Ch 17 (page 194)

Ch 17 Consolidation Ex (page 194)

1. a cone b cube c pyramid
   d cylinder e cuboid f sphere
   g triangular prism
2. cuboids 1
   cubes 2
   cylinders 3
   spheres 1
   pyramids 1
   cones 1
   triangular prisms - 1
3. 2 triangular faces and
   3 rectangular faces
4. a cuboid b cylinder
   c pyramid d triangular prism
5. a 12 b 0
   c 9 d 1

Chapter 17 Exercise 1 (page 195)

1. a 6 b 8 c 12
2. a 6 b 8 c 12
3. a 5 b 5 c 8
4. a 9 b 6 c 5
5. a 1 b 1 c 2
6. a 1 b 0 c 0
7. a 0 b 2 c 3
8. cuboid 6 8 12
   cube 6 8 12
   pyramid 5 5 8
   prism 5 6 9
   cone 2 1 1
   sphere 1 0 0
   cylinder 3 0 2
9. sphere, cone and cylinder

Answers to Ch 18 (page 198)

Ch 18 Consolidation Ex (page 198)

1. a 6 b 7 c 7
   d 8 e 6 f 5
   g 22 h 14 i 26
   j 27 k 7 l 9
   m 14 n 35 o 14
   p 11 q 27 r 200
2. a - b + c x
   d ÷ e + f -
   g x h x i ÷
   j ÷ k + l -
   m x n x o ÷
   p ÷ q + r x
3. 8 x 3 = 15 +9
   22 - 10 = 6 x 2
   21 ÷3 = 18 - 11
   18 ÷ 2 = 27 ÷ 3
   26 + 24 = 25 x 2

Chapter 18 Exercise 1 (page 199)

1. a 4 b 7 c 5
   d 8 e 7 f 8
   g 3 h 9 i 8
   j 12 k 21 l 56
   m 30 n 40 o 54
2. a 2 b 6 c 6
   d 4 e 7 f 9
   g 10 h 10 i 7
   j 27 k 40 l 60
   m 3 n 5 o 7

Chapter 18 Exercise 2 (page 200)

1. a + b - c x
   d ÷ e x f -
   g ÷ h + i x
   j + k - l ÷
   m x n - o ÷
2. a - b + c x
   d ÷ e ÷ f +
   g x h - i x
   j - k + l x
   m - n ÷ o x

Chapter 18 Exercise 3 (page 201)

1. 3 + * = 10, 7
2. 2 + * = 9, £7
3. 7 + * = 12, 5 mins
4. 11 + * = 17, 6 mins
5. 12 - * = 4, 8
6. 30 - * = 10, 20 cm
7. 14 - * = 5, 9
8. * - 8 = 12, 20

Chapter 18 Exercise 4 (page 203)

1. a = b > c = d =
   e < f < g = h >
2. a is smaller than
   b is greater than
   c is smaller than
   d is greater than

e is equal to
f is greater than
g is smaller than
h is smaller than

a < b > c = d <
e = f > g > h <

various - for example
5 x 9 > 40 - 4
99 ÷ 3 > 15 + 14
12 + 10 + 4 > 50 ÷ 2
2 x 11 > 23 - 4
3 x 6 > 8 + 9 - 5

pter 18 Exercise 5 (page 205)

a (i) 12 (ii) 32 (iii) 40 (iv) 100
b (i) 4 (ii) 7 (iii) 11 (iv) 30
a (i) 1 (ii) 7 (iii) 14 (iv) 19
b (i) 8 (ii) 20 (iii) 35 (iv) 100

a 8 b 8 c 14 d 5
e 15 f 9 g 40 h 7
i 22 j 25 k 49 l 6
m 28 n 11 o 56 p 6
q 9 r 240

a 7 b 6 c 14 d 5
e 15 f 9 g 20 h 6
i 32 j 13 k 28 l 9
m 50 n 15 o 64 p 6
q 63 r 10

a 6 b 5 c 3 d 9
e + 7 f - 6 g x h ÷
i + 12 j - 12 k 9 l 8
m - 36 n 3 o -10 p + 10
q ÷ r x

nswers to Ch 19 (page 211)

19 Consolidation Ex (page 211)

a calculator
b rowing boat
ladybird, pigeon, squirrel, horse, bison
red
a various b various
a 4 kg b 5 kg c 23 kg

pter 19 Exercise 1 (page 212)

biscuit - phone - camera - iron
a kg b g c g
d kg e g f g
g g h g i kg
j kg k g l kg

3. a 3000 g b 5000 g c 9000 g
d 10000 g e 4500 g f 6500 g
g 8500 g h 12500 g
4. a 2 kg b 4 kg c 7 kg
d 6 kg e $1\frac{1}{2}$ kg f $5\frac{1}{2}$ kg
g $8\frac{1}{2}$ kg h $9\frac{1}{2}$ kg
5. a 2 kg b 3 kg
c 4 kg d $6\frac{1}{2}$ kg
6. 4 kg
7. a 1500 g b $1\frac{1}{2}$ kg
8. 5500 g

Chapter 19 Exercise 2 (page 214)

1. a jug b skip c oil drum
d bath e freezer f trunk
2. lizard
3. elephant - cow - goat - hen - chick
4. a 6 l b 5 l
c $2\frac{1}{2}$ l d $\frac{1}{2}$ l

Chapter 19 Exercise 3 (page 215)

1. a litres b ml c litres
d ml e ml f litres
g litres h ml i ml or l
j l or ml k ml l l
2. a 2000 ml b 4000 ml
c 7000 ml d 12000 ml
3. a 3 l b 5 l
c 9 l d 11
4. a 3500 ml b 5500 ml c 9500 ml
d 14500 ml e $2\frac{1}{2}$ l f $6\frac{1}{2}$ l
g $8\frac{1}{2}$ l h $13\frac{1}{2}$ l
5. a 2 l b 3 l
c 5 l d $4\frac{1}{2}$ l
6. 75 ml
7. a 100 ml b 10 days
8. 1500 ml
9. a 2 b 10

Chapter 19 Exercise 3 (page 215)

1. a 4 cm^3 b 4 cm^3 c 5 cm^3
d 8 cm^3 e 10 cm^3 f 8 cm^3
g 14 cm^3 h 20 cm^3 i 16 cm^3
j 32 cm^3 k 7 cm^3 l 11 cm^3
m 15 cm^3 n 12 cm^3 o 15 cm^3
p 19 cm^3 q 13 cm^3 r 13 cm^3
s 20 cm^3 t 13 cm^3 u 21 cm^3
v 16 cm^3 w 14 cm^3 x 16 cm^3
2. a practical b i, k, s, w

Answers to Ch 20 (page 221)

Ch 20 Consolidation Ex (page 221)

1. a 4's b 18 c 18 d 6
2. a £90 b £150 c 4 nights
3. a 16 b 10 c 8 d 1
4. a 𝍸 || b 𝍸 𝍸 ||||
c 𝍸 𝍸 𝍸 𝍸 |||
d 𝍸 𝍸 𝍸 𝍸 𝍸 𝍸 |
5. see graph
6. a

Shampoo	Tally	Total
Alvive	|||	3
Radow	𝍸	5
E62	|	1
Touch	𝍸 ||||	9
Soapy	𝍸 |	6

b 1 c Touch d 24
e 3 f see graph

Answers to Ch 21 (page 224)

Chapter 20 Exercise 1 (page 224)

Some discussion might be required for the answers to this exercise

1. a certain b not likely
c impossible d likely
e not likely f evens
g certain h impossible
i certain j impossible
k not likely l evens
2. a unlikely b evens
c impossible d unlikely
e evens f likely
g impossible

3. Some possibilities are :-

a

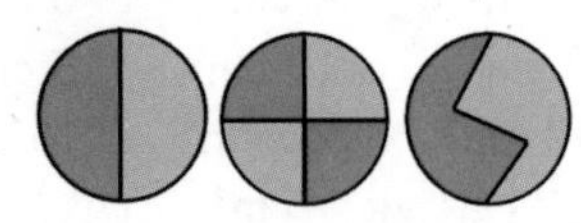

b

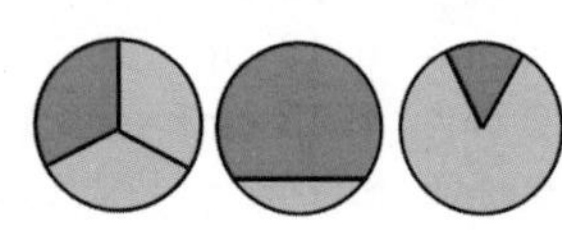

4. a various b various
5. a yes b no c no
6. 5

Chapter 20 Exercise 2 (page 226)

1. green
2. pink
3. red
4. less likely
5. less likely
6. a 1 b 3 c losing
7. C
8. less likely
9. a Mary b Change 1 Mary to Jed
10. a unlikely b evens
    c likely d impossible
11. blue is 3 out of 6 or evens
    yellow is 2 out of 4 or evens also

Chapter 20 Exercise 3 (page 228)

1. a 4 b 1 out of 4
   c 3 out of 4
2. a 8 b 1 out of 8
   c 7 out of 8
3. a 2 b 1 out of 2
   c 1 out of 2
4. a 8 b 5 out of 8
   c 3 out of 8
5. a 10 b 2 out of 10
   c 8 out of 10 d 4 out of 10
6. a 1 out of 5 b 4 out of 5
7. a 20 out of 30 b 10 out of 30
8. a 1 out of 6 b 3 out of 6
9. a 7 b 1 out of 7
   c 2 out of 7 d 4 out of 7
10. a 12 b 5 out of 12
    c 3 out of 12 d 7 out of 12
11. a 20 out of 100
    b 50 out of 100
    c 70 out of 100

Answers to Ch 22 (page 232)

1. a 70 b 300
2. 360 + 540 = 900
3. 6040
4. nine thousand one hundred and six
5. a 849 b 510
6. a 440 b 92 c 83 d 350
7. 130 litres
8. a 301 b 2560 c 17r2 d 140
9. 36 kg
10. $^{1}/_{7}$
11.

12. £60
13. 2
14. a £3·60 + £4·90 + £2·55
    = £11·05 b £8·95
15. ten to 5 or 4.50
16. 2345
17. 3.20 pm
18. Thursday
19. 30
20. Autumn
21. 5 minutes
22. 25 minutes
23. tape measure
24. 3 metres
25. 14 cm
26. bin - bucket - carton - ball
27. 15
28. 3 kg
29. 9 cm^2
30.

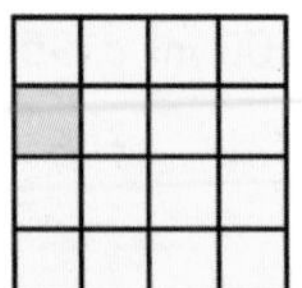

31. a 18, 21 b 52, 56
    c 52, 47 d Q, T
32. 82 ÷ 2, 8 x 5, 50 - 11, 8+9+10+11
33. a < b = c >
34. 50
35. 40
36. a 3 b 9 c 8
37. a + b x c ÷
38. a rectangle, b cylinder
    c triangle d triangle prism
39. square, circle, etc
40. cone, cube, etc
41. see drawing
42. forward 2, left, forward 3 rig
    forward 3, right, forward 5,
    right, forward 4
43. a lion b south
44. a doll b Db
45. a yes b no c yes
46.

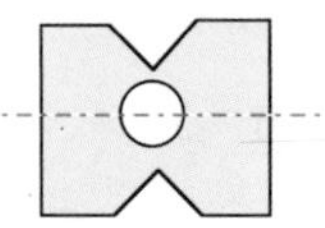

47. a Miss Glen b 8 c 4
48. a £6·50 b £35·50
49.

Number	Tally Marks	How Many
1	II	2
2	𝍸	5
3	𝍸 II	7
4	𝍸 𝍸	10

50. a impossible
    b likely c evens